Storytelling in Emergent Literacy

Fostering Multiple Intelligences

Early Childhood Education
providing lessons for life

www.EarlyChildEd.delmar.com

Storytelling in Emergent Literacy

Fostering Multiple Intelligences

Susan Trostle Brand, D.Ed.
Jeanne M. Donato, M.Ed.

Illustrated by Beth Gallo

DELMAR

THOMSON LEARNING

Australia Canada Mexico Singapore Spain United Kingdom United States

DELMAR

THOMSON LEARNING

Storytelling in Emergent Literacy: Fostering Multiple Intelligences
by Susan Trostle Brand and Jeanne M. Donato

Business Unit Director:
Susan L. Simpfenderfer

Executive Editor:
Marlene McHugh Pratt

Acquisitions Editor:
Erin O'Connor Traylor

Developmental Editor:
Melissa Riveglia

Editorial Assistant:
Alexis Ferraro

Executive Production Manager:
Wendy A. Troeger

Project Editor:
Amy E. Tucker

Production Editor:
Elaine Scull

Executive Marketing Manager:
Donna J. Lewis

Channel Manager:
Wendy E. Mapstone

Cover Design:
Joseph Villanova

For permission to use material from this text or product, contact us by
Tel   (800) 730-2214
Fax   (800) 730-2215
www.thomsonrights.com

Library of Congress Cataloging-in-Publication Data

Trostle Brand, Susan Louise.
   Storytelling in emergent literacy: fostering multiple intelligences / Susan Louise Trostle Brand, Jeanne M. Donato.
       p. cm.
     ISBN 0-7668-1480-7
     1. Storytelling.   2. Language arts (Elementary)   3. Multiple intelligences.
I. Donato, Jeanne M.   II. Title.
LB1042.T76 2000
372.6—dc21   00-064504

NOTICE TO THE READER

Publisher does not warrant or guarantee any of the products described herein or perform any independent analysis in connection with any of the product information contained herein. Publisher does not assume, and expressly disclaims, any obligation to obtain and include information other than that provided to it by the manufacturer.

The reader is expressly warned to consider and adopt all safety precautions that might be indicated by the activities herein and to avoid all potential hazards. By following the instructions contained herein, the reader willingly assumes all risks in connection with such instructions.

The Publisher makes no representation or warranties of any kind, including but not limited to, the warranties of fitness for particular purpose or merchantability, nor are any such representations implied with respect to the material set forth herein, and the publisher takes no responsibility with respect to such material. The publisher shall not be liable for any special, consequential, or exemplary damages resulting, in whole or part, from the readers' use of, or reliance upon, this material.

Dedication

This book is dedicated to
Jonathan David, my "Little Man"
and the light of my life,
and to Stephen, my "Big Man" and my rainbow's end.

All My Love,
Susan Trostle Brand

Dedication

This book is dedicated to John Donato,
our children,
and those who love storytelling.

With Blessings,
Jeanne M. Donato

Contents

Preface x

Acknowledgments xii

About the Authors xiv

Chapter 1 Emergent Literacy: An Evolving Process 1

　Reading and Preschool Children 3

　Reading and School-Aged Children 6

　Promoting Lifelong Reading 8

　Storytelling versus Story Reading 9

　Benefits of Storytelling.. 10

　Authentic Assessment of Literacy 11

　Summary 12

Chapter 2 The Use of Storytelling to Foster Emergent
　　　　　　Literacy Skills: Incorporating Brain-Based Learning 13

　Meaning and Comprehension.. 15

　Imagination, Emotion, Memory, and Learning............................... 15

　Gardner's Theory of Multiple Intelligences 16

　Storytelling and Learning.. 21

　Summary 22

Chapter 3 How to Tell a Story: Ten Exciting Approaches 24

　Background Information 26

　Purposes of This Chapter.. 26

　Preparing to Tell a Story 26

　Approaches to Storytelling.. 27

　Summary 39

Chapter 4 January: Winter Wonders.. 49

　The Purple Hat *(Chant)*... 51

　The Chinese New Year: How the Animals Were Chosen *(Traditional)*........... 55

　A Riddle for Winter *(Chant/Traditional)* 59

　I Have a Dream *(Puppetry)* 65

Chapter 5 February: Presents and Presidents 72

I Like You the Best *(Chant)* 74

Abe Lincoln and the Bullies *(Traditional)* 79

George Washington's "Lifeguard": The Legend of Simeon Simons *(Chant)* 84

The Frog Prince *(Chant/Pantomime)* 89

Chapter 6 March: Magic and Make-Believe 96

Daniel O'Rourke and the Pooka's Tower *(Traditional)* 98

Finn and Cuchulainn *(Group Role-Play)* 103

The Three Wishes *(Traditional)* 108

The Pot That Would Not Stop Boiling *(Character Imagery/Chant)* 111

Chapter 7 April: Spring into the Great Outdoors 118

Bojabi *(Felt Board/Chant)* 120

Kibungo: Beast of the Rainforest *(Musical/Group Role-Play)* 126

Jack and the Beanstalk *(Felt Board/Chant)* 132

The Lion and the Mouse *(Balloon)* 139

Chapter 8 May: Families Are Special 146

The City Mouse and the Country Mouse *(Puppetry/Chant)* 148

Why Not Call It Cow Juice? *(Draw Talk)* 153

The Little Bunny Who Wished for Red Wings *(Chant)* 157

The Brownies and the Tailor *(Chant)* 162

Chapter 9 June: Music and Poetry 170

Rattlin' Bog *(Balloon/Musical)* 172

Little Bunny Foo Foo *(Puppetry/Musical)* 178

It Could Be Worse! *(Group Role-Play/Musical)* 182

The Unicorn *(Musical)* 187

Chapter 10 July: America and Americans 192

Johnny Appleseed *(Group Role-Play/Character Imagery/Chant)* 194

Ida Lewis: Keeper of the Light *(Adapted Pantomime/Musical)* 199

A Yankee Doodle Legend *(Character Imagery/Musical/Chant)* 205

The Fourth of July *(Chant)* 211

Chapter 11 August: Oceans of Fun 218

Magic Fish in the Sea *(Musical/Chant)* 220

The Fairies, the People, and the Sea *(Puppetry)* 226

The Crab and the Lobster (*Group Role-Play/Pantomime*) 231

The War between the Sandpipers and the Whales:
  A Tale from the Marshall Islands (*Chant*) 235

Chapter 12   September: Making New Friends 242

The Three Billy Goats Gruff (*Puppetry*) 244

Pigs...Bears (*Chant*) 250

The Most Beautiful Thing in the World (*Draw Talk*) 257

How the Leaves Got Their Colors (*Traditional/Chant*) 263

Chapter 13   October: Shivers and Quivers 269

Old Rattle Bones (*Musical/Group Role-Play*) 271

Red Lips (*Chant/Adapted Pantomime*) 276

No Kids in the Gallery! (*Character Imagery*) 282

Skinny as a Spider's Waist (*Felt Board/Chant*) 287

Chapter 14   November: Food for Thought 294

The Little Red Hen (*Group Role-Play*) 296

Stone Soup (*Adapted Pantomime*) 300

Old Man Rabbit's Thanksgiving Dinner (*Draw Talk*) 305

The Strawberry Thanksgiving (*Traditional*) 314

Chapter 15   December: Holidays Around the World 320

Saint Lucia Day: A Swedish Tradition (*Traditional*) 322

The Kwanzaa Story (*Chant*) 329

A Baker's Dozen (*Traditional*) 333

A Stranger's Gift (*Puppetry*) 337

Glossary 343

References 348

Index 349

Preface

... It has now been established quite convincingly that individuals have quite different minds from one another. Education ought to be so sculpted that it remains responsive to these differences. Instead of ignoring them, and pretending that all individuals have (or ought to have) the same kinds of minds, we should instead try to ensure that everyone receive an education that maximizes his or her own intellectual potential (Gardner 1993, p. 71).

Students, in-service teachers, parents and caregivers will find a plethora of inspiring stories and extension activities within each page of *Storytelling in Emergent Literacy: Fostering Multiple Intelligences*. Consistent with the Constructivist approach to learning, this text guides rather than tells; the stories and activities allow for flexibility in grouping of students, use of settings, and props. Most importantly, the stories and activities encourage students to gain confidence in their own emergent literacy and areas of multiple intelligence abilities. Through exposure and practice, students gain skills in a naturalistic and meaningful way, beginning with a captivating story. Ultimately, students gain confidence in themselves and become lifelong learners and problem-solvers, realizing the inner-relationships of all learning and all the areas of multiple intelligence.

Storytelling in Emergent Literacy: Fostering Multiple Intelligences explores storytelling and emergent literacy using the foundations of brain research and multiple intelligence theory. The authors demonstrate creative applications of children's literature and folk tales to reading and literacy and to the other multiple intelligence abilities, such as social skills, nature, numbers and numeracy, music, visual arts, and movement.

The text acknowledges that emergent literacy is the day by day, gradual accumulation of skills and knowledge that leads to readiness for more formal reading instruction. Within the text, and throughout the set of three videotapes, the reader/viewer is provided with a wide array of information and tools which, when implemented, facilitate the learner's gradual accumulation of these essential early competencies and inspire a lifelong love of literacy.

Chapter 1: Emergent Literacy: An Evolving Process addresses the benefits of storytelling and compares the effect of storytelling with story reading on young children's comprehension and vocabulary acquisition.

Chapter 2: The Use of Storytelling to Foster Emergent Literacy Skills: Incorporating Brain-Based Learning presents information on Gardner's and other prominent researchers' theories of multiple intelligence. Brain development and related research are discussed in detail. The advantages of using storytelling are discussed in terms of cognition, brain development, and linguistic skills. Applications of both brain development and multiple intelligence theories to literacy and dramatic play settings for children conclude this chapter.

Chapter 3: How to Tell a Story: Ten Exciting Approaches delineates several approaches to storytelling. Suggestions for the storyteller preface the numerous approaches and include such considerations as costume, materials, props, voice control, use of stage, body positioning, audience involvement, facial expressions, using scripts, rewriting stories, creating unique stories, and learning to tell an effective, inspiring story. The various methods of storytelling include Traditional, Adapted Pantomime (using words), Character Imagery, Draw Talk, Puppetry, Chant, Felt Board, Balloon, Musical, and Group Role-Play. Multicultural, thematic children's literature selections, arranged by storytelling methods, are listed at the conclusion of Chapter 3.

Chapters 4 through 15 present 48 actual stories and, for each, three creative, multiple intelligence/content area activities. At the beginning of each chapter is a poem suitable to the chapter's theme. The stories and themes are arranged sequentially, according to the 12 months of the year. Photographs, recipes, songs, and illustrations accompany the stories and multiple intelligence activities and assist the Teller in applying the ideas to an actual classroom. For each of the 48 total stories, a description of the story, a thorough explanation of suggested props and the most appropriate method(s) of telling prefaces the story. This section is entitled, "Tips for the Teller."

An asterisk is used throughout the book to denote audience participation in the storytelling method through movement, words, or song. For simplicity, lines to be repeated in a chorus or chant are indicated with (2x) at the end of the line.

For the purposes of this book, the following definitions pertain to both the source of the original story and the author of the current format. The designation "By" refers to the originator of the story. "Retold by" implies that the story has been written by at least one author previously. The present author(s) made some minor content or sequence changes to the original story. An *adapted* story is one in which the formatting of the original has been changed to comply with one or more storytelling techniques but in which there are few or no changes to the content of the story. "Adapted by" signifies the writer of the reformatted story. A story that is both "Retold and Adapted" has been written by a previous author, has had minor changes made to the present story's content and/or sequencing, and has been reformatted for application to one or more storytelling techniques.

Finally, at the conclusion of each of the twelve sequential chapters is a chapter resources section, listing related, recommended books and audio recordings. A complete references list, a glossary, and an index conclude the text.

The Use and Enjoyment of the Three Storytelling Videotapes That Are Available to Accompany This Textbook

The three storytelling videotapes that are available to accompany this textbook will entertain, inform, and enlighten the storytelling student and instructor. Through viewing ten exciting and colorful stories from the textbook, each of which is told using a different storytelling method, students and instructors will learn how to implement the accompanying textbook descriptions. These ten complete stories from the textbook and the methods of storytelling used for each are demonstrated in the storytelling videotapes:

(1) Red Lips: Chant/Adapted Pantomime
(2) Jack and the Beanstalk: Felt Board/Chant
(3) The Pot That Would Not Stop Boiling: Character Imagery/Chant
(4) Why Not Call It Cow Juice?: Draw Talk
(5) The Three Billy Goats Gruff: Puppetry
(6) A Riddle for Winter: Chant/Traditional
(7) The Lion and the Mouse: Balloon
(8) Stone Soup: Adapted Pantomime
(9) Rattlin' Bog: Balloon/Musical
(10) Johnny Appleseed: Group Role-Play/ Character Imagery/Chant

A set of questions concludes each of the ten stories. These questions probe the students' understanding regarding characteristics of the preceding storytelling method, as well as foster a deeper comprehension for the viewer.

In order to maximize the use of the videotapes, students may follow this set of instructions:

(1) Carefully read Chapter 1 (an introductory chapter, called "Emergent Literacy" and Chapter 3 ("How to Tell a Story: Ten Exciting Approaches") of this text.
(2) Read the ten stories in this textbook that are also found on the set of three storytelling videotapes.
(3) Refer to your textbook while viewing each corresponding story in the set of videotapes.
(4) Pause the tape periodically in order to clarify a method and/or check your understanding.
(5) At the conclusion of each story, write (or orally answer) the set of questions relating to the storytelling method you viewed. If you are uncertain about the answers to some of the questions, refer to Chapter 3 for more information.
(6) Continue in this manner as you view the remaining nine stories.
(7) Decide which method you would like to use for your own storytelling. Allow this storytelling method preference to help determine your choice of story to perform for the class or audience.

Remember to have fun with storytelling and that it is not possible or even desirable to always tell a story the same way you read or heard it or viewed it on a videotape. Make the story your own. Your resultant enthusiasm, inspiration, and talent will reap the benefit of the children's sheer delight at your captivating performance!

Instructor's Manual

The Instructor's Manual, which also accompanies this text, features a multiple intelligence survey and steps to become a successful storyteller. A storytelling Rubric for assessing students' storytelling performances is useful to instructors of students who are learning to tell stories.

Also featured in this manual are multicultural literature references, a list of story-related organizations and publications, and a list of Web sites related to storytelling, storytellers, and children's literature. A video portion of the manual provides video presentation hints and answers to the questions presented in the videos.

Acknowledgments

Grateful thanks and hugs to my friends whose ongoing support helped to transform this book from a dream into a reality. I thank my parents, John and Lois Hewitt, who always taught me, by example, the role of faith and industry in pursuing one's dreams.

For her tremendous role modeling and boundless energy, kudos extend to Dr. Jane Madsen, my storytelling mentor at Penn State University and my lifelong friend. To the directors, children, and families at Redwood Library in Newport, Rhode Island, and to the University of Rhode Island's Early Childhood Cooperating Teachers, especially Mrs. Mikel Terluk, for their encouragement, suggestions, and use of facilities for this project, I extend warmest appreciation.

To my students—past, present, and future—at the University of Rhode Island, who continually amaze me with their talent and fresh perspectives, I thank you very sincerely. Michelle Berenson, Dana Hanley, and Cynthia Gaccione have earned a special note of appreciation for their creative contributions to this text and set of videotapes.

My secretary at the University of Rhode Island, Mrs. Reba Gould, has supported and guided me for the past 15 years. She has earned my admiration, heartfelt gratitude, and praise.

Thanks and praise are also due the editors and reviewers of this manuscript who provided excellent suggestions and insights throughout this project. We truly appreciate their attention to detail and their willingness to share their knowledge about formatting, activities, and stories, and for strengthening this book and the accompanying videotapes in many important ways.

To my wonderful husband, Stephen, whose wisdom, humor, gentle encouragement, and love brighten each of my days, I am eternally grateful. Last, but not least, my son Jonathan taught me the joy of reading together and the joy of motherhood. He is always a great source of inspiration and laughter for me. Stephen's and Jonathan's patience throughout the writing and revising process and their encouragement and belief in me were the keys which unlocked the doors to my writing this book.

Susan Trostle Brand

My love and devotion go to my husband, John Donato for his laughter, love, support, and all the dinners he cooked. I thank my children, Jeannie, Katie, and John-Paul for their love and understanding throughout the writing process. I am grateful to my parents, John and Lillian Mahaffey, who have nurtured us with love and encouraged us to follow our dreams.

I honor and bless Dr. Lillian Poston for her loving direction and inspiration, and Nancy and Dr. Robert Swegler for their friendship and professional assistance. Acknowledgment goes to the Educational Kinesiology Foundation and instructors for their excellent Brain-Gym® training. I thank Dr. Flora Joy for her expertise and innovative Storytelling Masters program at Eastern Tennessee State University, Dr. Joseph Sobol as he continues this work, and Dr. Wendy Nowlan for encouraging the use of "Whole-Brain" Storytelling in her Storytelling Institute at Southern Connecticut State University.

My gratitude extends to the librarians of Rhode Island and Connecticut for their help, especially Joan Gately, David Panciera, and Helen Mochetti, and the friends of the Westerly, Ashaway, and Redwood Libraries. Praise goes to the principals, teachers, students, and parents of Harbor, Jennings, and Westerly Elementary Schools, who worked on the storytelling projects for this text. I thank Jean Liepold for her musical editing and arranging. To my friends at the Connecticut Storytelling Center, I extend thanks for their innovative Tellers in Schools program, which enabled me to work with the teachers and students. To my storytelling communities— The Rhode Island Storytellers, Little Rest, the League for the Advancement of New England Storytelling (LANES), the National Storytelling Network (NSN)—and all who love storytelling, I thank you for your support and encouragement.

My heartfelt thanks goes to the artists, authors, reviewers, and professionals who contributed their time and work. I would like to thank our editors, Erin, Alexis, Amy, Elaine, and Melissa, and the other experts at Delmar for their belief, insight, and encouragement in developing this text. Their help was invaluable. My blessings extend to all.

Jeanne M. Donato

The authors and Delmar would like to express their gratitude to the following professionals who offered numerous valuable suggestions and strengthened this textbook:

Leanna Manna, M.A.
Villa Maria College of Buffalo
Buffalo, New York

Mary Clare Munger
Amarillo College
Amarillo, Texas

Mikel Terluk
Charlestown Elementary School
Charlestown, Rhode Island

Nina Mazloff, M.S.
Becker College
Worcester, Massachusetts

Loraine Phillips, Ph.D.
Blinn College
Brenham, Texas

Doris Walker-Dalhouse, Ph.D.
Moorhead State University
Moorhead, Minnesota

About the Authors

Susan Trostle Brand, D.Ed., is an Associate Professor of Education at the University of Rhode Island in Kingston, Rhode Island. She is a former teacher of primary age children in the public schools and has served as a Reading Specialist in grades Kindergarten through six.

Dr. Brand received her Bachelor of Science degree in Elementary Education at Indiana University of Pennsylvania in 1973. She earned her Master of Arts degree in Reading from West Virginia University in 1975 and her Doctorate in Early Childhood Education from Pennsylvania State University in 1984.

The author of two other textbooks and numerous chapters in books and articles on curriculum, play, and literacy, Dr. Brand enjoys reading, storytelling, kayaking, and traveling in her free time. She also enjoys spending quality time at home with her husband, Steve, her eight-year-old son, Jonathan, and her cats, Chelsea and Yogi.

Dr. Susan Brand with her son, Jonathan.

Jeanne M. Donato, M.Ed., holds a Masters degree in Reading/Story Arts and a Bachelor of Arts degree in Elementary Education. Her specialty is Storytelling in the Curriculum.

Jeanne M. Donato (photo by Susan Wilson).

She teaches Children's Literature at Southern Connecticut State University in New Haven, Connecticut. Jeanne is a former teacher in grades Kindergarten through six. She is a professional storyteller, Master Word Weaving Instructor, professional clown, and an award-winning Certified Master Balloon Artist, decorator, and designer. Mrs. Donato is a Specialized Educational Kinesiologist, certified Brain-Gym® instructor, and professional speaker, presenting workshops and lectures internationally.

Mrs. Donato has owned and operated her own company, Balloons by Joy-O-Loons, for more than 18 years, offering storytelling performances, workshops on professional development, and balloon decorating. She is an accredited Storytelling Artist on the Arts and Education Roster in Rhode Island, and the New England States Touring Artist Roster.

Emergent Literacy: An Evolving Process

Carly is now seven years old and reading at a tenth grade level. She began to read at age two. When asked how she became such a proficient reader, she replies, "Reading at our house happens all the time. It was easy for me to catch on!"

For Carly and other very successful readers, reading is an enjoyable process that evolves naturally and in an integrated fashion. For years, however, educators and theorists alike believed that children exhibited a readiness to read at an immediate and observable point in time. They advocated the identification and measurement of a child's readiness to read based upon a set of distinct and basically unrelated skills. Such individualized skills included **visual memory, visual discrimination, auditory memory, auditory discrimination, attention span, alphabet letter recognition,** and **comprehension.** Most often, these skills were introduced and taught in isolation. The skills were taught using a drill and practice approach, and often work sheets accompanied the lessons (Smith, 1983). Little attention was paid to linking the areas of reading readiness. Meaningful and real-life experiences were seldom provided as a means of fully engaging the child in the learning process (Fisher, 1998). The curriculum was planned in advance by the teacher and/or by a panel of experts. The focus was not on the process but rather on academics and skills. Providing time and resources for the children to plan their own activities in a **constructivist,** developmentally appropriate manner (Bredekamp, 1997) was the antitheses of past practices. In a constructivist approach children are actively involved in the learning process via hands-on activities.

Today's instruction of children differs markedly from the previous world of teaching and learning. Now the term **reading readiness,** which referred to the child's readiness to read at a predetermined age, is replaced by **emergent literacy,** a process-based approach that refers to the child's gradual acquisition of the literacy skills involved in formal reading. Research supports the belief that children's learning to read is not an end point, but rather an evolving process. Given the definition of emergent literacy, it is difficult indeed to determine exactly when reading begins for the child. Rather, we view the emerging literacy skills *collectively* and provide for closer and closer approximations of reading before the child begins to engage formally in independent reading.

Reading and Preschool Children

Practically from the moment they enter the world children prepare to read. When parents engage their children daily in meaningful learning experiences a number of positive results occur. These results may be either **explicit**—observable and significant—or **implicit**—not observable, but nonetheless significant. Reading aloud to children is one of the best means by which parents and caregivers foster a life-long love of reading in children (Gunning, 1998).

Benefits of Reading Aloud with Children

Children whose parents regularly read to them usually read more often and more extensively. In addition, reading to young children develops their language and conceptual skills. Children are thus better prepared to read independently. As children and parents or caregivers share read-aloud sessions twelve distinct benefits emerge. Reading aloud with children:

1. Expands schemata. Children's **schemata** (mental constructs) expand as the brain **assimilates** (recognizes, stores) new information and **accommodates** (reorganizes, adjusts) existing cognitive structures to incorporate new concepts and understandings. These changing and emerging schemata facilitate the child's framework for present comprehension and promote future learning. Thus, when schemata evolve and change, the child's understanding simultaneously is changed and enhanced.

2. Develops concepts. As adults read with children the children learn new concepts such as word opposites, human emotions, and informational facts about the world. Children learn to organize and categorize these new concepts through repeated exposures to books and reading.

3. Fosters a lifelong love of reading. Children's motivation to read is closely linked to the significant adult's attitude toward reading. Parents and caregivers who believe that reading is a source of entertainment have children with more positive views about reading than do parents and caregivers who emphasize the skills aspect of reading development (Baker & Green, 1987).

4. Enhances the child-parent relationship. Reading together provides a haven to both the child

Reading together enhances the child-parent relationship.

reuse the new words in real-life settings. When an adult continually establishes the connection between the vocabulary and concepts presented in literature and objects and ideas in the real world, the child builds strong and extensive vocabulary and comprehension skills.

7. Fosters comprehension. Comprehension competencies include the child's ability to classify information, to sequence or order events, to determine cause and effect, and to make comparisons. Through reading with a parent or other adult, the child extends factual information and learns to organize it into meaningful structures. Providing the older child with written **Concept Maps** and other organizers of information, following reading, assists the child in his or her recall and comprehension. Also, the adult who asks questions beyond the **literal** (factual recall) level provides support to all children in their related **higher-level thinking skills.**

8. Stimulates imagination. Reading aloud transports the child and the adult from the here and now to the then and there. Imagination is a precursor to **representational thought,** which characterizes all encounters with the spoken and written word. Representational thought transports the learner to symbolic experiences in lieu of direct experiences. Moreover, imagination and creativity are closely related for the young reader. The adult who facilitates an "as if" discussion, following the reading of a book, helps the child to visualize, to imagine, and to create. "As if" discussions might include the child's pretending to live in a particular time period, to have a particular skill, or to take the part of the main character of the story.

and the adult from the stress of daily living and routines. Through a shared, mutually satisfying experience, reading offers the adult and child a time to set aside for each other so that they might become acquainted and re-acquainted and experience entertainment and enjoyment. Constraints are lifted, and the two parties are, for a time, equal as together they explore the magic of books and reading.

5. Establishes links with life events. Reading provides explanations for children as they attempt to make sense of what may seem to be an overwhelming and confusing world. In the child's language, and through illustrations, books fill in the gaps and answer the numerous questions that the world creates every day in the child's life.

6. Expands vocabulary. As the child encounters new vocabulary words through books the parent or caregiver provides explanations and examples to clarify the words. Also, following the reading, the adult and the child use and

9. Provides **catharsis.** Children lack experience and confidence regarding many of life's events. Their frame of reference is egocentric and concrete. Through reading, children learn that other children experience the same emotions and fears as they do. They learn how to solve problems and confront and resolve fears. Children learn that it is acceptable to be different—physically, intellectually, emotionally, and linguistically.

10. Facilitates language and **expressive language skills.** When children listen to a skilled parent

or adult read a story with animation and expression, they eventually model these inflections and emotions. They learn to modulate their voices and to use volume and pausing as they read and communicate.

11. Promotes phonemic awareness. A child's familiarity with the alphabet and with letter-sound associations is closely correlated with his or her later success with beginning reading. In fact, one of the main distinguishers of early versus late readers is the early reader's acquisition of the alphabet and his or her **phonemic awareness,** or letter: sound correspondence (Adams, 1990, 1997).

When the child is engaged meaningfully and frequently with print, the child encounters many experiences with **phonemes,** or speech sounds. Beginning with ABC books, the child learns to associate letters with the written word and with familiar objects and persons. The adult provides game-like activities to extend reading, as well.

12. Correlates to later school success. Because a great deal of school involves reading for the student, the successful reader is often the very successful student (Clay, 1991). By naturally acquiring early skills and motivation in reading, the child is well prepared to enter the formal school setting in which reading and language is integrated throughout the day, and throughout all content areas.

It is clear from these benefits that early, frequent, and positive experiences with language, writing, and reading in the home or nursery school setting are critical to the child's literacy development. Children become proficient with reading and language through practice and through meaningful experiences related to their reading.

Maximizing Children's Potential

The following suggestions may enable parents and caregivers to maximize their children's potential for later literacy experiences:

1. Read every day. Replace television with books and real experiences related to literature. Visit your library early and often.
2. Read *with* your children. Keep them actively involved. Engage them in discussions after the reading and link the story to events that transpire in the children's own lives.
3. Be creative. Dress up in costumes, use animation, and make puppets. Use other props, too, to support concepts and vocabulary development.
4. Keep reading relevant and meaningful. Relate stories to actual events, to the child's interests, hobbies, dreams, and life experiences.
5. Use the three Rs: Rhyme, Rhythm, and Repetition. Big Books exemplify the three Rs, in which words rhyme, colorful phrases are repeated throughout the text, and the language is rhythmic and colorful. Children are naturally attracted to texts which are colorful and creative in their approach to pictures, words, and plot.
6. Keep reading fun, positive, and drill-free. Encourage the child's close approximations while the child learns to read independently. Mistakes are acceptable and expected aspects of learning for the child. Help the child to monitor his or her own progress with letters and sounds, with vocabulary, with picture identification, and with story comprehension.
7. Use expression and gestures while reading. Children benefit from experiences with skilled story readers. Readers themselves must convey interest and enthusiasm for the text. Texts are read with volume changes, use of hand and body movements to convey meaning, and vivid facial expressions. This enthusiasm sparks children's motivation and sustains their interest throughout the reading.
8. Always make reading a **horizontal learning experience.** In other words, extend reading into other life areas, linking all texts with content areas, even when the child is very young. Many books provide recipes, ideas for field trips, suggestions for art activities, music and sing-along appendices, and the like. These literacy extensions enable the child to later view reading as meaningful to the content areas and relevant to all of life's experiences.
9. Incorporate role-play and creative dramatics. At the conclusion of a story have the child dress up in old clothing as one of the characters. He or she can then ad-lib or rehearse the role and stage a show for friends. Such dramatic reenactments can be simple or compli-

A print-rich environment fosters children's literacy.

cated, brief or lengthy, as the child's interest and abilities dictate.

10. Keep your home or school environment print-rich. Model good reading habits yourself. Order children's magazines. Make word walls by filling your bulletin boards, refrigerators, and cupboard exteriors with words and with children's artistic and language displays.

11. Use the Language Experience Approach (LEA). The **Language Experience Approach (LEA),** while not a new learning activity, is still invaluable today as a tool for promoting reading and literacy. While the child describes a favorite or memorable event, the adult writes the child's words verbatim onto a large sheet of paper. Then the child uses this story as the basis for reading. He or she reads first with the adult and later independently. Finally, the child circles familiar letters and words within the LEA story and uses this skill practice to acquire punctuation, phonemic, and print-awareness.

Adults are primary facilitators of meaningful learning as they prepare children for later literacy experiences. As a result, children are well-equipped to become proficient language users upon their entry to formal schooling.

Reading and School-Aged Children

Children's proficient use of language is described by Cambourne (1988). Cambourne's model of language learning maintains that certain specific conditions characterize effective teaching and learning in **authentic settings,** which are settings closely approximating the learner's real world. These conditions include immersion, responsibility, use and practice, approximations, demonstrations and modeling, feedback or response, expectations, and engagement.

Immersion

Learners require immersion in texts of all kinds, including both expository and narrative materials. Picture storybooks, big books, and wordless picture books hold special appeal to young children. Other genres which appeal to children include poetry, folktales, fairy tales, myths, fables, historical fiction, and informational or concept books. Such immersion occurs as teachers provide time for Sustained Silent Reading (SSR) or Drop Everything and Read (DEAR), breaks, frequent visits to the school library, a classroom library and book display area, and opportunities for reading alone, with the teacher, with a buddy, with a small group, and in large-group settings.

Responsibility

In order to facilitate learners' **empowerment** (sense of control over life circumstances), teachers need to let learners make their own decisions about how to learn, what to learn, and when to learn the material which is presented. Learners who do not acquire this sense of responsibility are far more dependent upon others to make choices for them.

Use and Practice

In realistic and authentic settings, learners can use and practice their developing skills and literacy tools for practical purposes. For example, a class explores methods for improvement of the classroom book collection. In small, collaborative groups, students design their own ideas for classifying the collection of books. Upon presenting their ideas to the entire class, the students vote to select the method most practical and useful for indexing the books and providing accessibility to the students.

Approximation

Approximation involves making mistakes. Without practice and freedom to make subsequent mistakes, learners cannot explore their learning potential and exercise their unique learning style and sense of timing. Teachers assist children as they participate in these trials and errors through discussion, brainstorming reasons for results, guided questioning, and helping the student to rework ideas.

Demonstration and Modeling

Through frequent teacher demonstrations and modeling of the uses of text, students learn to apply these models to their own literacy development. Implicit modeling occurs, for example, when the teacher invites all students to Drop Everything and Read (DEAR), or when the teacher, sharing the big book *The Three Billy Goats Gruff* with the class, invites everyone to join in on the repetitive chants, "Trip-trap, trip-trap, trip-trap" and "Who's that tramping on my bridge?"

Explicit modeling occurs when the teacher demonstrates how to locate the answer to a ques-

tion raised at the conclusion of an expository text. Modeling also occurs as the teacher talks aloud as he or she reads a selection. For instance, the teacher reads aloud a section of *Mrs. Frisby and the Rats of NIMH* by Robert O'Brien. Then, at intervals, the children listen as the teacher may comment, "That part was interesting. I enjoyed learning about Mrs. Frisby's children. I wonder what will happen next in this chapter entitled, 'Mr. Fitzgibbon's Plow.' I predict that the farmer may be preparing to plow early this year. That will mean that Mrs. Frisby and her family will need to move to a new home soon. I think I will write my hunch on this prediction chart in my notebook." Thus, students have new tools for constructing meaning from text.

Feedback or Response

In a literacy-rich classroom teachers provide feedback, or response, to learners. When these responses are readily available, timely, appropriate to the issue, encouraging, and nonthreatening, children learn to monitor their own progress and achievements. They become self-regulating with a realistic view of themselves and their own strengths and weaknesses. The practice of providing ready feedback to learners also enables the teacher to monitor the climate of the classroom and to plan for individual, as well as whole-group needs.

Expectations

Closely linked to responsibility, expectation involves the learner's bonding with a significant role model. Such role models exert powerful influences upon children's behavior and learning. When high expectations exist in the literacy classroom and when the expectations are set by a closely bonded, significant model, the student more readily assumes responsibility for his or her learning and success.

Engagement

Finally, engagement for the learner occurs when the learner is convinced that he or she is the potential performer of the demonstrations observed. The learner must also hold the belief that engagement with these demonstrations will further the purposes of life without fear of physical or psychological hurt. The learner must recognize the value of close approximations, and in so doing demonstrate a willingness to explore, experiment, fail, try again, and eventually reach the intended goal.

When classroom teachers simulate these conditions for learners in authentic settings, children reap the benefits. Many classrooms now exemplify Cambourne's model. Today's children write their own stories. They become editors, making suggestions and offering encouragement to fellow writers. They work collaboratively on projects, on stories, and on researching topics that fascinate them. When children require further assistance a teacher, classroom aide, more advanced classmate, or parent volunteer works with them in a small group or individually. The ad hoc group uses life experiences, games, and other meaningful learning tools to acquire the skills. Children write and illustrate daily journals. They sit in claw bathtubs filled with cushions and read with buddies. They retell and rewrite favorite stories such as *Cinderella* or *Goldilocks and the Three Bears*. They make the stories their own. They bind these stories into big books for the class to share.

Today's children observe skilled and amateur storytellers, as role models, tell new and classic stories. They extend the stories with art, music, research, writing, and problem-solving activities. They work in large or small groups, at creative and colorful learning stations. The children themselves learn to become storytellers. They stage plays and puppet shows and tell and retell felt board stories to classmates. Through song, poetry, and chant, they become immersed and involved in the stories. Their alphabet, phonemic awareness, visual discrimination and other competencies are integrated in rich and meaningful ways, often through the medium of children's books. Learning today is a far cry from instruction in the early 1900s, and the change is welcome.

Promoting Lifelong Reading

Durkin (1993) and Routman (1988) build strong cases for using **authentic literature** in the primary grades in order to promote a lifelong interest in reading and literacy. Authentic literature uses characters, pictures, vocabulary, and stories that closely resemble those in the real world. Among the advantages of using a literature-based approach in the curriculum, Routman delineates the following:

1. **Language development.** Vocabulary and multiple meanings of words are best learned and applied through the context of reading and listening to authentic literature. As children experience **syntactic** (word order) and semantic (usage) patterns, figurative language, rhyming words, and repetition of vocabulary, their own skills and levels of expertise improve.

2. **Fluent reading.** When the teacher uses a strategy that requires predicting and sampling of appropriate words in context, the students learn to transfer this skill to their own reading. This transference of reading ability to other contexts is a highly important occurrence which gives children confidence and encourages independent reading.

3. **Emotional catharsis.** Authentic literature deals with emotions common to all humans. Anger, jealousy, sadness, and so on, capture children's attention immediately and sustain it throughout the reading. Through folk and fairy tales, children learn about longings, conflicts, and failings.

4. **Development of reading and comprehension.** Literature use promotes the child's continuous and related applications of text. This differs markedly from previous approaches in which unrelated, individual stories were used and, from these basal stories, skills were taught in isolation. In the literacy-rich classroom, children listen and read for meaning. Comprehension, and not a set of isolated skills, is the ultimate goal of the child's reading.

5. **Self-esteem.** When the best children's books are used in the classroom, student's failure rates drastically decline and success rates soar (Routman, 1988). When children view themselves as readers and writers from the first day of school this advantage carries over to other content areas. Because reading is infused throughout the curriculum, children who read well tend to excel in other content areas.

6. **Awareness of story structure, genre, style, and theme.** As students are exposed to a variety of writing models, genres, and authors of authentic literature, their own repertoire expands. Thus, students can glean under-

standing and relate what they learn to their own writing and illustrating of stories. **Story structure** refers to the organization or arrangement of a book's events or concepts. **Genre** refers to the form, type, or content of a book. **Style** refers to a book's mode and form of expression, as distinguished from its content. **Theme** refers to the subject or topic.

Research studies have also found that story reading is most beneficial when it is accompanied with extension strategies. For example, in primary classrooms in which children reflect on stories and respond to them using art, drama and music, children became more self-reliant and more able to recreate story events (Fisher, 1998).

Storytelling versus Story Reading

While story reading is traditionally the most popular method for using children's literature with young children, storytelling is an attractive and viable supplement to reading aloud for achieving specific language and comprehension goals (Glazer, 1991; Trostle & Hicks, 1998). Morrow (1997) compared storytelling with reading books aloud to children. The study discovered that more give and take exists between the audience and the storyteller during storytelling than during story reading. Thus collaboration between teller and students was increased among those who engaged in storytelling.

Storytelling is the oral interpretation of a traditional, literary, or personal experience story. It is a tale told in a natural manner with all the flavor and language of the particular tradition from which it comes. It is an interaction between teller and listener; at its best it becomes a mutual creation (Baker & Green, 1987). Storytelling began many years ago as oral tradition since writing and printing supplies were unavailable. Stories were passed on from one generation to another and were used for a variety of purposes. Three main purposes for storytelling were entertainment, scientific explanations, and projection.

Storytelling as Entertainment

Storytellers in medieval days roamed the lands, traveling from castle to castle in hopes of impressing the royalty and obtaining free lodging and meals. After a delicious banquet, a storyteller might use the **Traditional Storytelling** method (using gestures but no props) or the **Pantomime** method (using body movements, gestures, and expression to convey a story). This system worked very well, as long as the storyteller was deemed acceptable. Woe, however, to the poor storyteller whose stories were not sufficiently entertaining; a punishment as severe as death was the occasional unfortunate result.

Early forms of storytelling included fables, myths, epics, folktales, sonnets, and legends. In addition, storytelling was also later characterized by different genres, such as historical fiction, animal stories, stories of other lands, bible stories, realistic, and fantasy stories.

Nature-Related Explanations

Natural phenomena terrified people in primitive civilizations. Early civilizations believed that angry gods caused hurricanes, floods, tornadoes, and other natural disasters. Even the changing seasons, the phases of the moon, the tides, and high winds were met with apprehension and fear. Myths were created by the Greeks, Romans, and Norse in an attempt to explain these phenomena. Indeed, the Greeks and Scandinavians created myths that have shaped the language, literature, and mentality of Western man.

For example, "the gods are angry" explained a violent thunderstorm, while a rainbow was considered a sign from the gods of good fortune and promise. Greek shepherds and herdsmen made the gods in their own image; however, their gods were more handsome, taller, and closer to perfection then mere mortals. Therefore, their gods were considered less fearful and more benevolent than were the earlier gods. Such explanations gave these persons a sense of order and purpose; they attributed natural occurrences to the activities and feelings of higher beings and felt more secure in this knowledge (D'Aulaire & D'Aulaire, 1992).

Projection

Cinderella is a classic example of a story that allowed wishful thinkers to project themselves into a new role or way of living. **Projection-type** stories allowed folks with little means to imagine they were rich, famous and powerful. Many of the fairy and folk tales (e.g., *The Ugly Duckling, Hansel and Gretel, Beauty and the Beast,* and *The Three Billy Goats Gruff*) portray this ugly to beautiful and/or rags to riches theme. Such stories are popular even today, as readers and viewers enjoy projecting themselves into the roles of the rich, powerful, and famous.

> "Storytelling strongly attracts children to books. It has a power that reading stories does not, for it frees the storyteller to use creative techniques. It is one of the surest ways to establish rapport between the listeners and the storyteller" (Morrow, 1997, p. 167).

Storytelling, as an extension of children's literature, is one means by which children with diverse literacy levels and educational needs achieve unity of ideas and establish harmony, both within and among themselves. Storytelling is an effective and efficient learning tool that is not fully appreciated. It is a natural medium that endows a feeling of shared purpose on the children. Moreover, it is a fun and effective way to learn concepts, vocabulary, language, and to acquire comprehension skills (Strickland & Morrow, 1989).

Benefits of Storytelling

Storytelling brings children's literature to life for people of all ages and serves a variety of important functions today, as it has done for centuries. Although its purposes may vary from those of the past, storytelling today is no less valuable as an art form. Specifically, modern storytelling serves the following purposes: catharsis, comprehension of story line, expressive and receptive language development, and aesthetic enjoyment.

Catharsis

Stories about multiculturalism (e.g., *I Have a Dream,* see p. 65), emotional issues (e.g., *The Purple Hat,* see p. 51), relationships (e.g., *I Like You the Best,* see p. 74), physical or academic handicaps (e.g., *Crow Boy*), and peer pressure (e.g., *Swimmy*) help children to relate to the protagonists. Through stories that reflect events that occur in their own lives, children realize a sense of unity. Through story conflicts and solutions, children discover that they may take an active role in solving their problems (see Table 3–2, p. 42).

Stories that use catharsis are often successfully told using the **Character Imagery, Group**

Role-Play, and **Chant Storytelling** methods. Often assigning children roles or allowing them to select ones different from their own life roles helps them to understand other points of view. Conversely, role-playing their own life roles may help them and other classmates to look more objectively at themselves and their situations.

Comprehension

Storytelling, as compared to story reading, is often more dramatic, more colorful, and more active. As a result, children are more likely to tune in to a story well told than a story well read. This storytelling attention advantage is especially true for children who have short attention spans (e.g., slower academically, attention deficit, etc.) and for those with limited visual and/or auditory skills. With its use of large and bold visuals (as in **Draw Talk** and **Felt Board Storytelling**) and its expressive and action-oriented sequence of events (all methods) storytelling elicits and sustains attention. Children thus have many more avenues of comprehension available to them than they would have when merely listening to a story being read. Comprehension is specifically enhanced as children view, and later enact, the story's sequence, discover cause and effect, compare characters, and classify story elements. In addition, children learn to distinguish between the main idea and details.

In a recently conducted study (Trostle & Hicks, 1998), researchers explored differences in children's comprehension and vocabulary acquisition when they listened to stories read by an adult or, conversely, witnessed the same stories enacted (actively told) by an adult. The children employed for the study were 32 British primary school children. Over a six-week period of time, the 16 subjects in Group One, Story Tell group, were further divided into small groups of four children, so that they witnessed one of four story titles, told by a trained adult. The 16 subjects in Group Two, Story Read group, listened to the same four stories and viewed the book illustrations. Following each story enacting or reading, the researchers tested each child individually on a measure of comprehension and on a measure of vocabulary. Children who witnessed storytelling of a selected title scored significantly higher on comprehension and vocabulary than did children who listened to storybook reading.

Asking children to dramatize or tell the story is also an effective teaching and learning strategy. In a now classic study, Smilansky (1968) found that children used the same processes when they use symbols in dramatic role-play of stories as they use in reading. Therefore, children practice using symbols and abstract thinking during their role-play. Storytelling abilities and narrative skills, too, increase during children's dramatic play. During symbolic play of stories, children practice and extend their emergent literacy skills (Piaget, 1962; Johnson, Christie, & Yawkey, 1987).

Auditory, tactile, and visual experiences, which characterize storytelling, all enable the child to comprehend meaning using a multisensory approach. Developmentally, this approach is known to benefit children who function at the **concrete operations stage,** the stage from ages four through seven, approximately, in which children learn best through real experiences and tangible props. Aesthetically, this approach benefits all listeners who appreciate storytelling as an art form.

Expressive/Receptive Language Development

When a storyteller invites the audience to join in on the storytelling, children feel free to say the refrain along with all the others without fear of mispronunciations, forgetting the line, recognizable speech impediments, and other barriers to children's confidence in speaking before others. Children's expressive language (language they use aloud) is, therefore, enhanced. When children hear others telling stories and learn words and language patterns from listening, their receptive language (language they hear and understand) increases in both quantity and quality. When children role-play a favorite story, using creative dramatics or puppetry, they are no longer themselves but rather, imagine themselves to be the story's characters. The judgmental nature which characterizes some traditional reading performances diminishes. As a result, children frequently shed their inhibitions and join in on the fun.

Aesthetic Enjoyment

For many of the same reasons that people of all ages all over the world enjoy theater, they also enjoy quality storytelling. This is known as **aes-thetic enjoyment.** In theater, fantasy and reality combine in a captivating manner. The audience escapes from the worries of today's challenging world and settles in for a new glimpse of what has been, what is, and/or what might be. Through creativity, animation, art, music, scenery, expression, props, sequence of events, humor, conflict, resolution of conflict, and culmination, theater elevates its audience to new levels of understanding and new visions.

Likewise, storytelling affords its audience many of the same privileges as theater. Children and adults of all ages and all intellectual capabilities benefit from the many language, sensory, and artistic experiences that invite them to listen, observe, participate, and enjoy.

Whereas research supports traditional use of teachers' story reading for improving students' comprehension, enjoyment, and "awareness of print" (Clay, 1991), storytelling of selected titles may provide an even more engaging context for students' resultant vocabulary acquisition, collaboration, and comprehension. Specifically, while story reading may be a useful vehicle for developing children's concepts of print—book handling, word identification, use of picture cues, capitalization, and punctuation—storytelling may further enhance children's vocabulary and comprehension.

Therefore, both story reading and storytelling play prominent and important roles in the literacy-rich classroom. Facilitation of all children's emerging literacy competencies is best accomplished, then, by the teacher's use of a combination of reading and telling of stories. The application of related extension activities related to listening, thinking, reading, writing, and problem solving also plays a key role in making the literacy environment function smoothly.

Authentic Assessment of Literacy

With the advent of whole language and integrated learning experiences for learners emerged a new view of assessment, **authentic assessment**, which is now widespread (Valencia, 1994). Assessment of students using portfolio evaluation has gained recognition and merit. Authentic assessment includes the use of videotapes, audiotapes, checklists and **rubrics** (sequentially-numbered scoring devices which contain written criteria and descriptions for achieving each number), anecdotal records, behavior sampling, and criterion referenced testing in real learning situations. This type of assessment is consistent with the theory that children learn in a process-type approach, at their own rates, and through meaningful experiences. Portfolios are used as folders or showcases and as one means by which children's work and project samples are collected and displayed. Progress through the school year is easily retrieved through a perusal of each individual's sequentially-organized portfolio.

Gardner's Theory of Multiple Intelligences (1993) reinforces the idea that children learn at their own rate and in their own style. Rather than viewing intelligence as a single general capacity, Gardner posits the existence of several intelligences. To Gardner these several intelligences are not physically verifiable entities but rather, potentially useful scientific constructs.

This text addresses brain research and multiple intelligence theory. Through the use of several storytelling methods and extension learning activities, each identified intelligence construct is addressed for all types of learners. Chapter 2 reviews the various types of intelligences, derived from those introduced by Gardner (1983, 1993) and later revised by others.

Summary

Storytelling is currently an underused but valuable tool for teaching and student learning. The authors find that few educators are well-versed in storytelling and the variety of applications available to them. Yet, teachers who are trained in storytelling become excellent models of literacy for their students. All stories found in this text are told Family Style; i.e., they can be adapted for children of all ages and abilities.

Emergent literacy engages children in meaningful, developmentally appropriate experiences that include reading, writing, speaking, listening, and problem solving. Through using authentic literature in the classroom and extending storytelling experiences to include immersion, responsibility, use and practice, approximations, demonstration and modeling, feedback or response, expectations, and engagement, educators help to ensure children's lifelong love of, and success with, reading.

CHAPTER RESOURCES

Andersen, H. C. (1999). *The ugly duckling*. New York: William Morrow.

Asbjrnsen, P. C. T. B. B. (1998). *The three billy goats gruff*. New York: HarperCollins.

Baker, L., & Brown, A. L. (1984). Cognitive monitoring in reading. In J. Flood (Ed.), *Understanding reading comprehension* (pp. 21–44). Newark, DE: International Reading Association.

Brett, J. (1990). *Beauty and the beast*. New York: Clarion.

Brett, J. (1992). *Goldilocks and the three bears*. New York: Dodd, Mead & Company.

Brothers Grimm. (1986). *Hansel and Gretel*. New York: Dutton.

Butler, D., & Clay, M. (1979). *Reading begins at home*. Portsmouth, NH: Heinemann.

Disney, W. (1997). *Disney's princess treasury collection: Disney's Snow White, Disney's Sleeping Beauty, Disney's Cinderella*. New York: Mouse Works, a division of Disney Book Publishing.

Lionni, L. (1963). *Swimmy*. New York: Pantheon.

O'Brien, C. O. (1986). *Mrs. Frisby and the rats of Nimh*. New York: Aladdin.

Piaget, J. (1952). *The origins of intelligence in children*. New York: Norton.

Yashima, T. (1955). *Crow boy*. New York: Viking.

The Use of Storytelling to Foster Emergent Literacy Skills: Incorporating Brain-Based Learning

No study of emergent literacy would be complete without considering the current methods of achieving the literacy skills delineated in Chapter 1. Morrow (1989) defines emergent literacy as the accumulation of early knowledge on how to communicate, make sense of the world, attend to tasks, negotiate help, and ask questions. She believes that it is this base of early knowledge on which the child needs to build when he or she enters formal instruction. Educators in emergent literacy are concerned with how their students can best assimilate, relate to, and accommodate symbols, content, and meaning. Clay (1991) cites the need for educators to incorporate a diversity of experiences when teaching young children. She states that we need to offer more expert teaching and interaction for children who are not showing normal progress. Storytelling assumes a key role in facilitating the goal of maximizing students' full learning potential.

Meaning and Comprehension

According to Clay (1991), "Meaning is the most important source of information" (p. 292). It lies outside the text and depends upon what the reader is able to bring to it. As educators, we are challenged to help students find the relationships between symbols and sounds and between informational facts and their application to life experiences.

The search for meaning occurs through patterning, according to Caine and Caine's (1991) principles relating to thinking. They explain that the brain learns by patterning and **chunking** ideas that relate to each other naturally. This ability to chunk ideas together forms the pattern for the brain to chunk letters together to form words and gain phonemic awareness (Adams, 1990). Finding the pattern connects the information to other ideas in the brain through **neural pathways** to become part of the long-term memory (Fogarty, 1997). This template pattern depends on **linguistic awareness** from which the child can develop knowledge about the nature of his or her own language (Clay, 1991). Here, storytelling provides a logical framework for patterning ideas, with linear, winding, and circular tales. As the child becomes familiar with the story's framework, he or she is able to develop the skill of predicting outcomes.

Clay (1991) notes the need for children to experience and use natural language. This usage forms the base of knowledge from which the child is able to make syntactic predictions and develop patterns of **grammatical knowledge** necessary to construct sentences. Clay (1991) states, "The preschool child's language development is vital to his progress in reading....The more of this experience he enjoys, the more mature his language will be on entering school" (p. 37). Storytelling provides the experience to create this foundation.

Nelson (1989) maintains that the combination of language, story, and metaphors heightens the listener's awareness. She states further that through the listener's emotional involvement, literal and inferential comprehension are increased. As Kline (1988) puts it, "the structures we discover for ourselves give shape and meaning to experience." The patterning found in thematic and integrated teaching approaches enhances the pattern of learning and is more brain compatible.

This integrated, thematic approach is provided through stories and storytelling. "The storytelling experience, then, is a vehicle for enhancing comprehension, both literal and inferential: Motivating oral discussion; increasing perceptual knowledge of metaphor; explaining and promoting interesting language usage; and using children's personal experiences to instill deeper meaning" (Nelson, 1989, p. 388).

More than an ancient oral art form, storytelling has been used throughout the ages to effectively transmit cultural information and morals, and to entertain. It is this playful, entertaining aspect of storytelling that enables it to engage its listener's attention and convey information into long-term memory.

Imagination, Emotion, Memory, and Learning

Einstein said, "Imagination is more important than knowledge, for while knowledge points to all there is, imagination points to all there will be" (Hannaford, 1995, p. 63). It is this very imagination that created the computer.

The process of imaginative development and the development of play becomes the "essence of creativity and high level reasoning," according to MacLean (Hannaford, 1995). Play is yet another tool by which children can explore and learn about their world. When the brain is given the chance to examine and play with information, giving its own order and meaning, structured perceptions arise naturally (Kline, 1988). Whether they are listening or telling, storytelling engages children's minds in creative play. This play involves order, sequence, ideas, concepts, and information as the mind processes it into meaning.

The impact emotions have on our ability to think and learn is noted by Hannaford (1995). Educators and researchers have noticed the importance emotions play in retaining knowledge. When learners make an emotional connection to information in a positive and engaging way, it is retained in memory longer (Jensen, 1998). The learner makes this positive emotional investment when he or she responds to information through play, art, movement, or by internalizing it through storytelling. With storytelling,

15

children develop the creativity to comprehend sequence and detail. They also learn to imaginatively retell or create stories of their own.

Fogarty (1997) maintains that learning involves the entire physiology. Glasser (1986), in agreement, states:

> We learn:
> 10% of what we read
> 20% of what we hear
> 30% of what we see
> 50% of what we see and hear
> 70% of what is discussed
> 80% of what is experienced personally
> 95% of what we teach someone else.

Einstein approached learning with his maxim saying, "Learning is experience. Everything else is just information....In order to learn, think or create, learners must have an emotional commitment"(Hannaford, 1995, p. 56). For Hannaford, the involvement of the intellect, emotion, and movement are needed to anchor learning into our long-term memory.

Some researchers believe that the brain stores every experience and that it only requires the correct trigger to recall the information (Lazear, 1991). And yet, our brain acts like a sieve, filtering out information that it determines is not relevant within nine seconds (Fogarty, 1997). Because of this filtering system, a great deal of information is not stored in the learner's long-term memory. For educators, the challenge is how to provide learning experiences that fully engage students, so that the information becomes anchored into long-term memory.

Information passing from short-term memory into long-term memory is processed through the **limbic system,** where most emotional processing occurs (Kline, 1988). "If the information is valued and practiced, it becomes the template for reorganization of previous patterning" (Hannaford, 1995). Ninety percent of the base patterns upon which all future learning is attached are formed within the first five years of life (Hannaford, 1995). If all the information passing into long-term memory is processed through the limbic system, a positive emotional state would have a great effect on learning (Kline, 1988). Storytelling engages the imagination and emotions while conveying information, which facilitates the integration of comprehension into the long-term memory.

The memory theory presented in Robert Sylwester's book *A Celebration of Neurons: An Educator's Guide to the Human Brain* (1995), suggests that "the best school vehicle for this search for relationships is storytelling." He includes such elements as "conversations, debates, role playing, simulations, songs, games, films, and novels," in this broad concept.

Storytelling offers the child a natural structure for facilitating **cognitive learning.** It involves the sequencing of events and information relevant to the context of the story. It provides the child with syntactic (ordering parts of speech) and semantic (meaningful contextual) tasks. Storytelling lengthens the child's attention span. Thus engaged, the brain creates a storehouse of patterns from which the child can draw conclusions and predictions to find solutions. The information to be learned is thus anchored in the child's memory with emotion and meaning, as he or she is involved in the story. Cognitive language skills combine with the creative imaging process during storytelling to engage the child's many ways of learning.

Gardner's Theory of Multiple Intelligences

Recent studies on the nature of human intelligence have changed our whole way of looking at how one is intelligent. In 1983, Gardner introduced the paradigm of **multiple intelligences** in his *Frames of Mind: The Theory of Multiple Intelligences*. Gardner discusses the criteria for an ability to be called an intelligence and how learning occurs when presented to a learner in his or her most competent area of intelligence. He believes that each intelligence is closely interrelated, yet can function separately (Gardner, 1983). He posited that a blend of the intelligences must be present for significant learning to occur (Gardner, 1993). Examples of this interrelatedness are shown in this chapter's discussion of the Musical-Rhythmic Intelligence and throughout our storytelling activities.

Gardner maintains that there are many ways in which one understands and learns, beyond the measure of the IQ tests. According to Gardner (1983), assessment of the intelligences is valid only if it will help a child understand his or her subject better and allow the educator to decide effective entry points for that particular child. His research suggests that we respond in different ways to different kinds of content, such as math, language, or other people (Checkley, 1997).

Some of these ways of knowing or intelligences may be stronger in one individual than in another. Yet these various intelligences work as an integrated whole to accomplish a learning task or problem while simultaneously developing the weaker ones. It has been found that intelligence can be enhanced at any age and occurs in many forms (Lazear, 1991).

Musical-Rhythmic Intelligence

Scientists at Beth Israel Hospital in Boston concluded that some people are born with a sense of music that can be lost without early training (Livo, 1996). Gardner believes that the **Musical-Rhythmic Intelligence** is one of the earliest to emerge and observe. It evokes emotion which is central to communication of feelings (Sylwester, 1995). It includes competencies in pitch, melody, rhythm, rhyme, and timbre. Exposure to, and appreciation of, music, along with vocal and instrumental performance, tap this intelligence (Fogarty, 1997).

Recent studies have shown that listening to music (for example, Mozart) can increase one's IQ (Livo, 1996). Lozanov's research showed that "concert sessions," i.e., reading while using dynamic vocal patterns to match the text to music, immediately tap the long-term memory, teaching 60% of the material in 5% of the usual time (Kline, 1988).

Throughout his discussion on multiple intelligences, Gardner gives examples of how each intelligence is different, yet shows how they are interrelated (Gardner, 1983). In his discussion of the Musical-Rhythmic Intelligence, Gardner gives examples of how music and song are closely associated to the movement and dance of the **Bodily-Kinesthetic Intelligence.** He continues by relating it to the **Verbal-Linguistic Intelligence** through the oral/aural skills employed. Gardner links the **Logical-Mathematical Intelligence** to the Musical-Rhythmic Intelligence through the sphere of patterns and logic (Gardner, 1983). Researchers at the University of California, Irvine, found that preschoolers who take music lessons improve their mathematical ability to reason about how objects relate to each other (Livo, 1996).

Incorporating songs, refrains, and musical instruments during storytelling adds depth to the emotions that storyteller's words can evoke or the child's journal can capture. Basic musical chants and rhythms aid the students in accessing and

Incorporating musical instruments during the storytelling experience helps children tap into the Musical-Rhythmic Intelligence.

anchoring information into their long-term memories, tapping into Musical-Rhythmic Intelligence. Vocal and instrumental performance, along with exposure to music appreciation, also taps this intelligence (Fogarty, 1997).

This text offers the reader stories, books, and related activities that integrate themes throughout the curriculum. The approach is based on the multiple intelligences theory of learning. The stories and activities provide opportunities to capture the child's attention and facilitate the acquisition of literacy. This text incorporates themes for use throughout the year. It will enhance learning opportunities and increase the experiences the young child needs in order to create and project future patterns of learning. The chants, songs, use of instruments, dance, and games to selected musical pieces related to the stories and storytelling work to develop Gardner's Musical-Rhythmic Intelligence.

Logical-Mathematical Intelligence

The ability to work with numbers, identify patterns, and think logically belongs to the Logical-Mathematical Intelligence. This intelligence is tapped through the skills of debating, concluding, calculating, computing, solving problems, and arguing logically, as well as through theory, principle, and proofs (Fogarty, 1997). Storytelling provides a natural sequencing of events in following or telling a story. The "if-then" and cause and effect thought patterns in stories hold appeal for this intelligence. Mysteries, riddles, **pourquoi** or "why" stories and the use of chants, and rhythm in participation stories further engage children who learn through this profile. These stories facilitate the child's ability to comprehend long chains of reasoning, exercising logical-mathematical skills. Young children are able to make accurate predications of meaning through the support of repetitious language patterns and events in the cumulative stories (Nelson, 1989). Young and old alike are fascinated as they follow the logic of circle and chain of event stories. Dramatizing story problems in math class anchors solutions in the body and brain.

Within this text, other storytelling activities created to develop the child's Logical-Mathematical Intelligence include bar graphing, problem solving, geometric designing, comparing and contrasting quantities, sequencing, patterning, measuring, and ordering. Each activity relates closely to the theme of the accompanying story. However, opportunities also abound for the child to create his or her own learning experiences related to the storytelling experience.

Bodily-Kinesthetic Intelligence

Gardner's (1983) Bodily-Kinesthetic Intelligence addresses handling objects or controlling and interpreting physical movements. This intelligence lies in the muscle memory of the body for athletes, dancers, mimes, craftspersons, carpenters, and car mechanics (Fogarty, 1997). Changing awareness through breathing and walking, labs, role playing, mental imaging, skill practice, and use of hands-on materials are ways to utilize this intelligence (Lazear, 1991). Emergent literacy competencies of hand, eye, and body coordination, timing, balance, and power are well developed for the child whose primary learning profile is kinesthetic. The mime and movements involved in telling and participating in a limited pantomime story activate this intelligence. Choreographed movement during a participation story also anchors the information for

Bodily-Kinesthetic Intelligence addresses handling objects or controlling and interpreting physical movements.

listeners and helps to extend their attention span, further enhancing this area.

Stories and activities to expand on the strengths of this intelligence include cutting, play dough molding, group pantomiming of stories, use of felt pieces to create and tell a story, participation in group dramatics, and choreographing and dancing to a story's song.

Visual-Spatial Intelligence

The **Visual-Spatial Intelligence** is the ability to perceive an object and mentally visualize and imagine how it would look when turned (Snowman, 1996). These skills are found in visualizing or transforming or modifying images. Artists, actors, painters, sculptors, graphic designers, and photographers generally have these capacities highly developed (Lazear, 1991). This intelligence is thought to be mainly centered in the **gestalt hemisphere,** usually thought of as the right side of the brain; but the eye dominance of the individual child and his or her processing abilities under stress can alter the expected outcomes (Hannaford, 1995). Some of the skills that are present with this intelligence are the ability to form mental images; discover shapes, pictures, and designs; manipulate images and **graphic representations;** recognize relationships of objects in space, optical illusions, and accurate perceptions from different angles; perform creative drama and **mind-mapping;** and draw areas of concern for time and the future (Lazear, 1991).

Storytelling offers the framework to exercise visual perception when learning to tell a story. Drawing **story maps** and **story webs,** or creatively walking-through a story, both physically and in the mind's eye, aid the learning process. The child is challenged to visualize the stage and boundaries of his or her story, both physically in space and in mind. These activities, along with creating block characters, constructing replica houses and villages, and producing and analyzing works of art using a variety of media are included to promote and develop spatial functioning.

Intrapersonal Intelligence

Gardner's **Intrapersonal Intelligence** addresses the development of understanding our inner selves. Self-awareness, self-regulation, self-assessment, and metacognition are skills related to this intelligence (Fogarty, 1997). Research findings show that we have the ability to shift from one state of consciousness to another at will; we have hundreds of levels of awareness; we can improve the quality of our own thinking; we possess capacities for controlling many bodily functions that were thought to be automatic; and that creativity is a process that can be learned, improved, and taught throughout our lives (Lazear, 1991). Storytelling provides the vehicle for this emotional processing as the teller or listener identifies with the story's characters and their plights. This empathy for the character allows the student to vicariously experience, evaluate, and examine the character's actions and development. Focusing and concentration skills are reinforced through special types of **journal writing** and discussion of stories from history, folklore, or the future. Using **learning logs** and **personal portfolios,** and setting goals are other tools of the trade to tap this intelligence (Fogarty, 1997).

Interpersonal Intelligence

Interpersonal Intelligence involves learning through interaction with others. The ability to solve problems through group projects, the division of labor, collaboration of skills, and feedback anchor information for this learner. It involves noticing other people's feelings and being able to make distinctions between them. It includes learning how to form values, ethics, and to develop empathy for others. As Fogarty (1997) explains, "the skills of caring, comforting, collaborating, and communicating bring this intelligence into being." Researchers have found this function takes place in the neocortex as well as the frontal cortex of the brain (Russell, 1976). Storytelling and its extension activities allow the listener and teller to become aware of, and to explore, the characters' feelings. They can experience these emotions within the safety of the story structure. Child psychologist, Dr. Bruno Bettelheim, in his book, *The Uses of Enchantment* (1976), stresses the value of fairy tales as a unique way for children to explore and come to terms with the emotions and the dilemmas of their inner lives. Storytelling itself is built upon the interaction between the teller and listeners. Taking turns sharing a story with a partner or reading in a group, choral reading, class plays, and

Interpersonal Intelligence involves learning through interactions with others.

making a story web or map are some of the activities that will develop this intelligence.

Verbal-Linguistic Intelligence

The Verbal-Linguistic Intelligence is the one intelligence most often associated with emergent literacy skills. This intelligence is located mostly in the left hemisphere of the brain in the part of the temporal cortex known as Broca's area (Lazear, 1991). It involves the ability to listen with comprehension, speak in an articulate fashion, identify and relate word sounds, read purposefully, write and create stories and poetry, and use language and its expression. Semantics (the meaning of words), **syntax** (the order among words within a context), **phonology** (the sounds, rhythms, inflections, and meter of words), and **praxis** (the different uses of words) all function as an integrated whole in providing clues to help children devise strategies in Verbal-Linguistic skills (Lazear, 1991).

Language is what sets humans apart from other species (Fogarty, 1997). In the early years, the impact of language stimulation is so critical that the curriculum needs to focus around language experience. Clay agrees that the child's language growth is entirely dependent on how much, what, and how people speak to the child (Clay, 1991).

Storytelling provides this language experience using both natural language and literary language. Conversations, dialogues, speeches, poetry, and essays foster Verbal-Linguistic Intelligence (Fogarty, 1997). Nelson (1989) writes that storytelling integrates speaking, listening, reading, and writing, while affecting children emotionally, linguistically, and cognitively. As such, storytelling further integrates emergent literacy skills and the different intelligences.

Follow-up activities included in this text to facilitate this Verbal-Linguistic Intelligence include storytelling, choral speaking, poetry reading, acting and creative drama, **process writing** (a step-by-step, collaborative writing/publishing procedure), journal writing, comprehension exercises such as Concept Maps and **Venn diagrams,** vocabulary developing exercises, and reporting activities.

Naturalistic Intelligence

Gardner defines the **Naturalistic Intelligence** as the human "ability to recognize and classify plants, minerals, and animals, including rocks and grass and all variety of flora and fauna. The ability to recognize cultural artifacts like cars, or sneakers may also depend on the naturalist intelligence" (Checkley, 1997, p. 12). Gardner states that this intelligence developed from the need to survive. Much of consumer society exploits the naturalist intelligence, which can be mobilized in the discrimination among brands of cars, sneakers, makeup, airplane models, and the like. The kind of pattern recognition valued in certain of the sciences may also draw upon naturalist intelligence (Roth, 1998). Roth states that it involves one's ability to understand the patterns in nature, discern the differences in species, grasp relationships, classify forms, and understand the interrelatedness of nature, and man's basic survival instincts.

Ways to experience this intelligence are observing, planting, collecting, comparing, displaying, sorting, discovering, uncovering, matching, and relating (Roth, 1998). Biologists, farmers, chefs, gardeners, hunters, sailors, astronomers, and fishermen are among those who have this intelligence highly developed (Roth, 1998). Nature walks, field studies, weather forecasting, stargazing, rooms with living plants, flowers, animals, rocks, fossils, and seashells encourage this intelligence (Fogarty, 1997). Stories of the great naturalists John James Audubon, Albert Einstein, Charles Darwin, and their methods of discoveries inspire children to look at their surroundings and encourage them to discover their own patterns and associations. Stories from different cultures featuring animal characters and their characteristics and stories of natural events and their effects on history enrich this intelligence.

Existential-Spiritual Intelligence

The newest ability being considered is the **Existential-Spiritual Intelligence.** This ability allows one to know the invisible, outside world and asks fundamental questions about our existence and purpose in life (Checkley, 1997). As of this printing, Gardner has not accepted this as a formal intelligence, as there is no brain evidence yet on its existence in the nervous system—a criteria for an intelligence (Checkley, 1997). Therefore, for the purposes of this text only the eight established intelligences are addressed.

Educators benefit from the theory of multiple intelligences when they take individual differences among their students seriously and modify how they teach and evaluate particular children (Checkley, 1997). Integrating the multiple intelli-

gences into a curriculum focused on caring results is a powerful intellectual undertaking (Checkley, 1997).

The application of the multiple intelligence approach to learning emergent literacy goals enables the educator to reach the mentally challenged students who are mainstreamed into the classroom and to inspire the prodigies. Most importantly, in an inclusive classroom, the theory provides the educator effective methods for teaching the average student who may have various methods of learning that cannot be measured with standardized tests.

Storytelling and Learning

Storytelling and its related activities integrate the various multiple intelligences and approach the child through his or her preferred learning profile. The child's ability to translate, comprehend, and store the information presented are reinforced, as it becomes relevant to him or her. Studies find that listeners are more engaged by the 'gestalt hemisphere' elements of a story than the speaker's use of '**logic hemisphere**' language. (Russell, 1976). By engaging students in this way, the educator is able to develop emergent literacy skills and anchor the information into the child's long-term memory.

Storytelling and its related activities succinctly integrate the various brain-based learning theories, effectively bridging the gap between concept and meaning to instill comprehension and enhance learning. According to Fogarty (1997), "these experiences imprint on the mind and stimulate brain growth and neural connections just as the more formally planned experiences in the classroom do" (pp. 24–25). Storytelling combines the cognitive language skills in the logic hemisphere of the brain with the creative image process in the gestalt side of the brain to engage the listener and teller in a whole-brain experience. As such an experience, storytelling avoids the labeling of people as either logic- or gestalt-side dominant, thereby creating the opportunity for children to develop new learning strategies. It provides them with the experience of accessing both sides of the brain without stress. Storytelling and related activities foster the critical, creative thinking which involves participation in problem solving, supports communication, builds a knowledge base, and develops skills and attitudes conducive to emergent literacy (Fogarty, 1997).

The child's listening skills improve as storytelling engages, challenges, and extends his or her attention span. The creative images and ideas that occur in the child's mind's eye become relevant to him or her. Emotionally invested, the child becomes self-motivated to master the goals of emergent literacy in order to share and preserve these thoughts with others. Storytelling's long-term success lies in its structure, which provides the experience and relevancy to facilitate the cognitive learning skills necessary to develop emergent literacy skills.

Summary

This text incorporates the multiple intelligences into themed curricula to facilitate the integration of emergent literacy skills. This approach is best served through the medium of storytelling and its related activities.

The format follows monthly themes to stimulate and challenge the various learning styles present in the classroom. Because there are no standardized tests available to help develop an accurate learning profile for the individual child, the authors recommend that educators use observation, portfolio evaluations, and other types of authentic assessment in a naturalistic setting in conjunction with this text.

The following poem, "The Average Child" aptly describes the unfortunate implications of failing to address the potential within each of the children whose lives we touch.

THE AVERAGE CHILD

I don't cause teachers trouble

My grades have been okay

I listen in my classes

I'm in school here every day.

My teachers think I'm average

My parents think so too.

I wish I didn't know that

'Cause there's lots I'd like to do.

I'd like to build a rocket

There's a book that tells you how,

Or start a stamp collection

Well it's no use trying now.

'Cause since I found I'm average

I'm smart enough you see

To know there's nothing special

I should expect from me.

I'm part of the majority

That hump part of the bell

Who spends his life unnoticed

In an average kind of hell.

— ANONYMOUS
(RETOLD BY JEANNE M. DONATO © 2000)

CHAPTER RESOURCES

Birch, C. L., & Heckler, M. A. (1996). *Who says? : Essays on pivotal issues in contemporary storytelling.* Little Rock, AR: August House.

Buzan, T., & Buzan, B. (1993). *The Mind Map® book: How to use radiant thinking to maximize your brain's untapped potential.* New York: Plume.

Campbell, D. (1997). *The Mozart effect: Tapping the power of music to heal the body, strengthen the mind, and unlock the creative spirit.* New York: Avon Books.

Dennison, P. E., & Dennison, G. (1985). *Personalized whole brain integration.* Ventura, CA: Edu-Kinesthetics, Inc.

Gillard, M. (1996). *Storyteller storyteacher: Discovering the power of storytelling for teaching and living.* York, ME: Stenhouse.

Goleman, D. (1994). *Emotional intelligence: Why it can matter more than IQ.* New York: Bantam.

Jensen, E. (1998). *Teaching with the brain in mind.* Alexandria, VA: Association for Supervision and Curriculum Development.

Mason, H., & Watson, L. (1991). *Every one a storyteller: Integrating storytelling into the curriculum.* Portland, OR: Lariat Productions.

Robbins, J. (2000). *A symphony in the brain.* New York: Atlantic Monthly.

Schank, R. C. (1990). *Tell me a story: A new look at real and artificial memory.* New York: Scribner.

Stokes, G., & Whiteside, D. (1996). *Without stress learning can be easy.* Burbank, CA: Three in One Concepts.

Weaver, M. (Ed.). (1994). *Tales as tools: The power of story in the classroom.* Jonesborough, TN: The National Storytelling Press.

How to Tell a Story: Ten Exciting Approaches

Storytelling, as an extension of children's literature, is an excellent means by which children representing all walks of life and all types of abilities achieve unity of ideas and establish harmony, both within and among themselves. As it has done for centuries, storytelling delights audiences, both young and old.

Background Information

Storytelling in modern days has evolved into a multidimensional art. From traditional to puppetry to musical to chant, storytelling has become one of the most promising tools of the new millennium for serving the diverse needs of children in our homes, our schools, and our child care facilities. In this text, storytelling is examined in ten unique ways. Each method is defined and described for the teller. Next, step-by-step instructions are provided and a listing of trade books appropriate for each method follows.

Storytellers are frequently intrigued when teachers and others who work with young children exhibit little confidence about storytelling. In fact, most teachers and those who work with children are skilled storytellers in their own rights. As they instruct children in their projects and inspire them every day to question, laugh, problem solve, think, and imagine, teachers exhibit many of the qualities of the finest storytellers. As teachers share stories about their own lives and the events they learn about through the newspaper, the radio, the computer or television, teachers are storytellers.

Purposes of This Chapter

It is one purpose of this chapter to help students, teachers, and others who doubt their expertise in storytelling to define the wonderful dramatic qualities that are already present in their daily interactions with children. Second, this chapter will help the reader to learn new methods of presenting children's literature. A third purpose is for the reader to be able to recognize the qualities that make different books appropriate for given storytelling methods. A final, and most important purpose of this chapter, is to help the reader acquire a love for storytelling that will last for a lifetime. The joys of storytelling are truly capable of transforming your classroom and your children. Soon, with inspiration, practice, and perseverance, you will become a master storyteller.

Preparing to Tell a Story

Regardless of the methods of storytelling the Teller uses, he or she can enchant and delight children of all ages and abilities. Through the use of dynamic body movements, eye contact, an enthusiastic, welcoming smile, and expressive facial changes throughout the telling, the Teller has the power to transform, transport, inspire, and uplift. Use of an effective voice tone, clear pronunciation, and projection are three keys to successful storytelling as well. As the Teller projects the voice in ranges from a dramatic stage whisper to a squealing mouse, to a roaring, thundering lion, the audience becomes lost in the story and mesmerized by the sights and sounds.

Rarely maintaining a stationary position, the Teller hops, skips, jumps, squats, perches, climbs, and crawls around the room. The Teller also involves the audience whenever possible and remains ever alert to signs of confusion and/or boredom from the audience. The Teller knows how and when to adapt the story, by adding more dialogue, explanations, use of examples, and/or opportunities for audience participation. The successful Teller realizes when it is wise to elaborate or extend the story, and, conversely, when it is time to shorten and end the story. A Teller may never tell a story the same way twice! Vocabulary, plot, style, and even settings and characters may vary considerably between and among tellings of the same story.

Above all, the successful Teller exudes confidence in him- or herself and in the story being told. When the Teller loves the story, has experience with the story, and has learned the story well, it is difficult for the story to "fall flat" or not meet the needs of the children. The Teller practices first, using note cards which summarize important story events, before a mirror. When the Teller feels comfortable,. he or she then practices before a small audience or friend(s).

The Teller asks him- or herself and the sample audience the following questions during the practice:

1. Is my story visually appealing?
2. Is my telling authentic to the story?
3. Is my story creative?
4. Am I animated and enthusiastic?
5. Do I have fun with my story?
6. Is my story short/long enough and sufficiently entertaining?

With the above, general suggestions at hand, the Teller now examines the ten types of story-telling.

Approaches to Storytelling

Teachers become skilled story readers as they learn to develop the correct use of pausing, intonations, expressions, and pictures to accompany the text. Likewise, these same skills translate very effectively into storytelling approaches. The next discussion delineates several storytelling methods for pre-school and primary level children of all developmental levels, talents, and abilities. Although storytellers today often use even more approaches than this text can accommodate, ten exciting approaches are included: Group Role-Play, Traditional, Adapted Pantomime, Character Imagery, Draw Talk, Puppetry, Chant, Felt Board, Balloon, and Musical. Group/Dyad Telling methods are discussed following the descriptions of many of the preceding storytelling methods.

Group Role-Play

From a very early age children practice and develop skills in Group Role-Play Storytelling. When they point a garden hose at the neighbor's garage and yell, "Let's put out the fire!" or serve a tantalizing platter of plastic fruits and vegetables to friends at a backyard restaurant, children are engaging in authentic forms of Group Role-Play.

Later, as children develop and witness plays, read and listen to stories, and observe storytellers in action, they become more sophisticated in their Group Role-Play techniques. For example, they may follow a script, assign roles, use costumes and props, and change voices, expressions, and body positioning. Whether primitive or advanced, however, Group Role-Play is, simply, children's reenactment of a story they have heard or observed which involves characters, drama, dialogue, and a plot.

Group role-play of many stories is easily accomplished using the listing of stories found in Table 3–2. Stories told in the Character Imagery Storytelling method are often adapted for Group Role-Play, for example. Occasionally Traditional, Puppetry, and Musical stories are used for Group Role-Play, as well.

Each of the following storytelling methods is followed by opportunities for students to engage in their own telling of the stories, using a single method of storytelling or a combination of storytelling methods. Students who retell stories they have heard or observed, using one or more of the storytelling methods discussed in this chapter, are engaging in group/dyad telling.

Commonly children witness an adult or adults telling a story using one of the storytelling methods. Later the children themselves gather materials, rehearse the story, and tell the story to an audience or a small group using the same techniques they observed the more skilled story-teller use.

Traditional

We have all told stories in the Traditional style. Traditional storytelling involves, quite simply, no props. Yet, storytellers who pride themselves on vivid facial and voice expressions and hand gestures often excel in the Traditional method of

Use of gestures and expression in Traditional Storytelling.

storytelling. This oldest of all methods relies heavily upon an inviting plot with a few simple characters, an exciting sequence of events building to a climax, and a quick conclusion. The use of a repeated refrain (e.g., "Then he huffed and he puffed and he blew the house in!") adds to the listeners' attention and enjoyment.

Since no props are used in this method, vocabulary that is unfamiliar to children, such as multicultural words or phrases, needs to be explained within the context of the story or directly defined prior to or just after telling the story.

The storyteller simply sits or stands before the audience and, using expressive voice tones and gestures, tells the story. Memorization of the exact story line deters from the natural flow of the story; therefore, books that depend upon an exact rhyming sequence and/or precise wording are not recommended for the Traditional method.

A recommended procedure for telling folk and fairy tales, which constitute excellent Traditional material, is to introduce different versions and compare and contrast those from each country. Perhaps, for example, each day for three days, tell a different version of *Little Red Riding Hood* or *Cinderella*. An introduction including props related to the story, such as a wolf puppet, a basket of goodies for "Grandma," or a red cape for Little Red Riding Hood, helps set the stage for the Traditional story; however, these props are not used during the actual telling.

Multicultural stories that are rich in imagery, offer a cumulative plot, and are interesting to audiences of all ages, languages, and cultures are ideal for Traditional storytellers. For recommended titles, refer to those used throughout the months in this text as well as those listed in Table 3–2. Bear in mind, however, that many stories lend themselves to several of the storytelling methods and/or a combination of methods. As the Teller gains familiarity with the titles and storytelling methods, he or she will naturally discern the appropriate method or methods for any given children's literature title.

Group/Dyad Telling

As a follow-up to a story told in the Traditional style, the children may take turns being the storyteller. Or, perhaps, the children can each tell one part of the story in either a random or a preassigned fashion. The emphasis is not on telling the story exactly as the adult storyteller (or story reader) did; however, the adult may need to assist the students in keeping the plot in the correct sequence. Vivid facial and voice expressions are encouraged. As an alternative, the students may wish to retell the story using a revised sequence of events or simply to retell the story using a new ending.

Adapted Pantomime

As was the case for Traditional storytelling, Pantomime uses no props. Also, this method relies heavily upon vivid facial expressions. Most importantly, however, the storyteller uses expressive movement throughout the story. In a true Pantomime story, no words are spoken by the teller. He or she relies, instead, upon gestures and movement to convey the words, phrases, and sentences in the story. In the Adapted Pantomime method, oral language accompanies the gestures and movements, either partially or completely. In either case, the storyteller dresses in solid-colored, loose-fitting clothing, preferably in a dark color such as navy blue, brown, or black. All words and phrases are demonstrated throughout the story by the Teller; therefore, this method is especially appropriate for visually impaired and/or academically challenged children. Also, unusual vocabulary words and concepts about lifestyles and features of other cultures are clearly demonstrated, through gestures and body actions, in the Pantomime approach.

An example of an Adapted Pantomime approach with Tony Johnston's *The Quilt Story* is the following:

Abigail *(show girl with pigtails on side of head)* loved *(hug self)* the quilt *(show square frame with hands)*. Abigail *(show girl with pigtails)* wrapped *(pretend to wrap)* the quilt *(show square frame)* round *(show circle with hands)* her in the quiet *(put index finger to lips; whisper "shhhhh")* dark *(cover eyes)*. Abigail *(show girl)* saw *(finger points to eye)* a falling *(kneel or fall down)* star *(use both index fingers to "draw" star)*.

When preparing to tell a Pantomime story, it is helpful to rewrite the story and circle each verb and noun that can be depicted through gesture.

Solid-colored, loose-fitting clothing and optional use of words are characteristics of Pantomime Storytelling.

Practice several motions for the verbs and nouns, in front of a mirror, until you "capture" the word as vividly as possible. You will need to tell the story at a slow, clear, and deliberate pace, since many of the words in a story are pantomimed.

A Pantomimed story may be introduced as follows:

Step 1: Talk about the subject of the story and relate yourself to this topic.

Step 2: Talk about the subject of the story and relate your audience to the topic.

Step 3: Show the book. State title, author, and illustrator. State how the book relates to the aforementioned theme. Then, placing the book aside, begin to tell the story.

Group/Dyad Telling

Group storytelling following the adult use of the Pantomime method includes suggestions similar to those used for the Traditional method. The children may decide to dramatize the story one at a time, or they may collaboratively assign one child to one image in the story. The story is then staged in the same sequence as it was told to them earlier. The use of words, again, is optional, but may be preferable for younger, novice storytellers.

As a variation the children may elect to change the words, the sequence of events, and/or the ending of the story. Later, with practice, they will successfully create their own stories appropriate to the Pantomime method with little assistance.

Selected multicultural books appropriate to the Pantomime approach to storytelling appear in Table 3–2 at the conclusion of this chapter.

Character Imagery

Children delight in witnessing their teacher or another adult dress as the story's main character and act out the story from the point of view of this protagonist. Likewise, they enjoy imitating and becoming the main character. The Character Imagery method bears a resemblance to the Pantomime method, in that they both rely heavily upon gestures and body movements. The differences, however, are that the Character Imagery method is told from the perspective of the main character and uses verbal language and verbal expression to portray additional story characters. Children with mental or visual special needs espe-

The Teller "becomes" the protagonist in Character Imagery Storytelling.

cially benefit from this active, colorful method of storytelling. Learning of vocabulary words indigenous to other lands and cultures occurs naturally because the key words are dramatized and used concretely throughout the story.

In preparing to tell a Character Imagery story, the Teller first prepares the costume of the protagonist in the book. The Teller practices telling the story, in first person, past tense from the point of view of the protagonist. Occasionally, the Teller "becomes" a secondary character while telling the story. This is accomplished by changing voice, gestures, and body positioning. The protagonist may ease this transformation into other characters or by announcing, for example, "This is what the bear sounded like to me..."

While the Teller is talking, he or she pantomimes gestures of the main character of the story and, occasionally, the secondary characters. Feel free to use the entire room while telling the Character Imagery story, greeting members of the audience, running to escape from a predator, and tiptoeing in a wide circle, for instance.

The introduction to the Character Imagery method of storytelling is unique, in that the Teller dresses as the main character while telling about the story plot and activating listeners' prior knowledge. The steps in the introduction are as follows:

1. Show book. State author, title, and illustrator. (If no book is available, simply state the title of the story and, if possible, its derivation.)
2. Place book aside.
3. Begin dressing while discussing your own experiences with the theme of the story.
4. Continue dressing while discussing children's experiences with the theme of the story.
5. When nearly finished dressing, refer the audience back to the theme of the book. Tell them that you will be telling a story about this book and its main character.
6. Fully dressed, ask them, "How do you think I know so much about the main character in this story?" (Pause for responses.)
7. Proclaim, "Because I AM the main character, _____!" (state main character's name now and begin telling story.)

Group/Dyad Telling

For the Character Imagery follow-up method, the same guidelines as for Pantomime are followed. The exception is that the children may wish to incorporate props, such as hats, wigs, costumes, accessories, and the like. Vivid voice and facial expressions are encouraged as the youngsters reenact the story they have observed. Also, the adult may wish to coach the children on projecting the voice, positioning themselves so that all can see, and other stage techniques.

The use of a narrator to facilitate the creative dramatics is optional. Later, as the children become skilled at using this method of storytelling, they may be ready to invent and enact their own story lines, either using a prewritten script prepared in a collaborative setting, or through the unfolding of the story line in ad lib fashion.

Matinez (1993) provides excellent guidelines for using **dramatic story reenactments (DSRs),** explaining that using such techniques strengthens children's understanding of cause and effect, recall, and sensitivity to emotional responses of characters from all cultural groups.

Besides the stories found throughout this text, other excellent selections for the Character Imagery method include those listed in Table 3–2 at this chapter's conclusion.

Draw Talk

Frequently authors and illustrators on tour use the Draw Talk method of storytelling to tell

Character Imagery: One child, following the adult's lead, becomes the main character.

Draw Talk involves tracing over pre-drawn pencil lines to tell a story.

their story to an audience. Unless the novice storyteller is very skilled at drawing, the pictures from five or six main parts of the story are drawn lightly, in advance, using a pencil. The Teller uses five or six sheets of 24" x 36" white drawing paper or newsprint. Each of these pages represents one event from the story. Therefore, best story choices are those which are simple and contain a few major events suitable for illustration. The Teller uses no more than three wide-point liquid markers of bright or dark colors. Drawing of pictures is precisely synchronized to the words stated by the Teller. Therefore, this method is excellent for children with visual and auditory challenges, as well as for those who are academically challenged.

Once the five or six pages are pre-drawn, the Teller clips the pages, in order, to a large easel. Use of a cover or title page is optional as the first page of the story. The Teller stands to one side of the easel, so that the view of the audience is not obscured. The introduction to the story proceeds next, as follows:

1. Talk about the theme of story, relative to some event in your life. For example, in a story about wishes, the Teller might begin, "Sometimes it is difficult to believe my wishes will come true. Once I wanted a swing set for my birthday. I hoped and wished that I would get it. But my friends all told me that I would not."

2. Talk about the theme of the story, relative to some event in your listeners' lives. For example, continue, "Perhaps you have wanted something very much. But your family and friends may have said it could not happen. If this has happened to you, you will appreciate the story I am going to tell you."

3. Show the book. Point to, and state title, author, and illustrator. State, "In this book, the main character also wants something to happen. But his family and friends do not believe that it will. Watch and listen to my story and see what happens!" (Begin Draw Talk story)

Group/Dyad Telling

Involving the group or teams in a Draw Talk story is relatively easily accomplished. The adult or child may retell the story, using the same paper, colors, and lines that were previously drawn by the adult teller. The child simply traces over the original lines. As the child traces the lines, he or she retells the story. The other classmates each have five sheets of smaller, blank paper at their tables or desks. Using crayons, colored pencils, or liquid markers, they draw along with the child at the easel and, simultaneously, recreate the five-page story.

As a small group or dyad alternative, the children may take turns being the storyteller. They retell the story using large easel paper on which the guidelines have been previously lightly sketched by the adult or a talented child. One child may tell and draw the entire story or each child in a group of five may tell and draw one page. For dyads, the children may draw alternate pages.

With experience, children will create and tell their own Draw Talk stories. In the meantime, the adult can facilitate their development toward this goal by providing the children with many simple, basic books from which they can translate the words and pictures into large, Draw Talk images with a minimum of adult guidance.

Recommended multicultural titles for Draw Talk Storytelling include those found in the following text chapters. Also, in Table 3–2 at the conclusion of this chapter, the reader will find other stories appropriate to Draw Talk Storytelling.

Puppetry

Flexibility of setting, Tellers enlisted, and types of puppets used vary this storytelling method. Ranging from elaborate stages with curtains and painted scenery to no stage at all, or lap settings, puppetry is as simple or as complicated as the Teller desires. Likewise, puppet types range from finger puppets to papier mâché puppets to envelope puppets to sock puppets to felt or cloth puppets. The most important aspects of this method are expressive and definitive voices for each character, active and differentiated manipulations of puppets, and appropriate story choice. Also, successful puppeteers are certain that they can be heard and (for formal performances) not seen.

Select stories with a few main characters and settings. Stories with a good deal of dialogue work best. If the story you select has limited dialogue, you may, of course, rewrite it and add conversation. Next, decide which characters will enlist actual puppets and which may appear, instead, on a small or large crowd scene, either painted or colored on the background or held up on a dowel rod on poster board.

If your story uses only one Teller, the use of two puppets, at most, is most easily handled. For two Tellers, four puppets may be comfortably manipulated; for three Tellers, six puppets, and so on. After deciding which puppets will be constructed, think about your desired scenery. How many times will the scene change, necessitating a change of background? How will this background change without interrupting or delaying the story line?

If the Teller is using lap scenery, he or she holds several scenes, in the order in which they occur, on the lap while seated. Then, as the story unfolds, the Teller simply removes each scene after it is used, revealing the next scene underneath.

For stage puppetry, a bottom rim works well. Onto this ledge, on the lower part of the stage, place the scenes in the order of appearance. As the scenes are no longer needed, slide out the front scene to reveal the scenery beneath it.

The next step in preparing your Puppetry story is script preparation. Rewrite the book, noting parts for narrator (if any), and for each of the characters, in play fashion. Highlight in yellow the speaking parts of each character, and give each Teller his or her designated script. If you decide to add music and/or sound effects, note the occurrence of these background noises on each script. Assign a designated tape recorder operator and/or sound maker.

Finally, practice the show before a small audience for constructive criticism about voices and audibility, movements of puppets, clarity of story line, and scenery.

You are now ready to stage your show! For your introduction, proceed as follows:

1. Teller stands in front of puppet stage and introduces the book. Point to, and state, title, author, and illustrator.
2. Talk about yourself in regard to the story theme.
3. Talk about the audience in regard to the story theme.
4. Relate the theme back to the book and tell the audience that you will now perform a Puppet Show, which is about this theme.
5. You may introduce one or more puppets at this time, before you travel behind the stage and begin the Puppet Show.

Papier Mâché Puppets

Materials:

1. Newspaper
2. Masking tape
3. Pail
4. Wheat flour or plaster of Paris
5. Water
6. Wooden stirrer
7. Decorating materials
8. Toilet tissue rolls
9. Elmer's glue
10. Tempera paintbrushes
11. Styrofoam ball (optional)
12. Paper towels (optional)

Make Form:

1. Use empty toilet tissue roll.
2. Set newspaper or styrofoam ball on top of roll. Tape in place.
3. Mold features with newspaper.
4. Wrap features and secure in place with masking tape.

Cover Form:

1. Gather old newspapers.
2. Tear the papers into 6″ × 2″ strips. Set aside.
3. In a large pail, pour one package of wheat paste or plaster of Paris.
4. Add water and stir until consistency is fairly thick.
5. Place paper strips into pail with paste mixture. Soak.
6. Wrap paper strips (thoroughly moist) around prepared newspaper form. Add soaked paper towel strips, if desired.
7. Allow to dry for 3–4 days in a warm, dry spot.
8. Use tempera paint to cover entire form. Allow to dry.
9. Decorate form with yarn, buttons, cloth, and/or other materials. Use Elmer's glue and/or needle and thread.
10. Enjoy your puppet!

Instructions for making papier mâché puppets.

Group/Dyad Telling

The Puppetry method lends itself very naturally to group storytelling, with each child in a group of four or five manipulating one puppet as they retell the story. Subsequent retellings will ensure that every child in the larger group has at least one turn. Prior to their retelling the story, the children may meet as a collaborative group to write a script to follow during the enactment.

Children also delight in creating original puppet show scripts. Adults simply need to provide books, tapes, videos, and examples of real-life situations; children will relish converting these episodes into puppetry shows. The use of child-constructed puppets, props, and staging adds to the personalization and involvement of all children. The need for adult guidance may be relatively strong at first; however, as the children gain experience as puppeteers, the need for extensive guidance will diminish. Cross-ability grouping flourishes as the children collaborate to write scripts, practice lines, and strive to master the art of puppetry storytelling.

Suggested titles for puppet show recreating include those found in the following chapters as well as those listed in Table 3–2 at the conclusion of this chapter.

Guidelines for constructing papier-mâché and puppets are provided here.

Chant

The Chant method is similar to the Traditional method with a few important exceptions. First, the Chant method involves the use of a gesture, on the part of the Teller, indicating to the audience to join in on a certain sentence or phrase. This gesture is introduced before the telling begins and is practiced a few times with the audience immediately before beginning the Chant story.

Second, the Chant approach, unlike the Traditional approach, involves the mandatory use of a story with a repetitive element so that, approximately every fifteen seconds throughout the story, at the Teller's predetermined gesture, the audience helps to tell the story. The Teller ends the story with this gesture and the chant of the phrase or sentence by the audience.

Some editing of the story may be necessary in order to ensure sufficient and regular audience participation. In other words, the Teller may insert the repetitive phrase several extra times, to ensure maximum audience involvement and sustained interest.

As the Teller prepares the Chant story, he or she locates a copy of the book from which the story is derived. The Teller then rewrites the story onto a few pages, using the entire story, or editing the story for shortened length. Next, the Teller inserts the repetitive chant throughout the story, so that the audience is involved every 15 to 30 seconds, approximately. The Teller may wish to highlight the repetitive phrases in yellow so that during practicing the Teller will learn the appropriate places to pause from the telling, show the practiced gesture, and have the audience join in on the chant.

The introduction to the Chant method is as follows:

1. Talk about the story's theme, relative to some incident in your own life.
2. Talk about this same theme, relative to some possible incident in the children's lives. (You may ask the audience questions at this time. However, be prepared for the children to begin their own storytelling and allow extra time for this!)
3. Show the book or tell the title and origin of the story. State the book's title, author, and illustrator, if known.
4. Talk about the theme of the story relative to your incident and the incidents the children discussed. Tell the group that you will be telling them a story about this theme. Put book aside.
5. Ask the children to help you with one final aspect of the telling, before you begin. Show

them a signal (such as a thumbs up sign, rabbit ears, a clap, etc., depending upon your story theme). Ask them to say a given phrase or sentence each time you show this gesture or symbol. For example, in the story *Millions of Cats* by Wanda Gag, the Teller shows cat ears as the chant symbol. Each time the Teller shows cat ears, the audience chimes in on the oral phrase. For this, it is helpful to print the chant on a large poster in advance, and display it beside the Teller, or somewhere else easily visible. The chant for this story is "hundreds of cats, thousands of cats, millions and billions and trillions of cats; cats here, cats there, cats and kittens EVERYWHERE!"

For a story about love, the Teller might show the Sign Language symbol for "I love you" and invite the audience to sing along with the repetitious chant each time the Teller shows the signal.

Group/Dyad Telling

At times, a story may contain more than one repetitive chant. For Chant Storytelling, the Teller

Teller using "I love you" sign for Chant Storytelling.
(Courtesy of Joy-O-Loons).

may introduce and practice up to two chants with the audience before the telling begins. The Teller may use a different and separate signal for each of the two chants.

Group involvement in the Chant Storytelling approach occurs frequently in the original storytelling itself. However, if the teacher desires even more group involvement, he or she may encourage the child to become the storyteller. Changing the story line and/or the ending are other variations. One creative class, for example, changed the title of Viorst's *Alexander and the Terrible, Horrible, No Good, Very Bad Day* to *Alexander and the Wonderful, Marvelous, Awesome, Very Good Day*. Using the thumbs-up symbol, the storyteller cued the audience when it was time to join in on the phrase. The revised story event, which the children had written earlier in a collaborative group setting, depicted a day—unlike the original story—in which everything went "just right!"

Selected multicultural titles for the Chant method include those selected stories in Chapters 4–15 of this text. Other appropriate Chant stories are listed in Table 3–2 at the end of this chapter.

Felt Board

Often called flannel board, the Felt Board method involves the use of a large board (approximately two feet in width by three feet in length). This board is covered in a sheet of felt which is three inches wider and longer than the board, to allow for tucking the extra fabric behind the board. Use masking or duct tape to secure the felt sheet in place, making certain the felt is smooth and unwrinkled on the front side of the board.

A black felt board is most commonly used; however, the Teller may easily add another color to the board simply by covering the black layer with, for example, light blue, green, white, or any color which relates to the story theme and setting.

Felt pieces are cut from patterns or drawn free hand. If the book's illustrations are sufficiently large and clear, the Teller may place a sheet of tissue paper over top of the book's images. Then the Teller traces the desired patterns directly from the book.

Felt pieces are usually no smaller than three inches in size to allow for visibility to all viewers.

If decorations are desired on the felt pieces, the Teller may add rick-rack, yarn, rolling eyes, cotton, imitation jewels, fabric, or additional felt. Use of liquid markers and/or paint on the felt pieces is usually disappointing, as the effect is blurred and not as professional in appearance as the other materials.

When the background of your felt board is very close in coloring to the felt images which will be used, the Teller is wise to mount the entire felt piece on a contrasting piece of felt which is about 1/8 of an inch larger all around than the original felt piece. Consider, for example, the old story of *Anansi the Spider*. The black spider brothers and the father, Anansi, will not be clearly visible upon a black felt board. Yet, if the Teller wishes to use the black board, he or she can mount each spider upon a slightly larger white spider shape. Now, the white spiders' background will contrast very well with the black felt board background.

In preparing to tell the Felt Board story, the Teller decides how many scenes the story will have. The Teller then constructs the appropriate pieces. Next, the Teller writes out the story on a few pages of paper, highlighting each change of felt piece and/or scenery. It is imperative that felt pieces be given a "reason" (or cue) for both placement and removal, such as, "the brown, fuzzy rabbit hopped into the barnyard" (*place rabbit now*). For removal, the pieces are "eaten, walk away, disappear, leave to find a friend," and so on. Exact synchronization of felt pieces with words the Teller uses is also an important key to quality Felt Board Storytelling. Youngsters with mental, visual, behavioral, and/or auditory challenges, as well as children from all cultures and abilities, benefit greatly from this multisensory approach. Felt Board Storytelling is generally best suited to ages two through seven, because of its simplistic and concrete nature.

An introduction to the Felt Board approach might proceed as follows:

1. Discuss the story theme, relating an event in your own life to this theme.
2. Continuing with this theme, relate an event in the children's lives to this theme.
3. Show the book. State title, author, and illustrator. Explain that this book also relates to

the theme discussed earlier, and that you will be telling the group a story using the Felt Board method of storytelling. State a few reasons for the children to watch and listen as you tell the story.

Group/Dyad Telling

After observing a Felt Board story, children are invariably eager to manipulate and explore the beautiful and colorful felt pieces. This curiosity is easily channeled into their retelling of the story. One child may retell the entire story or children may decide, before the reenactment, to assign individuals with specific pieces and/or parts of the story. For example, Lee may manipulate all the scenery pieces, while Hans manipulates all the characters in the story. Each is also responsible for telling the story related to the placement of the pieces. Alternatively, Juan may tell the beginning, Maria may tell the middle, and Felicia may conclude the story. While telling, each youngster places the pieces on the felt board that correspond to these sequential parts of the story.

As a variation, invite the children to retell the adult's version of the story in a creative, new manner using the original pieces. After the children become experienced with the mechanics of the Felt Board method, the adult encourages them to write their own Felt Board stories and/or to transform existing stories they have written into Felt Board stories. Having glue, scissors, and felt available will encourage children to create their own felt board pieces to complement their original stories.

Selected Felt Board references for grades K–1 are contained in Table 3–2 at the end of this chapter. Throughout Chapters 4–15 of this text, several Felt Board stories are also included.

Words mounted on felt accompany felt pieces.

Balloon

Balloons are used by some storytellers to help create a story. As the story unfolds, twist and tie the balloons to replicate the shape of the main character or several characters in the story. You may wish to fill the balloon with air before your story begins; or, you might fill the balloons during the storytelling.

Another creative use for balloons during storytelling is to use the balloon for sound effects, such as a "Pop!", a squeaking mouse, etc. When used in this manner, an assistant may use the balloon(s) so that the audience does not see them. However, some stories lend themselves to the Tellers showing the balloons and how they create the sound effects.

For introducing the Balloon story, the Teller may follow the same format as used for Felt Board. However, adding a balloon figure as part of the introduction may provide an even more motivating beginning to a story told in this unique storytelling method.

Teller twists, turns, and ties balloons, creating characters.

Group/Dyad Telling

With the use of some creativity and imagination, Balloon stories are readily transformed into group and dyad storytelling methods. For example, in a balloon story give each child a balloon in the shape of the character or animal found in the story. Or, if they wish to and can manage the task, children may construct their own balloon characters. As you tell the story, the child holding the character which is named comes forward, to the center of the group, and pantomimes the actions of that character.

Selections for the Balloon storytelling method are found in Table 3–2 at this chapter's conclusion. Also, the reader will locate Balloon stories in Chapters 7 and 9 of this text.

Musical

A wide variety of stories can be told using music. As mentioned previously, Felt Board stories are often supplemented with a musical background. Likewise, a Chant story may use a ditty or song chant at the given signal by the Teller. Another use of music in stories is to assign different singing parts to various characters; throughout the story, they sing to each other.

Keeping an assortment of instruments from around the world intrigues children and invites them to participate. At the same time, Musical stories are enhanced by the wide variety of sounds these exotic instruments provide. Explore, for example, the sounds of maracas, kazoos, bagpipes, accordions, and African drums.

Use of homemade instruments is another option for the Musical story. Kitchen pans and spoons, aluminum foil, newspapers, and pie tins all capture both the children's imaginations and the story's adventure.

Group/Dyad Telling

In a Musical story, as the sound of a certain instrument is named, such as "the screeching wind," the child holding an instrument that replicates the sound steps forward and plays. For example, a violin may imitate this screeching sound; a bugle might represent the wake-up call; and a whistle may be a robin in a story about spring.

A final use of music is to assign children to musical instruments before they tell the story. Then, at their assigned times, the instruments are played in the background as the story unfolds.

The Musical story may be introduced as was Felt Board. Or, the Teller may sing a short song to further enhance the beginning of the story and stimulate the children's curiosity.

Selected titles for Musical Storytelling include those found in Chapters 4–15 of this text as well as those in Table 3–2 at the conclusion of this chapter.

Summary

Multicultural storytelling offers the young learner unique advantages that are unavailable from any other single source. The variety of storytelling methods described in this chapter, though far from complete, enables the child to benefit emotionally, cognitively, expressively, and aesthetically. In addition, all of the multiple intelligences are addressed when children as storytellers, problem-solve; work together to plan and collaborate; discover spatial abilities in designing scenery and puppets; learn more about themselves and their individual talents; and apply language, naturalistic, and mathematical skills to their script writing, reading, and editing.

Children also expand their awareness of cultural diversity as they observe and participate in stories that deal with people and places unlike those with which they are familiar. Through the multiple intelligence extension activities, children reinforce and expand their repertoire of understandings and skills relating to the stories.

In addition, children learn about story mechanics and story structure so that their retelling and inventing new stories for the selected methods evolve naturally. Most importantly, perhaps, they learn that stories are captivating and inspiring vehicles for learning about life. By carefully establishing literature-rich classrooms for children, teachers and caregivers enable students to become self-initiators in many exciting types of story reenactments. The foundation for a lifelong love of literature *and* a lifelong respect for diversity emerges.

An assortment of instruments may be used in Musical Storytelling.

Table 3–1 Summary of Storytelling Techniques

Storytelling Method	Characteristics	Groups or Individuals Best Served	Materials; Props	Emotional and Literary Areas Addressed	Characteristics of Books Best Suited to Method
Traditional	• Told in past tense • No props necessary • Expressive voice and facial features • Occasional gestures	• Advanced students • Multicultural students • Students who possess a broad experiential background	• None are required	• Expression • Imagery • Enunciation • Sequence • Vocabulary	• Repetitive element • A few main characters; a few minor characters • Colorful, interesting, exciting tales
Adapted Pantomime	• Words accompany gestures • Dramatic body movements • Solid-colored clothing worn	• Advanced students • Students who possess a broad experiential background • Visually-impaired students	• Plain, one-colored clothing (slacks and shirt)	• Imagery • Imagination • Sequence • Problem solving	• Vivid elements • Simple, recognizable themes • Simple plot
Character Imagery	• Told in first person, past tense • One main character; a few minor characters • Storyteller dresses up and talks as protagonist	• Students with emotional problems • All ethnic backgrounds • Students with short attention spans • Students with hearing and/or visual problems	• Costume to represent main character • Other props (optional)	• Summarizing skills • Catharsis • Identification with protagonist • Expression	• One main character • A few events and an exciting conclusion • A few minor characters in supporting roles
Draw Talk	• Voice and drawing are synchronized • Uses approximately five sheets of unlined newsprint • Uses an easel for display	• All ethnic backgrounds • Advanced students • Students with language-delays • Students with visual impairments	• Unlimited newsprint • Easel • Liquid markers (3)	• Vocabulary • Artistic expression • Summarizing skills • Aesthetic enjoyment • Sequence	• A few major events • Simple pictures • High interest, descriptive level
Puppetry	• Puppets are active when "talking," still when "listening," • Many variations of puppets and stages possible	• Students who are shy • Expressive students • All ethnic backgrounds • Students with short attention spans	• Puppets • Stage • Scenery (optional) • Props (optional)	• Role-taking • Identification with characters • Catharsis • Expression • Creativity	• Two to four characters • Exciting yet simple plot • Much dialogue

Table 3-1 Summary of Storytelling Techniques (continued)

Storytelling Method	Characteristics	Groups or Individuals Best Served	Materials; Props	Emotional and Literary Areas Addressed	Characteristics of Books Best Suited to Method
Chant	• Repetitive phrase throughout story • Periodic audience participation via "chant" • Signal used to invite audience to join in throughout story	• Students with short attention spans • Students with language impairments • All ethnic groups • Students who are shy	• None are required • Chant (previously written on chalkboard or large chart paper (optional)	• Oral expression • Good listening	• Within audiences' frame of reference • Repetitive phrase • Sequential plot • Interesting story line
Felt Board	• Voice and placement of felt pieces are synchronized • Felt pieces are colorful and contrast well with background felt board	• Students with short attention spans • Students needing concrete examples • Students with learning disabilities • Students with language impairments • All ethnic groups	• Felt board • Felt pieces • Felt board stand or easel • Table for felt pieces	• Summarizing skills • Vocabulary • Counting • Matching	• Cumulative quality • Sequential quality • Attractive, simple pictures
Balloon	• Balloons represent one or more characters • May use balloons for sound effects	• Students with short attention spans • Students requiring concrete examples or models	• Balloons: various sizes, shapes, colors	• Artistic expression • Imagery • Creativity	• Few main characters • Additional supporting characters • Repetitive sound throughout story
Musical	• Supplements several other storytelling methods • Uses singing and/or musical instruments throughout telling	• Musically talented • Auditory learners • Students with short attention spans	• Musical instruments and/or noisy household items	• Aesthetic enjoyment • Active participation • Attention span • Expression	• Repetitive, poetic, or music element • Musical parts for several children
Group Role-Play	• Parts are assigned in advance • Use of props (optional) • Use of narrator (optional)	• Students who are shy • Students with language impairments • Students with comprehension difficulties • All ethnic backgrounds	• None required • Possible use of stage and props	• Catharsis • Expression • Story sequence • Vocabulary	• Several characters for group • Two main characters for dyad • Much dialogue • Colorful, interesting main plot

Table 3–2 Creative and Thematic Approaches to Storytelling Methods

TRADITIONAL

Grade Level	Theme/Subject	Title
K–1	Animals; Foods; Music; Science; Social Studies; Drama	Brothers Grimm. (1974). *The Bremen-town musicians.* Illustrated by Jack Kent. New York: Scholastic. (German)
K–1	German foods; Shoes and Clothing; Health; Social Studies; Math; Drama	Brothers Grimm. (1960). *The shoemaker and the elves.* Translated by Wayne Andrews. Illustrated by Adrienne Adams. New York: Scribner. (German)
2–3	African culture; Spiders; Language; Social Studies; Science; Art	McDermott, G. (1972). *Anansi the spider.* New York: Holt, Rinehart & Winston. (Ashanti people/Ghana, Africa)
4–5–6	Tall Tales; Language; Art; Social Studies; (History); Math	Emberley, B. (1963). *The story of Paul Bunyan.* Illustrated by Ed Emberley. Englewood Cliffs, NJ: Prentice-Hall. (European-American)
4–5–6	Animals; Yiddish Songs; Families; Social Studies; Science; Music	Zemach, M. (1976). *It could always be worse.* New York: Farrar, Straus & Giroux. (Yiddish)

ADAPTED PANTOMIME

Grade Level	Theme/Subject	Title
K–1	Holidays; Animal Homes; Farming; Crops; Science; Social Studies; Drama	Potter, B. (1903;1971). *The tale of Peter rabbit.* New York: Scholastic. (Animals)
K–1	Independence; Imagination; Science; Social Studies; Drama	Hall, M., et al. (1965). *Play with me.* New York: Viking. (European-American)
K–1	Independence; Imagination; Science; Social Studies; Drama	Hall, M., et al. (1965). *In the forest.* New York: Viking. (European-American)
K–1	Seasons; Self-Concept; Physics (beginning); Science; Math; Social Studies; Drama	Keats, E. J. (1996). *The snowy day.* New York: Viking. (African-American)
2–3	Family; Moving; Life Changes; History; Social Studies	Johnston, T. (1996). *The quilt story.* Illustrated by T. De Paola. New York: Putnam. (European-American; Early settlers)
2–3	Eyes and Other Body Organs; Self-Esteem; Social Studies; Health; Inner-City Life	Keats, E. J. (1969). *Goggles.* New York: Macmillan. (European-American)
4–5–6	Counting Money; Occupations; Colors; Fabrics; Vocabulary/Language; Social Studies; Art; Math; Value Studies; Drama	Anderson, H. C. (1949). *The emperor's new clothes.* Illustrated by Virginia Lee Burton. Boston: Houghton Mifflin. (Danish)

CHARACTER IMAGERY/GROUP ROLE-PLAY

Grade Level	Theme/Subject	Title
K-1	Friendship; Fears; Self-Esteem; Health; Social Studies (families)	Waber, B. (1972). *Ira sleeps over.* Boston: Houghton Mifflin. (European-American)
K-1	Self-Esteem; Social Studies	Sharmat, M. W. (1977). *I'm terrific.* Illustrated by Kay Chorao. New York: Holiday House. (European-American)
2-3	Animals; Self-Esteem; Vocabulary; Friendship; Social Studies; Science; Value Studies; Drama	Freeman, D. (1964). *Dandelion.* New York: Viking. (Animals)
4-5-6	Homes; Families; Social Studies	Lionni, L. (1968). *The biggest house in the world.* New York: Pantheon. (Animals)

Table 3–2   Creative and Thematic Approaches... *(continued)*

DRAW TALK

Grade Level	Theme/Subject	Title
K - 1	Crops; Farming; Self-Esteem; Hopes and Dreams; Persistence; Science; Social Studies; Art; Drama	Kraus, R. (1978). *The carrot seed.* Illustrated by Crockett Johnson. New York: Harper & Row. Spanish Edition: La semilla de zanahoria. Translated by Argentina Palacios. New York: Scholastic. (European-American)
2 - 3	Imagination; Colors; Self-Concept; Travel; Moon; Oceans; Homes; Art; Social Studies; Science	Johnson, C. (1955). *Harold and the purple crayon.* New York: Harper & Row. (European-American)
4 - 5 - 6 and up	Self-Esteem; Self-Concept; The Animal Kingdom; Travel by Air; Science; Social Studies; Music	Bach, R. (1970). *Jonathan Livingston Seagull.* Photographs by Russell Munson. New York: Macmillan. (All cultures)

PUPPETRY

Grade Level	Theme/Subject	Title
K - 1	Friendship; The Animal Kingdom; Science; Social Studies; Humor	Lobel, A. (1970). *Frog and toad are friends.* New York: Harper & Row. (European-American)
K - 1	Friendship; Foods; Cooking; Cooperation; Decision-making; Humor; Social Studies; Science (Animals)	Lobel, A. (1979). *Frog and toad together.* New York: Harper & Row. (European-American)
K - 1 - 2	Homes; Occupations; Foods (e.g. fish); Imagination; Oceans; Social Studies; Language/Vocabulary; Sexism; (study for older children)	Littledale, F. (1989). *The magic fish.* New York: Scholastic. (European)
3 - 4 - 5 - 6	Self-Esteem; Talents; Music; Social Studies; Art (e.g., origami); Friendship	Yashima, T. (1955). *Crow boy.* New York: Viking. (Japanese)
4 - 5 - 6	Self-Esteem; Animals; Birds; Growing up; Growing older; Races; Social Studies; Science; Value Studies; Art	Andersen, H. C. (1969). *The ugly duckling.* New York: Scholastic. (Danish)

CHANT

Grade Level	Theme/Subject	Title
K - 1	Families; Self-Esteem; Friendship; Coping with Adversity; Vocabulary/Language; Social Studies; Health	Viorst, J. (1972). *Alexander and the terrible, horrible, no good, very bad day.* Illustrated by Ray Cruz. New York: Atheneum. (European American)
K - 1	Families; Self-Esteem; Changes/Growth from infancy to adulthood	Munsch, R. (1986). *Love you forever.* Ontario, Canada: Willowdale. (All cultures)
2 - 3	Pets; Animals; Counting; Loneliness; Old Age; Language/Vocabulary; Math; Art	Gag, W. (1928). *Millions of cats.* New York: Coward, McCann & Geoghegan. (European)
4 - 5 - 6	Animals; Big vs. Little; Social Studies; Science; Art; (e.g., wood blocks; wood carvings); Music	Brown, M. (1961). *Once a mouse.* New York: Scribner. (East Indian)

continued

Table 3–2   Creative and Thematic Approaches... *(continued)*

FELT BOARD

Grade Level	Theme/Subject	Title
K - 1	Safety/Security; Night and Day; Personal Belongings; Families; Health; Language/Vocabulary; Art	Brown, M. W. (1947). *Goodnight moon.* Illustrated by Clement Hurd. New York: Harper & Row. (All cultures)
K - 1	Clouds; Imagination; Shadows; Vocabulary/Language	Shaw, C. G. (1947). *It looked like spilt milk.* New York: Harper & Row. (All cultures)
K - 1	Cooperation; Team-Work; Families; Fish; Shapes; Shells; Ocean; Colors; Social Studies; Music; Science; Art; Math	Lionni, L. (1963). *Swimmy.* New York: Pantheon. (All cultures)
K - 1	Colors; Wind; Season; Holidays; Ethnic Minorities; Neighborhoods; Inner-City Life; Hats; Science; Social Studies; Art	Robinson, D. (1970). *Anthony's hat.* New York: Scholastic. (European-American)
K - 1	Beginning Science; Butterflies; Caterpillars; Changes in Lives; Growing Up; Growing Older; Waiting; Nutrition; Food Groups; Colors; Math; Art	Carle, E. (1979). *The very hungry caterpillar.* New York: Putnum. (All cultures)
K - 1	Animals; Farm Life; Baking and Cooking; Science; Social Studies; Language/Vocabulary; Drama	Schmidt, K. (1986). *The gingerbread man.* New York: Scholastic. (European)
2–3	Spiders; Africa; Friendship; Adventure; Family; Social Studies; Geography; Math	McDermott, G. (1987). *Anansi: the spider: A tale from the Ashanti.* New York: Holt, Rhinehart & Winston. (Ashanti people/Ghana, Africa).

BALLOON

Grade Level	Theme/Subject	Title
K - 1	Fears; Halloween; Suspense; Adventure; Social Studies; Art	Gackenback , D. (1978). *Harry and the terrible whatzit.* Boston: Houghton Mifflin. (All cultures)
K - 1	Halloween; Planting; Fall/Spring/ Seasons Science; Art	Titherington, J. (1986). *Pumpkin, pumpkin.* New York: Greenwillow. (All cultures)
2 - 3	Magic; Rodents; Lizards; Toys; Wishes; Social Studies; Health; Art	Lionni, L. (1969). *Alexander, the windup mouse.* New York: Pantheon. (All cultures)
2 - 4	Magic and Make-Believe; Freedom; Love. Language Arts; Social Studies; Music	Rogasky, B. (1982). *Rapunzel.* New York: Holiday House. (European)
3 - 4	Tall Tales; Natural Wonders; Human/Super Human Strength; History; Geography	Kellogg, S. (1984). *Paul Bunyan.* New York: Morrow. (European)

Table 3–2   Creative and Thematic Approaches... *(continued)*

MUSICAL

Grade Level	Theme/Subject	Title
K - 1	Animals and Arachnids; Farms; Food; Science; Music	Wescott, N. (1980). *I know an old lady who swallowed a fly.* Boston: Little Brown. (All cultures)
K - 1	Animals; Farms; Animal's Food Chain; Foods/Cooking; Transportation; Social Studies; Health; Science; Music	Schmidt, K. (1986). *The gingerbread man.* New York: Scholastic. (All cultures)
K - 3	Amphibians; Weddings; Science; Social Studies; Music	Langstaff, J. (1955). Frog went a-courtin'! New York: Rojankovsky, Feodor. (All cultures)
2 - 3	Yiddish Culture; Lifestyles; Noise Pollution; Social Studies; Math; Music; Language Arts	Zemach, M. (1990). *It could always be worse.* New York: Farrar, Straus & Giroux. (Yiddish)
2 - 3	Nature; Environment; Beauty; Multicultural Education; Social Studies; Health; Science; Music	Weiss, G. D., & Thiele, B. (1995). *What a wonderful world.* Illustrated by Ashley Bryan. New York: Atheneum. (All cultures)
1 - 4	Nature; Teddy Bears; Food; Imagination; March and Dance; Music; Physical Education	Kennedy, J. (1992). *Teddy bear's picnic.* New York: Holt. (All cultures)

CHAPTER RESOURCES

Arbuthnot, M. H., & Root, S. L. (1968). *Time for poetry.* Glenview, IL: Scott Foresman.

Armstrong, T. (1994). *Multiple intelligences in the classroom.* Alexandria, VA: Association for Supervision and Curriculum Development.

Baker, A., & Green, E. (1996). *Storytelling: Art and technique* (2nd ed.). New York: R. R. Bowker.

Banks, J. A. (1994). *An introduction to multicultural education.* Needham Heights, MA: Allyn & Bacon.

Bauer, C. F. (1977). *Handbook for storytellers.* Chicago: American Library Association.

Booth, D. (1994). *Story drama: Reading, writing and role playing across the curriculum.* Markham, Ontario: Pembroke.

Brothers Grimm. (1989). *Little Red Riding Hood.* Mahwah, NJ: Troll Communications.

Cooper, J. D. (2000). *Literacy.* Boston: Houghton Mifflin.

Disney, W. (1997). *Disney's princess treasury collection: Disney's Snow White, Disney's Sleeping Beauty, Disney's Cinderella.* New York: Mouse Works, a division of Disney Book Publishing.

Edwards, L. C. (1997). *The creative arts.* Columbus, OH: Merrill.

Ehrlich, A. (1985). *The Random House book of fairy tales.* New York: Random House.

Farrell, C. (1991). *Storytelling: A guide for teachers.* New York: Scholastic.

Fields, M. V., & Spangler, K. L. (2000). *Let's begin reading right.* Columbus, OH: Merrill.

Forston, L. R., & Reiff, J. C. (1995). *Early childhood curriculum.* Needham Heights, MA: Allyn & Bacon.

Fujikawa, G. (1976). *A child's book of poems.* New York: Grosett & Dunlap.

Gag, W. (1996). *Millions of cats.* Burnsville, MN: Econo-Clad Books.

Gardner, H. (1993). *Multiple intelligences.* New York: Basic.

Glazer, J. (1991). *Literature for young children.* Columbus, OH: Merrill.

Gunning, T. G. (1998). *Best books for beginning readers.* Needham Heights, MA: Allyn & Bacon.

Hamilton, M., & Weiss, M. (1990). *Children tell stories: A teaching guide.* Katonah, NY: Richard C. Owen.

Harste, J. C., Short, K. G., & Burke, C. L. (1988). *Creating classrooms for authors.* Portsmouth, NH: Heinemann.

Harste, J. C., Woodward, V., & Burke, K. C. (1984). *Language stories and literacy lessons.* Portsmouth, NH: Heinemann.

Hernandez, H. (1989). *Multicultural education: A teacher's guide to content and process.* Columbus, OH: Merrill.

Johnston, T. (1996). *The quilt story.* Illustrated by T. De Paola. New York: Putnam.

Lauritzen, C., & Jaeger, M. (1997). *Integrating learning through story.* Albany, NY: Delmar.

Lipke, B. (1996). *Figures, facts & fables: Telling tales in science and math.* Portsmouth, NH: Heinemann.

Lipman, D. (1999). *Improving your storytelling.* Little Rock, AK: August House.

MacDonald, M. R. (1993). *The storyteller's start-up book.* Little Rock, AK: August House.

McDermott, G. (1987). *Anansi: the spider: A tale from the Ashanti.* New York: Holt, Rinehart & Winston.

Merritt, D. D., Culatta, B., & Trostle, S. (1998). Narratives: Implementing a Discourse Framework. In D. D. Merritt & B. Culatta (Eds.), *Language interaction in the classroom.* San Diego, CA: Singular.

Miller, W. (2000). *Strategies for developing emergent literacy.* Boston: McGraw-Hill.

Mikkelsen, N. (2000). *Words and pictures: Lessons in children's literature and literacies.* Boston: McGraw-Hill.

Morrow, L. M. (1997). *Literacy development in the early years.* Needham Heights, MA: Allyn & Bacon.

Morrow, L. M. (1997). *The literacy center.* York, ME: Stenhouse.

Moss, A., & Stott, J. (1986). *The family of stories.* New York: Holt, Rinehart & Winston.

Oldfield, M. J. (1969). *More tell and draw stories.* Minneapolis, MN: Arts and Crafts Unlimited.

Ovando, D. J., & Collier, V. P. (1985). *Bilingual and ESL classrooms: Teaching in multicultural contexts.* New York: McGraw Hill.

Pellowski, A. (1987). *The family storytelling handbook.* New York: Macmillan.

Pflomm, P. N. (1986). *Chalk in hand.* Metuchen, NJ: Scarecrow.

Raines, S. C., & Canady, R. J. (1989). *Story stretchers.* Mt. Ranier, MD: Gryphon House.

Readman, G., & Lamont, G. (1994). *Drama.* London: BBC Educational Publishing.

Salinger, T. S. (1996). *Literacy for young children.* Englewood Cliffs, NJ: Prentice-Hall.

Sawyer, W., & Sawyer, J. C. (1993). *Integrated language arts for emerging literacy.* Albany, NY: Delmar.

Sawyer, W. E. (2000). *Growing up with literature* (3rd ed.). Albany, NY: Delmar.

Shelley, M. (1990). *Telling stories to children.* Batavia, IL Batavia Publishing.

Sierra, J., & Kaminski, R. (1991). *Multicultural folktales: Stories to tell young children.* Phoenix, AZ: Oryx.

Sierra, J., & Kaminski, R. (1987). *The flannelboard storytelling book.* Phoenix, AZ: Oryx.

Silverstein, S. (1981). *A light in the attic.* New York: Harper & Row.

Silverstein, S. (1985). *A child's book of poems.* New York: Grosett & Dunlap.

Sitarz, P. G. (1990). *More picture book story hours.* Englewood, CO: Libraries Unlimited.

Stangl, J. (1984). *Paper stories*. Belmont, CA: Fearon Teacher Aids.

Tiedt, P. L., & Teidt, I. M. (1990). *Multicultural teaching*. Needham Heights, MA: Allyn & Bacon.

Trostle, S. L., & Hicks, S. J. (1998, Fall). The effects of story reading versus storytelling on vocabulary and comprehension in British primary school children. *Reading Improvement, 35*(3), 27–36.

Viorst, J. (1987) *Alexander and the terrible, horrible, no good, very bad day*. New York: Atheneum.

Whitin, D. J., & Wilde, S. (1992). *Read any good math lately?* Portsmouth, NH: Heinemann.

Yashima, T. (1955). *Crow boy*. New York: Viking.

Yolen, J. (1981). *Touch magic*. New York: Philomel .

January

✿

Winter Wonders

SNOW-FLAKES

Out of the bosom of the Air,
    Out of the cloud-folds of her gar-
ments shaken,
Over the woodlands brown and bare,
    Over the harvest-fields forsaken,
Silent, and soft, and slow
    Descends the snow.

-HENRY WADSWORTH LONGFELLOW
(EXCERPTED FROM THE COMPLETE POEM
"SNOW-FLAKES")

New beginnings! The wonder of winter is a vision of rosy-cheeked children, sparkling snowflakes and hopes for the year ahead. "January: Winter Wonders" explores a young child's feelings, the excitement of the Chinese New Year, and presents seasonal riddles.

Chant, Puppetry, and Traditional Storytelling methods are employed. Dreams of peace for the world culminate the set of four engaging stories. Multiple intelligence activities for January include raps about hats, multicultural dancing, and strategies for peaceful conflict resolution. Bodily-Kinesthetic, Logical-Mathematical, Interpersonal, Intrapersonal, Verbal-Linguistic, Naturalistic, Visual-Spatial, and Musical-Rhythmic multiple intelligences are addressed throughout these activities.

May your new year of storytelling shine bright with promise and may your dreams come true!

The Purple Hat

(as told by the hat)

By Jonathan Brand and Susan Trostle Brand

STORYTELLING METHOD

Chant

The Purple Hat is based upon a true story of a little boy and the day he forgot to wear a fancy hat to school for "Hat Day." Children will relate to the emotions of feeling left out, lonely, and inferior which this story evokes. The clear message, that "beauty lies in the eyes of the beholder" is an important one for young children to learn and for adults to remember.

In preparation, the Teller might don a purple hat. Before beginning the story, the Teller may want to establish a signal such as a nod of the head, a hand gesture, or a touch to his or her hat to indicate that everyone can join in the chanting. An asterisk indicates the text in which the class or audience participates. This text is printed in advance on the chalkboard or a flip chart, so that the class or audience can easily see their part.

The Purple Hat

It was a frigid Friday in January. At Dunn's Corners School, the teacher said it was Hat Sharing Day. I was proud to be the hat on Jonathan's head. Jonathan and I have been good friends for a year now. He wears me often. I keep him warm. That makes me feel good. I feel warm inside too.

But for me, it became a Horrible Hat Day. You see, Jonathan's Mom forgot to give Jonathan a fancy hat to wear to Kindergarten. She just gave him a plain, old, purple hat: ME. At the bus stop, Jonathan saw Wesley wearing a crazy-looking, large hat with lots of flowers and wild colors. On his head, Devin donned a cool-looking Mickey Mouse. Jonathan was mad and sad.

The bus monitor, Mrs. D., was cheerful. She said, "Well, your purple hat matches your purple gloves." But her words didn't seem to help much. I felt ashamed of myself. I felt broken-hearted for Jonathan.

Jonathan climbed off the bus. He was still angry with me—his plain, old purple hat. I became very, very angry too. "I don't want to be part of this hat show anymore! In fact, I don't even want to be part of your household, Jonathan," I cried. "I thought we were friends!" Jonathan just sulked.

In Room Five, Jonathan's classroom, the hat situation changed from bad to worse. Jonathan and I saw

✱ **frilly hats, silly hats,**
  hats with flowers, hats with showers
  hats with blocks, hats with clocks,
  hats with trees, hats with bees,
  festive confetti hats and drippy spaghetti hats

and then, there was me... a plain, old, purple hat.

Jonathan plucked me off his angry head. He threw me onto the hard floor. Then my friend laughed at me and sneered, "Good riddance, ugly hat. Ha-ha-ha-ha-ha."

Mrs. Beaupre, the teacher, looked at Jonathan sternly. Jonathan picked me up and shoved me into his bright blue backpack. Safe inside, I turned myself inside out. I became a great, big, plain, old purple ball.

I tried to disappear. I pretended I was invisible. But I could not hide from the hurt I felt. I felt rejected. My body ached. My hot, wet tears filled Jonathan's backpack. I became wet and soggy.

Outside my clammy, wet haven, the children made lively noises. They played "Construction" and "Cooking Corner." Mrs. Beaupre was a fun and friendly teacher. I had met her before. I had met the other children too. But never before had I felt so lonely and so scared.

Next, I heard the children play "Duck-Duck-Goose." Then they played "Fast, Medium, and Slow." The children moved fast and medium and slow as the music played. When the music stopped, the children had to freeze! I felt frozen too. I was cold and wet and very lonely. Curled inside my purple mass, I huddled and shivered.

Finally, school was over. We were going back home, at last. I wondered what would happen next. What would become of me? Would he throw me away? Would he give me to the Salvation Army? Would I become a dish rag in the kitchen sink? Perhaps I would become a dust cloth and collect cobwebs.

Then, something awful happened, Jonathan pushed some writing papers into his backpack. He forced some snowman art projects in beside me too. But Jonathan forgot to zip his backpack. He ran fast for the minibus, headed home. Jonathan rushed up the steps onto the minibus. I heard Tish, the driver, shout, "Hi kids!" And suddenly, I fell out of the backpack. I landed softly on the concrete beside the bus. No one noticed me. The bus roared away, above me. One huge wheel barely missed running over my purple body!

When he arrived back home, Jonathan was still angry. "Mom," he stormed, "I am very upset about this hat! I'm going to throw it in the garbage. This is the ugliest, plainest, oldest hat in the whole class! Purple is a dumb color." And he reached into his backpack to pull me out. But of course, I wasn't there. He searched through his papers. No purple hat. He searched through his art projects. No purple hat.

Jonathan began to cry. He slumped down onto the couch. He hid his face inside his hands, "It's all my fault," he said. "I was very mean to my purple hat. And now I will never see it again." Jonathan slowly climbed the steps to his bedroom. For one hour, he cried. When it was supper time, Jonathan wasn't hungry. Jonathan's mommy knocked on his door. "Jonathan," she said, "Tish, your bus driver, just drove by the house. She was in her minibus. She thought you might be missing this."

Jonathan's Mom dropped me onto Jonathan's lap. I was still wet and cold. But all of a sudden it didn't matter anymore to Jonathan. Jonathan hugged me and squeezed me tightly. "I love you, purple hat!" he cried. "And I am so sorry for treating you the way I did! You may be an old, plain, purple hat. But you are my hat. And, to me, you are very beautiful!" I smiled from brim to brim.

I was so glad to be home. Then I began to cry again. But this time, I cried tears of joy and tears of love.

Jonathan's Mom unrolled me. She tossed me into the clothes dryer. I turned and tumbled, upside down and inside out, right side up. and all about. I felt warm and dry and a little sleepy.

Jonathan and his Mom hurried around the house. They searched for other purple things. "Purple things can be very special," they said. Jonathan showed me a big, round, purple eggplant. They found tasty purple plums and succulent purple grapes. They brought out a huggable, bright purple Barney doll. Jonathan has loved Barney since he was a small baby. Next they told me about kings and queens. For kings and queens, purple is the color of dignity and royalty. "And some soldiers earn purple hearts for being very brave," they explained.

Now I felt proud to be a plain, old, purple hat. I puffed myself up and smiled broadly.

Jonathan and I spent a lively three-day weekend together. Jonathan slept with me each night in his warm, cozy bed. I felt more and more beautiful each day. I glowed with happiness.

Back at school, on Tuesday, it was Hat Contest Day. All those same hats were back. We saw

❊ **frilly hats, silly hats,**
   hats with flowers, hats with showers
   hats with blocks, hats with clocks,
   hats with trees, hats with bees,
   festive confetti hats, and drippy spaghetti hats

and then, there was me... a plain, old, purple hat.

But Jonathan loved me the best of all. And I was not ashamed to be me.

The judges chose the winners. The festive confetti hat won first prize for "Fanciest Hat." The hat with trees won first prize for "Most Clever Hat." As for me, the plain, old, purple hat?

Why, I won first prize for the "Hat Most Loved."

"Hats off" to you, Jonathan!

And "hats off" to all you other wonderful—

❊ **frilly hats, silly hats,**
   hats with flowers, hats with showers
   hats with blocks, hats with clocks,
   hats with trees, hats with bees,
   festive confetti hats, and drippy spaghetti hats
   and to me, a plain, old purple hat!

53

The Purple Hat

 Create a Hat!
(Interpersonal; Intrapersonal; Bodily-Kinesthetic)

Invite children to dramatize the story wearing their own self-created hats. One child holds the role of narrator. For hatmaking, provide such supplies as tissue paper, confetti, construction paper, glitter, silk and plastic flowers, pom-poms, scissors, glue, and tape.

 Hat Raps.
(Musical-Rhythmic; Verbal-Linguistic)

Divide the group of children into smaller, cooperative learning groups of four or five members. Each group sits at its own table. At each table display the Frilly Hats chant, printed clearly for the group. Ask the children to create their own music (or use a familiar tune) and new words for a chant about hats. While the children brainstorm ideas, one child writes them down. Another child at each table reads the new hat chant to the entire group. Then together, the children from each table sing their hat song or rap. For example, Group One could rewrite the chant to be sung to the tune of "Row, Row, Row Your Boat," with words such as these:

We like ruffly hats, fancy hats are cool;
We wear them when we walk outdoors—
But we take them off in school!

 Hats for Sale!
(Logical-Mathematical; Interpersonal)

Read the story *Caps for Sale* by Esther Slobodkina. Using the example of the peddler, have the children create their own hat store. Provide paper and plastic money and a toy cash register. Use a book rack or table to display the hats. Each child determines the cash value of his or her hat and constructs a price tag for that hat. Children can then sell the hats they wear to school or the hats that they construct previously. Other customers line up to come to the store and, counting out the appropriate amounts of cash, purchase a hat of their choice. The storekeeper counts out the correct change for each customer. Children take turns being the storekeeper who calls out, "Hats for sale! Low-priced, medium-priced, and expensive hats!" (Tip: For hygiene purposes, do not let the children wear others' hats.)

TIPS FOR THE TELLER

The Chinese New Year: How the Animals Were Chosen

Retold and Adapted by Jeanne M. Donato

STORYTELLING METHOD

Traditional

Chinese New Year begins between January 21 and February 19. Each year of the Chinese calendar is named for a different animal during a twelve-year cycle. Many stories have evolved explaining how this came to be. In this retelling, the Rat wins the race and the honor of having the first year of the cycle named for him.

This is an excellent story for discussion about the use of different calendars and the various ways of keeping track of time and of the seasons. Display a picture of the Chinese solar calendar with the pictures and names of the animals. Blank calendars for the students to fill in, dowels, red crepe paper, and the music to the "Lovely New Year Flower" dance will help with activities. The Teller may wish to play the song, "Lovely New Year Flower" before telling the story.

Have the children research the animals' names in American Sign Language or make up their own signs. For the participation aspect of the story, the children discuss the signs and sounds for the different animals with the Teller ahead of time, so that they are prepared to make them for each animal as it is mentioned. The Teller may want to establish a signal such as a nod of the head or a hand gesture to indicate when the children may join in. An asterisk indicates the text that the children will sign.

As an alternative, tell the story first in true Traditional style, with no audience participation. Ask the audience to join in later, perhaps, after they are familiar with the story.

The Chinese New Year: How the Animals Were Chosen

In ancient China, when animals could speak, *Cat and *Rat were friends and lived in peace. In the heavens the celestial gods prepared a wondrous new calendar to celebrate Buddha's arrival. This new calendar followed the sun through twelve-year cycles, helping the farmers to prepare for the changing of the seasons.

When *Cat saw the calendar she purred and asked Buddha, "With a gift such as this, you could honor each of your faithful animal friends before you leave. I am known for friend-liness and prosperity. It is only right that the first year be dedicated to me!"

"That is all well and good my friend," cried *Rat. "But I am also known for prosperity and cleverness. To suggest that Buddha chose you over the other animals would not be fair. Buddha, there are more animals than years in the calendar's cycle. What do you suggest?"

Buddha answered, "You are right. There are many animals that have served me faithfully. To be fair, I propose a race. Announce that all my faithful animal friends who wish to compete should meet at the riverbank. The race will begin at dawn. The first twelve animals to cross over the river will win the honor of having a year named for each of them, in the order in which they arrive."

And so it was that early the next morning all the animals gathered at the river bank. The river was so wide the animals could hardly see the other side. Some of the animals decided that they would rather watch than race. Anxious to start, the *Horse neighed, the *Dragon snort-ed, the *Monkey chattered from tree to tree, the *Pig was off rooting around for food, but the *Cat was frantic. She hated water and could not swim. She begged her friend *Rat for help.

*Rat said, "Don't worry my friend. *Ox is a strong swimmer; before the race starts just quietly hang onto his tail. He has such poor eyesight, he will never see you. As for myself, I have offered to help guide him across the river in exchange for the ride. With *Ox's help, we will all be assured a year on the new calendar.

So *Cat shivered in the cold water next to *Ox's tail waiting for the race to start. When the sun crossed the horizon the proud *Rooster crowed to signal the start of the race.

The animals started with a splash! *Tiger was first to leap into the river's swiftly mov-ing waters. *Horse slid down the slippery bank and thrashed around in circles with *Mon-key hanging onto his neck screeching that he was not going fast enough. *Rabbit had quietly tucked himself behind *Dragon's wing, while *Snake wrapped himself around *Dragon's tail. *Pig and *Dog swam together, helping *Rooster as he fluttered along.

*Dragon puffed and complained about the hard work as he used his wings for oars to row across the river. *Goat pulled his head down and gallantly swam forward against the cur-rent. *Rat watched the others catch up as *Ox struggled against the current. *Monkey worried that *Horse would never get across and jumped onto *Goat when *Goat passed near by. *Goat was angry but too exhausted to fight him off. Without *Monkey to slow him down, *Horse was able to swim faster and passed *Goat. *Ox was a strong but slow swim-mer and the other animals were passing him.

Frantic, *Rat whispered into *Ox's ear, "See that tall tree way down the river on the other shore? Swim towards it."

"That's too far away" complained *Ox. "It's shorter to swim straight across like the others."

"It may look shorter to swim straight across the river but you will waste all your energy fighting the current. Swim with the current, at an angle. This way the current will help you. Listen to me and we will win" cried *Rat!

As *Ox pulled towards the other shore *Cat begged *Rat to help her up on *Ox's back. Her wet fur was dragging her under and the water was choking her.

Worried that they would not arrive first, *Rat whispered into *Ox's ear. "You would be able to swim faster if you did not have to carry so much extra weight. Look behind you. *Cat is hanging onto your tail dragging you back."

"What are you talking about?" raged the ✻Ox. "What extra weight?" ✻Ox turned and saw ✻Cat. He flipped his tail and off she flew, carried away by the current. Reassured, the ✻Ox diligently swam with the current and started to take the lead. When ✻Ox passed ✻Dragon and ✻Tiger, ✻Rat cried out from ✻Ox's back. "Look ✻Tiger, ✻Snake doesn't have to work at all. He is letting ✻Dragon do all his work for him!"

When ✻Tiger turned to look. ✻Ox started to climb up the muddy riverbank. ✻Rat jumped off ahead of ✻Ox declaring that he was first! "Clever and small I may be and first is how they'll honor me!"

✻Ox bellowed and started to complain, but Buddha gave him a stern look. ✻Ox watched as ✻Tiger came in third. They both stopped and watched ✻Dragon trying to shake ✻Snake off his claw and throw him back into the water. ✻Dragon did not notice ✻Rabbit jump out from his hiding place under ✻Dragon's wing to claim fourth place. ✻Dragon had to content himself with fifth place. ✻Snake slithered in sixth.

✻Horse neighed, clambered up the slippery shore, and came in seventh. ✻Goat lowered his horns into the water until ✻Monkey let go and finished in eighth place. ✻Monkey, chattering and complaining, managed ninth. ✻Dog helped ✻Rooster flapping and fluttering up the riverbank. ✻Rooster was content with tenth while ✻Dog was satisfied to be eleventh. ✻Pig, still hungry, stopped to root around in the mud looking for something to eat, and ended up in last place.

Poor ✻Cat arrived last of all soaking wet and shivering. Buddha was sad that he did not have an honored place for her on the calendar. All the while ✻Dragon complained, "It's not fair! ✻Rat, ✻Rabbit, and ✻Monkey cheated. They didn't swim across the river!"

✻Rat protested, "Buddha didn't say *how* we had to get across the river!"

Buddha shook his head and agreed. ✻Rat was right. ✻Dragon was furious that he didn't think of flying. He would have easily taken first place.

"Well, I am not so easily satisfied," hissed ✻Cat. "Fair or not, I will get even with ✻Rat for his deceit!" Stretching out her claws and showing her fangs, she leaped after ✻Rat. And that is how it has been between ✻Cats and ✻Rats ever since. So ends the tale of how the animals were chosen to rule to twelve years of the Chinese solar calendar.

MULTIPLE INTELLIGENCE ACTIVITIES FOR . . .

The Chinese New Year: How the Animals Were Chosen

1 Make a Chinese Calendar.
(Logical-Mathematical; Naturalistic)

In China it is believed that the year in which you are born determines your characteristics. These characteristics are thought to be the same qualities as the animal ruling that year. Arrange the pictures on the board in the order in which the animals arrived. Research the characteristics for each animal. List them on paper, and match them to the corresponding animal. Hand out blank Chinese solar calendars divided into twelve-year cycles. Have the students paste or draw each animal's picture in the proper sequence. Label their

The Chinese calendar.

names, and fill in their characteristics. If the year 2000 is the year of the Dragon, calculate what animal ruled the year you were born. Find out the birth year animals of members of your family. Research the different calendars and ways of keeping track of time that have evolved throughout history. Compare their benefits.

 Kung Hei Fat Choy.
(Verbal-Linguistic; Interpersonal)

This is the Chinese greeting for "Happy New Year." Have the class collect other New Year greetings from different countries. Display the collection on the board, Discuss the different dates other countries have for celebrating the start of

the New Year. Make long streamers from rolls of red crepe paper. Print, trace, or cut out and paste the letters to the words "Kung hei fat choy." Glue the streamers to wooden dowels or rulers to wave during the dance in activity three.

 The Lovely New Year Flower Dance.
(Musical-Rhythmic; Bodily-Kinesthetic)

Play the music, and teach the words to the song "Lovely New Year Flower." Then teach the children the movements to the dance. Have them practice by desks and then in a line, moving and bowing together while waving their streamers. Instructions for the dance are as follows:

Lovely New Year Flower

Chinese folk tune. Words by Madu Lee Wilson.

This love-ly New Year flow-er nod-ding here brings joy-ous wish-es— for the year:

say-ing, "Be well, in con-tent-ment dwell, fill all your days with peace and cheer.___

(Words by Madu Lee, Chinese Folk Song, from *Growing with Music, Book 3* by H. R. Wilson, W. Ehret, A. M. Snyder, E. J. Hermann, and A. A. Renna. © 1966 by Prentice-Hall, Inc. Used by permission.)

Dance: The children stand in a line all facing the same direction. Have them take the red streamers made in the second activity and hold them close at chest level. Tell them to take one glide step, starting with the right foot and closing it with the left foot. The next glide step starts with the left foot and closes with the right. Tell them next to stop, bow slightly forward (careful not to touch the person in front of them), and wave their red streamers once to the right, and once to the left. Instruct the children to hold the streamers with both hands at chest level and repeat the steps as the music proceeds. The effect is a graceful snake-like dance to celebrate the New Year's Flower of Friendship.

TIPS FOR THE TELLER

This story available on Storytelling Video!

A Riddle for Winter

By Doug Lipman

Retold and Adapted by Jeanne M. Donato

STORYTELLING METHOD

Chant/Traditional

This riddle story was developed following Doug Lipman's story *Riddle Story: In Summer I Die*. This story follows two children wishing for a snowstorm so school will be canceled. They find it challenging to pass the time without electricity and television. Their grandmother gives them a riddle, and when they discover the answer she agrees to get up and play with them. Along the way they make some surprising discoveries. This is a story that will set the whole group to chanting.

Preparation for the storytelling of *A Riddle for Winter* may include the Teller dressing in colorful winter clothing, possibly wearing a furry hat, wool coat, boots, gloves, or clothing with snowflake designs on it.

continued

59

TIPS FOR THE TELLER *continued*

The children will need an explanation that their participation is needed. Before beginning the story, the Teller may want to establish a signal such as a nod of the head or a hand gesture to indicate that the audience can join in the rhythmic chanting. An asterisk indicates the text that the audience recites. This text is printed on the chalkboard or a flip chart in advance so that the class or audience can easily see their part in the chanting of the riddle.

Winter Lady sharing a seasonal story: "A Riddle for Winter."

A Riddle for Winter

Once upon a time there was a Little Boy who worried about going back to school. His teacher told the class that the next time they met, they would have a test. "I really need time to study. Oh, I wish they would cancel school," he cried.

(Teller to audience: "Do you know what would make school close?" Audience replies. "You're right! Especially in the winter a blizzard would close school. Do you know different ways to make a wish come true?" Audience replies.)

"Well, the Little Boy gazed out the window searching the sky for the first star. That's it. He crossed his fingers." *(Invite the audience to repeat the chant with you.)*

He said,

✿**"Star light, star bright, first star I see tonight. I wish I may, I wish I might, have this wish I wish tonight. I wish we had a blizzard so big that they would have to cancel school tomorrow!"**

And then he went to bed.

The next morning when he awoke, the room was dark and soft with silence. When he looked out his window the streetlight wasn't shining, but in the dim light of dawn he could barely believe his eyes! Why it was so high it reached all the way up to the windowsill!

"Yahoo!" he cried, as he ran to his little sister's room. "Wake up, Wake up! You won't believe it! My wish worked! It's snowing! They'll have to cancel school!"

"Of course there's no school today," his Little Sister stretched and yawned. "Today is Saturday."

"Saturday!" shrieked the Little Boy, "Saturday! I wasted my wish on a Saturday! Oh, but look out the window. Look! The snow is piled up to the windowsill. Let's go watch cartoons!" But the TV wouldn't work.

(Ask the audience: "Why do you think the television wouldn't work?" Audience replies.)

"Well, let's play some video games!" suggested the Little Boy.

"Remember," said his Little Sister, "there's no electricity and there are no batteries. So let's read a story!"

After a while, the Little Boy said, "I'm bored. Let's wake Mama up to play with us."

So the Little Boy and the Little Sister ran into their parents' bedroom. They went over to Mama's side of the bed and gently shook her shoulder but she just rolled over, sound asleep. "It's going to take more than that to wake Mama up," said the Little Sister. "Do what I do, and sing with me." And the Little Sister started to shake the bed.

(Teller: "You can join in with me. Ready? Clap your hands on your lap as if you are shaking the bed. They sang: ❧**'Mama, Mama, will you please wake up? Mama, Mama, will you play with us?'"** *Nod to the audience to join you and repeat a second time,* "Mama, Mama, will you please wake up? Mama, Mama, will you play with us?")

Well Mama opened her eyes and said, "What time is it?"

The Children replied, "Why it's six o'clock in the morning."

(Nod toward the audience to invite them to repeat the chant with you: ❧**"There's snow piled high as you can see, there's no electricity, and no TV! Please get up and play with us!"***)*

Mama said, "It's six o'clock in the morning, I need a little more sleep. Go ask you Father." And she pulled the covers over her head.

So the children ran to the other side of the bed and started to shake their Daddy awake. *(Teller: "Ready? Clap you laps. They sang:* ❧**"Daddy, Daddy, will you please wake up? Daddy, Daddy, will you play with us?"** *Repeat twice.)*

Daddy opened his eyes and asked, "What time is it?"

The Children replied: "Why it's six o'clock in the morning." *(Nod toward the audience to invite them to repeat the chant with you):* ❧**"There's snow piled high as you can see, there's no electricity, and no TV! Please get up and play with us!"**

Daddy answered: "Oh, its too early to get up. It's Saturday. Go get your Big Sister to play with you, OK?" And Daddy pulled the pillow over his head.

They ran to Big Sister's room and stopped outside her door. "You know we're not allowed to go in her room," said the Little Sister.

"Well," answered the Little Boy, "Daddy said we could." So they opened the door and tiptoed into her room.

Big Sister's room was so neat and clean. Bottles of all sizes and colors were lined up on the dresser. "Look," whispered the Little Sister, "I wonder what this one smells like?" as she squeezed the bulb on top of one of the bottles. "Oooooh," she cried, "I smell like peaches now!"

"Look at all her stuffed animals! They're everywhere!" whispered the Little Boy. "Oooooh, look at those big bumps on her head with her hair tied around them. What's all that while stuff on her face? I bet she thinks it's supposed to make her beautiful. Yuck! Let's wake her up!"

(Teller: "Are you ready?" They shook Big Sister's bed and sang: ✲**"Sister, Sister, will you please wake up? Sister, Sister, will you play with us?"** *Repeat again.)*

Well, Big Sister sat up in bed and screamed, "Mother, Father, they're in my room again. Mother, Father!" Then she picked up a stuffed animal and threw it at them as they ran into the hallway laughing.

"Now what do we do? Said the Little Boy. "I'm bored!"

"Gramma is visiting for the weekend," said the Little Sister "Let's go wake her up. I'll bet she'll play with us." So they tiptoed into Gramma's room. On the nightstand next to Gramma's bed were her glasses and a glass of water with false teeth in it! *(Teller: Now, Gramma is hard of hearing so we'll have to sing even louder to wake her up. Ready? The Children shook the bed and sang:* ✲**"Gramma, Gramma, will you please wake up? Gramma, Gramma will you play with us?"** *Repeat twice.)*

Gramma sat up in bed and exclaimed, "Oh dear! Wait 'til I put my glasses on, so I can hear a little better. There now, what time is it, Darlings?"

The Children replied, "Why it's six o'clock in the morning" *(Nod toward the audience to invite them to repeat the chant with you):* ✲**"There's snow piled high as you can see, no electricity, and no TV! Please get up and play with us."**

"Why of course," Gramma replied as she hugged them. "You know Gramma loves to play with you. Why don't we play the riddle game?"

"What's a riddle?" the Children asked.

"A riddle is a word puzzle that describes something in a mysterious way," Gramma said. "The fun is, you have to really think about what it could be. We used to play riddle games when I was young. Here it is: I'm one in a million, unique am I; in winter I grow, in summer I cry."

(Teller: Now you say it with me: ✲**"I'm one in a million, unique am I; In winter I grow, in summer I cry."**)

"Good," Gramma said. "Now you both run along and look for it while Gramma takes a little nap. When you find it, I'll have another surprise for you."

The Children ran into the play room and looked all around repeating the riddle.

(Teller indicates groups to repeat the riddle: ✲**"I'm one in a million, unique am I; In winter I grow, in summer I cry."**)

"What could it be?" the Children asked.

"I know," said the Little Boy. "It's one of my puzzle pieces! When I put all the pieces together, the puzzle grows!"

"No," replied the Little Sister. "A puzzle doesn't cry in the summer."

(Teller asks audience "What do you think it could be?" Wait for responses. The Teller can extend or shorten the guesses while in the house.)

"Oh," cried the Little Sister as she ran into the kitchen and pointed to the refrigerator, "Look at the refrigerator! It sort of cries in the summer when it gets wet with moisture."

"No," answered the Little Boy. "A refrigerator doesn't grow in the winter. I'm getting tired of guessing. Let's go outside and play in the snow!"

(Teller to audience: "What did the Little Boy and the Little Sister need to put on to go outside?" Audience might respond that they have to put on their boots, etc. The Teller mimes putting on the suggested boots, coats, etc.)

The Children ran outside and sank up to their knees in the snow. They wondered at the trees bent over with piles of snow on them. The Little Sister made a snow angel and the Little Boy drew horns on top of the halo. They had fun throwing snowballs.

"Oh, it's snowing again! The snowflakes look like goose feathers!" cried the Little Sister. "Look at this one and that one! See how beautiful they are. My teacher said that no two snowflakes are ever alike."

"Each one is different? That makes each one unique!" replied the Little Boy. "Why there are millions of them! Did I say unique? Millions? Hey, that reminds me of Gramma's riddle! Can you say it again?"

(Teller gestures for the audience to join in and repeat the riddle twice: ✿**"I'm one in a million, unique am I; In winter I grow, in summer I cry."**)

The Children both cried out together, "I know what the answer is! It's a snowflake!" Laughing, they ran back into the kitchen. They ran right into Gramma's bedroom and started to shake the bed to wake her up.

(Teller nods to invite the audience to join in. They chanted: ✿**"Gramma, Gramma will you please wake up? Gramma, Gramma, will you play with us?"**)

When they repeated the rhyme again, Gramma sat up in bed and hugged them both. "Did you find out the answer to my riddle, Darlings?" she asked.

"Yes, Gramma, it's a snowflake!" answered the Children.

"Why you are right! Now run along back outside and bring me two handfuls of snow. I want to show you something we used to do when I was your age. And be careful not to get it all over the floor." Gramma smiled.

The Children ran outside, and each scooped up two handfuls of snow. They carried it into the kitchen where Gramma was waiting for them. "There now," she smiled, "put it in this big bowl." The children scooped the snow into the bowl while Gramma opened the refrigerator and took out a bottle of pure maple syrup. She reached into the cupboard and pulled out a box of ice cream cones. Scooping the snow into balls to fit the top of each cone, she poured the syrup over the top and gave them to the children to taste. "What do you think of that?"

"This is great, Gramma!" the Children exclaimed.

"About this time of year, when I was your age, my grandparents would take me to the woods where a friend used to make his own maple syrup. They would pour it over freshly packed snowballs. We didn't have fancy cones to put them in; back then we used tree bark. Oh my, why it's almost time for lunch! My, it's amazing how time flies when you're having fun!" Gramma laughed. She hugged the Children and said, "You are both certainly one in a million!"

MULTIPLE INTELLIGENCE ACTIVITIES FOR . . .

A Riddle for Winter

 Make a Riddle.
(Musical-Rhythmic; Verbal-Linguistic)

Display different riddles on the board. Encourage the children to clap out the rhythm of the various riddles as they chant them together. They may create their own rhythmic patterns and riddles. Write a riddle on a flap of a folded piece of paper. Then ask the child to draw a picture or write the answer to the riddle inside. Display these on the walls where others can read, guess, and then look to see if they were correct. Or maybe *their* answer is yet another good solution to the riddle. Print a class riddle book. Decorate the book cover with snowflakes cut from folded paper.

2 **How Would You Say It?**
(Naturalistic; Interpersonal)

Research snowflake facts and shapes in the library. Discovering the different names the Inuit (Native American Eskimos) have for snow. Encourage group discussion of findings. Write and display words for snow from other countries. Place colored pins on the world globe or map to indicate the country of origin of the words displayed on the board. Ask the students to write in their journals about how each individual, like a snowflake, is unique even among identical twins. Questions for them to consider: How are we all alike? How are you different?

3 **What Make a Difference?**
(Naturalistic; Logical-Mathematical)

Have the class measure and count how many pennies or grains of sand it will take to equal the weight of a half dollar coin. Use a real scale or handmade weighing device to determine relative weights. Discuss and discover how many pennies

it would take to fill a box. Have the class decide where they can donate the pennies collected to make a difference (the library, homeless shelter, etc.) Reflect and have the class write in their journals about how one small kindness, smile, or word can make a difference in their classroom, school and world as evidenced in the following story, told in the Traditional method.

The Weight of a Snowflake

Retold by Jeanne M. Donato (c) 1998.

Dove passed the long winter months nestled smugly among the protective branched of an old pine tree, encrusted with ice and snow. Safe and warm she watched the world and wondered.

When Crow stopped by for a visit, Dove asked, "What do you think it would take to make a difference in this world?"

"Since Noah's time you've been the authority on such matters. But even I know that it would take more than anything you or I could do," answered Crow.

"Oh," replied the Dove. "Tell me, what is the weight of a snowflake?"

"Why, nothing more than nothing," Crow quickly cawed. "Why do you ask?"

"I was just wondering," answered Dove. "Let me tell you this puzzling story. Yesterday, when it started to snow, the snowflakes floated down from the sky like fluffy goose feathers, soft and slow. Not having much to do, I started to count them as they settled on the needles of the branch below me. I counted them one by one, until they numbered exactly 3,456,789. But, when the next snowflake which, as you said, weighs 'nothing more than nothing,' touched that branch, the branch broke! Think about it, Friend," Dove continued. "If one small snowflake can help break a strong tree branch, then maybe all the world needs is just one small voice to speak up and bring peace to this world."

TIPS FOR THE TELLER

I Have a Dream
By Susan Trostle Brand

STORYTELLING METHOD

Puppetry

I Have a Dream is a moving story, enacted by puppets, of the life of a great leader and inspirer of peace in our nation and world. If very young children are not prepared to grasp the implications of Dr. King's assassination, the Tellers may instead substitute the sentence, "Martin Luther King died at a young age." When the students are more mature, the adult may explain the details of Martin Luther King's death. Students may then be better prepared to discuss the complication of his life and death.

The story contains suggestions for use of several scenery changes, puppets, and props. The Tellers my use more or fewer of these scenery suggestions and props, depending upon the degree of simplicity or complexity desired.

Suggested scenery includes the interior of Martin Luther King's house; generic school background; neighborhood scene with school and drinking fountain; plain blue background. As props, a cradle, diploma, mortar board, hospital bed with patient, school house, church, bus, the Washington Monument, or an inscribed gravestone might be used.

Puppets on stage in *I Have A Dream.*

Puppet suggestions are Martin Luther King, Jr. as a baby; Martin as a young boy; Martin as an adult; Rosa Parks; Martin's father, a pastor; Martin's mother; two young boys; and a narrator (optional). Papier mâché, sock, paper and stick, or doll figures are all puppet possibilities (see Chapter 3 for puppet-making tips.)

For ease of telling, Teller may clothe Martin in the same black cloth throughout his adult roles. For a stage, use an actual puppet theatre, with curtains. Or, for simplicity, cover the top

continued

TIPS FOR THE TELLER *continued*

and front of a long table with a plain table-cloth. The puppeteers kneel behind the table as they manipulate props and puppets. Two or three puppeteers work well for this story. For the most effective and stimulating presentation use loud, clear, distinctive voices and add your own spontaneous dialogue at appropriate times during the telling. Invite children to tell the story when they are familiar with script!

Before beginning the story, the Teller may want to establish a signal such as a nod of the head or a hand gesture to indicate that the audience can join in. An asterisk indicates the text that the audience recites. This text is printed on the chalkboard or a flip chart in advance so that the class or audience can easily see their part.

I Have a Dream

(Display background of interior of house.)

Narrator: On January 15, 1929 in Atlanta, Georgia, baby Martin Luther King, Junior was born. *(Enter Baby Martin in cradle).*

Baby Martin's father was a pastor named Reverend Martin Luther King, Senior. *(Enter Martin, Sr.)* His family was very happy. *(Enter mother; all stand close and mother and father hug.)*

Mother: We are so glad that you are our baby, Martin.

Father: Yes, Martin. We love you very much! We are truly blessed.

(Remove house background; add school background.)

Narrator: Martin became a young boy. *(Enter child Martin puppet.)* He went to school in Atlanta, Georgia. He studied hard and was a very good student.

Martin: All this studying takes time and much work. But it will be worth it someday. I am learning a good deal about the world. And I will be able to have a fine job someday, too.

Narrator: Martin went on to high school and later, college in Atlanta. The he traveled north to Pennsylvania. There, he attended divinity school. He studies to become a pastor, just like his father had been. His graduation was a wonderful event. *(Enter grown up Martin puppet donning graduation attire: Mortar board and black robe.)* Everyone celebrated Martin Luther King now. He was a Reverend. He was glad that he had studied so hard and so well.

Martin: I knew that if I studied hard I would succeed. This is a very happy day for my family and me. *(Remove mortar board. Remove school background; add plain blue background.)*

Narrator: As a pastor, Martin did many good works. *(Enter Martin and person in a hospital bed.)* He visited sick people in the hospital. His visits made them feel better.

Martin: How are you feeling today, Mrs. Ames? I brought you some flowers to cheer you. It's a lovely, spring day. Soon you will be well and able to enjoy nature again.

(Exit bed.) (Enter church.)

Narrator: At his church, he prayed with people. He sang with them and shared good meals with them. He visited them at their homes and talked with them. The people in Martin's church and in his neighborhood looked up to Reverend Martin Luther King, Jr. They trusted him and respected him. (Exit church.)

(Change background scene to neighborhood with houses, drinking fountain, and restaurants.)

Sometimes Martin would take walks in his neighborhood. He would see young people fighting. *(Enter two young boys.)*

Boy One: This book is mine. I had it first.

Boy Two: No; it's mine. You've had it for three days now. If ya don't give it to me, I'm gonna grab it right outta yer hands!

Narrator: This fighting troubled Martin.

Martin: Boys, boys. *(Stands between feuding boys.)* Now, how does all this arguing make you feel? *(Pauses for answers.)* Can each of you think of a way to settle this problem? I know that you can find a better solution than fighting. *(Boys nod heads and shake hands.)*

Narrator: Martin Luther King put an end to many fights. He helped people solve their problems in peaceful ways.

Our country had some laws that troubled Martin Luther King. One of these laws was that African American people had to sit in the back of the bus. *(Enter bus.)* They could not sit in the front like white people. Martin Luther King helped this law to change.

Martin: All people are created equal. All people should be able to sit in any empty seat they like on any bus.

(Enter Rosa Parks.)

Narrator: A lady named Rosa Parks also helped to change this law.

Rosa: I agree with Reverend Martin Luther King. Martin and I worked hard to change this law. Now all people, of all races and colors, can sit anywhere they like in any bus in our country.

Martin: Some other laws bothered me. In some places African Americans could not use the same drinking fountains as white people. Sometimes African Americans could not dine in the same restaurants as white people. Some hard working people and I helped to change these laws. Now all people can drink from the same fountains and eat in the same restaurants.

(Enter school house.) In some places black and white children could not attend the same schools. They had to go to different schools. Some of my young friends and I helped to change this law, too. Now all children can go to public schools together. *(Exit school house; replace neighborhood with plain blue background.)*

Narrator: Martin Luther King tried very hard to bring peace to the world. He marched with other people. He gave talks about peace and fairness. When Martin Luther King talked, everyone listened. *(Enter Washington Monument.)* In 1963, Martin Luther King gave his most famous speech of all. He was in Washington, D.C., the capital of our nation.

Martin: I have a dream. I dream that all people, everywhere, will learn to live in peace and harmony. *(Exit monument; Exit Martin.)*

Narrator: In 1968, something very sad happened. Martin Luther King was shot and killed. His friends gave him a special funeral service in Atlanta, Georgia, where he was born. Thousands of people attended the funeral. *(Enter inscribed gravestone.)* On his gravestone were these words, "Free at last, Free at last, Thank God Almighty I'm Free at last." *(Exit gravestone.)*

Martin Luther King was now free from fighting and meanness and from the worries and cares of the earth. But we remember the Reverend Martin Luther King, Jr. today for many reasons. He worked very hard for people's freedom. He helped people to get along with each other. He helped people to stop fighting and to live in peace. He helped all people to share the same drinking fountains and buses and restaurants.

In January, we remember Martin Luther King. We know that he did much to realize his dream. We honor him on his birthday by singing this song to him:

(enter birthday cake prop; invite audience to sing along.)

✿ **Happy birthday to you, happy birthday to you;**
Happy birthday, Dear Martin—Happy Birthday to you!

Using poster board to "publish" a *Big Book of Peace.*

MULTIPLE INTELLIGENCE ACTIVITIES FOR . . .

I Have a Dream

 My Dream for the World.
(Intrapersonal; Interpersonal; Verbal-Linguistic)

Read children several short stories from Durell's and Sachs's *The Big Book for Peace.* Hold a group discussion on what peace means to them. On the chalkboard or on a large sheet of plain paper, record and review the children's ideas. Then, invite them to use the ideas from the puppet show, the readings, and their own brainstorming to create a story and picture entitled *My Dream for the World.* When each child has contributed one page, bind the pages together to form a large book entitled, *Our Dreams for a Peaceful World.*

 Peacemaker Windsocks.
(Bodily-Kinesthetic; Visual-Spatial)

In advance, prepare several colorful strips of construction paper for the group, allowing about eight 12-inch strips of paper for each child. Each child also forms one cylinder-shaped form, approximately 7 inches in width and 14 inches in length, before stapling or gluing. The child writes the name of a famous peacemaker (past or present) onto the cylinder-shaped paper. He or she draws or glues a picture of this peacemaker. Then, onto each strip of paper, the child prints one fact about the life of this person and/or one contribution for which this person is noted. For example, for Martin Luther King, the child could include "Born in Atlanta, Georgia," "Became a Reverend," "Led Peace Marches," and "Helped All People Attend the Same Public Schools," etc. Attach a string or ribbon onto the top of the cylinder, and hang in a breezy area of the room.

 Let's Be Problem-Solvers!
(Interpersonal; Bodily-Kinesthetic)

Prepare, or have the children prepare, several scenarios of conflict—at home, school, or within the community. In small groups of four or five members, children review their conflict situations and generate the most acceptable and peaceful solution to the dilemma. Then, when each group has completed their reviews, they role-play their conflict scenarios and peaceful resolutions to the rest of the group. Allow each group approximately 30 minutes for rehearsal and preparation and approximately 10–15 minutes for the actual group dramatization.

   Ideas for home conflict situations: Arguing with a sibling about mutual property; meeting the needs of a seemingly demanding parent regarding time spent on homework; dealing with parents who argue with each other.

   Ideas for school conflict situations: Being the object of ridicule from a group of bullies; dealing with a difficult teacher or classroom aide; encountering unpleasant (and probably untrue) gossip about a good friend.

   Ideas for community conflict situations: Observing a person shoplifting in a store; witnessing a child crying when he or she is not selected for the baseball team; replying to an irate and rude person seated near you at a basketball game.

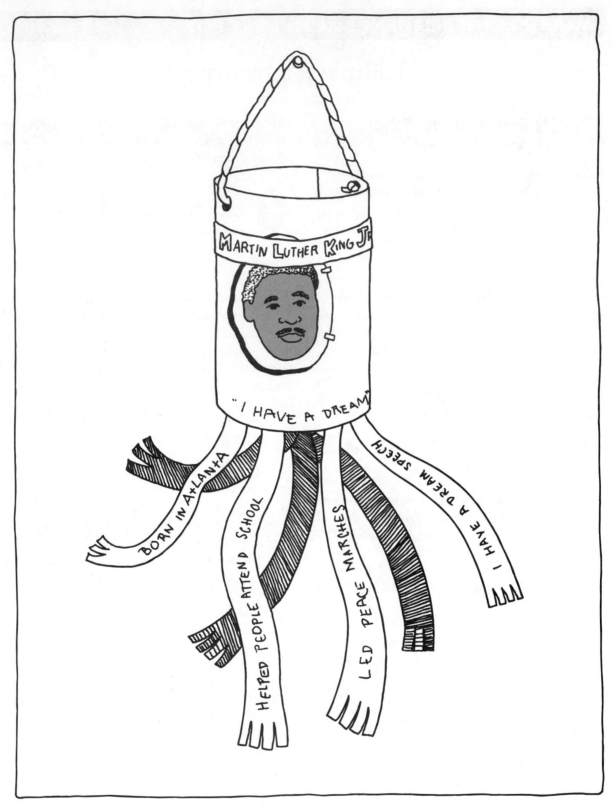

Martin Luther King, Jr. peacemaker windsock.

JANUARY CHAPTER RESOURCES

Amery, H., & Cartwright, S. (1994). *Usborne farmyard tales: The snow storm.* London: Usborne House.

Andersen, H. C. (1982). *The snow queen.* New York: Dial.

Bell, A. (1987). *Grimm Mother Holle.* London: Pelham.

Brett, J. (1985). *Annie and the wild animals.* Boston: Houghton Mifflin.

Brett, J. (1989). *The Mitten.* New York: Scholastic.

Brett, J. (1992). *Trouble with trolls.* New York: Putnam.

Carlson, N. (1997). *Snowden.* New York: Viking.

Cole, J. (1973). *Plants in winter.* New York: Thomas Y. Crowell.

De Gerez, T. (1986). *Louhi witch of north farm.* New York: Puffin.

Durell, A., & Sachs, M. (Eds.). (1990). *The big book for peace.* New York: Dutton.

Duvoisin, R. (1963). *Spring snow.* New York: Knopf.

Forest, H. (1995). *The blizzard witch of the north.* In H. Forest, Wondertales from around the world. Little Rock, AK: August House.

George, B. L. (1995). *In the snow: Who's been here?* New York: Mulberry.

Lipman, D. (1990, December) Riddle story: In summer I die. *Yarnspinner,* p. 5.

Littledale, F. (1978). *The snow child:* A Russian folktale. New York: Scholastic.

MacDonald, M. R. (1994). Little rooster and the heavenly dragon: A Chinese New Year celebration. In M. R. MacDonald, *Celebrate the world: Twenty tellable folktales for multiculural festivals.* New York: H. W. Wilson.

MacDonald, M. R. (1991). The snow buntings' lullaby: A Siberian tale. In M. R. MacDonald, *Look back and see: Twenty lively tales for gentle tellers.* New York: H. W. Wilson.

Marzzollo, J. (1993). *Happy birthday, Martin Luther King.* New York: Scholastic.

Mendez. P. (1989). *The black snowman.* New York: Scholastic.

Milton, J. (1987). *Marching to freedom: The story of Martin Luther King, Jr.* New York: Doubleday.

Peterson, H. (1970). *When Peter was lost in the forest.* New York: Coward-McCann.

Pinkwater, D. (1990). *Young Larry.* New York: Aladdin.

Robison, D. (1976). *Anthony's hat.* New York: Scholastic.

Schenk De Regniers, B. (1987). *The snow party.* New York: Lothrop, Lee & Shepard.

Sing, R. (1992). *Chinese New Year's dragon.* Cleveland, OH: Modern Curriculum.

Slobodkina, E. (1947). *Caps for sale.* New York: W. R. Scott

Tchin. (1997). *Rabbit's wish for snow: A Native American legend.* New York: Scholastic.

Tran, K. L. (1992). *Tet the New Year.* New York: Simon & Schuster.

Tresset, A. (1964). *The mitten.* New York: Mulberry.

Van Laan, N. (1989). *Rainbow crow: A Lenape tale.* New York: Knopf.

Yerxa, L. (1993). *Last leaf first snowflake to fall.* New York: Orchard.

Yolen, J. (1987). *Owl moon.* New York: Scholastic.

February

Presents and Presidents

ROMANCE

I will make you brooches and toys for
    your delight
Of bird-song at morning and star-shine
    at night.
I will make a palace fit for you and me,
    Of green days in forests
And blue days at sea.

-ROBERT LOUIS STEVENSON
(EXCERPTED FROM THE COMPLETE POEM
"ROMANCE")

resents of affection and our nation's presidents are often associated with the month of February. In this chapter, two stories addressing friendship and two stories addressing the presidents Abraham Lincoln and George Washington are presented. The storytelling methods of Chant, Traditional, and Pantomime are highlighted.

Multiple intelligence activities for February include constructing ceremonial masks, creating friendship bracelets, and learning dance steps to Lincoln's favorite folk song. The multiple intelligence areas are employed throughout the chapter, Naturalistic, Bodily-Kinesthetic, Interpersonal, Visual-Spatial, Musical-Rhythmic, Logical-Mathematical, Verbal-Linguistic, and Intrapersonal.

May friendship, love, and patriotism enhance your month of February storytelling!

TIPS FOR THE TELLER

I Like You the Best

By Dana Hanley

Adapted by Susan Trostle Brand

STORYTELLING METHOD

Chant

I Like You the Best is a simple and sincere story about self-esteem and the deep and enduring friendship between two young girls. Children will relate to this universal theme and will delight in the opportunities to chant along with the recurring statement, "I like you the best!"

Before beginning the story, the Teller may want to establish a signal to indicate when everyone can join in the chanting. An asterisk indicates the text in which the class or audience participates. This text is printed on the chalk-board or a flip chart in advance so that the class or audience can easily see their part.

For this story, clasping hands or linking the two pointer fingers in the sign language symbol for friendship may work well.

The Teller may also want to discuss friendship and love and may brainstorm with the group those qualities that characterize a good friend. Lead into the story by stating that today's story is about best friends; then teach the friendship signal and begin the telling!

I Like You the Best

Dana was a chubby, happy six-year-old. Dana's friend Michelle was a thin and happy six-year-old. Dana and Michelle were best friends.

One day at school, Dana would not play tag. Michelle asked her, "Why won't you play tag with us?"

Dana replied, "I cannot run as fast as you." Michelle smiled and placed her hand on Dana's shoulder. She said, "It doesn't matter, Dana. **✻I still like you the best!**"

The next day at recess, Dana would not jump rope. Michelle was in the middle of the rope singing," Teddy Bear, Teddy Bear, Turn Around...Teddy Bear, Teddy Bear, Touch the Ground!"

Michelle called to Dana, "Why won't you jump rope with us?" Dana replied, "I cannot jump as high as you." Michelle smiled and walked over to the steps where Dana was pouting.

She handed Dana one end of the jump rope and said, "I still want you to jump with me. *I like you the best!"

That weekend at the beach, Dana would not go swimming. Michelle dived into the waves. She swam onto the sandy shore with a very large wave. Michelle asked her, "Why won't you swim with us?" Dana replied, "I cannot swim as well as you." Michelle hurried to her friend. She put her tan arm around Dana. She said, "I don't care how well you swim. I want you to swim with me. *I like you the best!"

That night Michelle invited Dana to sleep over at her house. As they were lying in bed, Dana asked Michelle, "Why do you like me the best?" Michelle answered, "I do not care if you don't run as fast, jump as high, or swim as well as I do. There are many other things you are good at that I am not. You are my best friend and *I like you the best!"

The next school day, Michelle and Dana sat in the reading circle. The teacher, Mrs. Howe, asked Michelle to read. Michelle exclaimed, "I do not *want* to read." Dana looked over at her friend. She asked, "Why won't you read with us, Michelle?"

Michelle replied, "I can't read as well as you." Dana said, "I want you to read to me; come to my house and we'll read a neat book together tonight. *I like you the best!" Michelle glowed as she finished the whole story in reading group, all by herself.

The next day Michelle and Dana went to their art class. They made clay pots. Dana made the best pot in the class. It was yellow and white and had a nearly perfect shape. She proudly carried her pot to show her friend Michelle. Michelle wasn't smiling. Her pot was an odd gray-violet color and was leaning and misshapen. Dana asked Michelle, "Want to trade pots, so I can keep yours?"

Michelle replied, "Why? Your pot is so beautiful and mine is misshapen. All the other kids laughed at it!"

Dana smiled and set down her pot. She gave Michelle a big hug and said, "That's okay. You made it and I like it the best. That's because *I like you the best!"

MULTIPLE INTELLIGENCE ACTIVITIES FOR . . .

I Like You the Best

 Ceremonial Masks.
(Visual-Spatial; Bodily-Kinesthetic)

Locate other books about love and friendship, for example, *Mama Do You Love Me*, a story about a mother/daughter bond. This book is also rich in depictions of Inuit ceremonial masks. The symbols, materials, and decorations used in constructing the masks represent elements of nature, wishes, family history, tradition, and culture. Often used to ask the shaman for good luck, these symbols may represent such wishes as good game, abundant hunting, prosperity, and family happiness. (See the illustration that follows for more symbol writing.)

Place assorted craft materials (tissue paper, crepe paper, ribbon, stickers, and sequins) on a table. Encourage the children to think of wishes, hopes, and requests as well as elements of their own lives, talents, or family traditions. Invite them to create decorative and representative paper plate masks using the provided materials and glue. Secure masks behind heads with yarn or string.

Later, play appropriate tape selections from *Wee Sing Around the World* as children dance to the music donning their masks. After the dance celebration, display the colorful masks, complete with children's symbol-written explanations of their elements and decorations.

2 **Around the World Friendship Cookies**
(Visual-Spatial; Interpersonal)

Prepare (or purchase) plain sugar cookies. Purchase tubes of decorator's icing in a variety of colors, including blue and green. Children decorate the top sides of the cookies, depicting the water and land of the earth. Bake or locate small gingerbread person cookies and serve alone and/or secure into colorful frosting on sugar cookies. Hold a "Friendship Around the World" celebration, serving the cookies to parents and children. Add a tangy tropical fruit punch for added pleasure!

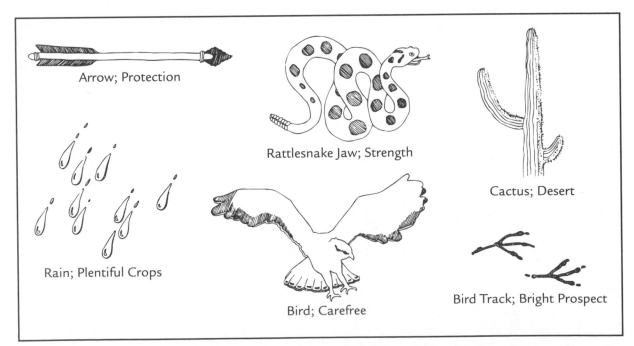

Arrow; Protection

Rattlesnake Jaw; Strength

Cactus; Desert

Rain; Plentiful Crops

Bird; Carefree

Bird Track; Bright Prospect

Native American symbol writing aids learning about diverse lifestyles.

Lightning; Swift

Big Mountain; Abundance

Man; Human Life

Crossed Arrows; Friendship

Thunderbird; Sacred Bearer of Happiness

Feathers; Status

Medicine Man's Eye; Wise

Deer Track; Plentiful Game

Horse; Journey

Butterfly; Everlasting

Sky Band; Leading to Happiness

Bear Track; Good Omen

Days and Nights; Time

Rain Cloud; Good Prospect

Native American symbol writing aids learning about diverse lifestyles.

Gingerbread Person Cookies

2 3/4 cups sifted flour
1/2 tsp. baking soda
1 tsp. ginger
1/2 tsp. cinnamon
1/2 tsp. salt
1/2 cup butter
1/4 cup packed dark brown sugar
3/4 cup dark molasses
1 egg, beaten
1 tsp. hot water
1 tsp. vinegar

Sift dry ingredients. Cream butter and sugar. Add molasses and egg, beating until smooth. Mix in dry ingredients. Then add water and vinegar. Chill dough two hours or overnight. Roll out on lightly floured board to 1/4 inch thick and cut with gingerbread person cutters (large and small sized). Place on buttered cookie sheet. Bake for 15 minutes at 350 degrees. Cool. Decorate with frosting if desired.

Around the World Friendship Cookies.

 3 I Love You Coupons.
(Interpersonal; Intrapersonal)

February is a great month for friends, parents, and children to express their feelings for one another. Prepare several oaktag or colorful poster board flower shapes with the youngsters. Each child should make seven flowers; one for each day of the week. Have them use liquid markers to write methods by which they will express their love to their parent(s) or guardians on the flower part of the paper. For example: Monday: I will make my bed; Tuesday: I will feed the cats; Wednesday: I will shovel the snow: Thursday: I will set the table; Friday: I will dry the dishes; Saturday: I will take out the trash; Sunday: I will give you hugs and kisses! Then, they can place the stems of the completed flowers into a heart-shaped envelope or pocket, so that just the top half of the flowers are visible. Each day, for one week, the adult may select one "love coupon" and the child performs this task, in response.

Abe Lincoln and the Bullies

Retold by Jeanne Donato

STORYTELLING METHOD

Traditional

Drawn from accounts of Abraham Lincoln's early years, this story focuses on Abe's yearning to strike out on his own and make time to read and study. He must learn how to make new friends and handle difficult people. How Abraham meets and deals with these new challenges offers children a model of creativity and compassion.

Referring to the Traditional telling model in Chapter 3, the Teller reviews unfamiliar vocabulary and phrases from Lincoln's era. A picture or model of a frontier town can be shown to the children to prompt a discussion of how frontier people needed to cooperate in order to survive. The Teller can then ask, "What makes a person difficult? What makes a bully? How do you think they feel? When Abraham Lincoln was a young man, he had to deal with bullies. Listen and see if you can think of other ways to handle the situation."

Abe Lincoln and the Bullies

Abraham Lincoln was twenty-two years old in 1831. He helped settle his folks on their new farm, wrapped all his belongings and books in a bandanna, and cut out on his own toward New Salem, Illinois.

New Salem was a little bit of a settlement, of twenty-five log houses, cut from the trees that clustered near the hills. There Abe found: a grist and sawmill, a tavern, grocery store, a cooper, blacksmith, minister, cobbler, cabinetmaker, constable, schoolmaster, and two doctors. The town was nestled on a bluff overlooking the Sangamon River and the prairie. New Salem was a sight bigger than what Abe was used to, yet slow enough to give him plenty of time to do what he loved most—read!

Denton Offutt owned the local sawmill in New Salem and figured the town could use a dry goods store. He would offer folks seeds, tools, food, felt hats, and other necessities. All Mr. Offutt needed now was help smart enough to run the store; sharp enough to work the mill; and strong enough to keep the Clary Grove Boys from bothering the customers.

These young men hung around New Salem and spent their time teasing and troubling other people. They didn't respect hard work or book learning. They believed that because they were the roughest and toughest around New Salem, they could do what they pleased. For sport, they would put a stone under a rider's saddle, crop horse tails, overturn outhouses, break windows, and bully anyone who tried to stand up to them. They challenged any newcomer to a wrestling match, to "set them straight" about who was the strongest.

Mr. Offutt had hired young "Slicky Bill Green" to help clerk the store but he was still one hand short. Mr. Offutt smiled when he saw the answer to his problem amble across the town field. He called out, "Why, Abe Lincoln! Is that you? You old rascal! What brings you 'round these parts?"

Abe Lincoln grinned. He pulled his black sunburned felt hat off his head revealing a shock of dark hair that didn't seem to know how to hide his big protruding ears. Standing six foot four inches tall, Abe's homespun shirtsleeves pulled several inches short of covering his long lanky arms. His pant legs fell high-water shy of ever tucking into his heavy leather boots. With his small bundle tucked under his arm, Abe held out one large work-hardened hand and gave Denton Offutt a powerful handshake. "Well Sir, it's mighty nice to see you again," Abe replied. "I'm looking for some work and wondered if you might be needing some help?"

Mr. Offutt replied, "I could sure use some good help around here! Can you read, write, and cipher?"

"Well, Sir, I can read, and write some. And I can cipher to the 'Rule of Three,'" Abe answered.

Mr. Offutt nodded and said, "That's good enough for me. I need an extra clerk 'round the store here and an extra hand to help me up at the mill. Now, I can't pay much. But I'll give you $4.50 a week. The bed in the back room next to the chimney is free if you don't mind sharing lodgings with 'Slicky Green' here. The Rutledge Tavern, across the way there, has good food, good rates, good company, and even some books I bet you ain't read yet. Job's yours if you want it." And with a clasp of a handshake, Abe was hired.

Well, it didn't take long for the folks 'round New Salem to start taking notice of the friendly gawky giant. He had a joke or story for everyone who came to the store. He seemed to always have his nose in a book. They got used to seeing Abe lying on his back in the grass with his long legs propped up the side of the tree trunk reading a book or curled next to the store window reading by the early morning light. The cooper even let Abe burn his leftover wood chips for a fire to read by late at night. Abe always had time to wait on his customers, spin a yarn, or play marbles with the children. He was right handy as any woman, with a needle, at quilting bees. Folks enjoyed his stitching and stories. But Abe always made time to read. He carried a book with him everywhere he went and read when there was a minute to spare.

One day, Abe was so interested in telling a customer about a story from a book he read that he forgot to take the measuring weight off the scales when he weighed out her tea. At the end of the day, Abe figured out that he had overcharged the lady by six cents. He walked three miles to her house and back to return her change. When the town folks heard that, they started calling him "Honest Abe."

Denton Offutt was so proud of his new clerk that he took to bragging about Abe to everyone, including the Clary Grove Bullies. "Why Abe Lincoln is just about the smartest, strongest man I know," Denton would brag. "The way I figure it, that Abe can out-talk, out-lift, out-run, out-throw, and out-wrestle any man in this here county." When Abe won at quoits, an old fashioned game similar to horseshoes, and a footrace at a town celebration, Mr. Offutt took to bragging even more!

But there were some things Abe preferred not to do. His favorite song was the "Blue Tail Fly" which he called the "Buzzin' song." He didn't like to dance, but he enjoyed watching others dance. Abe didn't mind wrestling matches, but he didn't put any store in wasting time wrestling himself. When Mr. Offutt tried to bring up the subject of a wrestling match, with one of the Clary Grove Boys, Abe would just shake his head and say, "I've got other things that interest me more." And he would go back to reading his book.

The Clary Grove Boys decided to put an end to Offutt's bragging about Abe and they figured it was time this newcomer was put in his place. Jack Armstrong was the leader of these bullies. And one day, he waited with the rest of the Clary Grove Boys, for Abe to lock up the store and start across the field to the tavern for his dinner.

"Hey Greenhorn," Jack called out to Abe. "I hear tell some folks are claiming you're the strongest man in New Salem and I'm fixing to prove 'em wrong. I challenge you to a wrestling match right here and now."

Abe looked Jack in the eye and replied, "Don't believe everything you see and half of what you hear. Now if you'll pardon me, I'm headed 'cross the way here for my dinner."

Abe stepped aside to walk around Jack, when Jack yelled, " I ain't never been thrown and I ain't about to let some yellow-bellied Greenhorn put down my reputation! I say we settle this right here and now!"

Abe smiled and said, "Now, I don't have any quarrel with you. And calling names is just that." Abe laughed and said, "Why that reminds me of a story 'bout an old…"

Before Abe could finish, Jack cut in " I'm here for a fight. No storytelling." And Jack knocked Abe's hat to the ground.

Abe slowly leaned over to pick up his hat, dusted it off and replied, "Now see here, I don't believe in woolin' and pullin'. Fighting just to fight never did anybody any good, I ever knew of. Now, if you'll pardon me…"

Abe started to walk away, when the Clary Grove Boys stepped in closer, forming a ring around Jack and Abe. They pushed Abe back towards Jack, cheering and jeering for the fight to begin. Jack tripped Abe to the ground and pounced on him. Abe took hold of Jack's arms and the two proceeded to wrestle. They tugged and pulled, stumbled and rolled for nearly an hour. Town folk gathered around to watch the fight. Finally, Abe said, "It doesn't really matter who's the strongest. Seems like I can't lick you and you can't lick me. Let's call it a draw and be on our way." Abe released his hold on Jack Armstrong and offered to shake his hand. But Jack threw a handful of dirt in Abe's face, shoved him to the ground and cried; "It matters to me! This ain't no draw. I ain't done with you yet!"

Folks say that Abe Lincoln clenched his fists till his knuckles showed white. He grabbed Jack Armstrong, raised him up over his head, shook him like a sack of potatoes and put him down. He offered Jack his hand saying, "I believe that we could go at this for hours and neither of us would win. I'd call it a draw. Wouldn't you?"

Shaken, Jack realized that Abe hadn't used his full strength till now. He was grateful that Abe was willing to call it a draw in front of everyone. Jack held his hand out and agreed, "It's a draw!"

Jack Armstrong and the Clary Grove Boys admired Abe from then on, even though he kept his nose in a book. They remained Abraham Lincoln's loyal friends and supporters for the rest of his life.

MULTIPLE INTELLIGENCE ACTIVITIES FOR...

Abe Lincoln and the Bullies

1 What Makes a Village?
(Visual-Spatial; Interpersonal)

Posing this question to the students, make a class listing of people, buildings, and professions frontier people would need to make an effective village. What would be most important? What would be the least important?

Make a class diorama of a frontier village. From the list made from the discussion, have the class decide what buildings, landscape, and people would best represent a frontier town. Divide into groups according to the list decided upon. Collect cardboard, shoeboxes, craft paper, milk cartons, clay, paint, and other useful craft materials and start to build.

2 You Were There.
(Intrapersonal; Verbal-Linguistic)

The teacher leads a group discussion on how Abe handled the bullies the way he did to gain insight into his actions. Discuss how bullies feel about themselves and why they act the way they do. What are the best ways to deal with bullies in our lives? Have the children share their feelings or experiences in dealing with bullies. Divide the class into groups of four and take turns acting out the confrontation between Abe and the bullies in slow motion, with each group using different ideas and solutions. Invite the class to share their ideas.

Frontier village shoebox diorama.

3 ## Abe's Buzzin' Song.
(Musical-Rhythmic; Bodily-Kinesthetic)

Discuss the different forms of entertainment such as quilting bees, barn dances, and community picnics that frontier settlers used to gather and meet the other people in their community. Play the "Blue-Tail Fly" on a recording or instrument for the class. Tell the children that they are going to learn Abraham Lincoln's favorite song and a dance to go with it.

Divide the class into two equal lines, line A and line B. Have them face each other in the middle of the room, leaving about 4 feet between the lines. The head couple is designated as the lead people from each line nearest the door. On the first stanza, line one skips backward to the edge of the dance floor. On stanza two, line two does the same. On stanza three, both lines skip back to the middle, leaving about 4 feet between the lines, and bow or curtsey to the opposite line. At the chorus both lines clap their hands in rhythm to the music while the line leaders join hands and skip-slide down the middle and take their new position at the end of each line. The dancers repeat the movements to each verse.

The Blue-Tail Fly

When I was young I used to wait on my mas-ter and give him his plate, and

pass the bot-tle when he got dry, and brush a-way the blue - tail fly.

Jim-mie crack corn and I don't care,_ Jim-mie crack corn and I don't care,_

Jim-mie crack corn and I don't care, my mas - ter's gone a - way.

"Blue-Tail Fly." (Traditional American Folksong. Melody arranged by Jean Liepold).

Dance Directions to Blue-Tail Fly:

1. When I was young I used to wait,   *(Line A skips backward)*
    On my master and serve his plate.   *(Line B skips backward)*
    And pass the bottle when he got dry,   *(Both lines skip forward)*
    And brush away the blue-tail fly.   *(Both lines bow and curtsey)*

    (Chorus)
    Jimmie cracked corn and I don't care,   *(Lead couple take hands and skip-slide*
    Jimmie cracked corn and I don't care,   *down the middle of the two lines*
    Jimmie cracked corn and I don't care,   *while the others clap hands)*
    My master's gone away.

2. My master rode one afternoon,   4. The pony ran, jumped, and pitched,
    I'd follow him with a hickory broom;   He tossed my master in a ditch.
    The pony being rather shy,   When he died, the jury wondered why—
    When bitten by the blue-tail fly.   The verdict was the blue-tail fly.

3. One day he rode around the barn;   5. They laid him under a 'simmon tree;
    Where the flies, they did swarm.   His epitaph you can see.
    One bit the master on the thigh;   "Beneath this stone I'm forced to lie,
    They blamed it on the blue-tail fly.   A victim of the blue-tail fly."

TIPS FOR THE TELLER

George Washington's "Lifeguard": The Legend of Simeon Simons

By Jeanne M. Donato

STORYTELLING METHOD

Chant

This original story was written from oral tradition and snippets of local lore passed down through the years. The memories of a young lad chosen to serve General George Washington during the Revolutionary War reflect the patriotism, pride, and dedication to duty during this turbulent time.

Before beginning the story, the Teller may want to establish a signal such as a nod of the head or a hand gesture to indicate that every-one can join in the chanting. An asterisk indicates the text that the audience recites. This text is printed on the chalkboard or a flip chart in advance so that the class or audience can easily see their part.

After the first telling, the class may want to act out the story with puppets, as suggested in activity three. To begin, discuss events leading up to the Revolutionary War. Artifacts suggesting this time period such as a tri-cornered

continued

TIPS FOR THE TELLER *continued*

hat, water bucket, and pictures set the scene. The Teller may want to dress in old-fashioned clothing like Susan Hall, or as a young boy. Ask the students: "What did the people think about the war?", "What was the difference between a Patriot or Tory?", and "What could women and children do to help in the fight for freedom?" Like many proud patriots of Simeon's time, no tombstone marks his grave. But a story carries his spirit for all to remember. Begin the telling by saying to the children, "Listen, and you will discover the honor given to one boy."

George Washington's "Lifeguard": The Legend of Simeon Simons

Susan Hall hummed as she snapped the fresh clean sheet up into the air. Slowly it billowed onto the bed like a soft cloud. "Now look sharp child!" Susan called. "Smooth the sheet out and tuck it under your side of the bed. Mind you, make it neat. We have a lot of chores to finish up here."

"But I don't want to work anymore." I moaned. "It's so cold I can see my breath in the bedroom! I wish summer were here. I hate February!"

"There's no use in fretting about what can't be. Why, February has lots of interesting surprises and stories." Susan smiled as she finished fluffing the feather quilts and plumping the pillows.

"Put on your hat, coat, and mittens" she ordered. "We're going outside and build a fire to boil the maple sap and make some sweet, thick maple syrup, for your Johnnycakes. And if you work hard, I'll fix you a treat my father would make for me. You can only make it in February, mind you."

"Did you know that February is maple syrup month? We celebrate Valentine's Day and it's the birthday of President George Washington. Why, I know lots of stories about George Washington!"

"How do you know those stories?" I asked.

Susan smiled and said, ❋"'Cause, Simeon Simons told me so!"

"Who is Simeon Simons?" I asked.

"You don't know who Simeon Simons was?" Susan exclaimed. "Why, he lived right here in Patchaug! Little Patchaug, I'm proud to say, had a lot of Patriots who served in the Revolutionary War. But I thought everybody round these parts remembered Simeon. Why, he served with General George Washington from the beginning to the end of the Revolutionary War."

"How do you know?" I asked.

Susan smiled and said, ✿ "'Cause, Simeon Simons told me so."

Susan put on her cloak and pulled a hat onto my head as she ushered me outside. Fresh snow covered the tree branches and crunched under our boots.

"This is perfect February weather!" Susan took a deep breath and said, "fetch me a bundle of kindling to start the fire. And I'll tell you the story. But first, we have to get a nice steady heat in the kettle to boil the maple sap. Then we'll need the larger logs. Hurry off now."

When I returned with the kindling and logs, I begged, "Tell me about Simeon Simons. How did he meet George Washington?"

Susan started, "Simeon liked nothing more than to talk about the Revolutionary War and serving his beloved chief. And this is how he told it to me."

"In the spring of 1775, war had broken out between the king of Great Britain and the American colonies. The Continental Congress elected General George Washington commander in chief of the Colonial army to make the British army leave Boston. At that time, the American colonies still belonged to Britain. They wanted the king of England to listen to their complaints and treat them fairly.

General George Washington left Philadelphia to join the Continental army near Boston, Massachusetts. He had stopped in Norwich, Connecticut, on his way for lunch, and word flew throughout the countryside that the General might stop to dine at the local tavern in Patchaug. People gathered from all over the countryside to get a glimpse of the famous man. The women spread blankets and set out picnics under shade trees next to the tavern. The children chased about while Simeon and the other young lads played quoits, wrestled, and raced on the town green nearby. The men gathered to discuss the war. They argued and debated the wisdom of declaring independence from the king. They all agreed that the people in Boston needed help while their sailing port was closed to trade by British troops.

Soon, Simeon stopped his sport and called out, 'Get ready! They will be here soon!' Everyone rushed along the road but they couldn't see anything. Just as they turned to walk away Simeon cried again, 'Look! Here they come!' A cloud of dust arose in the distance and the clatter of hoofbeats drummed through the hot dry air. The crowd started to cheer as they waved their handkerchiefs and hats in the air to greet the General.

The tavern owner and the local patriots rushed to escort the General and his officers into the tavern to refresh themselves before dinner.

Washington sat by the window upstairs and watched the crowd milling about waiting to get another glimpse of him. He was tired and anxious to be moving on. He watched the young lads wrestling, racing, and playing quoits on the green. One tall youth seemed to know that the great man was watching and he turned to salute and smile up at him. Something about Simeon Simons caught Washington's eye.

'Would that I had someone in my service with such energy and enthusiasm. Who is that young Indian lad over yonder?' Washington inquired. 'Such zest and enthusiasm! Bid him come here. I would have a word with him.'

The innkeeper noted that the General was pointing out Simeon and went outside to fetch him. Breathless and excited, Simeon entered the room, doffed his hat, and bowed.

Washington was so taken with his manners and bearing that he asked young Simeon if he would like to assist him as his personal 'lifeguard.' We would call him a bodyguard today," Susan added.

"How do you know?" I asked.

Susan smiled and said, ✿"'Cause, Simeon Simons told me so.'"

Susan continued, "The Revolutionary War lasted for eight years. And Simeon served Washington through it all. First he served Washington as his bodyguard. And then he was a soldier, when he was old enough to fight. Simeon stayed and served his beloved Chief Washington from the beginning to the end of the war.

Simeon carried water and watched as Washington rallied his troops until the British withdrew from Boston. During the battles around New York he was ever watchful, guarding Washington from the many Tories and spies who plotted to kill him. He was there when Washington had the Declaration of Independence read to all the troops in New York. Simeon told many harrowing tales of Washington's ingenious ideas and their narrow escapes from the British.

Crossing the Delaware River on Christmas Eve was one of his favorites. He could describe the dark ice-swollen river and the freezing rain that encased their boats, coats, and even their hair in sheets of ice. You could feel the cold and excitement as he related how their ragged, starving army surprised and defeated the British at Trenton and Princeton.

His heart would sing as he told of Washington's vision of freedom and liberty as this new country was taking shape. His stories of his Commander's courtesy and compassion kept us enthralled. He described countless details of his Commander's courage and compassion for his men. Simeon would say that when all felt lost, it was everyone's respect for this great man that held the ragged, starving army together through the brutal winter at Valley Forge, Pennsylvania.

Simeon was proud to serve as Washington's bodyguard. He met many brave men who served with Washington. Why, years later, the famous Marquis de Lafayette stopped in Patchaug on his way to Boston. He remembered Washington's faithful Simeon as he greeted all the other war heroes that gathered to meet him. I would say that makes Simeon Simons famous. Simeon just considered it his duty and a privilege. But my, how he loved to tell those stories!" Susan sighed.

"Come along and I'll show you Simeon's favorite February treat!" Susan hummed as she peeled some bark off of a birch tree and started to twist it into a cone shape. Next, she scooped some fresh snow into the cone. "Now, hold this snow cone while I pour some of this sweet maple syrup over it. Taste it. Isn't it grand?" Susan laughed. "Bet you won't ever hold February to be such a boring month after this!"

"I know," I answered, ✿"'Cause Simeon Simons told me so.But, tell me, how did you know Simeon Simons?" I asked.

Susan Hall smiled and answered proudly, "Oh I reckon I know all those stories ✿'Cause Simeon Simons told me so.And, I'm proud to say, he was my Pa!"

MULTIPLE INTELLIGENCE ACTIVITIES FOR . . .

George Washington's "Lifeguard": The Legend of Simeon Simons

 ### 1 What Did Simeon Simons See?
(Logical-Mathematical; Visual-Spatial)

To help the class visualize the events that occurred during the Revolutionary War, enlist their help to become history detectives! Discuss how a time line gives us a clear picture of ideas and events that took place over a period of time. A time line helps us to see a number of events in the order in which they happened. Tape a paper at the top of the wall around the classroom. Start with a dark marker and label the first line with the date 1775 and end with the year 1783. Leave room for months to be placed between. Attach a paper stating "Simeon Simons meets Colonel George Washington in Patchaug, Connecticut." Place it under the month of June in 1775. As the children review the story, they can add the events mentioned in his story. Have the class work as a group to discover other events that happened within this time period that are not mentioned in this story. Have fun discovering and collecting many of these dates.

Add a game of quoits to your time line fun! To play, make four circles out of rope about 15 to 18 inches long. Cover two of the ropes with red tape and two with black tape. Place a 20-inch stake into level ground. Draw a line about 20 to 25 feet away from the stake. The children should stand behind this line as they take turns trying to toss the quoit over the stake.

To score, two players or teams take turns tossing their two quoits from the tossing line to the stake, called a "hob." The closest quoit to the hob scores one point. Throwing a quoit over the hob is a "ringer" worth two points. Neither side scores if both teams score ringers. The first player, or team, to score 21 points wins the game.

 ### 2 Simeon's Tasty February Treat.
(Naturalistic; Interpersonal)

Display a picture of a sugar maple tree tapped for sugaring with the buckets attached. Label and identify the leaf and bark of a sugar maple tree. (Refer to *The Woodland Indians* for more information. Discuss how the early Native Americans and settlers used to collect and boil down the sap to make maple syrup and sugar. Sugaring involved the whole family and a division of labor. The maple syrup snow cones were a special treat during February, as the syrup was dependent on natural conditions for snow. There are options for collecting and boiling down your own maple syrup, watching a video on sugaring, or investigating the process in the library. Have the class decide how they will work together to make their snow cones. Materials needed will be: ice shavings, paper cups or ice cream cones, small wooden or plastic spoons, napkins, and maple syrup. Help the class make their own February maple syrup snow cones. Enjoy!

 ### 3 Be a Star.
(Bodily-Kinesthetic; Intrapersonal)

After the first telling, the class may want to act out the story with puppets. The following materials can make an instant background for a screen, or project the scene onto the back of a puppet stage or refrigerator box. Use an overhead projector and clear overhead sheets to draw the following backgrounds: the bedroom inside the house; outside with a fire, kettle, sugar trees in the background; tavern and outside scene; room inside the tavern; hill overlooking Boston; inside tavern scene for the New York scene; boats and Delaware River with ice in it; camp scene with snow for Valley Forge; inside tavern scene for Washington's farewell; outside tavern scene for meeting Lafayette.

Puppets on sticks might be made to show Susan; a child; Washington; Simeon Simons as a young boy; Simeon in uniform; Lafayette; groups of men, women, and children; a boat with soldiers on it; and groups of Patriot and British soldiers.

Arrange the story into a sequence of events. Have the students take turns with the puppets while one person tells or reads the story aloud. Write invitations to other classrooms or parents to see the show!

TIPS FOR THE TELLER

The Frog Prince

By the Brothers Grimm

Retold and Adapted by Susan Trostle Brand

STORYTELLING METHOD

Chant/Pantomime

A classic and humorous tale, *The Frog Prince* is a story of an unlikely friendship and romance between a princess and a frog to whom she is indebted for retrieving her golden ball. The frog insists that the princess keep her promise to befriend him, and comically sits at her royal table to dine. In the sleeping quarter, when the princess, in disgust and fury, throws the frog against the wall, he reveals his true identify: a prince, of course!

The story is great fun told in the Chant with Pantomime method. Before the Teller begins the story he or she asks or assigns six children to select and pantomime a part or action word they prefer, including the following:

When the story is new to the children you may wish to distribute copies of this story with each of the six children's parts highlighted in a different color. Invite all children to join in on the words and sound effects throughout the story whenever their preassigned words appear, indicated by an asterisk. One child may be the narrator of the story, pausing at appropriate times for the words and motions. The children sit in a circle to allow for selected children to come forth and pantomime at the predesignated times. Or, print the text on the chalkboard or a flip chart in advance so that the children can easily see their parts.

Key Word:	Sound	Motion
Frog	ribbit, ribbit	Hop twice
Splashing	splish, splash	Clap once; spread hands
Golden Ball	bounce, bounce	Jump once into the air
King	Oh, Royal one!	Bow or curtsey
Princess	Oh, Lovely!	Hold cheeks
Prince	Oh, Handsome!	One hand on hip; other arm outstretched

The Frog Prince

Once upon a time, in a faraway land, there lived a ✻King who had three daughters. Each of these daughters was beautiful. However, the youngest one was, by far, the most beautiful. Even the sun itself was amazed by the beauty of the youngest ✻Princess.

Near the ✻King's castle was a large forest. In the midst of the forest was a pond. In the midst of the pond was a fountain. On hot days, the ✻King's youngest daughter would run to the fountain to play, always taking along her ✻Golden Ball. Over and over, she threw the ✻Golden Ball into the air, and then she caught that ✻Golden Ball again.

Now one day, the ✻Golden Ball did not fall back into the hands of the ✻Princess. It landed, instead, into the deep waters of the fountain. The ✻Princess began to weep at the loss of her favorite toy.

Just then, out of the waters came a croaking voice. It said, "Why are you weeping, ✻Princess? Your tears cause even the stones to cry!"

The ✻Princess looked around. Behold! She saw a ✻Frog stretching his lumpy, ugly head from the waters. "Ah, ugly frog," said the ✻Princess. "So it was you who croaked and spoke to me just now. I am weeping at the loss of my ✻Golden Ball. It is somewhere deep in the waters of the pond.

"Do not weep, ✻Princess," croaked the ✻Frog. He ✻Splashed as he spoke, "I will fetch your ✻Golden Ball if you will, in return, do me a favor. You must let me be your royal friend, sit at your dinner table, and sleep in your bed. Will you promise to do these things?"

"Yes, yes," said the ✻Princess. "If you return my ✻Golden Ball to me, I promise to be your loyal friend, to allow you to sit at my dinner table, and to sleep in my bed." But, while she said these words, she was thinking, "Never, I will never allow that ugly, lumpy ✻Frog to set foot in our lovely castle!"

The ✻Frog did not know what the ✻Princess was thinking. He heard only her promise. So he quickly ✻Splashed down into the deep waters of the fountain and came up again. In his tiny hands he held the ✻Golden Ball. The delighted ✻Princess cried out for joy. She grabbed the ✻Golden Ball from the ✻Frog and ran with it through the forest without so much as a thank you or a good-bye to the ✻Frog.

"Stop, stop," called the ✻Frog. "Remember your promise to me! I must come with you to the castle!" Still, the ✻Princess kept running without seeming to hear her friend.

The next evening, when the ✻Princess was sitting with her father, the ✻King, at the dinner table, something came ✻Splashing up the palace stairs. It knocked on the dining room door and cried, "Let me in, ✻Princess. Let me in. Remember your promise about the ✻Golden Ball.

When the ✻Princess opened the door, there sat the ✻Frog. She slammed the door furiously and returned to the table. The ✻King asked, "Why are you so angry and frightened, daughter?"

The ✻Princess replied, "Oh, father, a horrid, ugly, lumpy ✻Frog has followed me home. I met him yesterday at the fountain and he rescued my ✻Golden Ball for me. In return, I foolishly promised him that I would be his friend."

The *King answered, "You must keep your promise, daughter. Open the door and let in the *Frog!"

The horrified *Princess opened the door and in hopped the lumpy *Frog. He followed her, step by step to her chair, *Splashing all the way.

"Lift me up," croaked *Frog. "I am not so large as you are." He *Splashed as he waited.

The *Princess waited and waited. Finally, the *King ordered, "Do it at once, daughter!"

The *Princess could not eat a single bite. But the hungry *Frog finished his entire meal and asked for seconds. "Carry me now to your room and then we will sleep in your royal bed, " requested the *Frog.

The poor *Princess began to cry. But she remembered her father's words. She picked up the *Frog with two fingers on one of his legs. It was still wet and *Splashing. She placed him in a far corner of her enormous and elegant room. "Put me on the pillow beside you," ordered the *Frog. "If you do not do as I ask, I will tell your father, the *King!"

This was all the *Princess could bear. She grabbed hold of the lumpy *Frog and threw him violently against the wall. "Now will you let me alone, you ugly *Frog?" she screamed.

But at that very moment, as the *Frog fell to the floor, something wonderful happened. The *Frog changed into a *Prince. He told the *Princess, "I have been under the spell of an evil witch. Only you, *Princess, the daughter of the *King, had the power to rescue me from the pond and turn me back into a *Prince."

The *Princess was delighted. A short time later the *Prince and the *Princess were married. And they lived happily ever after in the palace of the *King, who bestowed his richest blessings upon the happy couple.

So the next time you wander through the woods, near a pond, and see a *Frog, look closely and pay attention. It my really be a *Prince!

MULTIPLE INTELLIGENCE ACTIVITIES FOR . . .

The Frog Prince

 The Frogs Go Hopping.
(Musical-Rhythmic, Logical-Mathematical)

Sing this catchy song (to the tune of "When Johnny Comes Marching Home") with the children while pantomiming the motions. For each new verse, perhaps, add one new child to pantomime so that the numbers correspond to the sets in the verses.

The frogs go hopping one by one—hurrah,
   hurrah.
The frogs go hopping one by one—hurrah,
   hurrah.

The frogs go hopping one by one,
The little one stops to lie in the sun

Refrain:
And they all go hopping
Down to the pond to visit the toads.

The frogs go hopping two by two—hurrah,
   hurrah (2x)
The frogs go hopping two by two,
The little one stops to tie his shoe—

(Refrain)

The frogs go hopping three by three—
   hurrah, hurrah. (2x)

91

The frogs go hopping three by three,
The little one stops to climb a tree—

(Refrain)

The frogs go hopping four by four—hurrah,
  hurrah. (2x)
The frogs go hopping four by four,
The little one stops to eat a s'more—

(Refrain)

The frogs go hopping five by five—hurrah, hur-
  rah. (2x)
The frogs go hopping five by five,
The little one stops to take a drive—

(Refrain)

The frogs go hopping six by six—hurrah, hur-
  rah. (2x)
The frogs go hopping six by six,
The little one stops to pick up sticks—

(Refrain)

The frogs go hopping seven by seven—
  hurrah, hurrah. (2x)
The frogs go hopping seven by seven,
The little one stops to gaze at heaven—

(Refrain)

The frogs go hopping eight by eight—
  hurrah, hurrah. (2x)
The frogs go hopping eight by eight,
The little one stops to skate with her mate—

(Refrain)

The frogs go hopping nine by nine—hurrah,
  hurrah. (2x)
The frogs go hopping nine by nine,
The little one stops to send a valentine—

(Refrain)

The frogs go hopping ten by ten—hurrah, hur-
  rah. (2x)
The frogs go hopping ten by ten,
The little one stops to feed a hen—

(Refrain)

And they all go hopping
Down to the pond to visit the toads,
And take a cool swim—
I'm glad they're all friends!

(shout) The End!

2 Amazing Amphibians.
(Naturalistic; Verbal-Linguistic)

Invite children to research amphibians, which are animals that spend part of their lives on land and part in the water. Smaller groups of researchers may study and report on frogs; other groups may report on toads, using encyclope- dias, *Ranger Rick's* magazine, *The Big Backyard* magazine, and books about nature as resources. If possible, take a field trip to a local pond site or nature sanctuary to locate actual frogs and toads. Some interesting findings about frogs and toads include:

FROG FACTS
- There are about 2,000 kinds of frogs living today
- The largest frog is the giant frog which lives in West Africa
- Many frogs have poisons in their bodies; these poisons are used for protection
- The frog's tongue is sticky and catches insects and other moving animals
- The life cycle of the frog includes eggs, tadpoles in eggs, newly hatched tadpoles, tadpole with hind legs developed, tadpole with front legs developed, and adult frog
- Kinds of frogs are the bullfrog, the leopard frog or grass frog, the green or spring frog, the pick- erel frog, and the wood frog
- Frogs' skin is usually smooth and moist
- Frog legs are eaten in the United States and France; in Germany the entire frog is often stewed and eaten

TOAD FACTS
- The toad is a tailless animal that breeds in water, but spends most of its life on land
- The toad is more clumsy than the frog
- Frogs hop far and fast to escape their ene- mies; toads duck their heads when they are frightened
- Toads push away frightening or annoying objects with their front feet
- The toad has a long, sticky tongue; it uses its tongue to catch insects, as does the frog
- The toad has rough, warty skin; the warts are really glands that contain a poisonous fluid

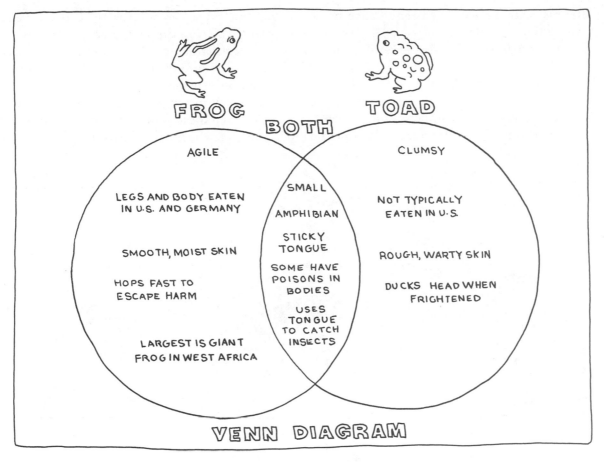

Venn diagram comparing frogs and toads.

When the research is collected, invite children to create a large-sized Venn Diagram, comparing and contrasting frogs and toads.

 Friendship Bracelets.
(Interpersonal; Visual-Spatial)

As a variation to making Valentines, children construct friendship bracelets. These bracelets fit nicely into Valentine envelopes, along with the Valentines, and provide lasting momentos of children's affection for one another. Purchase wooden or plastic colored beads with approximately 1/4-inch holes. You will also need string, yarn, shoestrings, gimp, or dental floss for stringing the beads.

Measure a length of string around the child's wrist. Cut the string 3 inches longer than the wrist size to allow for knotting when the bracelet is completed. Encourage children to be creative in their choices of designs and colors. Some may wish to use a pattern of colors, while others may decide to use a montage approach. Youngsters then exchange friendship bracelets with their best pals. (Important: Be sensitive to the feelings of all, making certain that each child receives a bracelet; this may take some advance organizing.)

Children will enjoy learning more about Valentine's Day traditions now. Share this historical background with them, perhaps, as they string their beads into friendship bracelets.

Most people believe that Valentine's Day got its name from a man named Valentine who lived 1700 years ago. He was a priest in Rome, Italy. At that time, Christianity was a new religion. Valentine was put to death for teaching Christianity. Legend also tells us that Valentine secretly married sweethearts who were ordered not to marry by Cladius II, who was the Emperor of Rome.

After his death, he was called Saint Valentine, the patron saint of lovers.

The ornaments that decorate valentines are symbols of love and friendship that began long ago. Valentine ornaments were crafted by hand. Each ornament had a special meaning. For instance, a fan on a valentine meant, "Open up your heart to me." A ribbon meant, "You are tied up," or "You are my sweetheart." Lace on the card meant "You have captured my heart."

At valentine parties romantic symbols were often baked into the cake. One lucky guest might receive an ornament of good fortune, such as a ring, which meant a forthcoming engagement, a coin, which meant a wealthy marriage, or a package of rice, which meant a wedding.

Friendship bracelets.

FEBRUARY CHAPTER RESOURCES

Aardena, V. (1984). *Oh, Kojo! How could you!* New York: Scholastic.

Adams, A. (1980). *The great valentine's day balloon race.* New York: Scribner.

Beall, P. C., & Nipp, N. S. (1994). *Wee sing around the world.* New York: Price Stern & Sloan.

Beim, J. (1955). *The boy on Lincoln's lap.* New York: Random House.

Brenner, B. (1994). *Abe Lincoln's hat.* New York: Scholastic.

Brothers Grimm. (1989). *The frog prince.* Mahwah, NJ: Troll Communications.

Bryan, A. (1967). *What a wonderful world.* New York: Simon & Schuster.

Buckley, H. (1963). *My sister and I.* Katonah, NY: Young Readers.

Bunting, E. (1990). *The wall.* New York: Clarion.

Clements, A. (1988). *Big Al.* Saxonville, MA: Picture Book Studio.

Clover, A. (1960). *Abraham Lincoln: For the people.* New York: Scholastic.

Flack, M. (1960). *Ask Mr. Bear.* New York: Macmillan.

Greenfield, E. (1978). *Honey, I love.* New York: Harper Festival.

Gross, R. B. (1973). *True stories about Abraham Lincoln.* New York: Scholastic.

Guilfoile, E. (1965). *Valentine's Day.* Champaign, IL: Gerard.

Hallinan, P. K. (1994). *Today is Valentine's Day.* Nashville, TN: Ideals Children's Books.

Harold, J. D. (Ed.). (1983). *The woodland indians: A history coloring book.* Groton, CT & Old Mystic, CT: Groton Public Library & the Indian and Colonial Research Center.

Heide, F. P., & Van Clief, S. W. (1968). *That's what friends are for.* Illustrations by Brinton Turkle. New York: Four Winds.

Ives, B. (1953). *Burl Ives song book.* New York: Ballantine.

Jeunesse, G. (1994). *Frogs.* New York: Scholastic.

Joosse, B. M., (1991). *Mama, do you love me?* New York: Scholastic.

Lionni, L. (1963). *Swimmy.* New York: Pantheon.

Lobel, A. (1970). *Frog and toad are friends.* New York: HarperCollins.

McDermott, G. (1972). *Anansi the spider.* New York: Holt, Rhinehart & Winston.

McGill, A. (1999). *Molly Bannaky.* Boston: Houghton Mifflin.

Noble, T. H. (1983). *Hansy's mermaid.* New York: Dial.

O'Brien, R. C. (1971). *Mrs. Frisby and the rats of NIMH.* New York: Simon & Schuster.

Perham, M. (1994). *The princess and the frog.* Leicestershire, England: Ladybird.

Pfister, M. (1992). *The rainbow fish.* New York: Scholastic.

Preller, J. M. (1995). *The boastful frog.* New York: Scholastic.

Sharmat, M. W. (1982). *The best valentine in the world.* New York: Holiday House.

Silverstein, S. (1964). *The giving tree.* New York: Harper & Row.

Trivizas, E. (1993). *The three little wolves and the big bad pig.* New York: Scholastic.

Udry, J. (1988). *Let's be enemies.* New York: HarperCollins.

Waber, B. (1972). *Ira sleeps over.* Boston: Houghton Mifflin.

Wells, R. (1985). *Hazel's amazing mother.* New York: Scholastic.

Williams, V. B. (1990). *More, more, more said the baby.* New York: Greenwillow.

Zolotow, C. (1969). *The hating book.* New York: Harper & Row.

March

Magic and Make-Believe

THE WIND

I saw you toss the kites on high
And blow the birds about the sky;
And all around I heard you pass,
Like ladies' skirts across the grass—

> O wind, a-blowing all day long,
> O wind, that sings so loud a song!

I saw the different things you did,
But always you yourself you hid.
I felt you push, I heard you call,
I could not see yourself at all—

> O wind, a-blowing all day long,
> O wind, that sings so loud a song!

O you that are so strong and cold,
O blower, are you young or old?
Are you a beast of field and tree,
Or just a stronger child than me?

> O wind, a-blowing all day long,
> O wind, that sings so loud a song!

—Robert Louis Stevenson

*B*ecome a toothless giant! Converse with a freckled leprechaun! In "March: Magic and Make-Believe," imagination abounds.

The four stories within this chapter are enacted by the Teller through Character Imagery, Chant, Traditional, and Group Role-Play Storytelling methods. Children discover giants, pookas, and wee folk.

Interpersonal, Visual-Spatial, Verbal-Linguistic, Logical-Mathematical, Musical-Rhythmic, Intrapersonal, Interpersonal, and Bodily-Kinesthetic multiple intelligences are engaged as children explore the mind's eye and their inner creativity, construct a puppet theater, and dance a jig at an Irish Festival.

Make your own rainbows in March through the magic of storytelling!

TIPS FOR THE TELLER

Daniel O'Rourke and the Pooka's Tower

Retold and Adapted by Jeanne M. Donato

STORYTELLING METHOD

Traditional

Daniel O'Rourke and the Pooka's Tower is an old Irish tale collected by T. Crofton Croker in the early nineteenth century. Daniel ignores his wife's superstitions and attends a party on a full moonlit night. His shortcut home past the ancient Pooka's tower takes him on a series of encounters with the Pooka in different forms. It ends with Daniel not sure whether his adventures were real or a dream.

This story lends itself to a delightful use of Traditional Storytelling as discussed in Chapter 3. The Teller, dressed as a leprechaun or as an Irish person dressed in green with shamrocks, presents the story as told by that character. The Tellers asks, "Ireland has many stories about magic and make-believe. Do you know the names of any of those characters?" Here the Teller can elicit class responses and introduce the vocabulary such as: lord, manor, bog, leprechauns, fairies, wee people, unicorns, and Pookas. A brief discussion may be required to give the background information needed for understanding and appreciating the humor in this tale. Tell the children, "Listen and see if you can recognize the different shapes the Pooka assumes to trick Daniel O'Rouke."

Daniel O'Rourke and the Pooka's Tower

The Teller begins, "As a Leprechaun (or Irishman), I've heard many a wild, fantastic tale about Daniel O'Rourke. And he'd be insistin', all the while, that they be true. But, I'll be lettin' that up for you to judge. He claims that it started out like this:

On the eve of Lady's Day, it was, a long time ago, the Lord of the manor, on the hill, invited everyone in the countryside, rich and poor alike, to a party. Now Daniel's wife, well she refused to be out and about late at night on the full of the moon. She feared the "wee folk" and the Pooka that was said to guard the tower in the forest nearby. But Daniel

O'Rourke begged, pleaded, and teased to go. He promised her that he would come home before midnight.

Now Daniel had been looking forward to all the singing, dancing, eating, and drinking. And at these he outdid himself the whole night long. He drank green beer, and dined on green cheese. He stuffed himself on roasted goose and steamin' puddings till the buttons fairly popped from his vest.

How the time flew he never knew. But, when the great hall clock chimed the midnight hour, Daniel fumbled to take his leave and stumbled into the cool March air. Down the drive and through the gates he hurried himself. And there, where the road split, he could see his own wee cottage nestled peacefully, down by the edge of the sea. Now, the main road went out and around the forest, while the shortcut passed through the woods where the ancient Pooka's tower stood. Chuckling at his wife's silly fears, Daniel turned himself onto the shorter path.

He could hear the stream gurgling over the stones, when something whisked by him and flew into the sky. When he looked up, all he saw was the crumbling rim of the Pooka's tower wrapped in a wisp of cloud. Daniel fancied the cloud was shaped like a unicorn. And he thought he heard someone whisper his name.

He made the sign of the cross for good measure and hurried himself across the stepping stones in the water. But a wind set him off balance. He lost his footing and tumbled headlong into the stream.

"Ah!" Daniel gasped "I'll be drowned for sure!" And just as he was about to give himself up for lost, he was washed ashore upon a desolate island surrounded by nothing but fog and bog.

Daniel found himself a rock to stand on but he noticed that it was slowly sinking down into the bog. Thinking that this would be his burying place he started to sing. Then next, wouldn't you know, says he, a great giant of an eagle pounced from the sky and cried, "Why, Daniel O'Rourke, how do you do?"

"Very well, sir. Thank you for asking. Though I wish I were safe at home" replied Daniel. And then he told the eagle how he had come to be there. All the while he was a wondering how an eagle could be talking and knowing his name.

"Well, Daniel" says the eagle, "That's a sad tale for sure. Hop up on my back. Hang on tight and I'll fly you out of this bog."

So Daniel thanked the eagle and said, "I'll gladly take your kind offer, sir." And before he knew it, he found himself flying high in the sky till they were far above the earth up into the heavens. "Whoa!" cried Daniel. "Where in the world are you going? This is not the way to my house!"

"'Tis been a long flight and here's the moon." cried the eagle. "Do me a favor and grab a hold of that reaping hook sticking inside of the moon and give me a rest."

"I'll do no such thing!" cried Daniel. "I might fall off!"

"Grab hold of the hook!" squawked the eagle, "or I'll be tossing you off. Now hang or fall. 'Tis no difference to me. I've nicked you right this time, Daniel O'Rouke! That's what you get for robbing my nest last year. Good riddance to you!" And the eagle flew off laughing, leaving poor Daniel dangling for dear life from the reaping hook, bawling and calling after the beast.

All at once a door opened up in the middle of the moon. A little man in the moon with a long white beard, a wee cap and spectacles on his nose greeted him saying, "Good morrow to you, Daniel O'Rourke. How are you faring this fine evening?"

"Why very well, your honor. And I hope that your honor's well," Daniel replied.

"How is it that you've come to be here?" the little man asked.

Well, Daniel related the tale of how he had gotten lost and been left on the moon.

"'Tis most curious indeed," replied the little man. "But 'tis my duty to tell you that you can't be staying here. You must be off."

"Now that's no way to be treating a stranded stranger with nowhere to go!" cried Dan. "I'll not budge. And you can't make me!"

"Say what you like. But off you must go! I thank you for your visit Daniel. Farewell!" he huffed. The little man gave the door such a bang after him that poor Daniel thought the moon would fall from the sky and him with it as he lost his hold of the reaping hook. Down he tumbled falling through the night sky.

"Well," cried Daniel, "this is a pretty pickle for a decent man to be seen in. I'll be smashed to a smitherin' pieces!" But no sooner were the words out of his mouth when, 'whiz,' a flock of wild geese flew by.

The lead gander looked up and honked, "Good morrow to you Daniel O'Rouke; how do you do?"

"Why very well indeed sir," replied Daniel "And I hope your honor can say the same."

"So I can," replied the Old Gander. "But, I think it is falling you are Daniel," says he. "Where are you going so fast?"

Well, Daniel related the whole sad tale of how he came to be tumbling through the night sky. "Grab hold of my leg and I'll save you" the Gander offered.

"Why thank you kindly, sir," Daniel cried. And away they flew as fast as hops till they passed over his own wee cottage. "We're home! Thank you kindly. You can put me down now. Stop here!" Daniel yelled. But, the geese just kept flying out over the deep ocean. "Now where do you think you going?" cried Daniel.

"To Arabia," replied the Old Gander.

"No, no," cried Daniel. "Put me down. Put me down at once, I say!"

"As you wish," said the Old Gander. And with a flip of his wing, he sent Daniel tumbling down till he hit the bottom of the sea and knocked the wind out of him.

"Well, there," thought Daniel. "'Tis the end of me for sure!" When a great white whale came along, scooped him up and tossed him high into the air above, soaking Daniel entirely.

"Now that's it!" sputtered Daniel, blowing the water from his nose. "I've had enough!"

"Oh you have had you!" came a voice calling his name and screeching "Come on! Get up you old fool! Get up I tell you! Are you crazy?"

It was his good old wife, Peg, a flinging a bucket of cold water all over him crying, "Have you no sense man? No man in his right mind would fall asleep under the old walls by the Pooka's tower! You've had me worried out of my senses! And I can bet you've not had a restful night's sleep here!"

"How right she was," thought Daniel. But he was so happy to see her, that he never minded the soaking nor her scolding the whole way home.

MULTIPLE INTELLIGENCE ACTIVITIES FOR . . .

Daniel O'Rourke and the Pooka's Tower

 ### The Magic Shamrock Game.
(Logical-Mathematical; Interpersonal)

This classroom game is based on an old game called Black Magic. It teaches observation of patterns and cooperation in the form of a game. The teacher takes two students (Number One and Number Two) aside and tells them how the game is played. Number Two goes outside with a cutout of a green shamrock, while Number One tells the class of an object that he or she is concentrating on to see if the magic shamrock will let Two know what it is.

When Two enters the room, One says, "Did I choose this chair?" One will continue to mention objects and Two pretends to listen to the shamrock and then guesses the correct object. They take turns until another student thinks they know how to arrive at the correct answer. This new student then takes One's place and the game starts again. The students are cautioned not to tell the secret until everyone has had a chance to play.

The pattern is: When One finally points to something green, the next object pointed out (for example, "Did I choose this pencil?") is Two's clue to pretend to listen to the shamrock and state that it is the correct answer. This game should be played gently and cooperatively until everyone can join in the fun once they understand the pattern.

 ### Lets Pretend.
(Visual-Spatial; Verbal-Linguistic)

Divide the class into groups. Several groups list the scenes as they occur in the story and each chooses a scene to depict. After they are com-pleted, they can tape the scenes together and attach them to the ends of two empty paper rolls. This creates continuous scenery for the background of the Puppet Theater. One group can practice being the narrators of each scene. Another group can color and cut out finger puppets from premade patterns or devise their own. Invitations to the play can be extended to other classrooms or parents to share in the final project.

 ### Find the Wee Folk.
(Verbal-Linguistic; Visual-Spatial)

Belief in "wee folk" is found in many cultures around the world. Through class discussion, list the names of these different wee folk and the countries from which they originate. Have the class research the stories from these countries. Examples may include: Scotland—Brownies; Ireland—Leprechauns; Denmark—Nisses; Sweden—Tomten; Scandinavia—Trolls, Dwarfs, and Elves; Germany, and Ireland—Changelings; Wales—Faeries; Spain and Northern Africa—Duende; France—Dracs; Finland—Para; United States—the tooth fairy. Native Americans too, have various names for "wee folk." These include: the Passamaquoddy—Nagumwasuck and the Mekumwasuck; The Wampanoags—Pukwudgies; the Mohegans—Makiawisugs. Among Hawaiian islanders, they are called Menehunes.

Display a map of the world. Cut out large shamrocks, write the names of the wee folk on them, and place them around the map. Attach green yarn to the shamrocks and tack the other ends to the country where each group originates. The students can lift the shamrock to see a drawing of the wee folk and/or read their story.

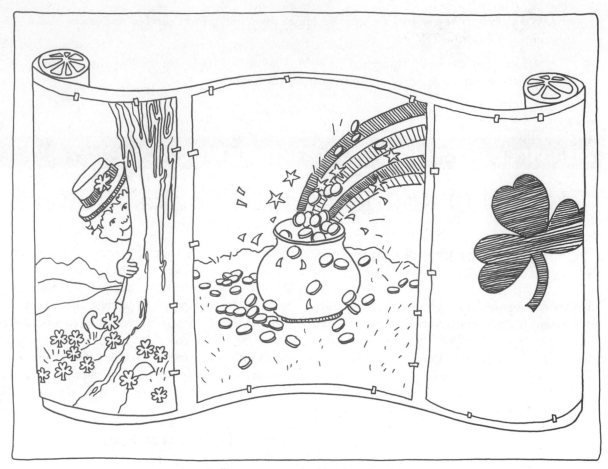

Rolling scenery created by class members.

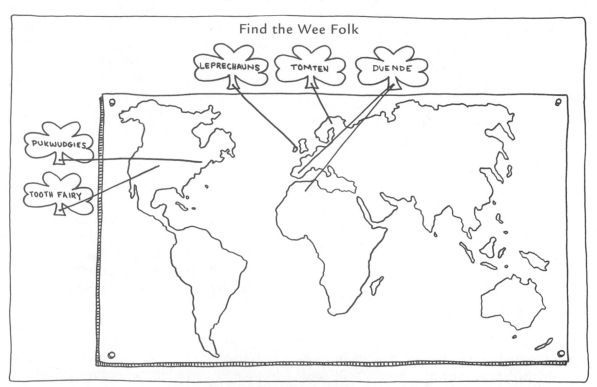

Find the Wee Folk

Locating groups of Wee Folks on a map of the world.

TIPS FOR THE TELLER

Finn and Cuchulainn

Retold and Adapted by Susan Trostle Brand

STORYTELLING METHOD

Group Role-Play

Finn and Cuchulainn is an amusing folktale about two giants from Ireland. Stories about Finn McCool have been passed down from generation to generation through oral tradition. Now, several trade books about the two giants are also available. Finn McCool is best known for his Giant's Causeway, the highway that, legend claims, he and other giants built between Scotland and Ireland.

Cuchulainn (pronounced Kuh-Hull-in) was the strongest giant in the world at the time. So far, he had beaten every other giant in Ireland. Now, his goal was to also beat Finn McCool, a fine and honorable giant who was married to a lovely Irish lass named Oonagh (pronounced OOH-nuh). When the scheduled day for the beating arrived, Oonagh thought of a clever scheme to outwit Cuchulainn. Finn, posing as a baby in a cradle, impressed Cuchulainn with his strength. Finally, Finn bit the terrible giant on his brass finger which contained the secret of his strength. The giant, weakened and terrified, fled from Finn's home, never to return.

In preparing to tell *Finn and Cuchulainn* for group role-play, you may wish to first read the story to the children. Tomie De Paola's version, *Fin M'Coul, The Giant of Knockmany Hill* (1981) and *The Legend of Knockmany*, retold by Judy Sierra (1993) are two excellent pre-acting, read-alouds of this popular story.

When the children are familiar with the story, ask one group to create a large "cradle" from an appliance box, such as a refrigerator or a stove. Decorate the cradle with colorful paint and trim, if desired. A second group selects Irish music and sound effects for the background. The third group makes the background scenery, such as Knockmany Hill (a hill near the town of Dungannon in Northern Ireland), the Giant's Causeway, and the home of Finn McCool and his wife, Oonagh. A fourth group prepares or creates the necessary props, such as papier-mâché loaves of bread, baskets, big white teeth, and white stones. A final group works on the costumes for two giants, a large baby, and Oonagh. The remaining four children prepare to role-play the parts of Finn, Oonagh, Cuchulainn, and a fellow Causeway worker.

Finn and Cuchulainn

(Display scenery of Giant's Causeway and workers)

Finn: *(pounding a hammer while working on the Giant's Causeway)*: I work so hard, all through the day; I'm building the Giant's Causeway!

Fellow Worker: You better watch out, 'tis the truth, Finn McCool. Cuchulainn's heard that there's a giant he hasn't yet beat. That would be you!

Finn: You give me a fright, wee man, that ye do! I've heard that Cuchulainn is so strong he can catch thunder in his hands and smash it flat as a pancake! I'd best be headin' home to m'lovely wife, Oonagh. Fare thee well!

(change scenery to Finn and Oonagh's house, atop a lush green hill)

Oonagh: M'dear Finn! You're shakin'. What might be wrong with you? And why are ye home while the sun's still high in the sky?

Finn: Oonagh, m' love. It's frightening news I have for ye. The giant Cuchulainn is after me! *(enters house; change scenery and add living room furniture and a cradle)*

Oonaugh: Oooooh, m' dear, Finn. Let's mull this over for a while. Let me bring you your slippers and pipe. Have a seat by the fire. Here's an Irish stout and a slice of soda bread. *(Finn sits down, "smokes" pipe, and eats bread)*

Now, let's talk. For years you've been worried about Cuchulainn. We've built our sturdy home upon a high hill so you'd be able to see him coming. Now, it is time to be brave and face him, Finn.

Finn: He's coming, Oonagh! *(covers eyes)*

Oonagh: Feemie, fimey, foomey, floo, Giant, this is the end for you!

Now, I will use my frying pans and my loaves of bread which I have saved for just such an occasion. *(place bread and pans on "shelf")* Into some of the loaves, marked with a "P," I will insert a frying pan!

Next, I will make some fresh cheese balls. *(display papier-mâché balls)*

I shall also need some round, white stones *(gather and display round white stones near cradle)*. These closely resemble the cheese balls. But the stones are marked with a small "S."

Finn, put on these baby clothes. *(Finn, looking puzzled, dresses in baby's clothing.)* Now, crawl into this cradle, and try to look like a helpless infant! *(Finn crawls into "cradle")*

(loud knocking sounds)

Finn: *(trembling)* Oonagh, he's knockin' at the door. Let's pray your plan works!

Oonagh: There's just one more thing, Finn. Cuchulainn's strength is in his brass finger on his right hand. Without use of this finger, Cuchulainn is a helpless weaklin'.

(More loud knocking; Oonagh opens door)

Oonagh: Well, hello, Cuchulainn. So you and I finally meet, we do. And a beaut of a day, it is, too!

Cuchulainn: *(wearing brass finger on right hand)* Spare me the small talk, woman. Where's that coward of a husband of yours, Finn McCool?

Oonagh: *(sweetly)* Oooooooooh, what a shame! Finn's out workin' on the Causeway. He won't be home until the sun lies low in the sky, that he won't. But, come on in anyway, Cuchulainn. Wait for him with me and the baby, won't you?

(Cuchulainn stomps in and sits in chair facing Finn in cradle)

(Oonagh places three loaves of bread on table)

Cuchulainn: I am a wee bit hungry. *(grabs a loaf marked "P" and takes a huge bite)*

Yoooooowwllllllll! What is this bread? I've lost two of my teeth trying to bite into it! *(giant displays two huge white teeth in palm of hand)*. Why, it's hard as iron!

Oonagh: Indeed! That's Finn's bread—the only kind he ever eats.

Finn: *(in cradle)* Hungry, hungry, hungry! Mama, bread!

Oonagh: Yes, m' darlin'. *(hands Finn bread with no "P" marking)*

Finn: Yummy, yummy, yummy! *("Eats" three slices of soft bread.)* Mama, play! *(Oonagh hands Finn two balls of "cheese." Finn crumbles each as water drops out. Finn "chews" and "swallows" each)*

Cuchulainn: I'll have a cheese ball, too. I'm still hungry!

(tries to bite into stone, marked "S," but loses two more teeth). Yoooowwllllllll! What is this cheese? My poor teeth, woman! *(displays two more teeth in palm of hand)*

Oonagh: Oooooh, I'm so sorry, Cuchulainn. That's the only kind of cheese me husband, Finn'll eat.

Cuchulainn: Wings-o-bats! What kind of teeth does that lad have? *(pretends to reach into Baby-Finn's mouth as Finn pretends to bite giant's brass finger. Brass "finger" falls to floor.)* AAAhhhh-hhhhhhh! My brass finger! And the rest of my teeth! *(Show handful of "teeth")* I'll not stay around to meet the father if the son can do these things. *(Cuchulainn exits, slamming door)*

(Finn leaves cradle and removes baby clothing)

Oonagh: Tea is served, m'love. Come keep me company.

Finn: Oonagh, you're my sweet Irish treasure, that you are!

(Irish music plays as Finn and Oonagh sit on couch with arms around each other)

105

MULTIPLE INTELLIGENCE ACTIVITIES FOR . . .

Finn and Cuchulainn

 Irish Tunes and Traditions.
(Visual-Spatial; Musical-Rhythmic)

Encourage children to research Ireland on a map and in reference books including encyclopedias. They will discover that Ireland is an island in the Atlantic Ocean just west of Great Britain. It is called the "Emerald Isle" because of its green countryside, farmlands, and hills. They may discover facts about the potato famine in 1840. They will report about Saint Patrick, the patron saint of Ireland. Saint Patrick introduced Christianity to Ireland long ago and, in his honor, Saint Patrick's Day is celebrated on March 17th, in many countries around the world.

Legend tells us that Saint Patrick chased the snakes out of Ireland. Also notable is the leprechaun, a tiny elf who hides treasures, and the good luck symbols of rainbows, pennies (heads up), and shamrocks.

Next, invite the class to learn a few Irish songs such as the "Wee Falorie Man," "Cockles and Mussels," "Londonderry Air," "Who Threw the Overalls in Mistress Murphy's Chowder," and other classical favorites.

 Me and My Giant Classroom Pen Pals.
(Intrapersonal; Verbal-Linguistic)

Introduce a poem about a child's friendship with a giant. Afterwards, invite children to create their own giants using mural paper and a variety of fabrics,

Giant classroom pen pals.

textures, and trimmings. Children write letters to their giants, telling them their wishes. An adult or older child responds to these letters, as the "giant," much to the children's delight! Later, display giants and letters around the room.

 Irish Festival.
(Logical-Mathematical; Interpersonal)

In advance, have the children prepare shamrock invitations and green Jello snacks for an Irish festival. (Children and adults prepare the Jello the day before.) Parents may help by preparing and serving corned beef and cabbage casseroles, along with carrots and potatoes, to the class. Play Irish background music, sing Irish songs, read Green poetry (see What is Green?), and culminate the festive event with bright green Jello desserts in shamrock molds, topped with whipped cream! Learn the "Jig!"

What is Green?

Green is the grass
And the leaves of trees
Green is the smell
Of a country breeze.
Green is lettuce
And sometimes the sea.
When green is a feeling
You pronounce it N-V,
Green is a coolness
You get in the shade
Of the tall old woods
Where the moss is made.

Green is a flutter
That comes in the Spring
When frost melts out
Of everything.
Green is a grasshopper
Green is jade
Green is hiding
In the shade—

Green is an olive
And a pickle.
The sound of green
Is a water-trickle
Green is the world
After the rain
Bathed and beautiful
Again.

April is green
Peppermint, too.
Every elf has
One green shoe.
Under a grape arbor
Air is green
With sprinkles of sunlight
In between.
Green is the meadow,
Green is the fuzz
That covers up
Where winter was.
Green is ivy and
Honeysuckle vine.
Green is yours
Green is mine...

"What is Green," from Hailstones and Halibut Bones *by Mary O'Neill and Leonard Weisgard, Ill., Copyright ©1961 by Mary LeDuc O'Neill. Used by permission of Doubleday, a division of Random House, Inc.*

The Three Wishes

Retold by Jeanne M. Donato

STORYTELLING METHOD

Traditional

The motif in this Old Spanish folktale can be found in many different stories around the world. It offers students a framework to work through the concepts of greed, selfishness, anger, understanding, reason, cooperation, values, and wisdom as the old couple develops ways of dealing with three free wishes. From the time the wishes are given and the pudding sticks fast to the wife's nose, until they find the wish that will bring true happiness, this tale offers children much about acquiring desirable values.

The Traditional method in Chapter 3 offers the Teller ideas on preparing to tell this tale. Its simple structure and brevity lends itself as a successful vehicle for this method. To prepare the listeners, the Teller will want to review where Spain is located on a map and any vocabulary the listeners may need to understand. The Teller may want to show a wand with a star on top and say, "What would you wish for if you were granted one wish? Imagine you were told that you could have one more wish only if you and a friend or your parents could agree upon it? Listen. I think the magic is starting!" Wave the wand and start.

The Three Wishes

One cool evening a long time ago, an old man named Diego, and his wife, Donna Isabella, sat before their cooking fire saying little and dreaming much. Instead of giving thanks to God for their blessings, they bickered and blamed each other, lamenting their bad luck and poor fortune.

Diego complained, "Wife, how is it that our neighbors have all the good luck? It isn't fair!"

"Aye!" agreed Donna Isabella. "You would think, that after all these years, fortune, herself would feel some pity for us!"

The words scarcely fell from her mouth when the embers spit and sparked on the hearth. A maiden, no larger than a hand, dressed in gossamer white appeared before them. A golden crown encircled her long dark hair and the tiniest ember sparkled on the end of her wand.

Speechless, the old couple listened. "I am Fortunata," said the tiny Fairy. "I have come to grant one wish to each of you. I will return at this time tomorrow to grant you a third wish, only if you can both agree on the same wish. Think carefully and guard your tongues. Remember, life is what you make of it." And with that, she disappeared.

"I must be dreaming, wife! Did you see and hear the same as I?" exclaimed Diego. "What would you wish for? What should we wish for? I wonder if it's true or if we have both been dreaming."

"What nonsense!" cried Donna Isabella. "Whoever heard of such a thing? But, just in case this is not a dream, I would wish for beautiful clothes, jewels, gold, carriages, and a castle! Oh, and I want an important title, like Contessa!"

"But that is more than one wish, Dear. We should be reasonable and make a list so we will know which three wishes to make. What good will any of these wishes do us if we do not have land, health, wealth, and a long life to enjoy all our riches? Don't even think of wasting your only wish on silly clothes or stupid titles! Oh," he yawned, "All this thinking has made me tired." And off to sleep he went, leaving Donna Isabella fuming.

"So he thinks my wishes are silly, does he? We'll see. My wish belongs to me. Only on one do we need to agree! I will do as I please!" And soon Donna Isabella fell asleep dreaming grand dreams.

The next morning, when the cock crowed, Diego slowly arose to do his chores, wondering if it had all been but a dream. He shook his wife and said. "I'm hungry. Where is my breakfast? Wishes or no, I must go out to milk the goats. Now hurry yourself!"

"Hurry, you say. Hungry are you? Would you expect a Contessa to cook your meals for you?"

"Contessa!" shouted Diego. "What good is a title when we don't have anything to eat for breakfast? I'm starving."

"Oh," grumbled Donna Isabella as she climbed out of bed. "I'm hungry too! I just wish I had a juicy black pudding so we could dine like rich people..."

Before she finished her sentence a juicy, plump, black pudding fell out of the air into the hearth. The woman's eyes opened wide with surprise!

Her husband leaped up with rage and screamed, "I can't believe it! See what you've done! You silly goose! You wasted your wish on a pudding! You had to stick your nose up and put on airs. I wish that stupid pudding was stuck right on that nose of yours!"

Kersplotch! The great, black pudding flew through the air and stuck fast to the end of Donna Isabella's nose as Diego watched in horror! No amount of pulling and tugging would budge it. All through the day they cut and pulled and still it stayed stuck to her nose.

Exhausted, they sat at the table looking at each other. Diego said, "Now, we must be reasonable. We have only one wish left and we mustn't waste it. What is it we both most want?"

"I can tell you right now," cried Donna Isabella. I can't go on like this. We will never be happy or have peace of mind until we use our final wish to get this hideous thing off my nose!"

Diego's eyes softened, then the ends of his mouth turned upwards into a smile. "You're right!" he agreed. "No amount of gold could make us happy with that silly pudding stuck on the end of your nose."

That evening, when the Fairy returned, the couple made their wish together. "We wish that this pudding would disappear from Donna Isabella's nose and leave us in peace and happiness."

Fortunata smiled and nodded her head. "A wise wish at last! Granted!"

The pudding whisked from Donna Isabella's nose and laughter and happiness filled their home till the end of their days.

MULTIPLE INTELLIGENCE ACTIVITIES FOR . . .

The Three Wishes

The Mind's Eye.
(Visual-Spatial; Intrapersonal)

The simple structure of this tale lends itself to this exercise. Type a beginning paragraph of the story in 14-point type on the bottom of a blank page. Explain that in telling a story some words may be added to or left out of the telling but that this will not affect the essence of the story. Distribute a copy of the story paragraph to each child. The Teller, not looking at the paper, proceeds to tell the excerpt from the story with lots of eye contact and gestures. The Teller uses his or her own words throughout the telling.

Explain to the students that as they listen to the story, they may imagine or see the scene with their "mind's eye" much like a camera films a movie. At the end of the page, everyone stops. Have the students use art material to create the scene they heard, as they visualized it. Proceed in a similar fashion for other important parts of the story. These visualizations may occur over a period of days, weeks, or all at once. Depending on the ability of the class, students may write changes in wording that they notice during the telling. After each story segment, students compare and discuss notes.

Oh, No!
(Bodily-Kinesthetic; Interpersonal)

This exercise builds on the first one. After the students have become familiar with the story, they are ready for the next step which involves creative group interaction and cooperation as they improvise the replaying of this story with a difference. Divide the students into groups of three. Either have prepared slips of paper with the following printed on them, or give the information orally to each group. Have the children discuss and plan an improvisation of *The Three Wishes* with one or more elements changed. Ask them to consider how the story might have turned out differently in light of the following questions.

1. What if the Fairy only gave them one wish?
2. What if the couple were just married?
3. What if the woman wished for something else? How would that affect the outcome?
4. What if the couple were loving and considerate? What wishes might they choose to help the world, or share with others?
5. What if the Fairy is out to play a trick on the couple?
6. What if the old couple were hard of hearing? How would this affect their comments?
7. What if you had to pantomime the story?
8. What if you mixed up the sequence of the story?

9. What if this story was set in modern times?
10. What if this story was set in your classroom and the teacher and class had to agree on three wishes?

3 You Don't Say.
(Verbal-Linguistic; Visual-Spatial)

Stories with similar motifs can be found in other cultures and countries. Collect a file of variants of this story. Margaret Read MacDonald's *The Storyteller's Source Book* is an excellent source for finding some of these variants. Motifs are the same and yet differ in content. Invite the students to search for variants or have a file of them already collected to read to them for comparison. Display a large world map. As the variants are collected they can be read to the class so that they may discuss what the stories have in common and what makes them different from each other. Identify the countries from which the stories come, and pin their titles or the story itself to the corresponding area on the map. Share the stories and the project with other classrooms that are studying those countries.

TIPS FOR THE TELLER

The Pot That Would Not Stop Boiling

Retold and Adapted by Susan Trostle Brand

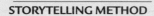

STORYTELLING METHOD

Character Imagery/Chant

The *Pot That Would Not Stop Boiling* is an old favorite tale about a magical pot that prepares spaghetti upon command when given a whimsical rhyme. It also ceases to boil upon a different rhyming command. All goes well with the owner of the pot, a young girl. However, when the young girl leaves home to visit a friend in another village, the girl's mother becomes hungry and tries the pot herself.

Unfortunately, the mother can only remember the first poem correctly. Therefore, plenty of spaghetti quickly becomes too much spaghetti as she tries, in vain, to recall the forgotten second rhyming chant.

The humor of this simple story increases when the Teller dresses as the mother, with a scarf tied around her head, a shawl, a long skirt and apron and, perhaps, a small cooking pot and a wooden spoon. The parts of the old woman who gives the daughter the pot and the daughter are role-played by the Teller at the appropriate times and with the appropriate voices. However, as in all Character Imagery stories, the Teller tells the story in first person, past tense, and takes on mainly the role of protagonist. If desired, the Teller may substitute a father for the mother in the story and dress, instead, as

Adult as peasant mother in "The Pot That Would Not Stop Boiling."

continued

111

TIPS FOR THE TELLER *continued*

a male character in boots, a wool shirt, trousers, and, perhaps, an Italian-style hat.

To begin the introduction, the Teller, while dressing, discusses spaghetti. He or she mentions that spaghetti is a form of pasta. Pasta is Italy's main food because the major grain product of Italy is wheat. The Teller continues talking about Italy and asks the children if any of them have traveled to Italy and/or have Italian relatives. Finally, the Teller, as he or she completes dressing as the protagonist, states, "In our story today, a mother (or father) and daughter live in Italy. Their favorite pasta is spaghetti. But they are very poor and rarely have enough food to go around. How do I know so much about this daughter and her mother? (pause) Because I AM the mother and I love spaghetti!"

Before beginning the story, the Teller may want to establish a signal such as a nod of the head or a hand gesture to indicate that everyone can join in the chanting. An asterisk indicates the text that the audience recites. This text is printed on the chalkboard or a flip chart in advance so that the class or audi-

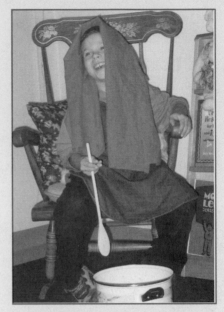

Child as peasant daughter in "The Pot That Would Not Stop Boiling."

ence can easily see their part. Children will, thus, be encouraged to join in the fun of making spaghetti appear and halting the pot, when finished.

The Pot That Would Not Stop Boiling

O nce *(hold up pointer finger)* upon a time *(point to watch),* not so long ago, my little girl *(show long ponytails with hands at head)* and I were very, very poor *(clasp hands; shake head).* Many times we had nothing to eat *(pretend to feed self).* We became quite hungry *(hold stomach).* One day, we could stand it no longer *(push hands apart).* I said, "Mama mia, Maria! *(shake hands beside head)* We are so poor *(clasp hands).* We are so hungry *(hold stomach).*

I am very weak and sick *(sick face)*. Please, go *(point outward)* out to the woods *(form trees with outstretched fingers)*. Gather *(place "berries" in "basket.")* some berries."

My daughter *(show ponytails)* was a very good girl *(nod head)*. She was happy to do as I told her *(smile sweetly)*. As she wandered *(walk around room)* along in the woods *(tree signal)* she heard singing *(hands to throat)* through the branches of the trees *(frame trees)*. She paused *(stop)*, listened *(hand to ear)*, and waited. The singing continued *(hand to throat)*. The girl walked *(walk to another room area)* closer to the beautiful voice and stopped *(stop and look surprised)*. An old, old woman *(take new position and hunch over)* came out from behind a group of trees *(trees signal)* and stopped. Maria looked at the old woman *(hands around eyes; change to old woman's position)*. The old woman *(hunch over)* looked at Maria *(hands around eyes)*.

Finally, the old woman *(hunch)* said, "Why are you out in the woods *(trees signal)* alone, my dear?"

Maria *(change position to Maria's and form ponytails)* answered sadly, "Because, you see, my mama *(hands cross chest)* is very sick *(sick face; cough)* and we are both quite hungry *(hold stomach)*. We have very little food to eat." *(pretend to eat while shaking head)*.

The little old woman *(hunch)* felt sorry for Maria *(ponytails)*. She lifted her heavy cloak *(lift apron)*. Underneath it was a cooking pot *(remove pot)*. She handed it to Maria *(hand pot)*.

"Here, my dear," she said. "Whenever you are hungry *(hold stomach)*, just sing this little song to it and you will have all the spaghetti *(pull arms apart to represent long spaghetti strand)* you wish *(sing to the tune of "On Top of Spaghetti")*:

❉ I love spaghetti, nice and hot—
  So boil me some, my cooking pot!

And when you have enough, all you need to say is this *(to the tune, above)*;

❉ The spaghetti was yummy, but my tummy is full—
  So that's all for now, pot; please stop and cool!

"Thank you!" *(clasp hands, jump up and down, and smile)* my daughter *(ponytails)* said to the little old woman. And she ran all the way home *(run to designated home area)* to me *(point to self)* with the little magic pot *(show pot)*.

When my daughter opened the door *(opening motions)* to our house, I asked her if she had found some tasty berries *(pantomime eating berries)*. When she replied, "No, Mama," *(shake head no)* I noticed that she was smiling and carrying something in her arms. I asked my girl, "What do you have there in your arms *(hold arms in circle)*, Maria?"

Maria *(ponytails)* explained that an old woman *(hunch)* had given her this magic pot *(point to pot)*. We decided to cook some spaghetti *(strand motion)* in it that very night to see if it was REALLY *(thumbs up)* a magic pot. We tried the song *(point to words on chart)*:

❉ I love spaghetti, nice and hot—
  So boil me some, my cooking pot!

It worked! *(clap)* Maria's pot filled with steaming, hot, delicious spaghetti! *(strands)* Maria sang something to make it stop *(hand up, vertically)* but I was too busy to listen *(shrug)*. She sang *(point to words on chart)*:

❉ The spaghetti was yummy, but my tummy is full—
  So that's all for now, pot; please stop and cool!

I didn't hear *(motion to ear)* what she said, but I do know that it worked *(arms outstretched in air)*. That wonderful little cooking pot stopped boiling and cooled off at once! *(fanning motions)* Every time we were hungry *(hold stomach)* for many days and many weeks, my little girl *(ponytails)* sang the songs and we had lots of fresh spaghetti *(strand motions)*. We were happy and healthy *(nod head; smile)*.

But one day *(pointer finger)* my little girl *(ponytails)* was invited to visit a friend *(hold hands)* in another village *(point into distance)* for lunch *(pretend to eat)*. I became very hungry *(double over and hold stomach)*. The thought *(pointer finger to temple)* of that delicious spaghetti *(show spaghetti strands)* was more than I could stand *(look desperate)*. So I took out Maria's little cooking pot *(hold pot)* and remembered the song:

❋ **I love spaghetti, nice and hot—**
  So boil me some, my cooking pot!

I ate and ate and ate *(eat and eat making munching sounds)*. At last, I'd had my fill of spaghetti *(hold stomach and puff out cheeks)*. But I had one *(pointer finger in air)* problem. I couldn't remember the song *(shake head and frown)* to stop the pot from cooking spaghetti! *(strands)* I tried this poem:

Halt, pot, halt pot—
I knew the verse, but I forgot!

This poem did not work. The pot kept boiling and boiling *(bubbling motion with hands)*. More and more long, thin strands of spaghetti *(demonstrate several long, thin spaghetti strands)* poured out *(gesture out motion)* of the magic pot. Mama mia! *(hit forehead)*. I tried another poem:

Cool down, cool down
My daughter's gone to another town!

This poem did not work either *(shake head and look worried)*. The pot kept boiling and boiling *(bubbling motions)*. Try as I might, I could not remember the words *(make fist and shake it a few times)* I'd heard Maria *(ponytails)* sing. So the spaghetti *(strands)* spread out over the kitchen floor *(stoop low and form spaghetti circles with hands)* It formed a huge mountain of pasta *(stand up and form mountain, pointing hands together)*. Soon the pasta filled up the entire kitchen *(walk around room area, gesturing kitchen parameter with hand)*. It grew so heavy *(pretend to hold heavy item)* that it pushed out the kitchen door *(pretend to knock down door)*. The pasta went rushing down the village street *(run down room, weaving and curing)*. And still, the little magic pot *(point to pot)* kept boiling *(bubbling motions)*. Soon the pasta ran *(run to another area of room)* into the next village. There my little girl *(ponytails)* Maria, and her friend were playing *(jump rope motions)* outdoors under the trees *(tree signal)*.

Maria *(ponytails)* saw the pasta *(strands)* pushing *(pushing motions)* its way down the street. She cried out, "Oh Mama! *(cross chest with arms)* You did not listen well *(shake finger)* to the songs. Now look at this spaghetti!" *(show several strands and gesture to street and mountains)*.

Maria *(ponytails)* ran home *(run to designate home area)* atop the spaghetti-filled streets. She could hardly keep her balance *(wobble)*. Once *(pointer finger)* she tripped *(stumble)* on some tangled strands of spaghetti and fell *(fall)* into the warm, sticky pasta!

Still, she ran and ran *(run fast and huff and puff)* until she waded *(walk as though in high snowfalls)* into the kitchen of our house.

Quickly, Maria sang the little song she remembered so well *(point to chart)*:

✽ The spaghetti was yummy, but my tummy is full—
So that's all for now, pot; please stop and cool!

At once, the pot stopped boiling *(wiggle and lower fingers; make fanning motions)*. But, unfortunately, the village was so full *(wide arms)* of spaghetti by that time that it took the village people three weeks *(hold up three fingers)* to eat their way out of it *(pretend to eat and eat)*. It was a very long time *(point to watch)* before we needed to use the magic pot *(point to pot)* to say *(point to chart)*:

✽ I love spaghetti, nice and hot—
So boil me some, my cooking pot!

MULTIPLE INTELLIGENCE ACTIVITIES FOR . . .

The Pot That Would Not Stop Boiling

 I'm Thinking of a Town...
(Visual-Spatial; Logical-Mathematical)

Display one large map of the world, or of a particular country, at each table of children. (Be certain that children have prior experience with map reading and with latitude and longitude.) Turn map reading into a fun guessing game. Ask children to each select one city or town on the map. The children do not reveal the identity of the town to the others; rather, they record its longitude and latitude on a slip of paper or index card which is then hidden from view. The first child then says, for example, "I'm thinking of a town in Italy that is 39 to 26 degrees north latitude and 16 to 23 degrees east latitude. It is near the toe of the boot. Can you guess my town?" The first child to correctly guess (e.g., Calabria) gives the next latitude/longitude/proximity clue.

For younger and/or less experienced children, begin with a large map of your own town or state. Children give clues about specific locations based upon streets and/or landmarks.

 Magical Mixables.
(Logical-Mathematical; Bodily-Kinesthetic)

Try these two recipes (one is edible; the second is non-edible!) with your youngsters, who may be curious about pasta and bubbles and their many shapes, sizes, colors, and uses.

 Spring into Pasta and Cheese

1 onion
6 oz. American cheese (block or slices)
2 cups spring pasta (rotini); may use elbow or bow-tie macaroni, instead
1/2 cup skim milk
Dash of pepper
Vegetables: green beans or broccoli (optional)

1. On a cutting board, cut onion into small pieces. Measure one-half cup of chopped onion.
2. Tear or cut cheese into bite sized pieces.
3. Cook pasta in saucepan following the package directions.
4. Add your chopped onion to the pasta in the saucepan, so that they cook together.
5. When macaroni is cooked (soft, but not mushy), turn off the burner.
6. Drain pasta and onions in a colander in the sink.
7. Return warm macaroni to pan. Stir in cheese, milk, and pepper.
8. Put saucepan back onto the burner. Cook for 4 to 5 minutes, stirring all the time, until cheese is melted. Remove saucepan. Serve with cooked green beans or broccoli. Enjoy!

Bubbles (non-edible)

(Suggestion: use these outside, on a mildly windy day)
Ingredients:
1/4 cup liquid detergent (preferably "Joy" or "Dawn")
1/2 cup water
1 tsp. sugar

Mix all ingredients in a flat dishpan or baking pan. Dip bubble wands or bubble blowers into the mixture. Wave the wands into the air. Make giant bubbles by waving or blowing very slowly; make smaller, multiple bubbles by blowing or waving quickly.

Household items easily transform into bubble blowers. Try using a bottomless paper cup, a slotted spoon, a drinking straw, a plastic berry basket, or a string looped onto a yardstick or dowel rod. Invite children to create giant bubbles that wrap around themselves using the yardstick bubble waver.

Bubbles are fun!

For more great recipe ideas, see the *Better Homes and Gardens New Junior Cookbook* (1997).

 ### My Story Map.
(Verbal-Linguistic; Intrapersonal)

Prepare two blank story maps for each child (see illustration). Use the book, *Strega Nona*. (In this story a character named Big Anthony gets into lots of mischief because he neither listens nor follows the rules.) The children work together or individu-

ally to complete the story map elements. When this is done, invite them to complete a personal story map, using a challenge or problem that they might overcome in their lives (see example). In keeping with the theme of magic and make-believe, encourage fantasy story reading, writing, and mapping later, as well.

STORY MAP

The Setting/Main Characters
Statement of the Problem
Event One
Event Two
Event Three
Event Four
Event Five
Event Six
Event Seven
Statement of the Solution
Story Theme (What is this story really about?)
Values Brought Out in the Story

Sample Personal Event Story Map

The Setting/Main Characters
My mom, my friend Kelsey, Kelsey's dad, me.

Statement of the Problem
My mom told me I couldn't go out. I wanted to go out, even though I had a bad cold. I was so bored.

Event One
It was a boring day in March. I had nothing to do. But Mom had told me I couldn't go outside, since I had a bad cold.

Event Two
Mom went downstairs to do laundry. She thought I was on the couch, watching television.

Event Three
I snuck outside. I went to the neighbor's house to visit my pal, Kelsey.

Event Four
Kelsey's dad didn't know I wasn't supposed to be there. He said it would be okay for Kelsey and me to go for a walk in the woods.

Event Five
We hadn't walked long before it began to rain. I wasn't wearing a jacket. I was cold. I

began to sneeze and my nose began to run. I coughed and coughed.

Event Six

I told Kelsey that I had to get back home. I hurried home. Mom was waiting for me. She looked really mad!

Event Seven

Mom scolded me for not obeying her rule about staying inside. I told her I was sorry.

Statement of the Solution

I had a three-day time out to think about what I had done wrong and how I could learn to listen better to my parents. I got pretty sick, too,

and learned that I should have stayed inside, just like Mom had told me in the first place.

Story Theme

This story is really about trust. I didn't follow a rule. My mom didn't trust me for awhile after that.

Values Brought Out in the Story

I learned that it's important to obey my parents; I learned that if I don't listen, I am punished and other bad things can happen. Being sneaky doesn't pay. I was like Big Anthony, who knew Strega Nona's rules but decided not to follow them. Next time, I'll be more responsible.

MARCH CHAPTER RESOURCES

Anderson, H. C. (1949). *The Emperor's new clothes.* Illustrated by Virginia Lee Burton. Boston: Houghton Mifflin.

Anderson, H. C. (1969). *The ugly duckling.* English version by Lillian Moore. Illustrated by Moneta Barnett. New York: Scholastic.

Babbitt, N. (1975). *Tuck everlasting.* Santa Barbara, CA: Cornerstone.

Babbitt, S. F. (1966). *The forty-ninth magician.* New York: Pantheon.

Baker, L. (1999). *Snow White and the seven dwarfs.* Amsterdam, The Netherlands: Mulder & Zoon.

Banks, L. R. (1980). *The Indian in the cupboard.* Santa Barbara, CA: Cornerstone.

Brothers Grimm. (1960). *The Shoemaker and the elves.* Translated by Wayne Andrews. Illustrated by Adrienne Adams. New York: Scribner.

Bunting, E. (1984). *The man who could call down owls.* New York: Simon & Schuster.

Croker, T. C. (1999). *Fairy legends and traditions of the south of Ireland.* Chester Springs, PA: Dufour Editions.

De Paola, T. (1975). *Strega Nona.* New York: Simon & Schuster.

De Paola, T. (1981). *Fin M'Coul, the giant of Knockmany Hill.* New York: Scholastic.

De Paola, T. (1992). *Strega Nona.* New York: Scholastic.

Dorland Darling, J. (1997). *Better homes and gardens new junior cookbook.* Des Moines, IA: Better Homes & Gardens.

Emberley, B. (1963). *The story of Paul Bunyan.* Illustrated by Ed Emberley. Englewood Cliffs, NJ: Prentice-Hall.

Ets, M. H. (1978). *Gilberto and the wind.* New York: Puffin.

Freeman. D. (1987). *Dandelion.* New York: Puffin.

Grimm, J. (1986). *Rumpelstilskin.* Retold and illustrated by P. O. Zelinsky. New York: Dutton.

Howe, R. (1993). *Rabbit-cadabra.* New York, NY: Morrow Junior Books.

Johnson, C. (1958). *Harold and the purple crayon.* New York: HarperCollins.

Kerr, J. (1968). *The tiger who came to tea.* London: Collins.

Langner, N. (1972). *Cinderella.* New York: Scholastic.

L'Engle, M. (1962). *A wrinkle in time.* New York: Farrar, Straus & Giroux.

Lobato, A. (1989). *Just one wish.* Saxonville, MA: Picture Book Studio.

Lobel, A. (1980) *Fables.* New York: HarperCollins.

Peet, B. (1970). *The wingdingdilly.* Boston: Houghton Mifflin.

Perrault, C. (1990). *Puss in boots.* New York: Farrar, Straus & Giroux.

Polocco, P. (1995). *My Ol' man.* New York: Philomel.

Sendak, M. (1963). *Where the wild things are.* New York: HarperCollins.

Sierra, J. (1993). *The Legend of Knockmany.* New York: Scholastic.

Simmons, S. (1997). *Alice and Greta.* Watertown, MA: Charlesbridge.

Souci, R. S. (1989). *The talking eggs.* New York: Dial.

Steig, W. (1969). *Sylvester and the magic pebble.* New York: Simon & Schuster.

Steig, W. (1984). *The amazing bone.* New York: Farrar, Straus & Giroux.

Van Allsburg, C. (1979). *The garden of Abdul Gasazi.* Boston: Houghton Mifflin.

Van Allsburg, C. (1981). *Jumanji.* Boston: Houghton Mifflin.

Van Allsburg, C. (1992). *The widow's broom.* Boston: Houghton Mifflin.

Weisner, D. (1991). *Tuesday.* New York: Clarion Books.

Wildsmith, B. (1965). *The rich man and the shoemaker.* Oxford, England: Oxford University Press.

Wood, A. (1996). *The flying dragon room.* New York: Scholastic Trade.

Zemach, M. *The three wishes: An old story.* New York: Farrar, Straus & Giroux.

April

Spring into the Great Outdoors

AUGURIES OF INNOCENCE

To see a world in a grain of sand
And a heaven in a wild flower,
Hold infinity in the palm of your hand
And eternity in an hour.

-WILLIAM BLAKE
(EXCERPTED FROM THE COMPLETE
POEM "AUGURIES OF INNOCENCE")

*S*pring is in the air and everywhere! April is daffodils and daisies, gentle breezes, and sunshine. Storytelling opportunities blossom as children and adults explore "April: Spring into the Great Outdoors."

Using Felt Board, Chant, Musical, Group Role-Play, and Balloon Storytelling methods, children experience four exciting outdoor stories. Discover an African Bojabi tree, a Brazilian rainforest, and a castle in the clouds, and tame an unlikely jungle friend in April's four captivating tales. As children enlist the Verbal-Linguistic, Visual-Spatial, Bodily-Kinesthetic, Interpersonal, Intrapersonal, Naturalistic, Logical-Mathematical, and Musical-Rhythmic multiple intelligence areas, they recycle, hunt for lions, and don talking book covers.

Spring showers us with storytelling fun!

TIPS FOR THE TELLER

Bojabi

Retold and Adapted by Susan Trostle Brand

STORYTELLING METHOD

Felt Board/Chant

Although preparing to tell a Felt Board story is time-consuming, the felt pieces are sturdy, fade and wrinkle resistant, and good for many, many years of retelling. Besides, the children's reactions to stories told in this method, and their love for using the felt pieces themselves to later retell the story, make the hard work and time well worthwhile!

Bojabi conveys a poignant message about the rainforests and the values of friendship and good listening. Used near Earth Day, many relevant activities surface as follow-ups to the story. Because of its easy sequence and colorful theme, it lends itself well to Felt Board Storytelling. Before beginning the story, the Teller may want to establish a signal such as a nod of the head or a hand gesture to indicate that everyone can join in the repetitive song. An asterisk indicates the text that the audience sings. This text is printed on the chalkboard or a flip chart in advance so that the class or audience can easily see their part. The children and Teller may rehearse the song before the story is told.

For optimal effectiveness and dramatics, the Teller may change his or her voice for each new animal character. The Teller also pauses occasionally to look at the audience and to allow the children to assimilate the story's message.

Cover a large felt board with a sheet of bright blue felt, to resemble the sky. The following felt board pieces are used for telling the story: trees, boa constrictor, monkey, elephant, gazelle, rat, tortoise, mother tortoise, canoe, waves, trees and flowers, bojabi tree, and sun.

Bojabi

In a lush, green rain forest *(place trees)*, in Gabon, Western Africa, a group of beasts lived peacefully. The beasts were: *(place each animal side-by-side as you name it)* a large gray elephant, a brown monkey, a brown and white gazelle, a pink and brown rat, and a green and brown tortoise. The trees in the forest *(point to trees)* supplied shade and food for all the creatures. They were happy and healthy.

Once, however, there was a drought in the forest. The rains did not fall. The sun shone brightly through the trees *(place sun)*. After many days and weeks of too much sun and too little rain, the animals became very warm and very hungry. Only one tree bore fruit now. This tree was an enchanted, magical tree *(place tree in background)*.

The round, red fruit of this great tree would not fall down, however. The animals needed to say its name to bring down the fruit *(point to each animal as you name it)*. But the elephant could not remember its name. The monkey could not remember its name. The gazelle could not remember its name. The rat could not remember its name. And, last of all, the tortoise could not remember the tree's name. So the fruit would not come down to earth.

The elephant thought and thought. Finally he said, "The only creature who knows the name of this tree is Mbama, the boa constrictor. She is wise in the ways of the forest. Send the gazelle to the boa. The gazelle is the swiftest of all the animals."

The gazelle left his friends of the forest *(place gazelle into canoe)*. He expertly paddled his canoe away from: *(remove each animal as you say its name)* the wrinkly gray elephant, the chattering brown monkey, the pink and brown rat, and the green and brown tortoise. When he reached the other shore, he spotted the boa constrictor *(add boa)*. "Mbama Boa Constrictor," said Gazelle, "we are in great trouble. The rain forest is dry and there is too much sun, too little rain, and no food. Only one tree bears fruit. This fruit is red and round. But none of the creatures knows its name. Can you help us?"

Mbama Boa Constrictor smiled and nodded. "Yes," she hissed. "The name of the tree is Bojabi. ✤**Remember it true and the famine is through!**"

As the gazelle paddled home, many huge waves pounded upon his canoe. One wave was especially large. Splash! He tried to remember the name of the tree. Jababi? Robaji? Abijorabbi? Oh dear! The wave had washed out the boa constrictor's words. The gazelle paddled away, swiftly but sadly *(remove canoe and gazelle from board)*.

Next, the animals sent the clever brown monkey to see Mbama Boa Constrictor *(place monkey in canoe on felt board)*. "Mbama, please tell me the name of the enchanted tree that bears the round, red fruit!" chattered the monkey. "We animals are so hungry and the famine lasts so long."

Mbama smiled. She replied, "The name of the fruit is Bojabi. ✤**Remember it true and the famine is through!**"

The monkey thanked Mbama and headed home in his canoe. Splash! A big wave encircled him. Oh dear! He forgot the name of the tree. Bobabi? Awabi? Shishkabobbi? He could no longer see Mbama. He paddled away *(remove monkey and canoe)*.

The animals looked around. The elephant was too large to fit into the canoe. Only the tortoise and the rat were left. The rat was clever and sharp. "Send the rat!" ordered the elephant. "Surely with his sharp mind and clever ways he can remember the name of the tree!"

(Place rat in canoe on board.) The rat began his journey to discover the name of the tree. When he reached Mbama Boa Constrictor, he sneered, "Mbama, I need to know the name of the enchanted tree with the round, red fruit. And I need to know it right now! We are all weak and sick with hunger!"

Mbama was a bit offended at the rat's rude manners. However, she answered with a smile and a hiss, "The name of the tree is Bojabi. ✤**Remember it true and the famine is through!**"

Unfortunately, some large waves crashed onto the rat's canoe. One wave was especially large *(add wave)*. Splash! The wave covered the canoe. Oh dear! The quick and clever rat forgot the name of the tree at once. Bibbidybob? Bobbidybib? Jobbityjib? The troubled and wet rat paddled away from the distant shore and from Mbama *(remove rat, canoe, and Mbama)*.

Who could the animals send next? Only the slow and thoughtful tortoise remained. "Let me try!" he suggested.

"No!" cried the gazelle *(add gazelle)*. "You are much too slow, tortoise!"

"No!" chattered the monkey *(add monkey)*. "You are not clever enough."

"No!" sneered the sharp rat *(add rat)*. "You take forever to do everything! We will surely starve before you return."

"Yes!" roared the elephant *(add elephant)*. "Let the tortoise try."

The animals walked back to their forest home to sleep *(name and remove animals, one by one, from left to right)*.

The tortoise was proud to be chosen by the elephant. But he was also worried. How could he remember the name of the tree? He plodded along to find his mother *(add larger tortoise)*. "Mother," said the young tortoise, "I have a very important job. I must paddle to Mbama Boa Constrictor and learn the name of the magical tree that bears round, red fruit. I am afraid that I will forget."

"Sing the name, darling," answered his mother. "Singing helps the mind to remember the words." With his mother's advice in mind, young tortoise said, "Farewell" to his mother *(remove mother)* and began his journey to visit Mbama.

After a long voyage, the tortoise finally reached Mbama *(add Mbama)*. "Mbama, please help me," cried the tired and weary tortoise. "The animals are all starving, the rain has not fallen, and the famine continues. What is the name of the tree that bears the round, red fruit?"

"The name of the tree is Bojabi," answered Mbama. **"✽Remember it true and the famine is through!"**

The tortoise headed home *(turn canoe and tortoise away from Mbama; remove Mbama)*. As he paddled, he remembered his mother's words. He made up a song to sing:

✽ **Bojabi tree, Bojabi tree—**
You will set the famine free!

Splash! A big wave hit tortoise's canoe *(add wave)*. Tortoise remembered the song:

✽ **Bojabi tree, Bojabi tree—**
You will set the famine free!

SPLASH! An enormous wave hit the canoe *(add larger wave)*. Still, tortoise remembered the song:

✽ **Bojabi tree, Bojabi tree—**
You will set the famine free!

A gigantic wave crashed onto the canoe *(add largest wave)*. Still, tortoise sang:

✽ **Bojabi tree, Bojabi tree—**
You will set the famine free!

Tortoise finally returned home to the land of the beasts *(place and name each beast, from left to right).*

"The name of the tree is BOJABI!" shouted the happy tortoise. All of the animals carried the tortoise to the Bojabi tree *(place tortoise in middle of circle of all other animals).* They sang together:

✴ **Bojabi tree, Bojabi tree—**
  You will set the famine free!

The round, red fruit tumbled to the earth *(peel some fruit pieces from tree).* Thoughtful tortoise carried some fruit to his mother to thank her for her wise advice.

And that is the story of how slow and thoughtful tortoise saved the day for all the beasts of the forest during the great famine.

Let's see if all of you remember the song! *(invite all to sing, one last time):*

✴ **Bojabi tree, Bojabi tree—**
  You will set the famine free!

MULTIPLE INTELLIGENCE ACTIVITIES FOR . . .

Bojabi

 1

Talking Book Covers.
(Naturalistic; Verbal-Linguistic)

Have the children write to The Children's Rain Forest at the following address in order to garner ideas for preserving our tropical rain forests:

The Children's Rain Forest
P.O. Box 936
Lewiston, Maine 04240

After sharing their ideas, children prepare body-sized poster board book covers (see illustrations). These covers depict a scene from the outdoors in a book they have read and enjoyed. They might use magazine pictures, liquid markers, tissue paper, fallen tree branches, and fabric remnants to decorate the fronts and backs of their covers. Encourage children to parade around the school and outdoors wearing their book covers, which are secured at the shoulders with string, ribbon, or yarn.

Talking Book Cover: Front.

Talking Book Cover: Back.

123

2 Recycle and Renew.
(Naturalistic; Visual-Spatial)

Collect empty cereal boxes, discarded papers, newspapers, and old magazine pages. Invite children to bring discarded papers and cardboard to the class or center. In addition to the recyclable papers mentioned, the project requires a blender, screens, trays or rectangular baking pans, a spatula, scissors, trimmings, and paper towels.

Children tear cardboard into small (about three-inch) pieces or strips and place the torn papers into a blender. Fill blender about 3/4 full and add water to fill to nearly the top. Turn blender on high and watch the paper become mushy pulp. When paper is completely mushy, pour pulp onto a fine, square or rectangular screen atop a baking pan to drain out water. Push down on pulp to completely remove all excess water. Carefully remove pulp square from screen. Place onto paper towels. Shape a picture mount-ing from the moist pulp, trimming with scissors if necessary. Press in leaves, flowers, fabric remnants, and/or ribbon trimmings to borders of picture. Allow to dry for a few days in a sunny area. If desired, once dry, glue on more trimmings. Secure a photograph or watercolor painting to the center of the picture mount. Frame, and proudly display, recycled creations! Discuss with children other materials that are recyclable.

3 Coffee Filter Butterflies.
(Visual-Spatial; Bodily-Kinesthetic; Logical-Mathematical)

Gather new, round, white coffee filters, one for each child. Prepare several bowls of diluted liquid tempera paint and place bowls on a table, atop newspapers. The children each fold a filter in half and then, again, in half. Next, they dip a small section of their folded filters in the

Recycling paper for picture mounts.

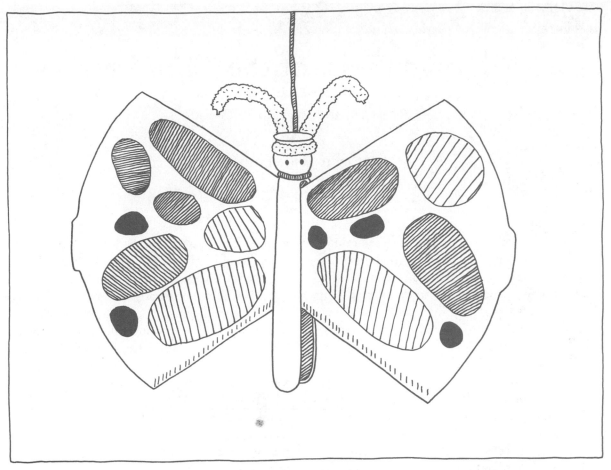

A coffee filter butterfly.

desired colored paints. Turn or partially open filters and dip again into desired colors. Open and/or turn again and dip again. Allow colors to run together and spread on newspaper or paper towels to dry. When dry, gather and secure middle section of butterflies with a wooden clothespin. To complete, add pipe cleaner antennae to top of clothespins. Creative and beautiful!

Outdoors, invite the children to fly their butterflies. Mark and measure the distance each butterfly flies before falling to the ground. Chart flying distances on poster board making a bar graph, perhaps. Compare and contrast flying distances when butterflies are flown on windy days versus non-windy days.

Kibungo: Beast of the Rainforest

By Claudia da Silva

Retold and Adapted by Jeanne Donato

STORYTELLING METHOD

Musical/Group Role-Play

This folktale from the Brazilian rainforest draws the listeners into the excitement of anticipation, improvisation, and participation as the students play, sing, and move to the rhythmic music. Of all the creatures in the rainforest, the most feared is a horrible monster called Kibungo. He captures and plans to eat all the animals in the rainforest. The tortoise Jabuti, the hero of the story, outwits Kibungo with a dance and song. Jabuti's song and his plan help himself and the other animals to escape to safety.

This story combines the Musical-Rhythmic Storytelling method with a modified Group Role-Play mentioned in Chapter 3. After a few tellings, and as it becomes a favorite with the students, the Teller will begin to feel comfortable adding even more ideas to the story's presentation.

The Teller may want to have some rhythm instruments available before the telling, for the children's use. Introduce the refrain "Kibungo oi! Bicho do mato" (pronounced: Kee boon go oi! Bee-shoo doo ma too), which means "Kibungo, beast of the rainforest." Have students search for pictures of animals that live there. This will aid in the improvisations during the story. Start with volunteers to play the rhythmic instruments as the class sings while holding pictures of different animals found in a Brazilian rainforest. Inform the students that Kibungo will be looking for different rainforest animals and that during the telling, if they raise their hands, they may be called upon to act like that animal, be captured, dance, and escape, all in character. A group warm-up of moving and acting like the different animals will help.

The Teller may want to teach a modified dance to the students so everyone who is selected to participate in this telling will be comfortable. The author, Claudia da Silva, retells this folktale in *The Singing Sack*. Her version offers a delightful, more complex, song and dance to challenge more advanced classes. The Teller will assume the role of Kibungo, Jabuti, and narrator, being careful to use voice, position of the body, and gestures to distinguish between the characters.

The Teller may want to use a tambourine to set the rhythm. Before beginning, the Teller may also want to establish a signal such as a nod of the head or a hand gesture to indicate when the students can begin each of the activities: playing the instruments, singing along, acting as an animal, or dancing. An asterisk indicates the text that the audience recites. This text is printed on the chalkboard or a flip chart in advance so that the class or audience can easily see their part. They are now ready to participate and enjoy it! For brevity, an asterisk will indicate a response from the students throughout this story. All other suggestions will also be noted in parentheses. The song and words are included at the end of the chapter and may also be heard on the cassette *The Singing Sack*.

Retold and adapted with permission from Claudia da Silva and Helen East. (1989). *The singing sack: 28 song-stories from around the world.* London: A & C Black.

Kibungo: Beast of the Rainforest

Rainforests differ around the world and yet have many things in common. This story is about the Brazilian rainforest, which is the largest rainforest in the world, and the animals that live there. The trees grow tall and close together, forming a green-roofed canopy that shuts out most of the sun and sky. Inside, the rainforest is warm, humid, dark, and teeming with life. *(Teller asks, "What kind of animals would you find in this rainforest?" Students suggest animals.)*

The Amerindian people, who have always lived in this rainforest, know and respect these animals. But there is one creature that even they mention only in stories. His name is Kibungo. *(Teller: "Can you repeat that for me?" Students respond. "Good!")* They even sing a song about him. I am going to teach you a refrain from that song. It goes like this *(Teller sings and plays the rhythm with the tambourine.)*: "Kibungo oi! Bicho do mato. Kibungo, oi! Bicho do mato." This means "Kibungo, beast of the forest." *(Teller: "Repeat after me:* ✽*Kibungo, oi! Bicho do moto. "* Teller: "Very good!")*

The reason no one speaks much of Kibungo is that he is such a horrible looking creature. Kibungo stands eight feet tall. He has four arms, on each side of his body! Kibungo has one eye in the middle of his forehead, his mouth is full of a thousand razor-sharp teeth, he is hairy all over, and he smells terrible! Oi!

Do you know what he eats? *(Students suggest answers.)* Why, he eats anything and everything when he gets hungry, and Kibungo is always hungry! Why, if he could catch you, he would take you back to his cave of bones and eat you! Everyone tries to stay away from Kibungo!

One day, Kibungo woke up feeling very hungry. "Me hungry. Me hungry enough to eat all the animals in the rainforest!" Kibungo threw his hunting sack over his shoulder and tromped down to the watering hole. The animals came there every day for a drink of fresh water. Kibungo snapped off the leaves of a smelly plant to disguise his odor. He wiped it all over the rocks and trees and then he hid in the underbrush and waited.

What rainforest animal do you think was the first one to come to the watering hole? *(Students suggest an animal.)* You're right! It was the *(Teller: repeat students' answer.)* The ✽[animal] stopped and sniffed the air. It looked around. The air smelled awful, just like Kibungo, but the ✽[animal] didn't see him. As soon as that animal went to take a sip of water *(Teller mimes sipping water, making loud slurping sounds from his or her hand, indicating to the students to join in.)* Kibungo jumped out from his hiding place. *(The Teller acts this motion out, grabs the student gently, and mimes throwing the animal into the hunting sack. The student feigns fear and stays on the ground where the Teller has indicated the sack is located. Make sure to keep this in the same general direction to help the class and animals visualize it clearly.)* Kibungo grabbed the ✽[animal] by the [arm, leg, tail, feathers, etc.] and threw it into his hunting sack. Not satisfied, Kibungo said, "Me hungry! Me wait for more!" And he crouched back into his hiding place.

What animal do you think came to the watering hole next? *(Students suggest another animal.)* Right! The ✽[animal] smelled a horrible smell and thought, "Oh, how it smells!" The ✽[animal] didn't see Kibungo anywhere and so it went to take a sip of water. *(Teller mimes sipping water, making loud slurping sounds from his or her hand, indicating to the students to join in.)* Mmmm. Good! Just then Kibungo jumped out from his hiding place and grabbed the ✽[animal] by the [arm, leg, tail, feathers, etc.] and threw it into his hunting sack. *(Teller mimes throwing the animal into his hunting sack.)* Not satisfied, Kibungo grunted, "Me hungry! Me wait for more!" And he crouched back into his hiding place.

(This part of the story may be repeated as many times as the Teller needs to include rainforest animals or as time allows.)

And so it went until all the animals were caught. Kibungo tied up his sack and dragged it along. On his way back to his cave of bones, Kibungo saw Jabuti the tortoise sunning herself on a rock. How Kibungo's mouth watered for tortoise soup!

Now Jabuti knew she could not get away, for Kibungo is very fast. Even though a tortoise is very slow, Jabuti is very clever, and she quickly thought of a plan.

"Kibungo!" Jabuti cried. "I am so happy to see you! I have just made a new song just for you! Would you do me the honor of dancing to it before you eat me?"

Kibungo looked puzzled and said, "Me no dance! Me hungry!"

"But Kibungo!" wheedled Jabuti, "Everyone says that you are the most graceful dancer in the rainforest. So agile! So handsome! So elegant! So..."

Kibungo had never heard such nice things said about him before and he began to feel very pleased with himself. "Me not sure about this dance thing. How you do this one? Remember now, no tricks. Me dance then me eat you!"

"Me trick you?" laughed Jabuti. "How? You are too smart for me, Kibungo!"

Scratching his sides, Kibungo said,"Yeah! Now how me do this dance?"

"Oh, it's very easy. It's the dance of the spinning top. Stand up on your toes, wave your arms high over your head, and turn around like a dainty dancing top, while I play my drum," Jabuti instructed as she started to sing, ✽**"Kibungo, oi! Bicho do mato."**

(The Teller indicates to the class to join in the singing and playing, while the Teller dances as Kibungo and plays the tambourine to establish the rhythm of the song.)

Kibungo stood clumsily up on his toes and flapped his arms up over his head while turning in circles. "Like this?" he questioned.

"Oh dear," said Jabuti, as she stopped playing and singing. "I'm afraid you can't do this dance after all."

"What you mean I can't do this dance? Watch me!" And Kibungo spun around flapping his arms. "Me like this. Now play!" ordered Kibungo.

"I'm sorry, I forgot," replied Jabuti. "You need a partner for the next part of the dance. You see, when I sing ✽**"Kibungo, oi! Bicho do mato"** a second time you are supposed to stop spinning and take your partner by the hand and the two of you are supposed to spin around and around as fast as you can. And as you can see, there is no one here to be your partner while I play the drum."

Kibungo raged, snarled and stomped and then he remembered his sack full of animals. He reached into the sack and pulled out....

(The Teller stops and asks the listeners, "What animal do you think Kibungo pulled out?" The students raise their hands, as arranged before the telling, and point to one student who answers with the name of an animal. The Teller replies, "You are right!" and then takes that student by the hand as if leading

him or her out of the sack and up to the front of the room beside the Teller/Kibungo. The Teller encourages the student to stand up on tiptoe, wave his or her hands in the air, and spin around. With the tambourine, the Teller is able to direct the singing and dancing while dancing with the animal, and while the class sings the refrain, "Kibungo, oi! Bicho do mato." After the first line, the Teller takes the student's hand and slowly spins him or her around while saying, "And they spun around, faster and faster, until the ✽[animal] fainted from the heat. The student then pretends to faint and drops to the ground. When Kibungo is busy dancing, the animal sneaks back to his or her seat.) The Teller says, "And while Kibungo went to search for a new partner, the other animal slipped quietly back into the rainforest.")

"More! Me need new partner! Me want to dance more!" cried Kibungo as he reached into the sack. *(This cycle is repeated as long as the Teller and the listeners wish to go on. The Teller brings it to an end.)*

Finally, Kibungo reached into the sack *(Teller mimes searching in vain)* and found it empty. He turned toward Jabuti and screamed, "They all gone! Me sack empty! Jabuti! You tricked me!" he gnashed his teeth. "Now me eat you!"

Jabuti stopped singing and started to crawl slowly backward, away from Kibungo. Kibungo started to stagger toward Jabuti. But he was so tired from the heat and all the dancing that he fell flat on his face, onto the ground, panting. And there he stayed until he could crawl home, very hungry and tired.

Jabuti just smiled and slowly crawled down to the bank of the Amazon, singing softly, **✽"Kibungo, oi! Bicho do mato. Kibungo, oi! Bicho do mato."**

Kibungo

"Kibungo" is used with permission from Claudia da Silva and Helen East. (1989). *The singing sack: 28 song-stories from around the world.* London: A & C Black. Available in the U.S. through Midpoint Trade Books.

MULTIPLE INTELLIGENCE ACTIVITIES FOR . . .

Kibungo: Beast of the Rainforest

 Kibungo's Animal Hunt.
(Visual-Spatial; Naturalistic)

Students cover a wall to make a rainforest mural. Have the class divide the task into sections with the idea of blending them into one large rainforest mural featuring the Amazon River. Have the students each find a picture of an animal of the rainforest, learn about it, and then report back to the class. They may cut, trace, copy, or draw the picture of their animal and then display it on the mural. For each report, or for every animal they study, they may also stamp a fire ant onto the mural to see how many ants they can get to cover the mural as an indication of their progress. When the students have added 10 or so reports, they may draw and color their own idea of Kibungo and hang him from the ceiling or around the mural as a frame.

 Save the Rainforests.
(Naturalistic; Interpersonal)

Share the book, *Amazon Diary,* by Hudson Talbott and Mark Greenberg. After reading, stop and consider the impact modern civilization is having on the rainforest and its people. Discuss what benefits the rainforest offers the world and how each one of us can make a difference in saving and preserving it. The address for the Rainforest Alliance is 65 Bleecker Street, New York, NY 10012; their Web address is www.rainforest-alliance.org. Ask the class what they can do to improve the ecology in the world around them. Suggest conserving water and electricity, picking up litter, etc. Help the students to arrive at a project that interests them and follow through with it. Tell them, "We can all make a difference."

 Play it Again.
(Musical-Rhythmic; Bodily-Kinesthetic)

Have the class collect materials to make their own drums, rattles, and rain and/or rhythm sticks. Listening to the tape, which accompanies the *Singing Sack,* the students are now ready to tackle the more intricate verses and add the extended dance into their story. Directions are given in the *Singing Sack.* After listening, and playing along with the tape, the students will feel more confident to combine the dance steps with the singing. Have the entire group practice singing, playing, and dancing and then for the play, divide into the groups they enjoy the most. This story lends itself to imaginative extensions in creative drama. As the class becomes familiar with the story, the roles of Kibungo and Jabuti can be added, along with a chorus of birds who escape Kibungo and comment on the action or act as narrators during the play.

To make a rainstick, you will need six paper cups, packaging tape, a small utility knife, and 1/3 cup uncooked rice.

Cut two half-moon shapes out of the bottom of four of the cups, keeping one strip of the bottom intact.

Fill one of the two uncut cups with the uncooked rice. Starting with the rice-filled cup on the bottom, stack the remaining cups on top of each other and tape as shown, ending with the second uncut cup on the top. Turn over to hear the rain!

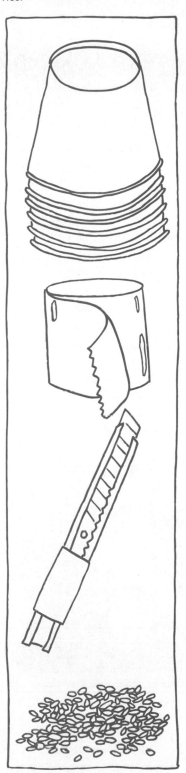

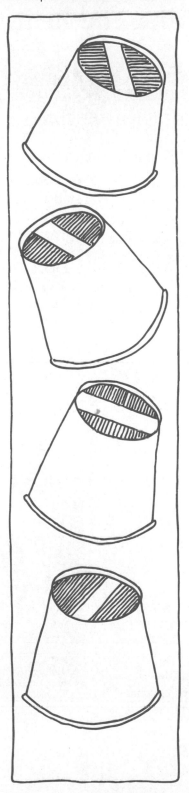

Steps in making a rainstick.

TIPS FOR THE TELLER

This story available on
Storytelling Video!

Jack and the Beanstalk

Retold and Adapted by Susan Trostle Brand

STORYTELLING METHOD

Felt Board/Chant

This Old English tale exaggerates the magic and wonder of spring and growth. Children through the ages have marveled at the beanstalk that grows and grows, and at the ominous and hungry giant who awaits curious Jack when he climbs to the top.

Told in the Felt Board Storytelling technique, the Teller needs the following pieces:

Jack
Hen and Golden Eggs
Jack's mother
Harp
Beanstalk (in pieces to show growth)
Beans
Axe
Cow
Giant
Old Man
Clouds
Giant's Wife
Castle outline, with oven inside (oven door should open)
Bag of Gold
Jack's house outline

An extra large, light blue felt board and large felt pieces work best with this story.

Before beginning the story, the Teller may want to bring in some beans and show them to the children. Ask them to describe the bean's appearance and to predict what might happen if they were planted in soil.

Next, the children briefly discuss their experiences with planting seeds. Tell the listeners that in today's story, *Jack in the Beanstalk*, a young boy plants some magical beans and has quite an adventure in store! Invite the children to join in on the giant's recurring chant, "Fee fi fo fum, I smell the blood of an Englishman. Be he alive or be he dead, I'll use his bones to grind my bread!" Before beginning the story, the Teller may want to establish a signal such as a nod of the head or a hand gesture to indicate that everyone can join in the chant. An asterisk indicates the text that the audience repeats. This text is printed on the chalkboard or a flip chart in advance so that the class or audience can easily see their part. Practice the chant together a few times, and then begin the telling.

Storyteller demonstrating the Felt Board method for "Jack and the Beanstalk."

Jack and the Beanstalk

Once upon a time, there lived a widow *(place Jack's mother)* in a small, red house *(add Jack's house)* who had a son named Jack *(place Jack)*. Their only earthly possession was a cow called Milky White *(place cow)*. They had very little food to eat and all they had to drink was the milk from the cow. But one morning Milky White gave no milk at all. Jack and his mother didn't know what to do.

"Do not worry, Mother," said Jack. I shall take Milky White to market today. I will sell her. Then we will have enough money to buy food. Perhaps we can also start a business with the money from the cow. Good-bye, Mother"*(remove mother)*.

So Jack took Milky White's halter in his hand. He set off to the market place *(move cow and Jack close together)*. Along his walk he met an old man *(place man)*.

"Where are you going, Jack?" asked the man.

Jack wondered how the man knew his name. But he answered, "I am going to market to sell my cow."

"Why bother going all the way to market, Jack?" asked the man. "I have something better for you than money."

Jack looked at the man. The man held five beans in his hand *(add beans)*.

"Plant these beans at night. By morning, they will have turned into a tall, tall beanstalk which reaches the sky," said the man.

Jack liked the idea of this magic beanstalk and quickly traded Milky White for the old man's five beans *(move cow close to man; move beans to Jack's hand)*. He bid the old man and Milky White farewell *(remove man and cow)*.

Jack returned home *(add Jack's house and place Jack and mother inside)*. There was his mother *(point to mother)* waiting for Jack and eager to see how much money he had fetched for the cow.

"Home so soon, Jack?" asked his eager mother. "How much money did you bring us? Can it be five pounds?"

"No," said Jack.

"Ten pounds?" asked his mother.

"No, not ten pounds," answered Jack, smiling.

"Surely not twenty pounds, Jack?" asked his mother in great delight.

"No, Mother," said Jack. "I have something much better than money. I traded Milky White, who gave us no milk lately, for these magic beans!"

"Foolish Jack!" screamed his furious mother. "You gave away our beautiful Milky White for a handful of beans? I'll show you what I think of that, you silly boy!"

With that, Jack's mother threw the beans out the window and sent Jack to bed without supper *(remove Jack)*.

In the morning Jack stepped outside *(add Jack)*. He couldn't believe his eyes!

There, before him, grew a huge beanstalk that went up and up and up and up and up *(add pieces of beanstalk, one upon the other)* until it reached the sky *(add large white cloud)*. Jack couldn't see the top of it. He was glad he had trusted the old man who gave him the beans. They were, indeed, magic beans!

Jack wasted no time. He climbed right onto the beanstalk. Higher and higher climbed Jack *(move Jack up the beanstalk)*. At the top Jack came to a large, great castle *(add castle in cloud)*. At the door of the castle stood a very, very tall woman *(place giant's wife)*.

"Good morning, ma'am," said Jack. "What a fine house you have here in the clouds! Do you think you could give me some breakfast? I am very hungry from all my climbing."

"You'll be eaten for breakfast, boy, if you don't hurry out of here. My husband is a mean giant. His favorite food is little boys, served on toast. You'd better hurry. He's on his way," said the giant woman.

"Oh, please," replied Jack. "I am willing to take a chance. I am so hungry that I will die, one way or the other."

The giant's wife agreed to hurry and feed Jack. She gave him milk, cheese, and bread. Jack had not quite finished his breakfast when he heard loud footsteps coming his way.

"Hurry," said the giant's wife. "You can hide in here." *(Put Jack into oven)*. Jack peeked out a crack in the door. There, before him, stood the largest man he had ever seen *(add giant)*. He was a giant, and a mean-looking giant, at that! The giant roared❀**"Fee fi fo fum, I smell the blood of an Englishman. Be he short or be he tall, I'll munch on him or nothing at all!"**

"It is only the little boy whom you ate yesterday, dear," lied the giant's wife. "Here, go and wash up and I will prepare your breakfast."

Jack waited inside the oven until the giant ate his breakfast *(make loud munching sounds)*, counted coins from a large bag of gold *(add bag of gold)*, and took his nap *(lay down giant horizontally and make loud snoring sounds)*. The Jack crept out of the oven and took the gold *(put gold in Jack's hand)*. He hurried away from the castle *(remove castle frame)*, away from the giant's wife *(remove wife)*, and away from the mean giant *(remove giant)*.

Down, down, down *(move Jack down the beanstalk)* climbed Jack. Finally he reached his mother *(add mother)*. "Look, Mother!" cried Jack. "The beans *were* magic. When you threw them from the window last night, they began to grow the huge beanstalk. I climbed it and at the top lived two giants, a husband and wife. The wife was kind to me, but the husband is ugly and mean. He has gold that once belonged to father. So I took it while he slept and brought it to you *(hand gold to mother)*. Now we will have enough to eat and drink for a long while."

The gold served Jack and his mother well for a few years. Finally, the gold was gone, and Jack and his mother became hungry. Jack decided to climb the beanstalk again.

Up, up, up climbed Jack *(move Jack up beanstalk)*, back to the castle *(add castle outline)*. Inside the castle *(move Jack into castle)* Jack saw the giant's wife *(add wife)*. "Good morning, ma'am," said Jack. "I'm very hungry after my long climb. Do you have a few morsels for me to eat?"

"You were here before, weren't you lad?" asked the woman. "My husband was missing a bag of gold when you left. He once said he stole it from a man. Was this man your father?"

When Jack said that it was, the woman said, "I'll feed you again, then. But hurry into the oven now, boy. My husband is coming. And he is very hungry." *(place Jack in oven and add giant).*

✱**"Fee fi fo fum, I smell the blood of an Englishman. Be he short or be he tall, I'll munch on him or nothing at all!"** roared the mean giant.

"No, dear," replied his wife. "It is simply the oxen I am broiling for your dinner. Here, it is ready. Come and eat."

The giant ate and ate and ate *(munching sounds).* Then he said, "Wife, bring me the hen that lays the golden eggs *(add hen).* "Lay!" he ordered the hen. And the hen laid a solid gold egg. Then the giant grew sleepy and took a long nap *(lay giant down and make loud snoring sounds).*

Jack knew that this was his chance. He grabbed the hen and hurried away from the castle *(remove frame),* the giant's wife *(remove wife),* and the sleeping giant *(remove giant).* He hurried back down the beanstalk—down, down, down he climbed. *(Move Jack with hen and golden egg slowly down beanstalk.)*

Jack's mother met him at the bottom of the beanstalk. She and Jack tried the magic hen. Each day Jack politely asked the hen to lay a golden egg. Each day, the hen did so *(show golden egg beneath hen).* Jack and his mother were never hungry now. But Jack was curious. And he was still angry with the giant for stealing his father's money long ago. He decided to climb the beanstalk once more.

Up, up, up climbed Jack *(move Jack up beanstalk).* When he reached the castle *(add castle)* he became worried. On his last visit, the giant's wife told him he was never to return. The giant would surely kill him if he ever dared to come back. So Jack hid outside the castle, near the window.

✱**"Fee fi fo fum, I smell the blood of an Englishman. Be he short or be he tall, I'll munch on him or nothing at all!"** roared the giant.

"Yes," agreed the wife. "I smell a boy, too. And if he is here, he is sure to be hiding in the oven!" The wife opened the oven *(open oven door).* Of course, Jack was not inside. He was watching everything through the window.

The giant searched the castle *(move giant around, inside the castle).* But he forgot to look outside where Jack was hiding. "Wife," called the giant, "the smell of that boy has me hungry. Fetch me dinner now." The giant ate and ate and ate *(munching sounds).* Then he asked his wife to bring his golden harp. The giant commanded the harp, "SING!" and the harp played the most beautiful music Jack had ever heard.

Soon the giant fell asleep *(lie down giant and make loud snoring sounds).* Jack lost no time. He waited until the wife was in another part of the castle *(move wife upstairs; place Jack inside castle).* Then he grabbed the large, golden harp and hurried away.

But the golden harp called, "Master, Master!" and the ferocious giant woke up. Before him ran Jack with his precious golden harp that had once belonged to Jack's father.

"STOP!" roared the giant. But Jack paid no attention and kept running. He ran away from the castle *(remove castle)* and away from the giant *(remove giant).* Down the beanstalk climbed Jack, with the heavy harp in his hands *(move Jack and harp down beanstalk).* But the giant was right behind Jack *(place giant on beanstalk).* The beanstalk swayed and bent under the weight of the heavy giant *(move the beanstalk back and forth).*

"Mother, Mother!" called Jack. "Come quickly and bring an axe!"

Mother came running with an axe in her hands *(add mother and axe)*. She was terrified and bade her son, "Be careful, Jack. The giant is right behind you!"

Jack jumped down at the foot of the beanstalk. He took the axe from his mother's hands and swiftly began to chop *(give Jack axe)*. "Chop, chop, chop," went the axe, and just in time. The beanstalk split in two *(remove top half of beanstalk)* and DOWN fell the giant *(place giant flat on ground)*. His huge body hit the hard ground. And that was the end of the giant. They never heard from him again *(remove giant)*. Jack and his mother chopped down the remainder of the beanstalk *(place axe on beanstalk)*. They carried the beanstalk away to the forest *(remove all parts of beanstalk)*.

Jack and his mother became very rich from the golden eggs and the money they made from the harp and its lovely concerts. And now, only in his dreams does Jack hear the giant's haunting words:

❋**Fee fi fo fum, I smell the blood of an Englishman. Be he short or be he tall, I'll munch on him or nothing at all!**

MULTIPLE INTELLIGENCE ACTIVITIES FOR . . .

Jack and the Beanstalk

 Showers of Flowers.
(Visual-Spatial; Naturalistic)

Purchase five clear or white shower curtain liners. Invite groups of "budding artists" to make vegetable and flower designs on construction paper. Each group may decide in advance which flowers and/or vegetables it will illustrate. When the decorations are complete, each group tapes its creations onto its shower curtain liner. Add typed or printed descriptions, poetry, and/or comments for added appeal. Hang liners on rods as a colorful and cheerful spring display!

 Whatif?
(Verbal-Linguistic; Intrapersonal)

Share the following poem by Shel Silverstein with children. Compare the poem with Jack's feelings in the story. The ask children to think of a time when they had fears. Record their fears on a large chart and /or ask each child to write and illustrate one fear on a large sheet of white paper. When the

pages are complete, bind them together into a large class book. A group or class "fear collage" might provide an intriguing cover for the book. This activity provides a great source of therapy for children, both in expressing their fears and in discovering that others also have fears.

Whatif by Shel Silverstein

Last night, while I lay thinking here,

Some Whatifs crawled inside my ear

And pranced and partied all night long

And sang their same old Whatif song:

Whatif I'm dumb in school?

Whatif they've closed the swimming pool?

Whaif I get beat up?

Whatif there's poison in my cup?

Whatif I start to cry?

Whatif I get sick and die?

Whatif I flunk that test?

Shower curtain art.

Whatif green hair grows on my chest?

What if nobody likes me?

Whatif a bolt of lightning strikes me?

Whatif I don't grow taller?

Whatif my head starts getting smaller?

Whatif the fish won't bite?

Whatif the wind tears up my kite?

Whatif they start a war?

Whatif my parents get divorced?

Whatif the bus is late?

Whatif my teeth don't grow in straight?

Whatif I tear my pants?

Whatif I never learn to dance?

Everything seems swell, and then

The nighttime Whatifs strike again!

"Whatif" by Shel Silverstein is used by permission of HarperCollins Publishers. Copyright © 1981 by Evil Eye Music, Inc.

 ### Spring has Sprung!
(Naturalistic; Logical-Mathematical)

Children paint tempera paint or permanent marker designs and pictures onto small, white plastic planting pots. When the paint is dry, they add soil to the pots. They plant carrots and other seeds of their choice into the soil. Place plants on a sunny windowsill. Children bar graph their plants' growth on a large sheet of poster board which is hung near the plants. Compare and contrast the speed of growth of same and different plants. Later, children take them home as treasured gifts for parents or friends.

TIPS FOR THE TELLER

The Lion and the Mouse

By Aesop
Retold and Adapted by Jeanne M. Donato

This story available on **Storytelling Video!**

STORYTELLING METHOD

Balloon

*T*he Lion and the Mouse is retold from *Aesop's Fables*. This age-old tale has many layers of appeal in its simplest form. The addition of the older and younger mouse characters enables both the younger and older students to enjoy a connection with the tale. Weaving the making of a balloon mouse into the storytelling attracts the attention of children of all ages. It captivates their curiosity and helps to immerse them into the possibilities of play offered by this story.

Children enjoy the mouse balloon in the *Lion and the Mouse* story.

Different ideas for incorporating the use of balloon animals either before, during, or after the telling, are addressed in the section on Balloon Storytelling in Chapter 3. The Teller may choose to start the introduction to the story by inquiring, "What qualities do you look for in a friend?" Or, the Teller may say, "Families come in all different sizes. How many of you are older brothers or sisters? How many do not have brothers or sisters? And how many of you are the youngest in your family?" A framed photograph of a friend or a family member could be displayed. Tell the students, "Today, we are going to meet Baby Mouse as he experiences the great outdoors and finds out what it takes to be a friend!"

At the beginning of the story, the Teller holds up a balloon inflated enough to make a mouse sculpture. Using the mouse-making instructions that follow the story (see illustration), twist a bubble into the balloon as each member of the mouse family is introduced. Display the finished mouse and continue with the story. When Baby Mouse is mentioned, the mouse balloon is moved around to show the action.

The Lion and the Mouse

A long time ago there was a little Baby Mouse who lived in a far away jungle with his Mother. He had a Big Brother Mouse and a Big Sister Mouse. They never let Baby Mouse go anywhere with them because he was too little.

One day, Mother Mouse said, "Little Mouse is old enough to go out into the jungle with you. Have fun and take good care of him. And be back in time for supper."

The three little mice crept cautiously through the tall jungle grass, around a tree trunk, under the leaves, and stopped. For there, out in the field before them, was a big Lion asleep, snoring in the warm sunshine. *(Teller: "Can you make big, loud, Lion snores? Good!")*

Baby Mouse was most excited seeing the Lion. But Big Brother Mouse pulled him aside and whispered, "Shhhh! Be quiet! If that Lion wakes up, he might eat us up! Don't move!"

Baby Mouse looked around and wondered, "What was there to be afraid of? A Lion that big wouldn't even notice a little Baby Mouse." He slipped quietly away through the grass. *(Move the balloon mouse as if weaving through the field grass.)* He climbed up on the Lion's back, *(move the balloon mouse up to the top of the Teller's head and wave back and forth)* and then up to the top of the Lion's head, and squeaked, "Look at me! Wheee!"

Just as he did, the Lion yawned and shook his head. Baby Mouse fell down the Lion's face and his tail tickled the Lion's nose. *(Demonstrate the mouse's tail tickling the Lion's nose.)*

The Lion opened up one Lion's eye and then the other Lion's eye. Reaching out, he caught Baby Mouse by the tail and gave a big Lion's yawn. *(Teller: "Can you show me a Lion's yawn? Good job!")*

"Who woke me up?" thundered the Lion. "What have we here?" he said as he held Baby Mouse up in the air.

"Why, sir," stammered Baby Mouse. "I'm sorry that I woke you up. I didn't mean to disturb your sleep. Please let me go!"

"Let you go!" laughed the Lion. "Why, when I wake up, I get hungry. And you will make a fine snack!"

Brother and Sister Mouse covered their eyes and cried, "Oh, no! He's going to eat him!" And away they ran. Whoosh! *(Snap the tail of the mouse for a sound effect.)* Zip! *(Snap the tail again.)* Around the tree they flew. Swish! *(Snap)* Through the grass they ran until they popped *(Snap!)* safely into their mouse hole.

Meanwhile, Baby Mouse, shaking, said, "Oh, please Mister Lion, Sir, if you let me go, I'll do you a favor sometime. Just let me go. I promise! You can depend on me. Why, I'll be your friend to the end!"

"What?" roared the Lion, showing all his great sharp teeth. *(Teller: "Can you give a big Lion roar?")* "What makes you think that someone as tiny as you could do me—the King of the Jungle—a favor?" And the Lion started to laugh. *(Teller: "Let's hear big Lion laughs. Good!")*

The Lion shook with laughter and Baby Mouse slipped between his paws. Like a flash, he dashed under the leaves! *(Snap the tail.)* Zip! *(Snap)* Around the tree he flew. Swish! *(Snap)* through the grass he ran and Pop! *(Snap)* He landed in the mouse hole panting for breath just as Brother and Sister Mouse were about to tell Mother what happened to Baby Mouse.

"Where were you?" Mother Mouse asked.

"Just having fun outside," Baby Mouse lied.

When Brother and Sister got Baby Mouse aside, they whispered, "What happened? How did you escape?"

"Escape?" Baby Mouse replied. "I didn't escape!" Baby Mouse stretched the truth a little. *(The Teller holds up the balloon and asks, "Is Baby Mouse telling the truth?" Then the Teller stretches the tail a little.)* "Why, I was just talking to the Lion." Baby Mouse stretched the truth some more. *(The Teller stretches the tail some more.)* "If you had stayed instead of running away, I would have introduced you to him," Baby Mouse bragged. *(Teller stretching the tail longer still.)* "The Lion and I are friends!" Baby Mouse bragged and bragged! *(Teller lets the tail snap.)*

"If that Lion is such a good friend of yours," Brother and Sister Mouse whispered, "then you can introduce us to him tonight after Mother goes to sleep!"

That night when the moon was full, Brother and Sister Mouse woke Baby Mouse up and they quietly slipped out of their mouse hole. The jungle took on an eerie glow in the moonlight. Cautiously they crept through the grass, around the tree trunk, and under the leaves to the edge of the field. *(Move the balloon mouse with shaking motions as if weaving fearfully through the dark jungle.)* They shook when they heard Lion's loud, angry roar cut through the warm evening air. *(Teller: "Can you make really loud, angry Lion roars? Really loud!")*

The three little mice looked out into the field but they could not see the Lion anywhere in sight. Shaking, Brother and Sister Mouse said, "It doesn't sound like this is a good time for you to introduce us to your friend. Maybe we should come back another time." And they turned to leave.

Baby Mouse was busy looking to see if he could find out where the Lion was hiding. The roars sounded so angry and loud. Certainly he had to be nearby. Just then Baby Mouse looked up. There, hanging in a hunter's net from one of the branches, was the Lion!

"Oh my," gasped Baby Mouse. "The Lion's trapped up there. He needs help!"

Before Brother and Sister Mouse could stop him, Baby Mouse scrambled up the tree trunk, out onto the limb, and down the rope and climbed onto the net near the Lion's ear. He squeaked, "Mister Lion! Oh Mister Lion! Could you please stop roaring so I can help you?"

The Lion and looked around and roared, "Who's up here?"

"Just me, your friend." replied Little Mouse. "Now would you please stop your roaring and shaking this net. You're making me dizzy!"

"You're too small to help me! I am in big trouble! When the hunters return in the morning, they will take me away from here! What can you possibly do to help me?"

"I may be small, but I have very sharp teeth that can gnaw through these ropes. I can make a hole big enough to set you free. Now hold still!"

All through the night, Baby Mouse chewed and gnawed on the ropes. *(Teller rubs the balloon near the nozzle "nose" end making a chewing sound, then pulls on the nozzle and lets it go, making a snapping sound for one of the ropes breaking. Teller repeats this sound and pantomimes a hole being made in the net.)*

141

The Lion fell through the hole in the net and landed in the grass and Baby Mouse fell next to him. The Lion picked up Baby Mouse and shook his mane. *(Teller holds the mouse up high.)* The Lion opened his mouth wide until his teeth shone in the moonlight.

Brother and Sister Mouse covered their eyes and cried, "Oh no! He's going to eat him!"

The Lion held Baby Mouse up high and gave a mighty roar. *(Teller: "Let's hear a really loud roar!" Next, the Teller holds the mouse on top of the Teller's head as if to give the mouse a seat of honor.)* "I want everyone in the jungle to know that this little mouse is a true friend! And that, from now on, we will be friends to the very end!" The Lion gave out one more big Lion roar. *(The Teller elicits one more roar from the listeners. With a nod, the Teller indicates that the story is finished.)*

MULTIPLE INTELLIGENCE ACTIVITIES FOR . . .

The Lion and The Mouse

 Make a Baby Mouse.
(Logical-Mathematical; Bodily-Kinesthetic)

You will need long, thin animal-making balloons, commonly called "260s." Use the mouse-making instructions that follow, and distribute copies of the instructions to the students. You may inflate and knot the balloons in advance or, if the students are skillful enough, let them do it themselves. Following the directions, measuring, and physically working with the balloons will strengthen students' manual dexterity. Encourage students to help one another until everyone has completed his or her own mouse. The color, shape, and feel of the balloons will cause excitement and entice the students to work with this model until they succeed.

 Create a Shape.
(Naturalistic; Visual-Spatial)

Play with the first activity until it has been completed successfully. Preinflate additional balloons with different amounts of air. Vary the balloons from 8 inches to 58 inches. Store these balloons in a large bag until needed. Display the mouse made in the first activity. Have the students work in groups to share ideas as they twist the balloons into different-sized bubbles and shapes found in nature. Invite them to observe and experiment with the sizes and work on creating different balloon animals or objects. This activity challenges the ability to see forms from the shapes in a playful way.

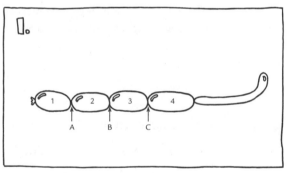

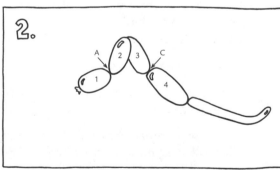

Creating a balloon mouse *(Courtesy of Wellsprings Design).*

1. Inflate 8 inches, leave a 12-inch tail. For head—at nozzle end twist a 2-inch bubble.

2. For ear—twist a 3-inch bubble. Hold bubbles #1 and #2 in your hand so they will not untwist.

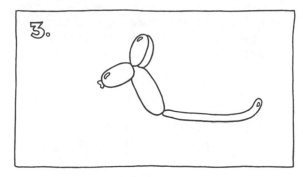

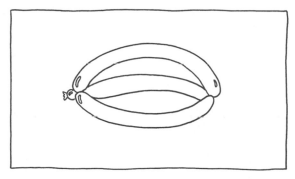

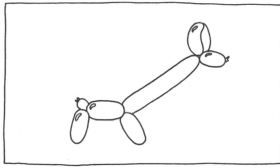

Creating a balloon mouse *(continued)*

3. Twist and connect points A & C to form ears. Pull ears (#2 and #3) apart and roll bubble #1 through them. This will lock them in place. Body is bubble #4.

Simple balloon creations.

3 Going on a Lion Hunt.
(Musical-Rhythmic; Bodily-Kinesthetic)

Following this interactive rhyme, taken from the oral tradition, the Teller assumes and models the leader's role while the class chants the responses, clapping the rhythm. When the class becomes comfortable with this, individual students take turns leading the class through it. As a variation, have the students create their own sequence of events leading up to finding the lion.

Verses for "Going on a Lion Hunt"

The Leader establishes a rhythm by alternating clapping the hands on the knees while seated. An asterisk indicates the text that the audience recites. This text is printed on the chalkboard or a flip chart in advance so that the class or audience can easily see their part. As the chant progresses, the asterisk substitutes for the text to be repeated.

Leader: "We're going on a Lion Hunt!"

Class repeats: ✳ **"We're going on a Lion Hunt!"**

Leader: "We're going to catch one, too."

Class repeats: ✳ **"We're going to catch one, too."**

Leader: "Then we'll take him to the zoo."

Class repeats: ✳ **"Then we'll take him to the zoo."**

1. Leader: "Oh! I see a FOREST in front of me."
   Class: ✳ **"Oh! I see a FOREST in front of me."**
   (Chorus)
   Leader: "Can't go over it." Class: ✳
   Leader: "Can't go under it." Class: ✳
   Leader: "Can't go around it." Class: ✳
   Leader: "Got to go through it." Class: ✳
   (Leader and Class pantomime chopping down trees in time to the rhythm.)

2. Leader: "Oh! I see a SWAMP in front of me."
   Class: ✳ **"Oh I see a SWAMP in front of me."**
   (Chorus)
   (Pantomime walking through mud.)

continued

3. Leader: "Oh! I see a RIVER in front of me."
   Class: ✿"Oh! I see a RIVER in front of me."

   (Chorus)

   (Pantomime swimming.)

4. Leader: "Oh! I see a JUNGLE in front of me."
   Class: ✿"Oh! I see a JUNGLE in front of me."

   (Chorus)

   (Pantomime hacking with a machete.)

5. Leader: "Oh! I see a LION in front of me!"
   Class: ✿"Oh! I see a LION in front of me."

   (Chorus)

   (Pantomime looking out toward the lion.)

(The verses unwind in reverse order at a faster pace. The chorus may be included to draw out the events and give students more time to anticipate the sequence of events.)

Leader: "Got to get out of here!" *(Increase pace of the rhythm!)*

Leader: "Run for your lives!" *(Pantomime running.)*

Leader: "Through the jungle!" *(Pantomime hacking through the jungle.)* ✿

Leader: "Through the RIVER...SWAMP...FOREST...SAFE AT HOME!"

Variation: Invite the class to make their own Lion hunt with different obstacles.

APRIL CHAPTER RESOURCES

Aardema, V. (1975). *Why mosquitoes buzz in people's ears.* New York: Dial.

Albert, R. (1994). *Alejandro's gift.* San Francisco, CA: Chronicle.

Allaby, M. (1996). *The environment.* London: Horus Editions.

Arnosky, J. (1993). *Crinkleroot's 25 birds every child should know.* New York: Bradbury.

Baker, J. (1991). *Window.* New York: Greenwillow.

Barrett, J. (1978). *Cloudy with a chance of meatballs.* New York: Macmillan.

Basker, J. (1987). *Where the forest meets the sea.* New York: Greenwillow.

Berstein, M., & Heffernan, E. (1974). *Coyote goes hunting for fire.* New York: Scribner.

Brett, J. (1992). *Berlioz the bear.* New York: Scholastic.

Brown, M. (1961). *Once a mouse.* New York: Scribner.

Brown, M. (1976). *Arthur's nose.* Boston: Little, Brown.

Brown, M. (1982). *Arthur goes to camp.* Boston: Little Brown.

Brown, M. W. (1947). *Goodnight moon.* New York: Harper & Row.

Brown, R. (1993). *The picnic.* New York: Dutton.

Carle, E. (1984). *The mixed up chameleon.* New York: HarperCollins.

Carlstrom, N. W. (1986). *Jesse bear, what will you wear?* New York: Macmillan.

Cherry, L. (1990). *The great kapok tree.* New York: Scholastic.

Cooney, B. (1982). *Miss Rumphius.* New York: Viking Penguin.

Dalgliesh, A. (1952). *The bears on Hemlock mountain.* New York: Scribner.

da Silva, C. (1989). Kibungo. In H. East (Comp.) *The singing sack: 28 song stories from around the world* (pp. 32–55). London: A & C Black.

Dayrell, E. (1968). *Why the sun and the moon live in the sky.* Boston: Houghton Mifflin.

De Paola, T. (1981). *The hunter and the animals: A wordless picture book.* New York: Holiday House.

East, H. (1989). *Songs from the singing sack: 35 songs from stories around the world.* On Tinderbox Music [cassette]. London: A & C Black.

Fowler, S. G. (1989). *When summer ends.* New York: Greenwillow.

Freeman, D. (1964). *Dandelion.* New York: Viking.

Freeman, D. (1977). *Dandelion.* New York: Puffin.

Freeman, D. (1976). *Bearymore.* New York: Viking.

Ganeri, A. (1992). *Focus on birds.* New York: Gloucester Press.

Gans, R., & Mirocha, P. (1996). *How do birds find their way?* New York: HarperCollins.

Gibbons, G. (1989). *The Monarch butterfly.* New York: Holiday House.

Henkes, K. (1985). *Bailey goes camping.* New York: Mulberry.

Henrietta. (1991). *A mouse in the house.* New York: Dorling Kindersley.

Hirschi, R., & Burrell, G. (1987). *Where do birds live?* New York: Walker.

Hirschi, R., & Burrell, G. (1987). *What is a bird?* New York: Walker.

Jeunesse, G., & Mettler, R. (1992). *The rain forest.* New York: Scholastic.

Kipling, R. (1985). *The beginning of the armadillos.* San Diego, CA: Harcourt Brace Jovanovich.

Kraus, R. (1945). *The carrot seed.* New York: Harper & Row.

Kraus, R. (1993). *The carrot seed.* New York: Scholastic.

Leonni, L. (1996). *A busy year.* New York: Scholastic.

Levinson, N. S. (1992). *Snowshoe Thompson.* New York: HarperCollins.

Lobel, A. (1978). *Grasshopper on the road.* New York: Harper & Row.

Locke, T. (1984). *Where the river begins.* New York: Dial.

Marzollo, J. (1994). *The rain forest.* New York: Scholastic.

Minarik, E. H. (1959). *Father bear comes home.* New York: HarperCollins.

Peet, B. (1970). *The wump world.* Boston: Houghton Mifflin.

Potter, B. (1971). *The tale of Peter Rabbit.* New York: Scholastic.

Ranger rick. National Wildlife Federation. 1412 16th Street, N.W., Washington, DC 20036-2266.

Rockwell, A. (1985). *First comes spring.* New York: Crowell.

Royston, A., & King, D. (1992). *Birds.* New York: Aladdin.

Shaw, C. (1947). *It looked like spilt milk.* New York: Harper & Row.

Stevens, C. (1974). *Hooray for pig.* New York: Seabury Press.

Suzan, G. (1994). *The bojabi tree.* New York: Scholastic.

Talbott, H., & Greenberg, M. (1996). *Amazon diary.* New York: Putnam.

White, E. B. (1980). *Charlotte's web.* New York: Harper Trophy.

Yashima, T. (1955). *Crow boy.* New York: Viking.

Your big backyard. National Wildlife Federation. 1412 16th Street, N.W., Washington, DC 20036-2266.

May

Families Are Special

LITTLE BIRDIE AND MOTHER

What does little birdie say
In her nest at peep of day?
Let me fly, says little birdie,
Mother, let me fly away.
Birdie, rest a little longer,
Till the little wings are stronger,
So she rests a little longer,
Then she flies away.

What does little baby say,
In her bed at peep of day?
Baby says, like little birdie,
Let me rise and fly away.
Baby, sleep a little longer,
Till the little wings are stronger.
If she sleeps a little longer,
Baby, too, shall fly away.

-ALFRED LORD TENNYSON

So she rests a little longer...

*M*ay is families and friendships, lilacs, lilies, and love. In "May: Families Are Special," Puppetry, Draw Talk, and Chant Storytelling methods lure us into stories about cousins, parents, siblings, and family capers in both traditional and nuclear family configurations.

Multiple intelligence areas Visual-Spatial, Bodily-Kinesthetic, Logical-Mathematical, Intrapersonal, Naturalistic, Verbal-Linguistic, Musical-Rhythmic, and Interpersonal are incorporated. Children enjoy creating family quilts and family trees, exploring figurative language, and constructing their own family board games

May warms us with storytelling possibilities!

The City Mouse and the Country Mouse

By Aesop

Retold and Adapted by Susan Trostle Brand

STORYTELLING METHOD

Puppetry/Chant

This classic folk story of a town mouse and her sophisticated city cousin endures and charms through the generations. The themes of this amusing tale are family differences and, "There's no place like home!"

Puppetry is the ideal method for telling this simple story, which involves few changes of scenery, an uncomplicated plot, and few characters. The use of a narrator, or a narrator puppet, is recommended. The story is further enhanced by the Tellers' use of scenery, background music, and props that the puppets manipulate. Also, throughout the story the audience may chime in, chant-style, on a recurring song. Before beginning the story, the Tellers may want to establish a signal such as a nod or a hand gesture to indicate that everyone can join in, chant-style, on a recurring song about the merits of "the good life" and the contrasting merits of "the country life." An asterisk indicates the text that the audience sings. This text is printed on the chalkboard or a flip chart in advance so that the class or audience can easily see their part.

Begin with an introduction and discussion of the theme of families. Brainstorm with the group about the various lifestyles that different family members enjoy. Children may wish to briefly discuss where grandparents, aunts, uncles, and other family members live. Next, the Tellers introduce the puppets by name and mention that these two mice are cousins and that each has a very unique lifestyle.

Four or five puppets work well in telling this story. The first puppet, a country mouse, is dressed in overalls, a flannel shirt, and a straw hat with, perhaps, a daisy on the top. The second puppet, the city mouse, is dressed in a lavish "fur" coat, a matching hat with a feather on top, and a "leather" designer handbag. The cat, created in orange, perhaps, is large and furry. The two dog puppets are black, large, and straight-haired, perhaps.

The mouse puppets are easy to create. They are probably easiest to manipulate when hand puppets are used (either sock, papier mâché, or fabric; see Chapter 3 for puppet-making suggestions). The cat and dog puppets are often constructed from poster board, which is colored or covered in fabrics and trimmings and then mounted on to dowel rods for easy and fast manipulation.

Two Tellers (or three, if one manipulates a tuxedo-clad narrator puppet) are enough for this story, speaking loudly behind the stage. The stage is a sheet-draped, rectangular table or a puppet stage, complete with curtains. The first scene is set in the country, the second, in the city. Finally, suggested props include a small suitcase and play food in the shapes of cheese, fish, cake, bread, corn, and wheat.

The City Mouse and the Country Mouse

(Display country scene)

Narrator: Once, in a large field of wheat, there lived a Country Mouse *(enter Country Mouse)*. She feasted on grain and barley and corn and other field crops *(mouse moves to scenery and/or holds props)* which the farmer planted. When the days grew short and cold, the Country Mouse went indoors, safe and warm in the farmer's house inside a hole in the kitchen wall *(mouse moves to house area of scenery)*.

Country Mouse: *(Sings to the tune of "Here We Go Round the Mulberry Bush")*:

✿ In summer time, I'm happy, eating wheat all day,
  And when I'm fed, I scurry round the field and play and play!
  In wintertime, when skies are gray, I run inside the house.
  I have a charming, easy life; I'm glad to be a mouse!

Narrator: Yes, the Country Mouse had a relaxed, safe and easy existence. One day, however, something very exciting happened. The cousin of the Country Mouse, the City Mouse, came to visit her *(enter City Mouse)*. She was dressed all in furs from her hat to her fancy red shoes.

City Mouse: Cousin, cousin! *(Hugs Country Mouse)*. It is wonderful to see you! It has been too long! Please, may I have a tour of your home? I must admit, also, that I am a bit hungry from all of my travels.

Country Mouse: Of course, Cousin! Come this way, into my pantry in the attic. Here are the cheese crumbs *(hold up a bit of cheese)*, here are the nuts and peas and wheat I've stored *(show food piles)*, and here are the tasty cake and bread crumbs the farmer drops while he eats *(show bits of cake and bread)*.

City Mouse: *(Nibbles meal with her cousin)* You poor little mouse! You must live on leftovers each day. You must store them in this dreary old attic. It is dark and musty here. Oh, come and visit me in the city. There I will show you a beautiful home and we shall have a REAL feast.

Country Mouse: *(sounding wistful and ashamed)* Yes, I suppose my house is rather simple to you. I would love to visit your home in the city, Cousin. Let's go today!

Narrator: The City Mouse and the Country Mouse gathered their luggage *(use luggage props)*. They were quickly on their way. When they arrived in the city *(change to city scenery)*, the Country Mouse beheld many amazing sights.

City Mouse: Well, here we are, Cousin. *(Sings to tune of "On Top of Spaghetti")*:

✿ Life in the city, suits me just fine,
  The scenery's lovely, the feasts are divine;
  There's more excitement than you've ever seen,
  I live in such luxury, I feel like a Queen!

149

Country Mouse: Goodness, Cousin! Your home is like a palace. No wonder you feel like a queen!

City Mouse: Come this way Cousin! *(Country Mouse follows City Mouse up staircase.)* Keep very still. The owners are having dinner. When they are finished, we can have all the food that they leave behind!

Country Mouse: They have all left the room, Cousin! And just look at all the food that remains on the table!

City Mouse: Hurry; it's time to dine, Cousin! *(City Mouse jumps upon table; Country Mouse follows her; mice munch greedily on large slices of cheese and pieces of fish.)*

Country Mouse: This is the life, Cousin! You are so fortunate!

(suddenly enter cat; pounces upon table behind mice)

Cat: MEEEEEOOOOOOOOOWWWWWWWWWWW!

(enter two dogs, barking loudly)

Dogs: WOOOOOOOOFFFFFFFF, WOOOOOOOOFFFF!

City Mouse: Hurry, Cousin! Run! Fast! *(both mice jump off table and scurry away quickly; move mice to another room of house)*

Country Mouse: That was a close call, Cousin *(shivers nervously).*

City Mouse: Nothing unusual, Country Cousin. We'll wait until the coast is clear. Then we'll go back to the table and finish our dinner.

Country Mouse: No thanks, City Cousin, We'll wait until the coast is clear, and then I'll go back to my country fields and hole in the wall and country pantry in the attic. *There* I am safe.

City Mouse: Very well, Cousin. I'm glad I traveled to se where you live. And I'm glad that you traveled to see where I live. But we have each learned an important lesson: *(mice wrap arms around each other and sway: both sing to the tune of "There's No Place Like Home"):*

✱ **We've both traveled far and wide**
So curious, we did roam;
Now, dear Cousin, fare thee well—
There's no place like home!

MULTIPLE INTELLIGENCE ACTIVITIES FOR...

The City Mouse and the Country Mouse

 Crayon-Press Class Quilts.
(Intrapersonal; Visual-Spatial)

This activity is relatively simple and yet the results are fascinating and lasting. Cut muslin into 5-by-5-inch squares. Cut finest grain sandpaper into four by four inch squares. Each child receives one square of sandpaper, one muslin square, and several fabric crayons. Onto the sandpaper, the child colors something positive about his or her family or self that is unique, different, and special. Remind the children to press very hard to ensure vivid colors on the fabric later on. Also, you may need to provide help with any lettering, as crayon letters will reverse themselves when they are pressed onto another surface. When the coloring is complete, an adult presses each sandpaper square, face down, onto the fabric with a very hot iron. Hold the iron down until the crayon image transfers vividly onto the fabric. (Be sure to keep children at a safe distance from this part of the activity.) Lift off the sandpaper and invite children to admire the colorful and interesting fabric squares. Sew the squares (by hand or machine) onto a contrasting fabric background to create a memorable class quilt. As a variation, children may each color six squares of sandpaper to create their own family quilt or wall hanging.

 Here, There, and Everywhere.
(Visual-Spatial; Logical-Mathematical)

Display a large map of the United States. Give the children stickers of different colors and/or designs onto which they can print their initials. Ask each child to place stickers on the map according to the places he or she has visited. When all children have placed all of their stickers, count the total number of places the entire class has visited. Tally results to see who has traveled the farthest west, the farthest east, south, and north, and so on. Transferring information onto a bar graph is an additional option. Ask each child to describe his or her most fascinating trip (real or imaginary) and to point to this location on the map. Next, as a comparison, ask children to describe what they like best about their home and/or hometown. Culminate this activity, perhaps, by using a large foam map puzzle of the United States which the children, in small groups, piece together on a large floor area.

 Nature and Family Trees.
(Naturalistic; Intrapersonal)

Distribute flat boxes or large bags to each group of four or five children. On a pleasant day, take a nature walk through the woods. Children collect leaves of various shapes and sizes. Upon their

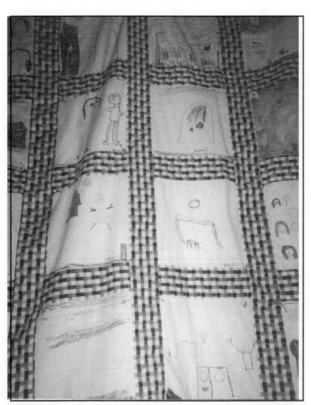
Crayon-press class quilt.

return, have them mount the leaves onto poster board trees (painting front and back leaf surfaces with white school glue works well). Print the name of the tree from which the leaf fell below each. Each child might be responsible for one type of tree. Compare and contrast the characteristics of various leaves using Venn Diagrams.

Discuss how the structure of family relationships is also like a tree. With parents' prior per- mission and information in hand, assist each child in writing the names of siblings, parents, grand- parents, and great-grandparents onto the tree's branches. (If children are adopted or otherwise estranged from their biological parents, they may complete only the information which they desire on their trees.) Share trees, add photos, if desired, and display on a large bulletin board or hang trees from a line or hooks near the ceiling of the room.

Oak and family trees.

TIPS FOR THE TELLER

Why Not Call It Cow Juice?

By Steven Krasner

Retold and Adapted by Susan Trostle Brand

STORYTELLING METHOD

Draw Talk

Family fun and figurative language appeal to young children. In Steven Krasner's story *Why Not Call It Cow Juice?*, a family discovers that many favorite expressions are not meant to be taken literally.

The Teller introduces the story by asking the children if they have ever given someone a hand around the house. When a few children have answered and explained how they have helped, show a large cutout hand encircling a model or paper house. Help them discover that "a hand around the house" has more than one meaning. Lead them into the Draw Talk Storytelling by telling them that more funny surprises await them in the story you are about to tell.

Six sheets of white poster or chart paper are needed, as suggested in Chapter 3. Two or three thick point liquid markers, preferably black, green, and yellow, are used to draw the illustrations, which may be sketched onto the paper before the telling.

Let the family fun begin!

The teller uses drawings to enhance the story
"Why Not Call It Cow Juice?"

Why Not Call It Cow Juice?

PAGE ONE: In a large white house *(sketch outline of house)* lived a happy family. In this happy family lived Father *(standing near house or inside house, draw and describe Father)* Mother *(draw and describe Mother)*, Jeffrey *(draw and describe Jeffrey)*, Amy, *(draw and describe and describe Amy)*, and Emily *(draw and describe Emily)*. One Saturday, the family climbed into the car *(draw* *car)* and went for a ride. In the car, they thought they would have some fun by playing a game. The children decided to try and trick Father and Mother.

PAGE TWO: "We are going to the farmer's market first," said Mother. "Oh, a farmer's market!" said Amy. "How many farmers are for sale?" *(draw a row of farmers underneath a large sign onto which you print: Farmers for Sale).* "No!" said Father. "The farmers are not for sale. The farmers are selling *food!*"

PAGE THREE: "Let's buy some ears of corn!" said Jeffrey. "It's my favorite food! These ears will keep my own ears warm, too!" *(Draw a farmer with one ear of corn covering each of his ears.)* "No!" said Mother. "The corn is shaped like large, pointed ears. But they are not *real* ears on your heads!"

PAGE FOUR: Emily pointed to some lettuce on a large wooden table *(draw table).* She said, "Let's buy some heads of lettuce for our salad tonight! We'll see eyes, noses, and mouths on the heads!" *(Draw several round heads, with faces, in the middle of each green lettuce shape.)* "No!" cried Father. "The heads have no faces. They are called heads of lettuce because they are round, like a head."

PAGE FIVE: On the ride home, the family became hungry. Father suggested that they stop at a sandwich shop for some snacks. Amy asked, "Is the sand witch friendly or scary? Will she share her sand toys with us?" *(Draw a large witch playing in the sand.)* "No!" said Mother. "A sandwich is not a witch in the sand. A sandwich is two slices of bread or toast with something tasty between the slices.

PAGE SIX: The waitress came to take the order. Amy ordered a slice of pie *(draw pie).* Mother ordered a sandwich *(draw sandwich).* Jeffrey ordered a dish of ice cream *(draw ice cream).* Emily ordered a piece of cake *(draw cake).* Father couldn't decide. At last, he made his decision. It was *his* turn to have fun with words. I'll have a large glass of cow juice!" he said. *(Draw a large cow sipping on a glass of white "juice," in the center of paper.)* "No!" shouted everyone. "That is not called cow juice, Father. That's milk!"

Father grinned. "We have discovered farmer's markets *(flip to page two),* ears of corn *(flip to page three),* heads of lettuce *(flip to page four),* and sand witches *(flip to page five).* So why *not* call milk "cow juice?"

MULTIPLE INTELLIGENCE ACTIVITIES FOR . . .

Why Not Call It Cow Juice?

 "Shake a Leg!"
(Verbal-Linguistic, Visual-Spatial)

Find and discuss other figurative and/or thought-provoking language expressions, such as the following: eyes of potato, barrel of fun, artichoke hearts, chocolate mousse, going batty, hoarse throat, frog in throat, yard sale, flea market, garage sale, mouth of the river, foot of the hill, long arm of the law, coat of arms, keeping an eye out for something, a hair raising experience, "I'm all ears!", under my skin, tiptoeing around an issue, walking on eggs, losing my mind, losing my voice, hot under the collar, "Don't sweat the small stuff," keeping a stiff upper lip, losing our cool, pipe down, grin and bear it, getting the upper hand, hang in there, and jump-start one's car.

Invite children to select one of the above, or a new one of their own, and draw it on a sheet of paper. The others try to guess the figurative saying that corresponds to each of the drawings.

2 Family Coat of Arms.
(Visual-Spatial; Verbal-Linguistic)

Briefly explain the history of family coats of arms, including the symbolism of the imagery (animals, military equipment, etc.) often contained in them. A book with illustrations of traditional coats of arms will help the children visualize the concept. Then have the children draw their own family coat of arms on plain white paper. They complete the information for each section and draw related illustrations (see illustration). When coats of arms are complete, mount them on heavy cardboard and share facts with friends. Display on a classroom bulletin board.

Family coat of arms.

Note: Because of the changing nature of families, adoption issues, etc., teachers may wish to consult with children's parent(s) prior to beginning this project. The information they provide will also assist children in identifying their nationalities and other important facts about family histories.

3 Life Goes On.

(Logical-Mathematical; Intrapersonal)

Invite children to bring in baby pictures with identifying information printed on the backs of each picture. Display all photographs on a large bulletin board. Be sure to include baby photos of teachers, the principal, and classroom aides, as well, for added fun. Children attempt to identify each classmate and teacher. Later, print names beneath each picture. Ask children to determine the total number of years in the class when all the children's ages are added together. Ask them the total age of the boys and the total age of the girls.

Tell them the years each teacher was born. Ask them to determine the age of each teacher, using subtraction. Invite children, in groups, to create their own math problems for others to solve

"Life goes on" necklace.

based upon ages, years of birth, and projected events in the future such as obtaining a driver's license, graduation and so on.

As a related activity, cut ten circles of colored construction paper (approximately 3 inches each in diameter) per child. Punch a hole in each circle near one edge. Help children to record the most meaningful events of their lives on the construction paper circles—one event per circle. For example, Kayla chose a blue circle to write, "I was born in Lexington, Massachusetts,

on April 4, 1994." On her next circle, a red one, she wrote, "My family and I moved to Arlington, Virginia, when I was two years old." Encourage children to add artwork to each event on the reverse sides of the circles. Children string and knot the circles with yarn, ribbon, or string, sequentially, into a necklace to wear throughout the day. Invite each child to choose at least two partners. Partners read their necklaces to each other; they ask questions and make positive comments about the life necklaces.

TIPS FOR THE TELLER

The Little Bunny Who Wished for Red Wings

Retold and Adapted by Jeanne M. Donato

STORYTELLING METHOD

Chant

This is a retelling of an old southern folktale. The story deals with a Little Bunny, who is not happy and wishes that he could be like other animals. He ignores his mother's assurances that she loves him just the way he is. He is able to wish for red wings and the results teach him to appreciate who he is and what he has. Children identify with the Little Bunny's wishing and longing to be anything but what he is. The children are able to vicariously experience his frustrations as he finally gets his wish and finds it's not what he really wanted. The story's conclusion leaves the listeners with a profound sense of knowing that self-acceptance and family love are what make for true happiness in this world.

The Chant Storytelling method explained in Chapter 3 will help the Teller to prepare for

the telling of this story. The Teller may introduce the story with a rabbit puppet or rabbit stuffed animal. As the children listen to the story, they will start to recognize its structure and delight in recognizing and anticipating the Mother's rhythmic reassurances of her love for her Little Bunny. Before beginning the story, the Teller may want to establish a signal to indicate that everyone can join in the chanting. An asterisk indicates the text that the audience recites. This text is printed on the chalkboard or a flip chart in advance so that the class or audience can easily see their part. When it comes time for Mother Bunny's answer, the Teller may want to pantomime her smile, and the way she folds her arms around Little Funny Bunny, with a nod towards the children or a self-hug, as a signal, to give them a cue to join in.

The Little Bunny Who Wished for Red Wings

Once upon a time, there was a Little Bunny with long pink ears, a whiskery little nose, a bit of a powder puff tail, and the softest of cuddly fur. He lived with his Mummy in a cozy little hole at the foot of an old butternut tree. But he was not happy, for he was always wishing that he could be like someone else.

One day Little Bunny and his Mummy saw their neighbor, Mr. Bushy Tail, scampering from limb to limb gathering nuts. "Oh, Mummy!" cried Little Bunny. "I wish that I had a tail like Mr. Bushy Tail's. Then I could climb trees!"

His Mummy just shook her head, folded her arms around him, and said, ✱ **"Funny Bunny, I love you just the way you are!"**

Down by the pond Mrs. Puddle Duck was teaching her fuzzy little ducklings how to swim. Little Bunny said, "Oh Mummy, I wish that I had red rubber-duck shoes like Mrs. Puddle Duck! Then I could swim!"

Mummy Bunny just shook her head, folded him into her arms, and said, ✱ **"Funny Bunny, I love you just the way you are!"**

When he saw Mr. Porcupine, Little Bunny sniffed, "I wish I had a prickly coat, like Mr. Porcupine's. Then no one would ever bother me."

Mummy Bunny just shook her head, folded him into her arms, and said, ✱ **"Funny Bunny, I love you just the way you are!"**

They had to plug their noses when Mr. Skunk passed by. And Little Bunny sniffed, "I wish that I could spray, like Mr. Skunk! Then no one would dare to come near me!"

Funny Bunny's Mummy shook her head, folded him into her arms, and said, ✱ **"Funny Bunny, I love you just the way you are!** Now, why don't you go off and play? But remember. Be home before it gets dark."

Little Bunny twitched his nose and hopped away to play. Old Mr. Groundhog heard Little Bunny saying, "I wish I wasn't a bunny!"

"Is that so?" replied wise Old Mr. Groundhog, as he slowly pulled out a large gold pocket watch. He opened it and held it closely to his nose. "You should be careful what you wish for, you know. It might come true."

Old Mr. Groundhog snapped his pocket watch closed and said, "If it's a wish you want, follow the path through the forest to the clearing. There you'll find a magic wishing pond in an old mossy stump. Look at your reflection in the water. Make a wish. Turn around three times. And your wish will come true."

"Thank you Mr. Groundhog!" Little Bunny called as he hopped away. He came to a clearing where sunlight shone down through the trees onto the wishing pond. Little Bunny thought to himself, "My Mama always says, ✱ **'Funny bunny, I love you just the way you are.'** But I wish I wasn't a bunny."

A little red bird was perched on the edge of the stump, splashing in the sparkling water. "Oh my," cried Little Bunny! "I wish that I had red wings like that little bird!"

Little Bunny hopped up to the stump and gazed into the water until he saw his reflection. "I wish, I wish, I wish, I had red wings!" he said. He turned himself around three times—

One...two...three...and waited. Very soon his shoulders started to feel strange, like when a tooth is growing in. "Oooh! Oooh! Oooh!" he squeaked. "What is happening?"

When the Little Bunny peered into the magic wishing pond he saw two great enormous red wings! "Oh!" squealed Little Bunny with delight as he flapped his wings. But instead of flying he flopped on his nose. "Oh my," cried Little Bunny. "This will take some getting used to!" And off he hopped and flopped to show his Mummy.

By the time Little Bunny got home it was so dark that he could hardly see his little house. When he knocked on the door his Mummy opened it. But the white fur with flapping red wings frightened her. "A monster!" she cried and locked the door.

A tear dropped from Little Bunny's eye. His own Mummy didn't know him! He was all alone in the dark with nowhere to go. Flapping his wings, he fluttered up into the treetop where Mr. Bushy Tail lived. He knocked on the door and called out, "Mr. Bushy Tail, may I please stay with you tonight? My Mummy doesn't recognize me. She always told me,✣ **'Funny bunny, I love you just the way you are!'** Now I am different, and I have nowhere to spend the night!"

Mr. Bushy Tail poked his head out of his hole and scolded, "You're not Little Bunny! Bunnies can't fly! Go away!" And he slammed his door.

Little Bunny dropped to the ground and cried. Where could he go? He hopped and flopped down to the pond. But when poor Mrs. Puddle Duck saw him coming, she honked and hissed, flapping her wings to keep him away, for she had never seen such an odd looking thing in her life.

No one recognized Little Bunny with his flapping red wings. Mr. Porcupine rolled into a prickly ball and Mr. Skunk started to lift his tail when he came near. Crying, Little Bunny stumbled along in the dark until he came to Old Mr. Groundhog's hole.

"Oh Mr. Groundhog sir," cried Little Bunny. "I wished for red wings and now no one knows who I am, not even my Mummy. She always told me,✣ **'Funny Bunny, I love you just the way you are!'** It's cold and dark and I have nowhere to go! May I please stay with you?" begged the Little Bunny.

Wise Old Mr. Groundhog recognized Little Bunny's voice and answered, "Certainly! Come right in."

But Little Bunny could not fit into Mr. Groundhog's house. "I can't get in!" cried Little Bunny. "My wings are too big!"

"Fold them up." called Mr. Groundhog. Little Bunny folded up his wings and crawled into Mr. Groundhog's hole.

Now, Groundhogs like to sleep on beechnuts but they make a lumpy bed for little bunnies with bumpy red wings. All night long, Little Bunny tossed and turned.

The next morning, Little Bunny was crying, "Oh, Mr. Groundhog, I wish I never had red wings! Why my own Mummy doesn't even know me and I don't know what to do! She always told me,✣ **'Funny Bunny, I love you just the way you are!'"**

"Are you sure you don't want your red wings?" asked Mr. Groundhog.

"I'm sure!" cried Little Bunny. "I was happier when I was a bunny!"

Wise Old Mr. Groundhog pulled out his pocket watch and looked at it carefully. He nodded his head and said, "Hum. Let's see here. There may still be enough water left for one more wish, if you hurry.

"Thank you Mr. Groundhog!" cried Little Bunny and off he hopped and flopped back to the wishing pond.

There Little Bunny found just enough water to see his face in it and wished his red wings off. He turned around three times—one...two...three! And soon they were gone.

Little Bunny hopped home and his Mummy recognized him right away. When he told her the whole story she nodded her head, folded him in her arms, and said, ✽ **"Funny Bunny, I love you just the way you are!"**

And Little Bunny never wished to be like somebody else ever again.

MULTIPLE INTELLIGENCE ACTIVITIES FOR . . .

The Little Bunny Who Wished for Red Wings

 ### Make a Whatsit.
(Naturalistic; Logical-Mathematical)

Creating and manipulating this toy involves students in the concepts of thirds, groupings, cubes, surfaces, top, bottom, width, length, and shapes. Opportunities for using the imagination abound, as well.

Ask each student to collect three cleaned milk cartons and one paper towel tube. Students cut, fold, and tape the milk cartons into cubes. Cut slits on the tops and bottoms of the three cubes so that a paper towel tube may be inserted into them. Attach flattened clay knobs or cardboard squares at the ends of the tubes to hold cubes in place.

Pre-draw and photocopy pictures of Little Bunny, the red-winged bird, Mrs. Puddle Duck, and Mr. Bushy Tail. Distribute one set of all four pictures to each child. Each picture should be 4 1/2 inches in height for most milk containers. Invite students to color all four animals. Then ask them to cut each picture into three equal (1 1/2 inch) parts. Providing pre-drawn, dotted guide lines for this horizontal cutting task is helpful.

Children then glue all the heads of the characters on the top four sides of the cube; they glue the middle sections on all four sides of the middle cube; and they glue the bottom of the characters onto all four sides of the lowest cube.

When the glue is dry, the children are ready for the fun. They can turn the cubes to change the heads, middles, and bottoms of the four animals. Encourage students to discover how many different animals they can create and to name each new creation. Calculate the total possible number of animal combinations.

Develop a class story about the Mixed-Up Bunny. Enjoy, play, and explore the possibilities. For a challenging variation, encourage the children to design and create their own animals.

 ### A Co-Op Play.
(Interpersonal; Bodily-Kinesthetic)

The premise for this activity is to enjoy the learning process and not to be overly concerned with the product, which is to present the Little Bunny story as a formal play. It offers many opportunities for group cooperation and creation along with movement exploration as a way of evoking the mood and development of each character. Have the children do group warm-up exercises before each play opportunity. Set to music played in the background, the group can move and explore being each of the characters.

This story involves two characters in each scene. Discuss the story with the class and have them break it down to scenes, as found in a play. Ask them to list the scenes and count how many there are. Next the teacher can divide the class into two groups. Elect a "Director" to oversee the groups. Divide the other students into groups of two for each scene, giving everyone a chance to participate. The Little Bunny and Mother will change with each scene. Let the students decide

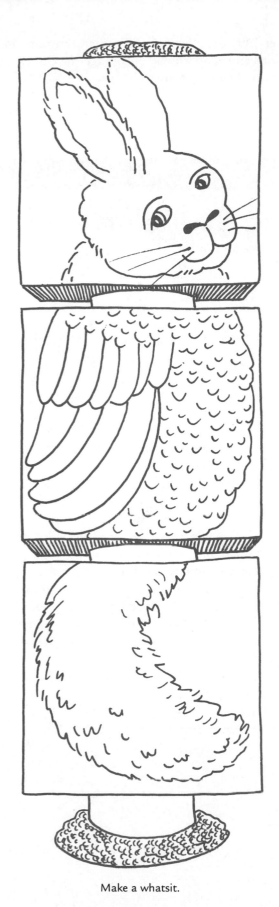

Make a whatsit.

where each scene will be located—the room, stage, or gym. Use a minimum amount of props to encourage full bodily expression through pantomime. The "Director" reads the story while the others enact it until they become familiar with the story. Improvisation of dialogue will naturally evolve. This allows each student to add his or her ideas. The groups will adapt and incorporate these ideas as they evolve into a full playful expression of the story.

3 The Wishing Game.
(Logical-Mathematical; Verbal-Linguistic)

Have the class collect and compare different games. Discuss what elements a game board needs to make it function smoothly. On a plain piece of paper draw a curving trail from Little Bunny's home, to Mr. Bushy Tail's tree house, to Mrs. Puddle Duck's pond, to Mr. Porcupine's log, to Old Mr. Groundhog's home, to the forest, and ending at the wishing pond. Draw approximately 20 egg shapes (large enough to contain letters or words) along the path. Label the shapes yourself in advance, or let the students decide how to label their playing board. They may also color and decorate the board. Label the first one "Start" and the last one "Finish." Place a lower case letter of the alphabet in each of the other eggs. Mark one shape "move ahead 2 spaces," another "go back 4 spaces," and another "take an extra turn." The spinner may be an arrow and circle cut out of tag board, divided into six pie shapes numbered 1–6. A brass paper fastener pushed through the arrow and loosely fastened through the center of the circle will allow the arrow to spin around on the circle. Dice may also be used to determine the number of spaces moved. The class decides on a procedure for choosing which member goes first. Next, the class decides on six categories, such as animals, foods, people, places, toys, etc. These may be listed on the board to be changed with each playing or instead on the bottom of the paper in words or pictures, depending on the level of the students. When a player lands on a shape with a letter, he or she may choose a category, or spin to choose one. Then, the player must name something from that category beginning with the letter he or she landed on. For example, if the letter is *W* and the category is birds, the answers might be, "wren, woodpecker, whippoorwill, etc." Allow each group to decide on questionable answers. The player to reach the wishing pond first is the winner. This game lends itself to many creative additions and adaptations. Encourage the children to create their own games.

TIPS FOR THE TELLER

The Brownies and the Tailor

Retold and Adapted by Jeanne M. Donato

STORYTELLING METHOD

Chant

The *Brownies and the Tailor* explores the idea of working to help others. The Tailor in this story, a single father, needs his children's help to keep the house neat and clean now that their Grandmother is aged. The Grandmother and Father tell a story about helpful brownies that used to do all the chores when their father was a young boy. The children are determined to find these Brownies and invite them back. They discover the satisfaction and happiness that comes from helping others.

Following the model in Chapter 3 for Chant Storytelling the Teller asks the students how many of them are or have been Brownie Scouts.

Begin the telling with the following speech.

"In the olden days, people used to tell stories about the wee folk. They used to do all sorts of helpful things, like red up the house for people. Do you know what "red up a house" means? It's an old fashioned word that means to clean up. Pancheon is another old word for pan. In Old England people gathered turf to burn in their fireplaces. They would cut the turf from the moors, which are open areas of land that often have wet patches that are also called bogs. Listen to this story for these old words. Would you like to have a Brownie live in your house?"

Before beginning the story, the Teller may want to establish a signal such as a nod of the head or a hand gesture to indicate that everyone can join in the chant. As asterisk indicates the text that the audience repeats. This text is printed on the chalkboard or a flip chart in advance so that the class or audience can easily see their part.

The Brownies and the Tailor is adapted and reprinted with permission from the *Brownie Girl Scout Handbook*, copyright 1986, Girl Scouts of the United States of America.

The Brownies and the Tailor

Once upon a time, in the North Country of old England, there lived a poor Tailor with his elderly mother and two children, Jeannie and Danny.

The Tailor worked from dawn till dusk then slowly turned his hand to the cooking and cleaning while his children played. The Grandmother sewed and did what she could to help but her aching bones kept her close to the warm fire and her rocking chair.

When asked to help with the chores, Jeannie would complain that it was Danny's turn. Danny would howl that he did it last and it wasn't fair. Then they would both whine and wheedle to play just a little longer. And as they ran off, so did all thoughts of their chores left undone. Sadly, the Tailor would complete the tasks.

"Children certainly are a lot of work," complained the Tailor one evening.

"Children can be a blessing and a help," replied the Grandmother. She smiled and said, "Do you remember the Brownies that lived in our house when you were little?"

"Brownies?" muttered the Tailor. "Ah, yes! My Brownies, how I've missed them. Let's see now, how did their old rhyme go? ❋**'Twist me and turn me...and show me an elf. I looked in the water and saw...'** Ah, yes, I remember my Brownies well," and he smiled.

That evening as the Tailor was getting his children ready for bed they squealed, "Papa, tell us a story please?"

"Oh, I am too tired to tell stories." Then he stopped and said, "Maybe your Grandmother can tell you one."

"I believe I have one. Come here, Children," Grandma called. "Your poor father is tired. I certainly miss the days when we had Brownies to help us around our house. I wonder where they've gone?"

"Brownies!" squealed the Children, "What are Brownies, Granny? Please tell us!"

"When your father was little we used to have Brownies in our house. We were very lucky. Brownies are very helpful little persons. They would do all sorts of things just for the love of helping others. They would sweep the floor, fetch the water, lay the turf by the fireplace, set the table for breakfast, and have the house red up by morning. Sometimes, if you were careful, you could hear them laughing and playing about the house at night. But they would run off before anyone could see them. They expect the people of the house to leave a little pancheon of clear water and a tiny bowl of bread and milk or cream out on the doorstep for them in the evening."

"Really!" the children exclaimed. "What happened to your Brownies, Granny?"

"Oh, Brownies only stay in homes where children believe in them." Grandma replied. "My children grew up and our Brownies moved on."

"But, we're children!" cried Jeannie and Danny. "And we have plenty of work for them here! Tell us where we can find some," begged the Children.

"That was a long time ago, Children. I suppose only the Wise Old Owl remembers how to find them now," Grandma nodded.

"Where does the Wise Old Owl live?" asked the Children.

"I don't know if he is still there anymore. He used to live out on the moor in the old barn down by the pond. He called, 'Hooo, hooo!' But on the full of the moon, they say you could hear him speak. Now it's time for bed. Off with both of you!" Grandma laughed.

"We need to find some Brownies!" called the Children as they set out a pancheon of clear water and a tiny bowl of bread and cream on the doorstep.

That night Jeannie and Danny lay awake up in their loft, thinking of Granny's story about the Brownies. The moon shone full and flooded the night with her silvery light. Jeannie and Danny silently climbed down the ladder from their loft and crept out of the house through the mist-filled moor. They looked like whispy white sprites in their long nightshirts and stocking caps.

Suddenly, the sound of flapping wings soared with a shadow that sailed swiftly over their heads and whooshed into the old barn. The Children followed. As their eyes adjusted to the moonlight filtering through the cracks of the barn, they saw two large, yellow eyes blinking at them down from a beam in the hayloft.

"Hoo, hoo! Hoo, hoo!" came the deep voice of the Old Owl. "Come up! Come up!" she called hoarsely.

"She can speak!" whispered Jeannie and Danny as they climbed the ladder to the hayloft and sat carefully on the beam next to the Old Owl.

"This must be the Wise Old Owl Granny told us about!" Danny whispered.

"Now, what do you want?" said the Old Owl. "Come on! Speak up!"

"Please," said Jeannie, "would you tell us where we can find some Brownies to come and live with us?"

"Hoo, hoo! Hoo, hoo!" called the Old Bird. "That's it? I know where you can find two!"

"Hurrah!" cried Danny. "Where do they live?"

"Why, in your own home!" cried the Owl.

"In our house!" cried the Children together. "But why don't they help us?"

"Perhaps they don't know what should be done," said the Old Owl.

"Just tell us how to find these Brownies," said Danny.

"And we'll tell them what to do!" cried Jeannie.

The Wise Old Owl ruffled her feathers and called "Hoo, hoo. You do? Hoo, hoo!" so that the Children were not sure if she was hooting or laughing.

"I can tell you where to find these Brownies. But if you want to tell a Brownie what work you want done, you must each catch your very own Brownie," nodded the Owl. "Remember now, follow my instructions exactly. Go to the north side of the pond in the woods when the moon is full. Close you eyes and turn yourself around slowly three times while you say this charm:

✽ **Twist me and turn me and show me an Elf.**
   I looked in the water and saw_____.

"Then carefully look into the pond and say the word that rhymes with Elf. That's it! At that very moment you will see your very own Brownie. Hoo, hoo! Hoo, hoo! Be off with both of you!"

Thanking the Wise Old Owl, the two children scampered to the pond on the edge of the woods as they chanted:

❋ **Twist me and turn me and show me an Elf.**
I looked in the water and saw... hmmm.

❋ **Twist me and turn me and show me an Elf.**
I looked in the water and saw _____.

The children knew the pond well, for there was a fine echo that lived there that they enjoyed playing with. The moon shone in the still dark pond like a silver dish in the stillness of the night. They stood on the north side of the pond when Jeannie whispered, "I'll try the rhyme first." She closed her eyes and turned around slowly, three times (one...two...three) while she recited the rhyme.

❋ **Twist me and turn me and show me an Elf.**
I looked in the water and saw _____.

When she opened her eyes and looked in the water she cried, "Why, I don't see anyone but myself! I must have done it wrong!"

"Wrong!" sang the Echo.

"Oh You!" cried Jeannie.

"You!" replied Echo.

"What can that word be? What rhymes with Elf? Belf! Helf! Kelf! Melf! Pelf! Zelf! All I see when I look in the water is myself!" cried Jeannie.

"Myself!" answered Echo.

"Did you hear that?" whispered Danny. "The Echo said it too! Myself rhymes with Elf! That's the rhyme. Come on let's try it together!" So the children closed their eyes, turned slowly around three times (one...two...three...) while they said:

❋ **Twist me and turn me and show me an Elf.**
I looked in the water and saw myself!

When they opened their eyes, all they saw was their reflections staring back at them.

"It didn't work!" cried the Children.

"Work" cried the Echo.

"There aren't any Brownies here, Danny. Let's go back and ask the Wise Old Owl again!" cried Jeannie.

The children ran back to the barn and climbed up beside the Wise Old Owl.

"Hoo, hoo! Hoo, hoo! How did you do?" said the Old Owl.

"All we saw were ourselves," replied the Children.

"And what did you expect to see?" hooted the Owl.

"We expected to see a Brownie. We did everything you said!" pouted Jeannie.

"And pray, what are Brownies?" inquired the Owl.

"Granny says they are most helpful little people," answered Danny.

"And the ones you saw in the pond are not?" hooted the Owl. "Are you sure you didn't see any Brownies?"

"We only saw ourselves. And we are not Brownies!" cried the Children.

"Are you quite sure?" questioned the Owl. "Didn't you find a word that rhymes with Elf?"

"Not really," said Jeannie. "The only word that made sense was *myself.*"

"Well, if myself rhymes with Elf, it seems to me you have found your answer," hooted the Wise Old Owl. "All children can be Brownies, hoo, hoo! Couldn't you sweep the floor, fetch the water and the turf, set the table, and red up the house? Couldn't you? Couldn't you?"

"Yes, but we would rather have the Brownies do that for us!" replied the Children.

"And what would you be doing? Do you want to be the kind of children who idle away their day, making work for others and never helping?" hooted the Owl as she ruffled her feathers.

"Oh no!" cried the Children. "We don't want to be like that. We would rather be helpful like the Brownies." They yawned as their eyes weighed heavy with sleep and their heads started to nod.

"Hoo, hoo," called the Owl. "Climb up on my back and I will fly you home. Hoo, hoo. Hoo, hoo!"

The Children drifted into the Wise Old Owl's soft feathers and before they knew it, they were back in their own snug little beds. They awoke in the early morning and crept silently downstairs. Quickly they cleaned and red up their little cottage till it shone. All the while they laughed and chanted their rhyme:

❋ **Twist me and turn me and show me an Elf.**
   I looked in the water and saw myself!

That morning when their Father came into the kitchen, he could hardly believe his eyes. "Mother, Jeannie, Danny!" he called. "Come and see! Our home has Brownies again! We are so lucky!" And laughter filled their home.

If you listen, you can still hear them chanting:

❋ **Twist me and turn me and show me an Elf.**
   I looked in the water and saw myself!

MULTIPLE INTELLIGENCE ACTIVITIES FOR . . .

The Brownies and the Tailor

 The Dance of the Brownies.
(Musical-Rhythmic; Bodily-Kinesthetic)

For a warm-up exercise, have the group stand in a circle and pantomime washing windows, dusting, washing dishes, ironing clothes, making a fire, cooking dinner, etc. Play the music "Rondo Alla Turca" from *Mozart in Motion,* Volume 3 of *The Mozart Effect: Music for Children,* or any similar sprightly music. Lead the class in pantomiming being a troop of Brownies sneaking into the house and doing different chores until the father comes in and discovers them as they scurry away.

 Twist Me and Turn Me.
(Interpersonal; Bodily-Kinesthetic)

As a class, discuss different ways Brownies could help in the classroom, at school, or at home. Make a list or draw pictures of some of these ideas that would help make life more pleasant. Play some reflective music in the background and give the students some time to think of other ideas. Draw or print these ideas under the categories of Home, School, and Classroom. Cut out stars in three different colors to represent each category. Paste the ideas on the stars. Next, place a large Mylar (nonbreakable) mirror in the corner of the room and decorate it with grass, leaves, and plants to make the Brownie's pond. Spread the stars with the Brownie deeds over the mirror. Choose however many students you wish to participate in a daily or weekly choosing ceremony. You may use the whole class at once or take turns. Gather the class around the "pond." Blindfold the children one at a time, or have them cover their eyes with their hands, while the class chants the Brownie rhyme found in the story. Have each student look into the "pond" and choose a star with its good deed. At the end of the day or week, have the class meet and share their good deeds, what they observed, and if they were seen. The "good deed star" is then pinned up on the bulletin board with the student's name on it.

The Rhyming Song.
(Verbal-Linguistic; Musical-Rhythmic)

Explore what makes a rhyme. Discuss how the children tried to discover different rhymes for Elf in the story. What other methods could they have used? This can lead into a unit on rhymes.

Using the following song as a model, encourage the students to fill in the last stanza of the tune with their own ideas. The model offers the name of an animal (using three or four syllables), doing or wearing something that rhymes with the animal's name (again, using three or four syllables). A discussion of syllables may be in order with the use of hand clapping and tambourines so that the children can feel the rhythm of the rhyme. A few examples are included.

The rhyme follows the first few stanzas of the tune "Turkey in the Straw."

Words by Jeanne M. Donato

Well I went to the pond / One moonlit night
To dance with the Brownies / And see the sights!
But when I got there / I had to stare
At a _____ [an animal using three or four syllables]
[Wearing or doing something in three or four syllables.] _____.

Examples:

1. At a lit tle old fly (Four syllables)
   Wear ing a tie. (Four syllables)

2. At great big ants
   Wear ing red pants.

3. At a pur ple whale.
   Tel ling a tale.

4. At a flock of crows
   Tap ping their toes.

MAY CHAPTER RESOURCES

Aardema, V. (1984). *Oh, Kojo! How could you!* New York: Scholastic.

Appelt, K. (1999). *Someone's come to our house.* Grand Rapids, MI: Eerdmans.

Babitt, N. (1994). *Bub or the very best thing.* New York: HarperCollins.

Bailey, C. S. (1987). *The little rabbit who wanted red wings.* New York: Platt & Munk.

Bartone, E. (1993). *Peppe the lamplighter.* New York: Lothrop, Lee & Shepard.

Behrens, J. *Soon Ling finds a way.* San Carlos, CA: Golden Gate.

Bradby, M. (1995). *More than anything else.* New York: Scholastic.

Brown, M. W. (1942). *The runaway bunny.* New York: Harper & Row.

Brown, M. W. (1947). *Goodnight moon.* New York: Harper & Row.

Bunting, E. (1978). *Magic and the night river.* New York: Harper & Row.

Bunting, E. (1986). *The mother's day mice.* New York: Clarion Books.

Burton, V. (1942). *The little house.* New York: Houghton Mifflin.

Campbell, D. (1997). *The Mozart effect: Music for children: Vol 3. Mozart in Motion.* Pickering, ON: The Children's Group.

Chorao, K. (1977). *Lester's overnight.* New York: Dutton.

Curtis, J. L. (1996). *Tell me again about the night I was born.* New York: Joanna Cotler.

De Paola, T. (1973). *Nana upstairs and Nana downstairs.* New York: Puffin.

De Paola, T. (1981). *Fin M'Coul.* New York: Scholastic.

Eastman, P. D. (1960). *Are you my mother?* New York: HarperTrophy.

Eastman, P. D. (1968). *The best nest.* New York: Random House.

Edens, C., & Lane, D. (1994). *Shawnee bill's enchanted five-ride carousel.* New York: Simon & Schuster.

Flack, M. (1960). *Ask Mr. bear.* New York: Macmillan.

Freeman, D. (1968). *Corduroy.* New York: Viking.

Gag, W. (1956). *Millions of cats.* New York: Scholastic.

Gardella, T. (1993). *Just like my dad.* New York: Trumpet Club.

Gaylord-Porter, L. (1991). *I love my daddy because....* New York: Dutton.

Gaylord-Porter, L. (1991). *I love my mommy because....* New York: Dutton.

Geil, K. M. (1992). *Grandma according to me.* New York: Doubleday.

Girl Scouts of the United States of America. (1986). The brownie. In *Brownie/girl scout handbook.* New York: Author.

Greenfield, E. (1988). *Grandpa's face.* New York: Trumpet Club.

Hill, E. (1994). *Spot bakes a cake.* New York: Putnam.

Hoffman, M. (1991). *Amazing grace.* New York: Scholastic.

Johnston, T. (1985). *The quilt story.* New York: Putnam.

Joose, B. (1991). *Mama, do you love me?* San Francisco: Chronicle.

Keats, E. Z. (1973). *Over in the meadow.* New York: Four Winds.

Krasner, S. (1994). *Why not call it cow juice?* East Greenwich, RI: Gorilla.

McCloskey, R. (1969). *Make way for ducklings.* New York: Puffin.

McCloskey, R. (1948). *Blueberries for Sal.* New York: Viking.

McDermott, G. (1972). *Anansi the spider.* New York: Holt.

McDermott, G. (1990). *Tim O'Toole and the wee folk.* New York: Viking Penguin.

McDermott, G. (1986). *Daniel O'Rourke.* New York: Viking Penquin.

McGovern, A. (1967). *Too much noise.* New York: Scholastic.

McPhail, D. (1990). *Lost!* Boston: Little, Brown.

Munsch, R. (1980). *Love you forever.* Ontario, Canada: Firefly.

Munsch, R. (1986). *Siempre te querré.* Ontario, Canada: Firefly.

O'Neill, M. (1961). *Hailstones and halibut bones.* New York: Doubleday.

Polacco, P. (1988). *The keeping quilt.* New York: Simon & Schuster.

Polacco, P. (1993). *Babushka Baba Yaga.* New York: Scholastic.

Potter, B. (1993). *The tale of Peter Rabbit.* Lincolnwood, IL: Weber.

Raffi. (1988). *Down by the bay.* New York: Crown.

Sciezka, J. (1989). *The true story of the three little pigs.* New York: Scholastic.

Sendak, M. (1963). *Where the wild things are.* New York: HarperCollins.

Sierra, J. (1993). *The legend of knockmany.* New York: Scholastic.

Steig, W. (1969). *Sylvester and magic pebble.* New York: Scholastic.

Tompert, A. (1990). *Grandfather Tang's story.* New York: Crown.

Trivizas, E. (1993). *The three little wolves and the big bad pig.* New York: Scholastic.

Turow, R. (1977). *Daddy doesn't live here anymore.* Matteson, IL: Great Lakes Living Press.

Viorst, J. (1971). *The tenth good thing about Barney.* New York: Macmillan.

Viorst, J. (1972). *Alexander and the terrible, horrible, no good, very bad day.* New York: Atheneum.

Waber, B. (1972). *Ira sleeps over.* Boston: Houghton Mifflin.

Waters, K. (1993). *Samuel Eaton's day.* New York: Scholastic.

Wells, R. (1995). *Lassie come home.* New York: Holt.

Wells, W. (1985). *Hazel's amazing mother.* New York: Scholastic.

Wescott, N. B. (1988). *Down by the bay.* New York: Crown.

White, E. B. (1976). *The trumpet of the swan.* New York: Scholastic.

White, E. B. (1945). *Stuart little.* New York: HarperCollins.

Williams, V. B. (1990). *More, more, more said the baby.* New York: Greenwillow.

Williams, V. (1982). *A chair for my mother.* New York: Greenwillow.

Wood, A. (1984). *The napping house.* San Diego, CA: Harcourt Brace.

CHAPTER 9

June

Music and Poetry

SUMMER SUN

GREAT is the sun, and wide he goes
Through empty heaven without repose;
And in the blue and glowing days
More thick than rain he showers his rays.

Though closer still the blinds we pull
To keep the shady parlour cool,
Yet he will find a chink or two
To slip his golden fingers through.

The dusty attic, spider-clad,
He, through the keyhole, maketh glad;
And through the broken edge of tiles
Into the laddered hay-loft smiles.

Meantime, his golden face around
He bares to all the garden ground,
And sheds a warm and glittering look
Among the ivy's inmost nook.

Above the hills, along the blue,
Round the bright air with footing true,
To please the child, to paint the rose,
The gardener of the World, he goes.

–Robert Louis Stevenson

School's out! Music dances in the air and poetry fills the soul. June is strawberry picking and the sweet, fragrant aroma of honeysuckle. June is bicycling and chasing butterflies under skies of brilliant blue.

This month is alive with the storytelling methods of Puppetry, Musical, Balloon, and Group Role-Play. Songs and stories happily intertwine with surprises and fun.

Youngsters benefit from engaging in Visual-Spatial, Naturalistic, Interpersonal, Verbal-Linguistic, Bodily-Kinesthetic, Logical-Mathematical, and Musical-Rhythmic areas of multiple intelligence.

Enrich your storytelling repertoire with the joys of music and poetry this month!

TIPS FOR THE TELLER

Rattlin' Bog
Retold and Adapted by Jeanne M. Donato

STORYTELLING METHOD
Balloon/Musical

Child is a balloon tree.

This traditional story-song's repetitive structure builds upon cumulative verses and frees the listener to anticipate and participate in its telling. Done for the sheer fun of the gathering details and rousing tune, rote memory is developed. This process aids the listener, through repetition, to lay down neural pathways of communication between the left and right hemispheres of the brain. For some students this will be a challenge. For all of the students it will be fun as they learn through play. Using the Balloon Storytelling method to introduce this song to children adds to the fun, as they are called upon to step forward with their balloons and act out the roles of the bog, the tree trunk, limbs, branches, and a leaf, as well as a nest, an egg, and a bird.

In order to proceed with the balloon aspect of the storytelling, count out and inflate enough 260s, which are balloons designed for making balloon animals, for each student to have one. Leave a one-inch tip uninflated in each. Use mostly green, yellow, and brown balloons to suggest colors found in a bog.

For the tree trunk, take three separate brown 260s. Inflate them, leaving a one-inch tip on the end of each balloon. Knot the nozzle and tip together to form a circle. These three circles will fit over the student's body, suggesting the rings and bark of a tree's trunk.

Two or three limbs should be sufficient for a tree-like look. Two or three students will hold up the limbs when called for. Inflate the 260s, leaving a one-inch uninflated tip at the ends. Tie, twist, or knot three brown 260s together at the nozzle ends. Braid these three strands. At the end of the strand twist the three 260s together, turning at least three times. You may want to pull one of the ends through the last opening of the braid to lock it tightly in place and prevent it from untwisting. Have the students decide where these limbs would best be placed around the "tree student" for the best view and tree-like shape.

The branches are single green or multicolored 260s. A few students holding two or three balloon branches near the limbs will give the suggestion of tree branches.

The use of one leaf helps focus the activity on the objects following it. Inflate a 260, leaving one-inch tip at the end. To make a leaf, tie the nozzle and tip of the green 260 together, forming a circle. Fold the circle in half lengthwise with the tied ends together at one end. Squeeze the opposite end several times. The warmth from your hand along with squeezing the air will make a pointed end and

continued

TIPS FOR THE TELLER *continued*

suggest a leaf. During the appropriate verse one student holds the leaf over one of the branches. Consider the height that the branch and limb should be held at to accommodate the other students who will hold up the nest, egg, and bird.

The nest is a braid formed like the limb is, but twist and knot the tip and nozzle ends together to form a circle. This is to be held over the balloon leaf when called for.

The egg is simply a small round balloon inflated to a 4- to 6-inch size. The student may step forward to show the egg right before the end of the chorus to act as a memory prompt for the newest item to be added.

Teller singing the repetitive song "Rattlin' Bog."

Making a balloon nest.

Inflating a 260, leaving a two-inch tip uninflated, forms the bird. You may simply fold the 260 in half and curve each side to suggest wings. The student may hold the 260 by pinching the middle with his or her hand. The hand becomes the body of the bird. Any color may be selected.

A large plastic garbage bag is an excellent place to store the inflated balloons until you need them. Take two uninflated 260s and tie them together until they form a circle like a large rubber band. Place this around the outside of the plastic bag. It will help contain the balloons and keep them from floating out of the bag.

It is best to go over ground rules for respecting other people's space and place before distributing the balloons and beginning the song. This will encourage group cooperation and reduce the possibility of the bog balloons being used to distract other students. Have the students being the bog practice by "rattlin'" and waving to give the illusion of the bog moving and swaying. Going over the placement of the students portraying the different parts of the bog and tree will help the story flow. Introduce the story, with the text provided, and sing it through the first time without the balloons. Students will join in the singing of the chorus—and perhaps even the verses!—as they discover the cumulative pattern.

The second time, form the different objects out of the balloons and ask for volunteers to act out the parts of the story when called for. Have the students hold their object out of sight or on the floor until needed. It works smoothly if the students who are portraying the tree trunk, limbs, branches, nest, egg, and bird balloons sit on the floor behind a line of students who will be holding up their balloons to make up the "rattlin' bog." The student who is going to be presenting the next object should stand up and hold up his or her balloon part as the chorus is just ending. This will serve as a memory prompt for students to follow along as everyone joins in. After a few

continued

TIPS FOR THE TELLER *continued*

rounds, rhythm instruments can be added. Use of an autoharp or guitar or singing a cappella with a tambourine are all natural extensions that enrich the telling.

Before beginning the song, the Teller may want to establish a signal such as a nod of the head or a hand gesture to indicate that everyone can join in singing the chorus. An asterisk is used in the text for both the chorus and the individual parts to indicate to the Teller when the students participate. The text of the chorus is printed on the chalkboard or a flip chart in advance so that the audience can easily see their parts.

Now you are ready to start!

Rattlin' Bog

(The Teller should begin with the following instruction.)

The *Rattlin' Bog* is a traditional story-song, that came to the United States with immigrants from Scotland and Ireland. To start this story-song, I will need your help and cooperation.

First of all, can anyone define the word bog? A bog is made up of plant material that has decomposed and formed uneven layers. It looks like an open stretch of wet, soft, spongy ground. A bog builds up and grows over stagnant ponds, marshes, and some solid ground. This ground cover compresses to form peat. When peat is cut into sections and dried out it can be burned as fuel in fireplaces. Peat, or turf, fires are smokier than wood-burning fires. But in Scotland and Ireland, wood is scarce and too expensive for use in a house's open fireplace.

On a bog, the ground underneath would literally shift, shake, or sink, "rattling" as you walked along. The people who lived near these bogs were wise to the lay of the land. They knew where it was safe to walk. They were familiar with the paths and with the patches of solid ground, and they could avoid the mud holes and quicksand that would trap and swallow an unwary traveler.

Only the very bravest or most foolhardy of souls would dare to travel the bogs at night. The people imagined that all sorts of fearsome things roamed above and below the bog. Many people feared digging for peat even in the daylight until they learned to respect and appreciate the bog. For them it was a means of making a living. They came to appreciate the natural beauty found out in the bog. Rare is a word they used to mean beautiful. To calm any uneasiness and pass the time while working to gather peat they used to sing this rousing cumulative story-song, adding verses as they went.

Rattlin' Bog

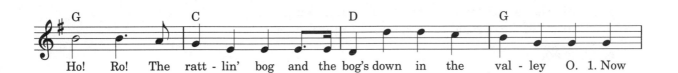

Ho! Ro! The ratt-lin' bog and the bog down in the val-ley O,

Ho! Ro! The ratt-lin' bog and the bog's down in the val-ley O. 1. Now

in that bog there was a tree, a rare tree, a ratt-lin' tree; The

tree's in the bog And the bog's down in the val-ley O. Ho! Ro! The

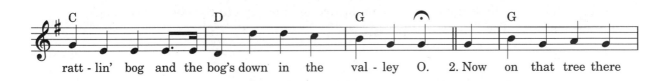

rat-lin' bog and the bog's down in the val-ley O, Ho! Ro! The

ratt-lin' bog and the bog's down in the val-ley O. 2. Now on that tree there

was a limb, a rare limb, a ratt-lin' limb. The limb's on the tree And the

tree's in the bog And the bog's down in the val-ley O.

* This measure is repeated an additional time for each verse.

Rattlin' Bog

Chorus:

✽ Ho! Ro! the rattlin' bog,
And the bog down in the valley oh
Ho! Ro! the rattlin' bog,
And the bog down in the valley-O.

1. Now in that bog there was a ✽**tree**, a rare tree, a rattlin' tree.
   The tree's in the bog and the bog's down in the valley-O.

✽**(Chorus)**

2. Now on that tree, there was a ✽**limb**, a rare limb, a rattlin' limb
   The limb's on the tree and the tree's in the bog and the bog's down in the valley-O.

✽**(Chorus)**

3. Now on that limb there was a ✽**branch**, a rare branch, a rattlin' branch.
   The branch's on the limb and the limb's on the tree and the tree's in the bog and the
   bog's down in the valley-O.

✽**(Chorus)**

4. Now on that branch there was a ✽**twig**, a rare twig, a rattlin' twig.
   The twig's on the branch and the branch's on the limb and the limb's on the tree and the
   tree's in the bog and the bog's down in the valley-O.

✽**(Chorus)**

5. Now on that twig there was a ✽**nest**, a rare nest, a rattlin' nest.
   The nest's on the twig and the twig's on the branch and the branch's on the limb and the
   limb's on the tree and the tree's in the bog and the bog's down in the valley-O.

✽**(Chorus)**

6. Now in that nest, there was an ✽**egg**, a rare egg, a rattlin' egg.
   The egg's in the nest and the nest's on the twig and the twig's on the branch and the
   branch's on the limb and the limb's on the tree and the tree's in the bog and the bog's
   down in the valley-O.

✽**(Chorus)**

7. Now on that egg, there was a ✽**bird**, a rare bird, a rattlin' bird.
   The bird's on the egg and the egg's in the nest and the nest's on the twig and the twig's
   on the branch and the branch's on the limb and the limb's on the tree and the tree's in
   the bog and the bog's down in the valley-O.

✽**(Chorus)**

("Rattlin' Bog Song" from the Oral Tradition. Melody line arranged by Jean Liepold.)

MULTIPLE INTELLIGENCE ACTIVITIES FOR . . .

Rattlin' Bog

 1 **A Dandy Bog Salad.**
(Naturalistic; Visual-Spatial)

The common dandelion is a native of Europe and is naturalized all over America. Its edible parts include the young leaves and the unopened flower buds. The leaves are rich in iron and vitamin C.

Pioneers had to learn to adapt their eating to make use of the plants native to their location. Discuss and research different wild and natural foods that grow native to your area. Collect old recipes that incorporated the natural native plants grown in your area.

Dandelions can be picked throughout the growing season, but the young tender leaves are the best. Locate areas that have dandelions. Make sure the area has not been sprayed with pesticides. Collect the necessary materials. Choose a day to fresh-pick the dandelions, mix them up, and enjoy a "dandy" salad.

 Dandy Bog Salad

Utensils needed: a basket for collecting the greens, a large mixing bowl, salad fork and spoon to toss and serve the salad, colander, paper towels, paring knife, cutting board, lidded glass jar (8- to 12-ounce size), measuring cup, spoons, and enough napkins, paper plates, and plastic forks for the class. Don't forget to take along a camera with film to record the day!

Ingredients needed: enough fresh-picked dandelion greens for the class, a variety of leaf lettuce, 1 can of chickpeas (drained), sliced cucumbers and tomatoes, a small onion or fresh scallions, 1 clove of garlic or fresh-picked wild garlic, 1 cup of cold-pressed olive oil, 6 tablespoons of balsamic vinegar, a dash of sea salt, and ground peppercorns.

Dressing recipe: (Students may make this with supervision.) Cut up some wild garlic and onion.

If not available, cut up scallions and a clove of garlic. Add these to 5 to 6 tablespoons of balsamic vinegar mixed with 1 cup of cold-pressed olive oil. Add a dash of sea salt and a twist of ground peppercorns. Shake and let stand overnight in a sealed glass jar.

Salad recipe: Gather the tender, young dandelion greens, wash them, drain in a colander, and pat dry. You may also add sliced tomatoes, chickpeas, cucumber, watercress, and different varieties of leaf lettuce. Shake the jar of oil and vinegar. Pour over the salad. Toss and serve!

 2 **You've Got to Have a Habitat.**
(Naturalistic; Interpersonal)

A bog is a quagmire, a piece of wet, soft, and spongy ground where the soil is composed mainly of decaying and decayed plant life, peat being an example.

A bog is just one of many habitats. Look around you. List all of the habitats in your area; for example, city, garden, woodland, desert, farm, mountain, seashore, swamp, pond, polar, etc. Get ready to explore, observe, and understand the animals and plants that live in habitats in your area.

Arrange to share your observations and findings with another school in a different part of the country. Offer to exchange with them the information you collect on the habitats in your area. Write letters sharing your observations.

Observation materials you will need: appropriate clothing, binoculars, camera, magnifying glass, storage containers, plastic zip-lock bags, a field guidebook, and a field notebook for sketching animals and plants, recording notes and details of the conditions, and describing places you visit. In the classroom you will need an index card file to store your notes in alphabetical order, a supply of lined index cards on which to write your observations, and an area to assemble and display your findings. File cards may include information such as type of habitat, place, date, time, weather conditions, plant or animal observed, its scientific name, description, and how it moved or where it grew, along with any other special observations.

Make a mural of each habitat you observe. Include the plants and animals you observe. As a class write a letter describing the habitat. Locate the habitat on a map; include some pictures taken on your field trips.

Remember that it is important to protect our habitats. Use common sense, dress sensibly for your field observations, make no unnecessary noise, return everything to its rightful place, do not litter, be wise, and use your eyes.

3 Be a Bog!
(Musical-Rhythmic; Verbal-Linguistic)

After you have become familiar with the story-song about *Rattlin' Bog*, practice it in different groups, taking turns using rhythm instruments, singing, and becoming the bog, tree, etc. with the balloons.

Write invitations to another classroom, parents, or several classes, to share your story-song. Follow the preparations for the first telling in the Tips for the Teller section. Take pictures for your classroom scrapbook and display.

TIPS FOR THE TELLER

Little Bunny Foo Foo
Retold and Adapted by Susan Trostle Brand

STORYTELLING METHOD

Puppetry/Musical

This simple but enchanting story invites musical audience participation. Told with papier mâché, sock, or sewn fabric puppets, the story's main theme is good versus naughty. Specifically, the good fairy gives three warnings to Bunny Foo Foo to stop bopping various animals on the head. However, when the Bunny does not heed the fairy's warnings, he pays the consequences and learns that he is "Hare today and Goon tomorrow!"

Before beginning to tell the story, the Teller may sing the recurring song, which may also be written on a nearby chart, for the children. The Teller may inform them that if they listen for the words, "And you know what happened next, don't you?" and the words, "And the good fairy sang...," they will know when to chime in on the song. An asterisk indicates the text that the audience sings. Then the Teller and the children practice the song before the Teller(s) hide behind a puppet stage to enact this amusing and captivating story. Developmentally, preschool and young primary school-aged children are especially fond of this simple story.

The book *Little Rabbit Foo Foo,* by Michael Rosen, may be introduced either before or after the puppet show. Since children will be familiar with this story and song, they will enjoy reading it themselves or with buddy readers. You may also provide puppets for the children to use during their subsequent retellings of the story. Characters include the Bunny, animals, the Good Fairy, a Goon, and a narrator.

Little Bunny Foo Foo

Narrator: Once, in a deep green forest, on a bright summer day, there hopped a naughty little bunny. His name was Bunny Foo Foo. He liked to eat carrots. *(Bunny appears, munching a carrot.)* He liked to hop and explore and sniff the grass. *(Bunny hops and sniffs.)* But he had one very bad habit. He liked to bop lots of other little harmless animals on the head! Now, the Good Fairy saw Little Bunny Foo Foo. And what she saw did not make her very happy at all!

So she told him one day that he must stop bopping animals on the head. But the next day, down flew the Good Fairy. And she noticed that Little Bunny Foo Foo was still up to his mischievous behavior. *(enter three field mice)* Three field mice came along. And you know what happened, don't you?

✽Little Bunny Foo Foo, hopping through the forest, scooping up the field mice and bopping them on the head!

And the Good Fairy sang:

Fairy: ✽Little Bunny Foo Foo, I don't like your attitude, scooping up the field mice and bopping them on the head! *(Bunny swoops up field mice and bops them each on the head.)* I'll give you three chances. And then, if you still have not learned to behave, I will turn you into a GOON! *(exit field mice)*

Bunny Foo Foo: Okay, Good Fairy. You are right. I am wrong. I will never bop another animal on the head as long as I live!

Narrator: But Little Bunny Foo Foo soon forgot his promise to the Good Fairy. Along came some wiggly worms. And you know what happened, don't you? *(enter wiggly worms)*

✽Little Bunny Foo Foo, hopping through the forest, scooping up the wiggly worms and bopping them on the head! *(Bunny bops worms)*

Narrator: The Good Fairy was not pleased. She flew down to Little Bunny Foo Foo and the wiggly worms. And the Good Fairy sang:

Good Fairy: ✽Little Bunny Foo Foo, I don't like your attitude, scooping up the wiggly worms and bopping them on the head! I will give you two more chances to behave properly. If you do not, I will turn you into a GOON! *(exit worms)*

Bunny Foo Foo: I am SO sorry, Good Fairy! I promise you, I will NEVER, EVER bop another animal on the head.

Narrator: But the next day, along came some blue birds. And you know what happened, don't you?

(enter blue birds)

✽Little Bunny Foo Foo, hopping through the forest, scooping up the blue birds and bopping them on the head! *(Bunny bops blue birds)*

Narrator: Down flew the Good Fairy. She wanted to see the Bunny and the poor, harmless blue birds. And the Good Fairy sang:

Good Fairy: ✱**Little Bunny Foo Foo, I don't like your attitude, scooping up the blue birds and bopping them on the head!** I caught you again, Little Bunny Foo Foo! You have not kept your promises to me. I will give you only one more chance. And if you do not behave, I will turn you into a GOON! *(exit blue birds)*

Bunny Foo Foo: Oh, Good Fairy, please forgive me. I promise to NEVER, EVER bother another living creature. You have my word.

Narrator: But the next day, Little Bunny Foo Foo noticed some friendly frogs leaping by the edges of the forest, near the bubbling brook. He remembered the warning from the Good Fairy. But he just couldn't resist those friendly frogs. And you know what happened, don't you?

(enter friendly frogs)

✱**Little Bunny Foo Foo, hopping through the forest, scooping up the friendly frogs and bopping them on the head!** *(Bunny bops frogs)*

Narrator: Now, as you might imagine, the Good Fairy was very displeased. She flew down to see Bunny Foo Foo and those poor friendly frogs. And the Good Fairy sang:

Good Fairy: (holding magic wand) ✱**Little Bunny, Foo Foo, I don't like your attitude, scooping up the friendly frogs and bopping them on the head!** I gave you three chances to behave. But you chose to be naughty, instead. So now, I will have to keep MY promise and turn you into a **GOON!** *(exit frogs)* POOOOOOOOOFFFFFFFFFF! *(Magic wand touches bunny; exit bunny and fairy; enter large, gruesome goon)*

Narrator: And the moral of this story is:

HARE TODAY...GOON TOMORROW!

MULTIPLE INTELLIGENCE ACTIVITIES FOR . . .

Little Bunny Foo Foo

 ### **1** **Bunny Hop Tag.**
(Bodily-Kinesthetic; Interpersonal)

Instruct the children to play a unique game of tag, in which each child is a bunny, and five children are Good Fairies. When the Good Fairy tags a bunny, the tagged child, face down, makes a body bridge in which the hands and feet are spread apart and touching the ground. This child stays in this bunny position until another bunny hops underneath him or her. At this time, the bunny is "rescued" and free to hop again. If any bunny needs a rest during this fun-filled game of cooperation, he or she simply curls into a tight "ball" on

the ground for a maximum of thirty seconds. Be sure to alternate Good Fairies so that everyone gets a turn to be the "tagger!" (Some folks also call this type of tag Frog Tag or Turtle Tag.)

 ### **2** **Bunny Baskets.**
(Visual-Spatial; Logical-Mathematical)

To accompany the story about a naughty rabbit, children enjoy constructing spring or summer baskets from clean, empty milk cartons. Have the children lay milk cartons on their sides so that the edges of the triangle formed by the tops on the unopened sides are flat on the table. Then, with the help of an adult, children may cut into two sides of the milk carton to form a square, so that there is a basket-type opening for straw, grass, or torn-up pieces of paper. To make the head, push the open spout of the milk carton all the way out so that the triangle sticks up on top. The ridge that remains is taped down so that the children can glue on decorations. Have the children cut out and attach bunny ears to the top of the head. Add pink felt to the insides of the ears, and glue on rolling eyes, pipe cleaner whiskers, and pom-pom noses. Youngsters count out and glue 30 cotton balls on each side of the rabbit and another 30 cotton balls on the edges of the top, head, ears, rear, and tail. Later, the children can fill each basket with paper straw.

Before filling the rabbit baskets with straw, the children can gather in small groups to create number stories using small prizes, counters, or candies to fill their gift baskets. For example, Carlos tells Anna, "Your rabbit eats five red candies. Next she eats four blue candies. Finally, she eats three yellow candies. (Anna places candies as Carlos names them.) How many candies did your rabbit eat in all? (Anna counts them and replies, "12 candies!")

③ Magic Wands.
(Verbal-Linguistic; Musical-Rhythmic)

Create a sparkling magic wand using a cardboard star shape secured to a ruler or dowel rod. Display a stuffed "Rabbit Foo Foo." Brainstorm with the children about different types of animals they observe on a nature walk. Also, ask them to think of scary creatures and list them in

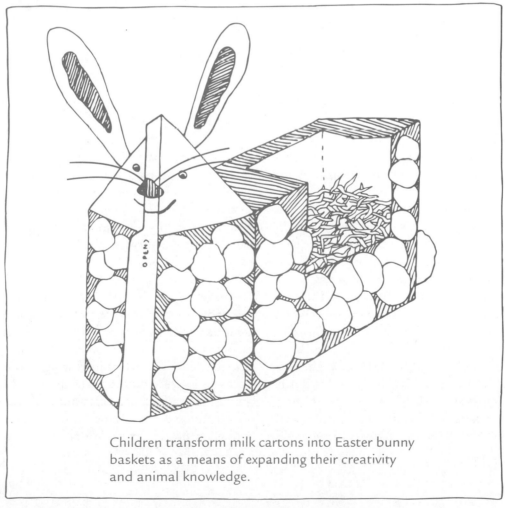

Children transform milk cartons into Easter bunny baskets as a means of expanding their creativity and animal knowledge.

A Bunny Basket.

181

separate columns on a large chart. The children substitute the animal of their choice as they re-sing the song. Then, using the magic wand, they pretend to transform Rabbit Foo Foo into another creature or animal, just as the Good Fairy transformed Bunny Foo Foo into a Goon. You can type a work page for them where they can fill in the names of the substituted animals before singing the song. Then, invite the young-sters to sing:

"Little Rabbit Foo Foo I don't want to see you, scooping up the _____ (name animal) _____ and bopping them on the head! I'll give you three chances, and if you don't behave, I'll turn you into a _____ (name creature) _____ !"

Note: The music and words to "Little Bunny Foo Foo" can be found on the *Wee Sing Silly Songs* cassette and booklet by Pamela Beall and Susan Hagen Nipp. The song is sung to the tune of "Down by the Station."

TIPS FOR THE TELLER

It Could Be Worse!
Retold and Adapted by Susan Trostle Brand

STORYTELLING METHOD

Group Role-Play/Musical

Retold and adapted from a traditional tale, *It Could Be Worse!* depicts a Yid-dish family that, in the ears of the father, is too noisy. Much to the father's dis-may, the local rabbi whom he consults about his problem, provides puzzling advice. He tells the old man to go home and add chickens, a rooster, and a goose to his hut. When things do not improve, the rabbi tells the man to bring a goat into his hut. Life is much noisier still, and yet the rabbi tells the man to add a cow to his menagerie of animals and people in the hut. Bewildered, the man does as he is told. When life becomes unbearable, the man returns in desperation to the rabbi. Stroking his long, white beard, he tells the man to go home and let out all of the animals. Although his hut is now the same as it was when the story begins, the man realizes that his life is peaceful, quiet, and uncrowded. The man returns to the rabbi to thank him for improving his life, realizing that, "it could be worse!"

It Could be Worse! provides an ideal format for group dramatic role-play with music. In this text, the story is adapted for Musical Sto-rytelling by substituting the playing of musical instruments for the sounds of the animals in the original story. For the first telling, howev-er, the original format is followed, using the original storybook for reference. Invite the children to select the roles of narrator, man, mother, wife, six children, rabbi, four chickens, one rooster, one goose, one goat, and one cow. Rehearse voices and animal sounds with the actors and actresses several times before stag-ing the show so that, increasingly, the din becomes louder and louder as more and more animals are added. Create a hut from a sheet strung along a clothesline. Animal homes are located at nearby "barns" or areas underneath

continued

tables. The rabbi might sit at a card table. As costumes, the rabbi dons a long black robe (perhaps a graduation gown), a wide-brimmed black hat, and a long, white beard and mustache. The wife, mother, and girl children wear long skirts, bandannas in their hair, and bare feet. The boy children wear shirts, colorful cotton trousers with suspenders (optional), and bare feet. The man wears a brown jacket and matching brown hat over his tattered trousers and long boots. For the animals, costumes are constructed from paper bags, fabric, felt, feathers, paper plates, and the like. For a professional-looking production, the narrator may decide to wear a suit and tie or bow tie.

For alternate tellings, substitute friends who play musical instruments for the animals. Provide cymbals, wood blocks, maracas, kazoos, drums, accordions, and other instruments as explained in the following revised story.

It Could Be Worse!

Narrator: Once upon a time, in a small village, a poor unfortunate man lived with his mother, his wife, and his six children in a little one-room hut. It was crowded, and the man and his wife, often argued *(husband and wife argue)*. The man's mother complained *(mother grumbles)*. The children were noisy and they fought *(children pretend to punch and fight)*. The hut was full of crying and quarreling *(noise continues)*. One day, when the poor unfortunate man couldn't stand it any more, he ran to the Rabbi for advice.

Man: Holy Rabbi! Life is in a bad way. And things are getting worse. We are so poor, and we live in a tiny hut. It is crowded, and all day and all night, my wife and I argue, my mother complains, my children fight, and there is *too much noise!*

Rabbi: *(stroking beard)* Is it possible, dear man, that you have some friends? Perhaps these friends play musical instruments?

Man: *(puzzled)* Yes, Rabbi. I do have some friends who are musicians. They play the kazoo, in fact. And one plays the wood blocks!

Rabbi: Ah, fine! Now go to the houses of these friends. Invite them to your home to live with you.

Man: *(looking surprised)* Yes, indeed, Rabbi. *(man visits four friends and invites each to come and live with him. He asks each to bring their kazoo or wood blocks. The man's friends, playing their instruments, follow him into his hut.)*

183

Narrator: When some days or a week had gone by, life in the hut was worse than before. The mother complained. The man and his wife argued. The children fought. And it was hot and crowded. To make things worse, the friends never stopped playing their kazoos and wood blocks (*characters argue and play instuments as they are named*).

Man: *(running to rabbi)* Holy Rabbi! See what a misfortune has befallen me! Now with the crying and quarreling, the complaining and musical instruments, it couldn't be worse! Please help me, Rabbi!

Rabbi: *(looking thoughtful)* Tell me, dear man. Do you happen to have any friends who play the accordion? And perhaps you have a friend or two who play the maracas?

Man: Yes, I have some friends who play the accordion and maracas.

Rabbi: Then hurry to the homes of these friends. Invite them to bring their instruments and come live with you and your family.

Man: Ah, no! Do you really mean it, Rabbi?

Rabbi: Come, come now, my good man, and do as I say at once.

(The man hurries to homes of friends who play accordion and maracas. He invites them to live with him and to bring their instruments. Each friend follows the man, playing his or her instrument.)

Narrator: When some days or a week had gone by, life in the little hut was much worse. Now, with the crying, quarreling, fighting, and complaining (*children, wife, and mother make appropriate noises*), the hut seemed smaller and the children grew bigger. And the sounds of the kazoo, woodblocks, accordion, and maracas was unbearable (*instruments play together loudly*).

Man: *(running to rabbi's table)* Holy Rabbi! Your help I do implore! Now the noise is even worse than before! There's arguing, complaining, fighting. And there's too much noise— kazoos, woodblocks, accordions, and maracas. I am going out of my mind!

Rabbi: *(stroking beard)* Ah, dear man. I hear you. Tell me, do you have any other friends? Perhaps some of them play the drums and the trumpet?

Man: *(fearfully)* Well, yes I do, Rabbi. But.................you don't mean........

Rabbi: Now, dear man. You did come to me for assistance, did you not? Follow my instructions quickly. Go to the homes of these friends. Ask them to bring along their drums and their trumpets and to come and live with you.

Man: Oh, no, surely not, Rabbi!

Rabbi: Do it at once!

(The man trudges to friends' homes and reluctantly invites them to come live with him.)

Narrator: When some days or a week had gone by, life in the hut was very much worse than before. The mother complained. The wife and husband argued. The children fought. The kazoo and the woodblocks, the accordion and maracas, the drums and the trumpet created an awful din. (*characters and instruments make respective **loud** noises*). The man was at his wit's end. He *had* to see the rabbi.

Man: *(at rabbi's table)* Holy Rabbi! Help me! Save me! The end of the world has come! My mother does nothing but complain. My wife and I argue constantly. My children toss and tumble, fighting, all day. And those instruments! *They never stop playing! It is horrible!*

Rabbi: *(pauses thoughtfully before speaking)* Go home now, my poor, unfortunate man. Ask all of your musician friends to leave your hut.

Man: I will! I will! I will do it right away! Oh, thank you Rabbi!

(The man hurries home and asks all his friends to return to their homes with their instruments.)

Narrator: That night, with all the noisy friends and their noisy instruments gone, the poor man and his family slept peacefully. There were no tooting kazoos, no thumping wood blocks, no screeching accordion, nor rattling maracas. There were no blaring trumpets and no pounding drums! The very next day, the man returned to the rabbi.

Man: Holy Rabbi! You have made my life so sweet for me. With only my family in the hut, it's so quiet, so roomy, so peaceful. What a pleasure!

Rabbi: You have learned your lesson well, dear man. From this day on, remember, that as bad as things seem, **"It could be worse!"**

MULTIPLE INTELLIGENCE ACTIVITIES FOR . . .

It Could Be Worse!

 The Barnyard.
(Verbal-Linguistic; Naturalistic)

Visit a local farm or petting zoo. Have the children observe the mannerisms and sounds of various animals. Upon their return, encourage them to participate in the following traditional poem by Maude Burnham, with the children speaking the part of one barnyard animal each, plus the narrator, and the farmer. An asterisk indicates the text to be recited by the children. This text is printed on the chalkboard or a flip chart in advance so that the children can easily see their parts.

The Barnyard

By Maude Burnham

When the Farmer's day is done,

In the barnyard, ev'ry one,

Beast and bird politely say,

✱**"Thank you for my food today,"**

The **cow** says, ✱"Moo!"

The **pigeon**, ✱"Coo!"

The **sheep** says, ✱"Baa!"

The **lamb** says, ✱"Maa!"

The **hen**, ✱"Cluck! Cluck!"

✱"Quack!" says the **duck**;

The **dog**, ✱"Bow Wow!"

The **cat**, ✱"Meow!"

The **horse** says, ✱"Neigh!

I love sweet hay!"

The **pig** near by,

Grunts in his sty.

When the barn is locked up tight,

Then the **Farmer says**, ✱"Good night!"

Thanks his animals, ev'ry one,

For the work that has been done.

Body Beat.
(Bodily-Kinesthetic; Musical-Rhythmic)

Ask the children to stand in a circle as they read and use their bodies to enact this poem.

Body Beat

By Susan Trostle Brand and Jeanne M. Donato

Do you feel the beat?

Now, tap your feet!

Hear the cymbals slam?

Then clap your hands!

Want to shake like jelly?

Now pat your belly!

See the swaying trees?

Then bend you knees!

Feel the body beat......

Feel the body beat......

 Story Frames.
(Verbal-Linguistic; Interpersonal)

Youngsters complete a Fictional Story Frame about the story, *It Could Be Worse!* A **story frame,** which is similar to an outline, provides part of the story for the student, allowing the student to complete the sequential story details in writing. Invite them to share their ideas, noting that different children's Frames may differ slightly, depending upon their interpretations of the story. Then, ask them to think of a problematic situation in their own lives and how it was resolved, and then to think of that life event in terms of a story. The children write factual stories on Factual Story Frames. Later, these their Factual Story Frames provide an excellent outline for process writing and published stories that the young authors create!

Story Frame for Fictional and Factual Life Event Stories

The story takes place _____

_____

_____ .

_____ is a character in the story who _____ .

_____ is another character in the story who _____ .

A problem occurs when _____

_____

After that, _____

and _____

_____ .

The problem is solved when _____

_____

_____ .

The story ends with _____

_____

I learned from this story that _____

_____

_____ .

Story Frame.

TIPS FOR THE TELLER

The Unicorn

Words and Music by Shel Silverstein
Retold and Adapted by Jeanne M. Donato

STORYTELLING METHOD

Musical

The Unicorn captures the ears and imaginations of students. It offers a creative venue for communication in sign language and oral expression. The sheer play and energy that this story-song offers, appeals to the different ways of knowing and opens up many valuable venues for extending the learning benefits.

Following the Musical Storytelling method in Chapter 3, the Teller may want to sing or play the song for the class. Each animal in the chorus is assigned a hand sign to help in remembering the list of animals. The class can make up their own signs for each of the animals or they can do a class research project to look up and use the signs for each of the animals listed in any of the American Sign Language books. The Teller should demonstrate and review the signs for the animals before the telling. Assigning individuals or groups of students to each sign helps in the enjoyment and memory of the animals in the chorus. Before beginning the story-song, the Teller may want to establish a signal such as a nod of the head or hand gesture to indicate that everyone can join in singing the chorus, and a separate signal to indicate when the class will use the animal signs. An asterisk indicates the text that the audience will recite. The words may be handed out to the class, and each group may take a verse to learn and act out as they sing it. Playing with this story-song unleashes many possibilities and variations in the presentation. The Teller may want to introduce this story-song with a short story before singing it.

The Unicorn

A long time ago when the earth was young there lived a man called Noah. As he was walking through the desert the Lord called his name. "Noah! This is the Lord speaking. I am not pleased with the way things are going in this world. I am going to wash everything away with a great flood and start over again. But since you and your family have been so good, I am going to have you build me an ark to keep you and your family safe along with two of all the animals in the world. Then you can start over again."

"Lord," said Noah, "what is an ark?"

"It's a big boat, Noah. I'll give you all the details on how to build it. I need you to round up all of the animals, two by two, nice and orderly. But don't forget my lovely unicorns!"

Noah started to build the ark and round up all of the animals. He found green alligators, long-necked geese, humpty-back camels, chimpanzees, cats and rats and elephants, but as sure as he was born, Noah couldn't find those silly unicorns. They were too busy playing games in the rain to pay attention to Noah. And this is the story-song of what happened to them because they didn't listen.

(The Teller continues: "I will need people to help us remember the signs for each animal that Noah put on the ark. They will help us and we can all help them to remember the signs by doing them together. We decided on the signs for the animals. Can anyone remember the sign for green alligators? Good! Next, we need someone to come up and help with the sign for the long-necked geese. Show me the sign. Very good! Noah got humpback camels. Let's practice that sign together. What comes after the camels? Yes, chimpanzees, you are right! Show me our sign for chimpanzees. Next, we have cats and rats. Who can remember the sign for cat? Very good! And now the sign for rat. Yes, now elephants come next. Show me your sign that show the elephants' trunks. Very good! And last but not least, the unicorn. The unicorn was a large white horse with a large horn growing out of the middle of its forehead. What sign could we use for the unicorn? Good job! Now, let's review all our signs for the animals to help us with our story-song.")

The Teller reviews the signs for the animals and then plays or sings the chorus to introduce the melody. After one more rehearsal singing using the signs it is time to start.

The Unicorn

world was be - ing born, And the love - li - est of all was the U - ni - corn.

Faster, slowly last time

Verse

1. There was green al - li - ga - tors and long - necked geese
   But the Lord seen some sin - nin' and it caused him pain He says

Hump back cam - els and chimp - an - zees Cats and rats and el - e - phants, but
"Stand back, I'm gon - na make it rain. So hey Broth - er No - ah I'll

Fine last time

1. sure as you're born The love - li - est of all was the U - ni - corn

2. tell you what to do Go and build me a float - ing zoo.

"The Unicorn" (Words and music by Shel Silverstein. TRO - © Copyright 1962 [Renewed] 1968 [Renewed] Hollis Music, Inc., New York, NY. Used by permission.).

2. And you take two ✲alligators and a couple of geese,
   Two hump back camels and two chimpanzees,
   Two cats, two rats, two elephants, but sure as you're born,
   Noah, don't you forget my unicorns.
   Now Noah was there and he answered the callin',
   And he finished up the ark as the rain started fallin',
   Then he marched in the animals two by two,
   And he sung out as they went through.

3. Hey Lord, I got you ✲two alligators and a couple of geese,
   Two hump back camels and two chimpanzees,
   Two cats, two rats, two elephants, but sure as you're born,
   Lord I just don't see your unicorns.
   Well, Noah looked out through the drivin' rain,
   But the unicorn was hidin'—playin' silly games,
   They were kickin' and a-splashin' while the rain was pourin',
   Oh them foolish unicorns.

189

4. Then the ducks started duckin' and the snakes started snakin',
   And the elephants started elephantin' and the boat started shakin',
   The mice started squeakin' and the lions started roarin',
   And everyone's aboard but them unicorns.
   I mean the✻two alligators and a couple of geese,
   The hump back camels and the chimpanzees,
   Noah cried, "Close the door 'cause the rain is pourin',
   And we just can't wait for them unicorns.

5. *(Begin with music of Introduction—slowly, ad lib)*
   And then the ark started movin' and it drifted with the tide,
   And the unicorns looked up from the rock and cried,
   And the water came up and sort of floated them away,
   That's why you've never seen a unicorn to this day.
   You'll see✻a lot of alligators and a whole mess of geese,
   You'll see hump back camels and chimpanzees.
   You'll see cats and rats and elephants but sure as you're born,
   You're never gonna see no unicorn.

MULTIPLE INTELLIGENCE ACTIVITIES FOR . . .

The Unicorn

① Author, Author!
(Verbal-Linguistic; Interpersonal)

Some interesting and fun stories and songs have known literary authors but they have been taken in to the oral tradition of a people so that people do not recall who the author is. Copyright laws are a way of giving credit to the originator of the story or song. Ideas cannot be copyrighted, but the style or accompaniment can be. Copyrights credit the author's work by assigning specific rights when it comes to republishing or crediting the work. If you write an original story or song, you may want to officially register your work with the government under a copyright. Some stories and songs are so old, they belong to the oral tradition and may not have a known author. Stories and songs change as they move from the author's print to the oral tradition found in schoolyards, camps, and anywhere people gather.

Have the class play the game "telephone," while seated in a circle. The leader thinks of a specific message and whispers it to the person next to him or her. The message is whispered and passed on around the circle. The student at the end announces the whispered message aloud. The leader confirms if there have been any changes to the message and announces what the original message was. Folktales and songs have a certain element or motif. Their content varies as they take on the customs of the countries to which they migrate, but the motif remains identifiable. Compare the difference between how these folktales have changed and how *The Unicorn* is starting to change. Read, or give a printed version of the song "The Unicorn" and the poem "The Unicorn" to the students. Have them read or listen to see if they can detect where the two start to change. Ask the class if they have ever heard the song sung in a manner different from how they've just sung it. Like the game of "Telephone," this is how stories start to change. More advanced classes may then go to the library and research to find folktales and songs that have changed when found in different countries.

② Did You Hear the News?
(Interpersonal; Verbal-Linguistic)

Have the students pretend to be newspaper reporters who interview the animals (extinct or imaginary) that didn't answer the call to get on the ark. Have the students draw pictures of these animals and tell or write their stories. Publish them in a classroom newspaper, big book, or display them on the wall in newspaper format. Feature one or two reporters and their stories each day.

 ### 3 Math Sleuths.
(Logical-Mathematical; Bodily-Kinesthetic)

How did Ancient Man count and measure? Where did these terms originate?

The class researches and displays examples of counting to ten from different cultures such as: Babylonian, Mayan, Chinese, Egyptian, Greek, and Roman.

Divide the math measurement terms among groups or as a whole class project. Students discuss and list math measurement terms to discover how they got their names and how they were used. For example: the word foot comes from the measure of the king's foot; hands are still used to measure horses; yard came from the measure from the nose to the tip of an outstretched arm; cubits, etc. Decorate the classroom with pictures of other cultures and traditions. Make physical examples of the different measures.

JUNE CHAPTER RESOURCES

Adams, R. (1970). *Fidels.* New York: Lothrop, Lee & Shepard.

Alexander, L. (1967). *The truthful harp.* New York: Holt, Rinehart & Winston.

Appelt, K. (1995). *Bayou lullaby.* New York: Morrow.

Aylor, J. (1992). *Twinkle twinkle little star.* New York: Morrow.

Baer, G. (1989). *Thump, thump, rat-at-tat-tat.* New York: Harper & Row.

Beall, P., & Nipp, S. H. (1988). *Wee sing silly songs.* Los Angeles: Price Stern & Sloan.

Berenstain, S. (1998). *The Berenstain bears go platinum.* New York: Random House.

Bratton, J. W., & Kennedy, J. (1985). *The teddy bear's picnic.* In *The Readers' Digest Children's Songbook* (p. 98). Pleasantville, NY: Reader's Digest.

Carter, D. A. (1992). *Jingle bugs: A merry pop-up book with lights and music.* New York: Simon & Schuster.

Cohn-Livingston, M. (1989). *Dilly dilly piccalilli: Poems for the very young.* New York: Simon & Schuster.

Cravath, L. W. (1998). *Over the river and through the woods.* New York: Harper Festival.

Dobrin, A. (1971). *Scat!* New York: Four Winds.

Fink, C. (1994). *Nobody else like me: Songs that celebrate diversity.* Hollywood, CA: A & M Records.

Gross, R. B. (1974). *The Bremen-town musicians.* Illustrated by Jack Kent. New York: Scholastic.

Hogrogian, N. (1965). *Always room for one more.* New York: Holt, Rinehart & Winston.

Keats, E. J. (1973). *Over the meadow.* New York: Scholastic.

Kessler, E. (1994). *Is there a gorilla in the band?* New York: Simon & Schuster.

Larrick, N. (1991). *Let's do a poem.* New York: Dutton.

Martin, S. C. (1991). *Old mother Hubbard and her wonderful dog.* New York: Farrar, Straus & Giroux.

McGovern, A. (1967). *Too much noise.* New York: Scholastic.

Milne, A. A. (1980). *Pooh's bedtime book.* New York: Dutton.

Moss, L. (1995). *Zin! Zin! A violin.* New York: Simon & Schuster.

Oram, H. (1993). *Out of the blue: Poems about color.* New York: Hyperion.

Palacios, A. (1979). *Los musicos de Brema.* New York: Scholastic.

Potter, B. (1994). *Little treasury of Beatrix Potter nursery rhymes.* New York: Derrydale.

Provost, G. (1994). *Popcorn, popcorn.* New York: Bradbury.

Raffi. (1980). *Baby beluga.* Universal City, CA: MCA.

Raffi. (1987). *The second raffi song book.* New York: Crown.

Raffi. (1987). *Down by the bay.* New York: Crown.

Raffi. (1988). *Wheels on the bus.* New York: Crown.

Rosen, M. (1990). *Little rabbit foo-foo.* Illustrated by A. Robins. London: Walker.

Schulz, C. (1971). *Play it again Charlie Brown.* New York: World.

Silverstein, S. (1981). *A light in the attic.* New York: Harper & Row.

Silverstein, S. (1974). *Where the sidewalk ends.* New York: Harper & Row.

Simms, T. (1967). *Too much noise.* Boston: Houghton Mifflin.

Sweet, M. (1992). *Fiddle-I-fee: A farmyard song for the very young.* Boston: Little, Brown.

Tripp, W. (1995). *Roses are red, violets are blue.* Boston: Little, Brown.

Weidt, M. (1996). *Daddy played music for the cows.* New York: Lothrop, Lee & Shepard.

Zemach, M. (1990). *It could always be worse.* New York: Farrar, Straus & Giroux.

CHAPTER 10

July

America and Americans

JULY IS . . .

July is sunshine, smiles and songs;
July is parades with lively throngs.

July is picnics and Bar-B-Ques;
July is straw hats and new, white shoes.

July is pride in our country's past,
A pride that, through the years, will last.

July is our flag—red, white and blue;
July is loving our land anew.

-SUSAN TROSTLE BRAND

*J*uly marches to the patriotic beat of "America and Americans." Picnics, parades, and fireworks ignite the spirit this month.

As children encounter the Liberty Bell and meet a Yankee Doodle Dandy, Johnny Appleseed, and New England's Ida Lewis, they learn more about their country. Storytelling methods for these tales are Group Role-Play, Adapted Pantomime, Character Imagery, Musical, and Chant.

Festive July multiple intelligence activities include constructing lighthouse keepers and marching in a patriotic jug band. Highlighted are Bodily-Kinesthetic, Logical-Mathematical, Naturalistic, Verbal-Linguistic, Intrapersonal, Interpersonal, Musical-Rhythmic and Visual-Spatial intelligences.

This July, celebrate America through the excitement of storytelling!

TIPS FOR THE TELLER

Johnny Appleseed
Adapted by Susan Trostle Brand

STORYTELLING METHOD

Group Role-Play/Character Imagery/Chant

Johnny Appleseed was the name given to Johnny Chapman, who was a pioneer, healer, and preacher of the Ohio River Valley. Chapman has become a legendary figure in American history because of his dedication to planting apple seeds throughout the Midwest. He accepted almost any amount of money or object in return for his apple seeds and seedlings. Upon Chapman's death in 1845, Sam Houston stood tall in Congress and proclaimed, "Farewell dear old eccentric heart. Your labor has been a labor of love, and generations yet unborn will rise up and call you blessed."

Johnny Appleseed is humorously and poignantly told when the Teller dons a large, upside down pan on the head, an earth-colored belted tunic and matching ragged trousers, a large shoulder pouch for apple seeds, a second pouch for money and objects acquired, and a walking stick. The Teller's feet remain bare.

Brainstorm and print the names of farmers and townspeople on a large chart. An adult or older child becomes Johnny Appleseed. Provide pioneer dress-up clothing and, if desired, construct a covered wagon from a large, empty refrigerator box and a sheet. Of course, you'll want to have apple seeds and apple seedlings on hand to enhance the play! Before beginning the story, the Teller may want to establish a signal such as a nod of the head or a hand gesture to indicate that everyone can join in chanting Johnny's recurring phrase. An asterisk indicates the text that the audience recites. This text is printed on the chalkboard or a flip chart in advance, so that the class or audience can easily see their part.

Group Role-Playing of *Johnny Appleseed*.

Johnny Appleseed

Narrator: This is the story of Johnny Appleseed.

Johnny Appleseed: ✱**Give me money, or give me naught. Apple seeds are what I've got!**

My name's Johnny Chapman, but folks have come to call me Johnny Appleseed, 'cause apples are just about my favorite thing! Sure, I look a little odd, what with this upside down pan on my head and these ragged clothes. But I don't mind. You see, I have a mission in life. I need to help the settlers in their covered wagons. They have a difficult job ahead as they settle in the West. It's my callin' to help these folks! And I also tell them stories about God and His miracles.

(enter family in covered wagon)

Ma: Now, Sarah, quit your whinin'. We'll be in Indiana within three more days. I know you're hungry. But your brother Thomas is hungry, and he's not whinin'. Your Pa and I are hungry, too. We've just gotta be patient and have faith.

Pa: Look ahead. What is that? Why, by thunder, it looks like a man wearin' a pan on his head!

Thomas: *(covering eyes)* I'm scared, Pa.

Sarah: Oh, Tommie—that fellow looks silly, not scary!

Ma: He's throwin' somethin' from his pouch onto the ground. Wonder what it could be?

Thomas: Help! He's comin' closer! *(clings to Ma)*

Johnny: (approaching wagon) Howdy, folks! What are your names? *(all tell names)* No need to be afraid, boy. My name's Johnny Chapman, but folks call me Johnny Appleseed. That's because I'm spreadin' apple seeds all over the land so folks won't go hungry. ✱**Give me money, or give me naught. Apple seeds are what I've got!**

Sarah: Why do you wear that pan on your head, Johnny?

Johnny: That's so's I can cook me own dinner whenever I gets hungry.

Thomas: Where do you sleep, Mr. Johnny?

Johnny: I sleeps under the stars.

Ma and Pa: Where are you headin' Johnny?

Johnny: I'm headin' west, just as far as these ol' legs o' mine'll take me. God has told me to help my fellow man, and that's what I'm intendin' to do! Now, here, take these seedlings. *(Removes seedling plants from bag.)* Set them deep into the earth. Then, with proper care, these seedlings'll become nature's treasures! Why, you can make apple sauce and apple butter!

Sarah: Yes, and apple pie!

Thomas: Right, and apple cobbler! Yum!

Ma: I'll make apple jelly and apple jam. I may even make some delicious apple tarts, or perhaps an apple salad!

Pa: I'll make some tasty apple cider. Johnny, here is twenty cents for your apple seedlings. God bless you and keep you safe!

Johnny: You're very generous! Thank you, and fare thee well, Ma, Pa, Sarah, and young Thomas. And now, I must be movin' on. I've got lots of work to do.

(Johnny walks away reciting chant): ✳**Give me money or give me naught. Apple seeds are what I've got!**

(The play may continue with Johnny meeting more families, if desired)

Narrator: Many years have gone by. Ma, Pa, Sarah, and young Thomas are now safely settled in Indiana.

(family is seated around table)

Ma: Just look outside at those apple orchards! If it weren't for Johnny Appleseed, we might be poor and hungry today.

Pa: Yes, we owe Johnny a great deal. He cared enough to devote his whole life to the good of others.

Sarah: I wish Johnny would visit us here in Indiana!

Thomas: Yes! I'd give him a big slice of this delicious apple pie!

Ma: Remember what Johnny always said?

All: ✳Give me money or give me naught. Apple seeds are what I've got!

Narrator: All across America, people just like Ma, Pa, Sarah, and Thomas, point to apple orchards and say, "Johnny Appleseed planted these trees." Thank you, Johnny Appleseed!

MULTIPLE INTELLIGENCE ACTIVITIES FOR . . .

Johnny Appleseed

 The United States.
(Musical-Rhythmic; Visual-Spatial)

Children will feel pride and a great sense of accomplishment when they learn the words to "The United States" by Pamela Conn Beall and Susan Hagen Nipp. The accompanying *Wee Sing* audio tape is equally delightful and contains many new and favorite songs and quotes about America, such as a John F. Kennedy quote, a Statue of Liberty excerpt, the Preamble to the Constitution, and, of course, the complete "Yankee Doodle!" To accompany the song, display a large map of the United States in a prominent place. Children place stickers or thumb tacks on the states in which the early settlers traveled, especially noting Johnny Appleseed's birthplace (Leominster, Massachusetts) and the site of his plantings in Ohio and Indiana.

The United States

The U-ni-ted States, the U-ni-ted States, I love my coun-try, the

U-ni-ted States. There's Al-a-bam-a, A-las-ka, Ar-i-zo-na, Ar-kan-sas, Cal-i-for-nia, Col-o-ra-do,

Con-nec-ti-cut and Del-a-ware, Flor-i-da, Geor-gia, Ha-wai-i and I-da-ho,

Il-li-nois, In-di-an-a, I-o-wa and Kan-sas. Ken-tuck-y Lou-i-si-an-a,

Maine, Ma-ry-land, Mas-sa-chu-setts, Mich-i-gan, Min-ne-so-ta, Mis-sis-sip-pi, Mis-sour-i, Mon-

-tan-a, Ne-bras-ka, Ne-vad-a, New Hamp-shire, New Jer-sey, New-Mex-i-co, New

York, North 'n' South Car-o-li-na, North Da-ko-ta, South Da-ko-ta, O-hi-o, O-kla-hom',

Or-e-gon, Penn-syl-va-nia, Rhode Is-land, Ten-nes-see, Tex-as, U-tah, Ver-mont, Vir-gin-ia,

West Vir-gin-ia, Wash-ing-ton, Wis-con-sin, Wy-o-ming, The U-ni-ted States, the

U-ni-ted States, I love my coun-try, the U-ni-ted States, Yeah.

197

2 Apple Graphing.
(Logical-Mathematical; Naturalistic)

During a class visit to an apple orchard or farm, purchase several varieties of apples, including Red Delicious, Golden Delicious, Granny Smith, McIntosh, York Imperial, Jonathan, and Winesap. Place sections of each type on labeled trays for the children to sample. Then ask children to place apple stickers labeled with their initials on a bar graph, according to their favorites. Later, compare and contrast apple flavors and favorites. (While slicing, be sure to demonstrate the "magical star" inside the apple, which becomes apparent when the apple is sliced horizontally.) Invite the class to make tasty applesauce with the varieties of apples.

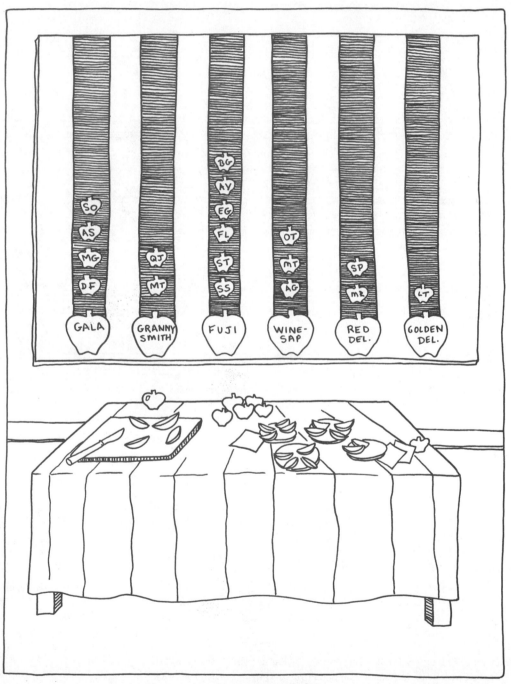

Apple favorites bar graph.

Johnny Appleseed Meets Miss Rumphius.

(Verbal-Linguistic; Intrapersonal)

Read the story of *Miss Rumphius* by Barbara Cooney. After the children have performed the play *Johnny Appleseed,* invite them to compare and contrast Johnny's story with that of Miss Rumphius. Next, have the class write an innovative script for a play for the story of Miss Rumphius, who meets Johnny Appleseed, combining elements of both stories and adding events to create a new story. As a meaningful ending, each child may add what he or she will do to make the world a more beautiful place, using Johnny Appleseed and Miss Rumphius as role models. For example, one child may decide to end the war on hunger; one may fight homelessness; one may promote peace efforts; and another may plan to replace ghettos with art museums and music recital halls.

TIPS FOR THE TELLER

Ida Lewis: Keeper of the Light

By Jeanne M. Donato

STORYTELLING METHOD

Adapted Pantomime/Musical

This original story is about Ida Lewis, a real-life heroine and lighthouse keeper, who lived in Newport Rhode Island. It takes the listener through some of the highlights of her daring rescues. It includes pantomime along with the chorus to further participation.

This story includes ideas from the pantomime and musical models discussed in Chapter 3. Before beginning the story, the Teller may want to establish a signal such as a nod of the head or a hand gesture to indicate that the chorus is approaching and that everyone can join in. An asterisk indicates the text that the audience sings. This text is printed on the chalkboard or a flip chart in advance, so that the audience can easily see their part. The Teller can sing a cappella or use a musical instrument for accompaniment. Have the listeners join in with the singing of the chorus as they pantomime boat rowing motions. Crossing the middle finger over the index finger is the sign for "R". Holding three fingers down into a fist leaving the baby finger extended up is the sign for "I", the initials for Rhode Island. Hooking thumbs under pretend suspenders and moving left to right may suggest a hero. Rehearse the pantomimes with the class.

Displaying sea adventure books, a picture or model of a typical lighthouse (or Ida's lighthouse), a map showing the location of Rhode Island, and other items suggesting a nautical theme would help to set the mood and theme of this story. A picture of Ida may be found at the Web site http://www.vais.net/~cypress/ida.htm. Introduce any vocabulary that might be new for the listeners, such as the words bow, stern, keeper, buoy, trimming wicks, etc.

The Teller may want to show or draw a picture of a rowboat and demonstrate how to pull the oars in rhythm, pulling down into the

continued

TIPS FOR THE TELLER *continued*

water with a push and pull motion using both hands. The Teller may want to knot a towel around the shoulders like Ida, always ready for an emergency. It was considered an "Ida Lewis fashion" to wear a towel tied draped around the shoulders and knotted in front. Invite the listeners to step back in time and note her duties along with her rescues. Introduce the chorus.

Ida Lewis

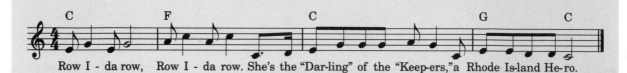

Row I-da row, Row I-da row. She's the "Dar-ling" of the "Keep-ers," a Rhode Is-land He-ro.

"Ida Lewis" (Word and music copyright © 2000 Jeanne M. Donato. Melody line arranged by Jean Liepold.)

Ida Lewis: Keeper of the Light

In 1842, Idawalley Zorada Lewis was born in Newport, Rhode Island. She was named after her Mother and they called her Ida for short. Ida was five years older than her brother Rudy, and then came her little brother Hosea and her sister Hattie.

When Ida was twelve years old, her father, Captain Hosea Lewis, was appointed the keeper of the Lime Rock beacon light. Every evening, Captain Lewis would row the little lifeboat 300 yards out to the Lime Rock, light the beacon, and wait in a shed. At midnight, he would fill the lamp and trim the wick to keep it burning. It was his duty as keeper of the light to stay in the drafty old shed all night in case the light needed tending. At five o'clock in the morning he extinguished the light, prepared the lamp for the evening, polished the brass and lens, and trimmed the wick. When he was finished, he would row back to Newport harbor and walk home to eat breakfast with his family.

On warm summer days he would take the children over to spend the night on the rock while he tended the beacon light. Ida loved to help row the boat.

✤**Chorus:**
Row Ida, row! Row Ida, row!
She's the "Darling" of the "Keepers,"
A Rhode Island Hero!

When Ida was sixteen, her family moved into the brand new lighthouse built on Lime Rock out in the harbor. The only way to get to town was by rowboat.

Lime Rock was just large enough to hold their tiny two-story house with the beacon light attached to it, a small shed, a chicken coop, an outhouse, and a small dock for their boat. There wasn't much room to run around. Yet Ida and her family loved living out on the wide-open harbor.

A few months after they moved in, Captain Lewis suffered a stroke and could not walk without help. Mrs. Lewis and Ida took over the lighthouse keeping duties. That meant that Ida had to drop out of school to help her parents.

She would row the children to school every morning and row back in the afternoon to bring them home. Captain Lewis worried when the seas would churn up during a storm and send giant, freezing waves crashing over the tiny rowboat. The children dried their frozen clothes over the wood-burning stove while their Mother prepared cookies and hot tea for them. Life on the Lime Rock Lighthouse was always an adventure. And the Captain could be heard to brag, "My, but that girl takes to them oars like she was born to it!"

❀Chorus

That first year out in the lighthouse Ida watched four boys fooling around on a small sailboat. One crawled to the top of the mast and rocked the boat until it capsized. Ida was out the door in a flash. She launched the lifeboat and rowed out in time to save all four of the boys from drowning. Nothing was ever said about that daring rescue until many years later.

❀Chorus

Fort Adams lay across the other side of the harbor from the city of Newport. One winter it got so cold that the whole harbor froze up. One foolish soldier from the fort tried to walk across the harbor ice and fell through. Ida grabbed a rope and her boat and slid across the ice to rescue him.

❀Chorus

The next year was a busy one for Ida. Three men were herding an expensive ewe from the Belmont estate. When they got near the harbor the sheep jumped into the water. A heavy gale was blowing and the poor sheep was swept out to sea. The terrified men grabbed a boat and attempted to rescue the ewe but the waves capsized them. Ida rushed to save the grateful men. Then she returned to save the floundering sheep.

Soon after, a man who had stolen and wrecked a boat was rescued by Ida. She could not understand why the man was in such a hurry to leave, until the rightful owner explained what happened.

In November, two soldiers took Rudy's boat to row to Fort Adams. One of them was so nasty that he stomped a hole in the boat and it sank. Again, Ida was off to the rescue.

❀Chorus

Ida loved living and working at the lighthouse. Ida raised chickens. Her brothers fished, and gathered clams and lobster for dinner. Rescuing people was just part of a keeper's job. She thought nothing of it and the rest of the year passed peacefully.

One March night in 1869, things changed, and Ida Lewis's life would never be the same. It was a raw and bitter cold evening. Suffering from a severe cold, Ida was huddled next to the stove when her mother went up to light the lamp. From there Ida's mother could see a small rowboat struggle through the raging winds and capsize in the harbor. As soon as she called out, Ida dashed out of the house in her stocking feet, without even covering her head. She managed to pull the two heavy soldiers aboard her little "Refuge" as she called her boat. Only the boat's pilot was lost before she could reach them. With the help of her brother, Rudy, they dragged the soldiers into the lighthouse, where they revived them. Ida was so cold that her Mother had to cut her frozen stockings off her legs to warm her up.

The two grateful soldiers gave Ida a handsome gold watch and reported her heroism to their commander. Newspapers and magazines spread her picture and story all over the country. America took Ida to its heart as the "Darling of the Keepers."

❋Chorus

One of the rules for lighthouse keepers required the keeper to be courteous and polite to all visitors and show them everything about the station as long as it did not interfere with the lighthouse duties. Keeping a lighthouse required a lot of work, and that became harder to do as news of Ida's fame spread.

That summer, visitors poured in from everywhere, anxious to meet her. Susan B. Anthony, Vice President Colfax, millionaires, theatrical agents, and tourists all visited Ida. Captain Lewis counted over 9,000 people visiting Lime Rock Lighthouse that summer. When President Grant visited, he stumbled and got his ankles wet. It was reported that he said he was willing to get soaked up to his armpits to see Ida Lewis.

There seemed to be no end to the publicity. The "Ida Lewis Waltz" was published and was all the rage. The people of Newport held the Fourth of July parade in her honor. They declared an Ida Lewis Day. The boys wore Ida Lewis caps and the girls wore towels draped around their shoulders like Ida. They presented her with a fancy new lifeboat named the "Rescue." It had red velvet cushions and fancy gold trim. Ida preferred to use her old dependable boat, the "Refuge," for her daily chores.

❋Chorus

The United States government awarded Ida a gold medal of the First Class, the first of its kind ever given to a woman. Of all the medals and honors Ida was awarded, they say the award she cherished most was the silver-plated teapot the soldiers from Fort Adams gave her for saving their fellow comrades.

Congress appointed Ida's mother as the official keeper of Lime Rock Lighthouse and Ida helped as her assistant. When her Mother retired, Congress appointed Ida as the official keeper. Ida continued to perform rescues and tend the light faithfully every night for many years. And the people of Newport harbor slept securely knowing that Ida was there.

When Ida died in 1911, the Rhode Island legislature officially changed the name Lime Rock to Ida Lewis Rock. The Lighthouse Service renamed the lighthouse in her honor. She is the only keeper to have a lighthouse named after her. And the Coast Guard named a new class of buoy tenders for Ida Lewis. Ida's lighthouse was automated and then officially taken from service. It is now the home of the Ida Lewis Yacht Club. Her light is kept burning brightly.

❋Chorus
Row Ida, row! Row Ida, row!
She's the "Darling" of the "Keepers,"
A Rhode Island Hero!

MULTIPLE INTELLIGENCE ACTIVITIES FOR . . .

Ida Lewis: Keeper of the Light

 Cute Keepers.
(Visual-Spatial; Interpersonal)

Lighthouse keepers were mostly men. Sometimes their wives and families were allowed to continue on as keepers after the illness or death of their husband. Research what kind of uniform the keepers wore. Did women have a uniform? How did they dress? What would it be like to wear clothes like that and perform the hazardous duties of a keeper? Now for some fun! Instead of a ship or message in a bottle, make a keeper display! Collect enough one liter plastic bottles and wooden spoons for each student. An assortment of colored cloth, markers, buttons, gold trim or wire, felt, glue, cotton or felt for hair, and any other items for decorating will be useful. Decorate the neck and base of the bottle as the body of the keeper. Draw a face on the back of the wooden spoon. Glue cotton, yarn, or felt for hair, hats, etc. Insert the decorated wooden spoon into the clean, dry bottles and glue in place. Place finishing touches on the keeper and display around the room. Encourage written or transcribed descriptions of the keepers describing life in a lighthouse or some part of their duties. Invite parents in to see the display and to enjoy the class joining in the story.

 Row, Ida, Row.
(Logical-Mathematical; Intrapersonal)

Ida's lighthouse was 300 yards from shore. Every morning she had to row her brothers and sister to shore for school and then row back in the afternoon to bring them home. Sometimes the waves were so tall that her parents couldn't see the rowboat when it was hidden between the huge waves. All of this exercise helped her to become an expert rower and enabled her to perform her daring rescues. How many miles did Ida have to row in one day, week, month, or year? If you lived in a lighthouse and could only get food supplies twice a year, what would you order? A lighthouse keeper's typical list of supplies is indicated here.

Cute keepers.

Supplies:

200 lbs. pork	50 lbs. sugar
100 lbs. beef	2 barrels of flour
10 gal. beans	24 lbs. coffee
4 gal. vinegar	2 barrels of potatoes
50 lbs. rice	10 oz. mustard & pepper
	1 bag of salt

Make up your list in units of pounds and dozens. Your list must allow for feeding a family of four for six months. Find out how other keepers stretched their food budget. They were paid $500 a year. What could you trade or barter with other people on the mainland? Remember that the Lighthouse Commission had you on a budget.

Conduct research to find out what the children did for entertainment. What would you do to keep yourself occupied? What games would you play? Some children who lived at Ida's lighthouse used to ride their mother's ironing board down the stairs for fun (when their mother was away). The keepers, in Ida's time, had no electricity (they used oil lamps), no running water (they collected rainwater in a cistern in their basement), and no indoor plumbing (they used outhouses). Since there was no electricity, why not add to your experiment by turning off the TV for the week? Now how would you spend your time after school—after your lighthouse chores were done? Keep a journal for a week. Write down your thoughts, or draw pictures of what you would do. What do you think Ida and her brothers and sister felt like? Add your thoughts and feelings. Share any interesting comments with others in your class.

3. Keep it Ship Shape.
(Bodily-Kinesthetic; Visual-Spatial)

Lighthouse Inspectors would hold surprise inspections on the keepers and their families. They would come at any hour of the day and expect to find the lighthouse in Shipshape condition! One even wore white gloves when checking windowsills for dust! The Keeper could lose points for dust, not keeping the light burning, unpolished lamps, or a messy house. After all, the Lighthouse was government property. Would your classroom, whether public or private, pass inspection?

Make a list on a chart of all the housekeeping duties needed to make the classroom Shipshape. Divide the class into different sets of Keepers, one group for each task on the list. Trace and cut out shapes of the different kinds of lighthouses, one for each set of lighthouse keepers. Have the crews look up names of lighthouses, choose a name and label their lighthouse. The teacher will act as the Lighthouse Commissioner and rotate the lighthouse chores each day for two weeks. Invite the principal or maintenance person to play the role of the Inspector General. The inspector may declare a surprise inspection and inspect the classroom at any time of the day during the week. The Inspector General will decide if the classroom is shipshape and passes inspection according to each job listed on the chart. At the end of the two weeks the classroom should be shining! Congratulate yourselves! Hold a seafood festival and celebrate with blue Jell-O, or blue ice pops, goldfish-shaped crackers, or maybe even a cake in the shape of a lighthouse!

TIPS FOR THE TELLER

A Yankee Doodle Legend
Retold and Adapted by Jeanne M. Donato

STORYTELLING METHOD
Traditional/Musical/Chant

There are many legends about the origin of the song "Yankee Doodle." This story is a retelling of a legend about how it was composed. As the listeners follow the telling, they come to appreciate the ability of the Patriots to take a song meant to tease them and turn it into a source of national pride. It demonstrates American ingenuity and resourcefulness, and stands as a mark to our courage against all odds.

Chapter 3 outlines the Traditional Storytelling method. Many methods overlap and the Teller will be incorporating chant, audience participation, and music as a surprise ending to the story. The Teller can be dressed in patriotic colors or choose a tricornered hat or Colonial dress to introduce this story. It is best not to introduce this story by the title, in order to sustain the surprise or anticipated ending of the story by encouraging everyone to sing the song "Yankee Doodle." Prepare the audience with questions about life in the early Colonial days when this story takes place. Ask them to wait until the end of the story if they guess the ending so everyone can appreciate it together. As asterisk in the text indicates where the students can join in singing "Yankee Doodle." However, the Teller might work this in his or her own way to maximize the surprise.

Introducing some vocabulary from Colonial times will help young listeners to enjoy the story. A discussion on how words have changed meanings is a good introduction to this. Dandy meant a young gentleman who wore extravagant clothing. Macaroni was a name given to the fancy trimmings they wore on their clothes and hats. Doodle was a word of ridicule that people used for a fool or half-wit. Yankee was a name that referred to New Englanders or Northerners and later came to be used by people from other countries as a name for people who live in the United States.

A Yankee Doodle Legend

In 1756, the British and French were fighting for control of the New World's wilderness along the western colonies. The British issued a call for help. The colonies responded by sending volunteers to Fort Crailo, across the Hudson River from Albany, New York.

Each colony sent what help they could. Rhode Island's regiment arrived in uniform with tents and equipment, ready to fight. This is the legend of what happened to the Connecticut volunteers.

Young Colonel Thomas Fitch was the son of Connecticut's colonial governor, Thomas Fitch. Eager to prove himself, Colonel Fitch put a call out for volunteers throughout the colony. Young farmers eager to seek adventure and protect their homeland dropped their plows and gathered in New London, Connecticut, to march on to Colonel Fitch's family farm in Norwalk. Colonel Fitch realized that these young farmers had little schooling and no military experience. They wore the clothes that they farmed in. Their horses were used to pulling plows. Their guns were fit for shooting turkey and wild game. Shoes, back then, would fit either foot. The men did not know their left foot from their right foot, but they were smart farmers. They could tell the difference between hay and straw. Anxious to get his men formed into a proper marching unit, Colonel Fitch ordered the men to tie hay on one foot and straw on the other. Now when he gave orders to march he would shout, "Hay foot, straw foot, hay foot, straw. Hay foot, straw foot, hay foot, straw!" By the time they reached his home in Norwalk, Connecticut, they were just beginning to get used to marching.

Colonel Thomas Fitch's little sister, Elizabeth, was just sixteen years old. When she saw her brother with his "army" she ran up to greet him squealing with excitement, "Tommy's home, Tommy's come home! Look!"

Thomas Fitch, with reddened cheeks, greeted his little sister with all the dignity he could muster and said, "It's Colonel Fitch! Now compose yourself and tell Father that the Connecticut regiment is here to collect more volunteers before we leave for Fort Crailo in New York."

Elizabeth ran off to help with the preparations. She suggested to her mother that she go to the village to get more help for this great army. Running into town, she spread the news among her friends. She called out, "My brother Tommy has come home! He's a real colonel now and he has brought a whole army of men with him to the farm. Mother and I need all the help we can get to look after them. Wait till you see all the men; you won't believe it. Hurry!" The young girls from the village flocked to the Fitch's farm.

When her brother announced that they would soon be leaving, Elizabeth protested. "But they have no uniforms," she said. "You must stay until we can make them some proper uniforms. Why, they look like plain farmers!"

"The British need us. We don't have time to waste on uniforms!" Colonel Fitch replied. He gave orders for the men to prepare to move out.

"Wait!" cried Elizabeth. "Wait!" She called her girlfriends together and they ran to the barnyard. There arose a great protest of clucking and squawking with chicken feathers flying everywhere. When the girls returned, their aprons were filled with chicken feathers. "Here," Elizabeth exclaimed. "Your men must have some kind of uniform. Soldiers should wear plumes! So here!" Elizabeth insisted, and the other young women shyly smiled as they placed the chicken feathers on the hats of the blushing young men. Colonel Fitch's soldiers, young and old alike, gallantly accepted the token as they marched off to New York.

Two well-dressed sentries, with their bright red uniforms, gleaming boots, and polished brass buttons were standing guard duty. The urge to laugh was pressed hard in their throats. Word flew ahead of the motley Connecticut Irregulars as they approached General Abercrombie's headquarters at Fort Crailo. Other British soldiers rushed to gape and ridicule them. "What are those Yankees wearing? Why, they all have chicken feathers in their hats! What Doodles! They must think that's fancy macaroni! What a bunch of Dandies! This bunch are real Dudes! Look what they have tied to their feet. That's so they can mind their step! Oh, help us!" the British soldiers howled with laughter. "These are our reinforcements?"

A British army surgeon, Dr. Richard Shuckburg, came out of his tent to see what was causing the commotion. He was overheard to say, "Why, stab my vitals, they're macaronis!" Dr. Shuckburg sat down and quickly penned a few lines to a song from a well-known children's game called "Lucy Locket Lost Her Pocket." He called out, "Come, my merry comrades, and listen to my ditty."

Yankee Doodle went to town,
Riding on a pony,
Stuck a feather in his cap,
And called it macaroni!

♣Chorus:
Yankee Doodle, keep it up,
Yankee Doodle dandy,
Mind the music and the step
And with the girls be handy!

It was rumored that, when the war was over, the Rhode Island and Massachusetts volunteers followed the Connecticut Irregulars home whistling "Yankee Doodle" along the way.

When General Gage closed the Boston harbor and occupied the city, he had the tune "Yankee Doodle" played. And again it was played as the Redcoats marched to Lexington and Concord. The story goes on to say that the Patriots whistled this tune as a taunt when they shot at the British, from behind stone walls, as they retreated back to Boston. General Gage exclaimed, "I hope that I shall never hear that tune again!"

Yankee Doodle had become the rallying song for the Colonial troops during the Revolutionary War. The Patriots, in typical Yankee fashion, took the very song created to ridicule them and added verses to it until it became synonymous with American pride and spirit. Even a British officer admitted this, as he wrote, "It was not a little mortifying to hear them play this tune, when their army marched down to our surrender."

In 1979, the Connecticut General Assembly made "Yankee Doodle" their official state song.

MULTIPLE INTELLIGENCE ACTIVITIES FOR . . .

A Yankee Doodle Legend

1 ### A Patriotic Jug Band.
(Musical-Rhythmic; Visual-Spatial)

The class can do these activities together or in small groups. Materials needed: paper towel tubes, wax paper, rubber bands, glue, colored paper, stars, and glitter. Cut the paper towel tubes in approximately 6-inch lengths. Fold wax paper tightly over the end of the tube and fasten tightly with rubber bands, glue, and tape. Punch a hole in the side of the tube within 1 inch of the wax paper. This will let excess air escape. Decorate with patriotic colors and hum the tune into the open end of the tube. It will give off a vibrating kazoo sound. You are ready to march. Empty coffee cans and round oatmeal boxes can be collected and decorated for drums. Rice can be put inside small, decorated boxes for rattles. Old pan lids become cymbals. Blowing on the edge of different-sized bottles creates varied sounds for wind instruments. Old buttons can be threaded on elastic thread with bells for rhythmic rattles. Sandpaper fastened with tacks to wooden blocks creates a rhythmic sound when the blocks are scraped together. The Patriotic Jug Band is ready to play "Yankee Doodle" or "The World Turned Upside Down," which was played by the British when they surrendered to the Americans during the Revolutionary War.

The World Turned Upside Down

If but-ter cups buzz'd af-ter the bee, if boats were on land, church-es on sea, if

po-nies rode men and if grass ate the cows and cats should be chased in-to holes by the mouse,

if the ma-mas sold their ba-bies to the gyp-sies for half a crown, if

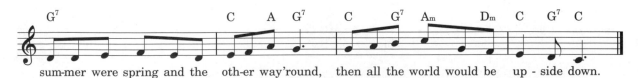

sum-mer were spring and the oth-er way'round, then all the world would be up-side down.

"The World Turned Upside Down" (Traditional English Folksong. Melody line arranged by Jean Liepold.)

JULY

 Hay Foot, Straw Foot.
(Bodily-Kinesthetic; Logical-Mathematical)

Colonel Fitch had trouble getting his Colonial troops to march in formation. Watch films of local bands marching and military units parade drills. Considering the total number of students in the class, decide which parade grouping would be best: Groups of three, four, or five persons long and three, four, or five wide. Measure the space allowed for the parade and design a simple marching formation. For more of a challenge, have the class design some variations on marching drills, turns, marching in place, and splitting the group to circle the room and rejoin while staying in step. In a gym or multipurpose room have the class form the marching units they have designed. If there is an extra person, they may be the leader, or Colonel Fitch. Play some brisk marching songs by John Philip Sousa and at the leader's signal, start the marching. When the class has had enough practice, you may elect to add rhythm instruments.

For a fun variation, add sound effects to your celebration! Place balloons, which have been twisted into bubbles, on the floor. When the children stomp on them they "pop," sounding like firecrackers!

③ Make a Quill Pen.
(Naturalistic; Visual-Spatial)

Colonists used different feathers for different types of writing. They preferred crow feathers for their fine lines. Do not collect feathers from outdoors, due to diseases they may carry. Collect and compare goose, turkey, seagull (if applicable), crow, and other large bird feathers from the craft section of a store. A good quill pen is at least 8 inches long. Materials needed: large feathers at least 8 inches long; scissors, craft knife (used by teacher only);

Smiles galore with balloons on the floor.

209

Making a quill pen.

cutting board; paper; bowl of warm tap water; ink; and scrap cotton or felt. For 15 minutes soak the tip of the quill in a bowl of warm water, to soften it. Trim 3 to 4 inches of feathers from the quill end of the feather. The nib is the curve cut from the end of the quill to the side, shaped like the letter *c*. Use a cutting board and have the teacher do the cutting. Next, cut a small slit in the center of the nib. This helps control the flow of the ink. Dip the nib end of the quill into a bottle of ink and blot gently on a scrap of felt or cotton. You can achieve different-sized lines by holding the quill at different angles. Re-dip and blot as often as necessary. When the nib becomes soft, the teacher can cut a new c-cut or nib on the same quill. Practice different styles of letters. Compare the different scripts for one or more letters. Display your findings and examples for all to see.

You may want to label, compare, and display the shapes and sizes of the different feathers collected by mounting them on paper. Below, using that feather quill, write your findings.

TIPS FOR THE TELLER

The Fourth of July
Retold and Adapted by Jeanne M. Donato

STORYTELLING METHOD

Chant

This story weaves historical legends and facts with fictional characters to explain how the Fourth of July was chosen as our country's official birthday. This tale is based on a legend about the Liberty Bell's old bell ringer and his assistant. The assistant to the person who rang the Liberty Bell on July 4, 1776, is now a grandfather. His young grandson is his assistant, helping him with the ringing of the bell to celebrate the Fourth of July. The young lad wants to know how a nation can have a birthday and why ringing this particular bell is so important to his Grandfather. In answering his grandson's questions, the Grandfather tells of the events leading up to the Fourth of July.

Chapter 3 refers the reader to the use of the Chant Storytelling method. The Teller may want to dress in patriotic colors or wear a colorful vest with American symbols on it. The Teller may want to have the American flag, along with pictures of earlier American flags and a picture of the Liberty Bell, on display. A birthday cake decorated like a flag or with red, white, and blue frosting and candles suggests celebration and anticipated fun!

Explain to the children that a chant response will be used throughout the story. Before beginning the story, the Teller may want to establish a signal such as a nod of the head or a hand gesture to indicate that everyone can join in the chanting. An asterisk indicates the text that the audience recites. This text is printed on the chalkboard or a flip chart in advance so that the class or audience can easily see its part.

Ask questions such as: "What do people do to celebrate a birthday? What does your family do to celebrate on the Fourth of July? Do you know how the Fourth of July came to be known as our country's birthday?" Have the children listen to this story as Daniel learns about the birth of our country.

The Fourth of July

✿ **Chant:**
"Ring the bells and clap your hands
For Liberty throughout the Land!
Let freedom ring for liberty
Let freedom ring for you and me!" (2x)

Daniel thought, "I bet that's just what Grandpa is saying right now," as he scraped his shoe in the dirt. Daniel was waiting for the man on the platform to finish his speech. As soon as it was over Daniel had to run and tell Grandpa that it was time to ring the Liberty Bell. The waiting seemed to take such a long time.

Just then the speaker stopped and the people clapped. "Oh my!" cried Daniel, "I'd better hurry!" And he started to run up the bell tower steps calling, "Ring the bell, Grandpa! It's time! The speech is over!"

The great bell started to clang before he reached the top step. Then all the other bells in Philadelphia joined in. The air reverberated with bells ringing, guns shooting, and people cheering and clapping. Daniel fairly shook with each stroke of the bell's clapper. He could feel it from head to toe even with his hands held tightly over his ears. "My, that bell is loud! No wonder Grandpa is hard of hearing," thought Daniel. He watched his Grandfather pulling the bell rope. He could see his lips moving and the pride in his smiling eyes. Daniel knew that his Grandpa was reciting his favorite rhyme. Grandpa used to say that if you listened to the Liberty Bell, when he pulled its rope, you could hear it ringing and singing.

✿ **(Chant)**

Looking out of the tower, Daniel could see the crowds gathered below to watch the parade pass by. How exciting! When the ringing stopped in their ears, Grandpa asked, "Did you hear it sing, Son? Come on! Sing it with me again!" Then he and Daniel would both sing it out as they waved to the people down below.

✿ **(Chant)**

Daniel asked, "Grandpa, how did the Liberty Bell get it's name? And why is it the first bell that rings to celebrate the Fourth of July?"

Grandpa answered, "Read the words written on the bell, Daniel."

Daniel slowly read the inscription: "Proclaim liberty throughout all the land unto all the inhabitants thereof."

Grandfather continued, "It used to be called the Old Statehouse bell. The people who had that inscribed on this bell believed in freedom for all. When the colonies united to declare their independence from England, this bell was the first one to ring out the news to the world! It was the first bell to ring when the colonies voted on the Constitution to form the United States of America. And now it rings each Fourth of July to celebrate our country's birthday. It truly is a Liberty Bell! And folks just got to calling it that."

"Were you there when the United States was born?" Daniel asked.

"I certainly was, son," Grandpa replied.

"How was our country born?" Daniel questioned.

"Hold on now," Grandpa laughed. "Now let me see...Countries are not born the way people are born. It takes a long time for people to come together and realize that they share common goals and ideals about how they would like to govern themselves.

"Before the United States was formed," Grandpa continued, "our country was made up of 13 colonies ruled by the king of England. People from many different countries settled here seeking religious freedom, land, or an opportunity to better their lives. The king did not give the colonists any say in the laws and taxes that he imposed on them and eventually they grew resentful. As the laws and taxes became more intolerable, the colonies started to protest them. Even George Washington thought that if the colonies united and presented their protests to the king, that he would change his mind. Some colonists wanted to remain loyal to the king. Some colonists wanted freedom from England and the right to govern themselves. Still others had no opinion. They just wanted to be left in peace.

"The word congress means a coming together. And that is exactly what the colonies did. Each colony sent delegates to the Continental Congress, right here in Philadelphia, to discuss their different opinions and see if they could agree on how to deal with the king of England and his soldiers."

"How did they ever reach an agreement?" Daniel asked.

"It took the colonies a long time to make up their minds. The delegates agreed to honor the vote of the majority. They also agreed not to talk about the discussions outside of the Congress. They wanted to be free from public pressure, to think and discuss the issues sensibly.

"During the Congress, people would gather outside. They wondered and worried. They were anxious to know what Congress would do. The delegates said that when they made up their minds they would send word and have the bell in the Statehouse rung.

"Mr. McNair was the official bell ringer. He needed someone on the steps below to run up and let him know when to ring the bell. I was his assistant, just like you helped me today. Every day Mr. McNair would wait up in the bell tower and I would wait at my post by the door. Congress had some big decisions to make, but no one ever thought it would take so long."

Daniel asked, "How long did you have to wait?"

Grandfather laughed and shook his head. "Back in 1776, as far as I can reckon, we waited about six weeks. We started waiting back around May 15. On July 2, Congress voted for independence and even John Adams thought that would be the day everyone should celebrate. But on Thursday, July 4, Congress voted on the completed Declaration of Independence. That was the day they told me to give the signal for Mr. McNair to ring the bell for liberty! And when it rang out all the other bells in Philadelphia joined in.

"Congress has copies of the Declaration made so it could be read to people in all the colonies. We rang the bell on Monday, July 8, when the Declaration was read to the people gathered outside the Statehouse. George Washington and his troops celebrated on July 10, when he read it to his troops. We rang the bell and celebrated again on August 2, when the delegates gathered to sign it."

"With all that celebrating, how was July 4 chosen as the date for our country's birthday?" Daniel puzzled.

"Things were pretty confusing back then. The War for Independence lasted eight years. But even during that time some folks took to celebrating our country's independence on July 4 with bell-ringing, cannons, gun salutes, and illuminations."

"What's an illumination?" asked Daniel.

"Illuminations are candles placed in the windows and along the streets to light up the cities and towns for special celebrations," Grandfather answered.

"There wasn't any set holiday until Thomas Jefferson, who wrote the Declaration of Independence, was elected president. He thought July 4 should be the official celebration. Yes, sir, ever since then this old bell has been ringing and people have been singing.

❋**Chant: Ring the bells and clap your hands**
"For Liberty throughout the Land!
Let freedom ring for liberty
Let freedom ring for you and me!"

MULTIPLE INTELLIGENCE ACTIVITIES FOR . . .

The Fourth of July

 1 Symbol Savvy.
(Naturalistic; Verbal-Linguistic)

What are symbols? What do they mean? Research the meaning of a symbol. Display pictures of the Liberty Bell and our flag as examples of symbols. Some symbols are identifiable by their shape or color. To encourage students to explore the impact symbols have in our lives, divide the class into two teams and have them collect and bring to class as many symbols as possible which are used in their everyday lives. Children can either find pictures or draw the symbols. For each symbol or logo the team brings in, they may receive a Liberty Bell icon, or some other symbol, to display under their team name. This acknowledges individual efforts. Duplicate symbols can be eliminated.

Have the children use the symbols they have collected to design a board game. Instruct the teams to display, draw, or trace the symbols about 6 inches in size and arrange them down the left side of the board. Either a bulletin board or a pocket board (see illustration) will work well as a game board. In a column down the right side of the board, have them attach printed cards with the meanings of the different symbols in a mixed-up order. The team with the most Liberty Bells goes first. Each member takes a turn. Team A's representative draws a line from one symbol to its meaning. If it is correct and Team B challenges it, Team A gets a point plus another turn. If the answer is incorrect, and the team is challenged, the other team gets a point if they get it right plus another turn. The team with the most correct answers wins. The board may be scrambled to play again.

Examples of symbols include: a stop sign, a yield sign, the Statue of Liberty, the Bald Eagle, an American Flag, five-pointed stars for each state, the Star of David, a Christmas tree, skull and crossbones, birthday cake, a witch on a broom, a Jack-O-Lantern, an Easter egg, a hospital "H" sign, a library sign, a traffic light, a peace sign, etc.

 2 The Colonial Twist.
(Bodily-Kinesthetic; Logical-Mathematical)

Many students have trouble identifying the states. Becoming familiar with the original thirteen is a great beginning. Play this game using a spinner and the body.

Trace the outline of the 13 original states on an overhead projector transparency, and direct the image onto a wall until it is about 6 feet long. Hang an old sheet or oilcloth on the wall and trace only the outlines of the states. Remove the sheet from the wall and place on the floor.

Next, draw a circle on heavy cardboard. Divide the circle into 13 pie-shaped wedges and

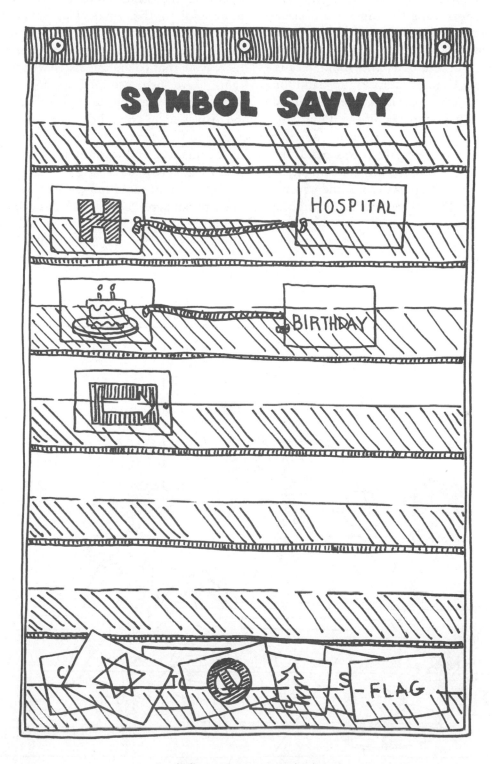

Symbol savvy may use a pocket board.

label the name of a state on each wedge. Each state is worth one point. Attach a cardboard arrow to the circle to make a spinner. Make sure it can spin around easily. Two players can play this game. One player does the twisting and the other person spins, calls the moves, and keeps score. The first move is always the right foot, then the right hand and next, the left foot and the left hand. For example, the spinner calls, "Right foot on Connecticut; Right hand on Pennsylvania; Left foot on Delaware; Left hand on New Jersey!" The order is repeated until the player falls over. A player scores one point for each state that he or she correctly touches. If the player chooses the wrong state by touching it, he or she must stop, add up the score, and become the scorekeeper. The player with the highest score is the winner.

 Fly Your Flag.
(Intrapersonal; Interpersonal)

After discussing what symbols can stand for, encourage the students to reflect on what is meaningful in their lives. Play some reflective music and have them draw a list of symbols that would represent qualities that are important to them. Note that colors can also have some significance. Have them use their symbols to create a personal flag. They may draw their flags on paper and display them around the room. Next, create a classroom flag. Let the students experience reaching a consensus and learning the art of compromise. In order to make a classroom flag, they must suggest different ideas and debate them until the majority can agree. Other delegates debated what should be in the Declaration of Independence after Jefferson wrote it. Talk about what it may have been like going through that process.

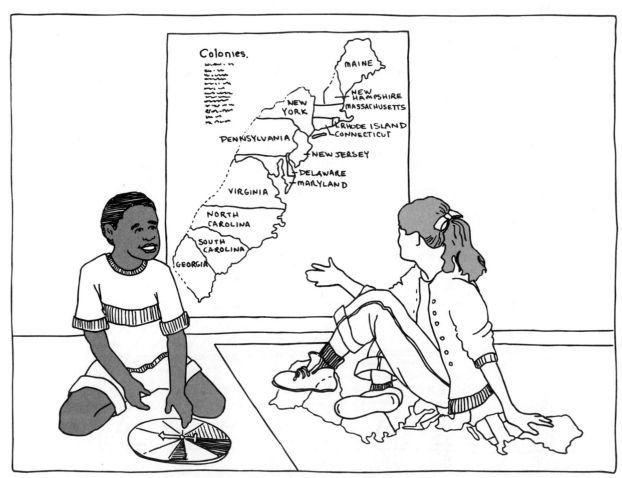

Playing the Colonial Twist.

JULY CHAPTER RESOURCES

Alderman, C. (1969). *The Rhode Island colony.* New York: Macmillan.

Aliki. (1963). *The story of Johnny Appleseed.* Englewood, NJ: Prentice-Hall.

Ardizzone, E. (1968). *Tim to the lighthouse.* New York: Henry Z. Walck.

Asimov, I. (1963). *The kite that won the revolution.* New York: Houghton Mifflin.

Beall, P. C., & Nipp, S. H. (1987). The United States. In *Wee Sing America.* New York: Price Stern, & Sloan.

Beals, C. (1970). *Colonial Rhode Island.* Chicago: Nelson.

Bennett, W. (1998). *Children's book of America.* New York: Simon & Schuster.

Bennett, W. (1997). *Children's book of heroes.* New York: Simon & Schuster.

Blos, J. W. (1996). *Nellie Bly's monkey: His remarkable story in his own words.* New York: Morrow.

Borden, L. (1988). *Good-bye, Charles Lindbergh: Based on a true story.* New York: Simon & Schuster.

Brenner, B. (1994). *If you were there in 1776.* New York: Macmillan.

Chlad, D. (1982). *Matches, lighters and firecrackers are not toys.* Chicago: Children's Press.

Cohn, A. L. (1993). *From sea to shining sea.* New York: Scholastic.

Cooney, B. (1996). *Eleanor.* New York: Puffin.

Cooney, B. (1982). *Miss Rumphius.* New York: Puffin.

Copeland, P. (1988). *Story of the American revolution coloring book.* New York: Dover.

Crews, D. (1983). *Parade.* New York: Greenwillow.

Dalgliesh, A. (1995). *The Fourth of July story.* 2nd ed. Illustrated by Marie Nonnast. New York: Aladdin.

Devlin, W. (1992). *Cranberry summer.* New York: Four Winds.

Epstein. S. (1966). *Young Paul Revere's Boston.* New York: Garrard.

Fradin, D. B. (1988). *The flag of the United States.* Chicago: Children's Press.

Fradin, D. B., & Fradin, J. B. (1995). *From sea to shining sea: Rhode Island.* Chicago: Children's Press.

Furlong, W. R. (1981). *So proudly we sail: The history of the United States flag.* Washington, DC: Smithsonian Institution Press.

Gay, K. (1995). *Revolutionary war.* New York: Twenty-First Century Books.

Giff, P. (1992). *Yankee doodle drumsticks.* New York: Dell.

Gleason, S. C. (1991). *Kindly lights: A history of the lighthouses of southern New England.* Boston: Beacon.

Glubok, S. (1969). *Home and child life in colonial days.* New York: Macmillan.

Gregary, K. (1996). *The winter of red snow: The revolutionary war diary of Abigail Jane Stewart.* New York: Scholastic.

Hicks, R. (1994). *The big book of America.* Philadelphia, PA: Courage.

Holland, J. F. R. (1989). *Great American lighthouses.* Washington, DC: The Preservation Press.

Houck, E. L. (1993). *Rabbit surprise.* New York: Crown.

Joose, B. M. (1995). *Fourth of July.* New York: Knopf.

Keller, H. (1985). *Henry's fourth of July.* New York: Greenwillow.

Krone, C. (1990). *United States of America.* Austin, TX: Steck-Vaughn Library.

Lasky, K. (1991). *Fourth of July bear.* New York: Morrow.

Marsh, V. (1994). *Paper-cutting stories for holidays and special events.* Fort Atkinson, WI: Alleyside.

McGovern, A. (1964). *If you lived in colonial times.* New York: Scholastic.

Minahan, J. A. (1999, September). Ladies of the house. *Rhode Island Monthly,* pp. 51, 102, 106.

Morgan, H. (1987). *Symbols of America.* New York: Penguin.

Morse, S. S. (1996). *Ida Lewis: Heroine of Lime Rock Light.* Marion, MA: Lime Rock Lighthouse.

Nolan, J. (1963). *The shot heard around the world.* Chicago: Messner.

Penner, L. R. (1998). *The liberty tree.* New York: Random House.

Pomeranc, M. H. (1998). *The American wei.* Morton Grove, IL: Albert Whitman.

Pyle, K. (1965). *Once upon a time in Rhode Island.* Chicago: Rand McNally.

Quackenbush, R. (1976). *Pop! Goes the weezle and Yankee Doodle.* New York: Lippincott.

Rappaport, D. (1998). *The Boston coffee party.* New York: HarperTrophy.

Raslin, J. (1976). *Spies and traitors: Tales of the revolutionary and civil wars.* New York: Lothrop, Lee & Shepard.

Rosenblum, R. (1993). *Stars and stripes and soldiers.* New York: Scholastic.

Shortall, L. (1975). *One way.* Englewood, NJ: Prentice-Hall.

Skrepcinski., D. (1998). *Silly celebrations.* New York: Aladdin.

Swanson, J. (1990). *I pledge allegiance.* Minneapolis, MN: Carolrhoda.

Watson, W. (1992). *Hooray for the fourth of July.* New York: Clarion.

Webb, G. (1990). *Great stories of the American revolution.* Nashville, TN: Rutledge Hill.

Zion, G. (1995). *The summer snowman.* New York: Harper & Row.

217

August

Oceans of Fun

AT THE SEA-SIDE

When I was down beside the sea
A wooden spade they gave to me
To dig the sandy shore.
My holes were empty like a cup,
In every hole the sea came up,
Till it could come no more.

–Robert Louis Stevenson

In August we ride the waves and squish the sand between our toes. August is vacations and beaches, fishing and waterslides.

"August: Oceans of Fun" investigates whales, crabs, lobsters, magical fish, and sea fairies. Storytelling methods for the four nautical stories are Musical, Chant, Pantomime, Group Role-Play, and Puppetry.

The multiple intelligences Verbal-Linguistic, Naturalistic, Visual-Spatial, Interpersonal, Logical-Mathematical, Musical-Rhythmic, and Bodily-Kinesthetic are covered as youngsters explore pollution and create nautical t-shirts in the related activities.

Make a splash with storytelling in August!

Magic Fish in the Sea

By Heather Forest

Retold by Jeanne Donato

STORYTELLING METHOD

Musical/Chant

The Magic Fish is Heather Forest's adaptation of the Brothers Grimm's tale "The Fisherman and His Wife." Forest added her gift of music and song to enhance the storytelling. Stories and songs change from Teller to Teller and this story has evolved from Forest's version. Listeners begin to anticipate and participate in this story with the help of the repetitive song and story pattern. In this story the Old Fisherman and his Wife come to terms with the concept of happiness verses greed.

The Musical Storytelling method in Chapter 3 will help to guide the Teller. The music that accompanies this story uses only four chords. They are easily accessible on the guitar or autoharp. To build mood and momentum, the Teller might strum the chords lightly while telling the story. The Teller may also want to break out of the narrative and ask the audience members what they think might happen next.

Before beginning, the Teller may want to establish a signal such as a nod of the head or a hand gesture to indicate when the audience may join in the singing, perhaps assigning separate signals to differentiate between the different characters' parts. An asterisk indicates the text that the audience sings. This text is printed on the chalkboard or a flip chart in advance so that the audience can easily see the different characters' parts.

The Magic Fish

"The Magic Fish" (Heather Forest © 1989).

Fish: Part I (2x)

Old Man: Part I (1x); Magic fish would you grant this wish. For we now want more than we had before

Fish: Part II (1x)

Old Man: Part I (1x)

Fish: Part II (louder) (2x)

Magic Fish in the Sea

(Strum alternating chords: Em and D)

Once upon a time there lived a little Old Fisherman and his Wife. They lived by the edge of the sea in a little glass-vinegar-bottle house. And they were happy. Each day the Old Fisherman would leave his house and climb up the hill and down the hill to the sea. He cast his net into the water, hoping to catch a fish for their dinner.

One day, as the Fisherman was pulling in his net, a golden flash caught his eye. Then he heard, ❀**"Let me go! I'm a Magic Fish. If you let me go I will grant you a wish."**

"A wish? What would I wish for? We are already happy. I'll let you go for free!" cried the old man as he tossed the Fish back into the sea.

(Teller asks: "Now if a Magic Fish gave you a wish, what would you wish for?" Elicit responses from the audience.)

221

The Fish flipped its tail on the surface of the sea and disappeared as the Old Fisherman turned for home. There he found his wife waiting for him in the doorway.

"I have a cup of tea for you. How was your day, dear?" his Wife asked.

When the Old Fisherman told his Wife about the magic fish she cried, *(chanted alternating chords Em -Am)* "A Magic Fish could grant a wish and you didn't ask for anything? Are you crazy?"

"But I thought we were happy!" protested the Old Fisherman.

"Happy?" shrieked his Wife. "Happy? How could you expect me to be happy living in this old, broken down, glass-vinegar-bottle house? I want a cottage. Yes, a cottage with flower boxes in the windows, pigs and chickens in the yard, and a picket fence all around. You tell that Fish, that is my wish! Now, go!"

Bewildered, the Old Fisherman trudged over the hill and back to the sea. He called, ✱**"Magic Fish, can you grant this wish? For we now want more than we had before."**

The Magic Fish appeared on the surface of the sea and asked, "What is it that you wish of me?"

Reluctantly, the Old Fisherman explained to the Magic Fish his Wife's wish. The Fish slapped his tail on the water and sang, ✱**"Go home, old man, and you will see the wish this Fish has given thee."**

The wind blew at the Old Fisherman's coat as he walked back home. When he got there his vinegar-bottle house was gone! And there, in its place, stood a beautiful little cottage. It had flower boxes in the windows, pigs and chickens in the yard, and a white picket fence all around. In the doorway stood his Wife and on her face there was a _____.

(Teller asks: "What look do you think was on his Wife's face?" Pause to elicit responses from the audience. "Maybe some of you don't know this little old woman. On her face there was a frown!")

His Wife complained, *(Chanted alternating chords Em - Am)* "A Magic Fish could grant this wish and this is all you asked for? Are you crazy?"

"You're not happy?" the Old Fisherman asked, incredulous.

"Happy? How could you expect me to be happy in this miserable little hovel of a cottage? I want to live in a city with a castle! I want to be queen! I want to sit on a tall throne and wear a golden crown! You go back and tell that Fish, that is my wish! Now, go!"

"But Wife!" protested the Old Fisherman. "I thought you said this would make you happy!"

"Happy, is it?" cried his Wife! "I won't be happy until you tell that Fish my wish! Leave! Now!"

The clouds in the sky hung low over the sea. The Old Fisherman sang out ✱**"Magic Fish, can you grant this wish, for we now want more than we had before?"**

The wind blew a mist into the Old Fisherman's face as the Magic Fish came to the surface of the sea. Angrily he asked, "What is it that you want of me now, Old Man?"

"I'm sorry," apologized the Old Fisherman, wiping the mist from his face. "My Wife is not happy. She wants a city, and a castle. She wants to be a queen with a throne and a crown. She says that will make her happy. Can you help me please?"

The wind blew stronger and the sea started to churn. The Magic Fish sang out,✱**"Go home, Old Man, and you will see the wish this Fish has given thee!"** Then with a smack of his tail on the water he dove from view.

The little Old Fisherman buttoned his coat around him and leaned into the wind as he struggled up the hill. When he got to the top of the hill he could see that his cottage was *gone!* There in its place was a city with a castle! Guards lined the hallway and snapped to attention when the Old Fisherman passed by. At the end of the long throne room, he saw his wife sitting on a high throne. On her head there was a crown and on her face there was a *(pause to elicit answers from the audience)*

(Teller: "Ah, I see you are starting to get to know the Old Fisherman's Wife! You are right! On her face there was a frown!")

His Wife shrieked, *(Chanted with chords Em-Am)* "A Magic Fish could grant this wish! And this is all you asked for? I want more! More! More!"

"But Wife dear," the Old Fisherman questioned, "I thought you would be happy now."

"Happy? Happy?" screamed the Old Woman. "How could I possibly be happy like this? Do you have any idea how time consuming it is to order all these people around all day? Why, I don't have any time for myself! I am not happy! The only way I can possibly be happy is if you go back and tell that Fish to make me the empress of the air and sea. Until then I can't be happy!"

"Oh, but dear," protested the Old Fisherman. "I can't possibly go back and ask that Fish for another wish! I won't go!"

The Queen thundered, "It's 'Your Majesty' to You! Won't go, will you? Guards! Off with his head!"

The little Old Fisherman ran down the aisle, out the door, and over the hill to the edge of the sea. The clouds were dark and heavy. Thunder rumbled in the distance. The sea was churning black with whitecaps. And the wind blew cold.

The Old Fisherman, his voice quivering, called out,✱**"Magic Fish, will you grant this wish? For we now want more than we had before."**

The Magic Fish rose up from the surface of the sea and asked, "What is it you ask of me *now*, Old Man?"

"I beg your pardon, sir," the Old Fisherman shook. "But my Wife is still not happy. She says she can only be happy if you make her the empress of the air and sea; of you and me!"

"What is it that you want Old Man?" thundered the Fish.

"Oh," cried the Old Fisherman. "I just want her to be happy. Please, sir, can you help me?"

Lighting flashed and the thunder roared as the Magic Fish replied,✱**"Go home, Old Man, and you will see the wish this Fish has given thee!"**

(Here the Teller can continue the same chord pattern to simulate the storm.)

Darkness closed in around the Old Fisherman as the rain and the wind whipped at his coat. He struggled to reach the top of the hill. He couldn't see anything in the driving rain. Sliding through the mud, he came to the bottom of the hill.

(Here, the Teller may choose to return to the gentle, slower-paced Em-D chords to simulate the storm breaking and the rain stopping.)

223

The clouds lightened and the rain slowed to a drizzle. There where the city had been the castle was *gone!* The cottage was *gone!* And there standing before him was just his little old glass-vinegar-bottle house. His wife was standing in the doorway looking out all the while. And on her face there was a *(pause and then add the answer)* "smile!"

"Oh, dear Old Man!" cried his Wife with relief. "I worried that you were lost or drowned in the sea! But now that you are home safely, I am so *happy!* Come, I have a cup of tea waiting for you. There now, tell me about your day."

MULTIPLE INTELLIGENCE ACTIVITIES FOR . . .

Magic Fish in the Sea

About Fish.
(Logical-Mathematical; Visual-Spatial)

Little fishy in the sea
Turn around and follow me!
Move his eye and three lines.
About face he swims each time!

–Jeanne M. Donato

Cut yellow, or golden, construction paper into strips. Make the strips equal in length and width. Arrange the students into small working groups and hand out *eight* paper strips to everyone, and a black circle for the eye, along with a drawing of the golden fish to use as their pattern (see illustration). To make their own golden fish, instruct the students to arrange the strips and the circle following the pattern on the drawing swimming to their left. The Teller may want to arrange the sample drawing on an overhead projector so all students have a chance to follow along. Now, reciting the above rhyme, challenge the groups to work together to turn their fish around so it is swimming to their right, by moving only *three* of the paper strips and the circle. (The three strips that must be moved are shown in darker print in the illustration.)

Sea Chants.
(Musical-Rhythmic; Verbal-Linguistic)

Divide students into groups of two. Distribute individual sheets with a copy of the Sea Chant Partner Activity to fill in and illustrate. The partners brainstorm for possible answers to the chant. They may want to refer to charts or books that have the names of sea and air creatures to make choices easier. As authors, the students each write their own chant on their paper. Then, they may exchange papers, and as illustrators determine what medium to use to illustrate their partner's ideas. The possibilities include watercolors, crayon, marker, collage, pencil, ink, etc., to illustrate their partner's chant. Have the students sign their names as the author or illustrator and display the chant posters on a board for all to appreciate. Playing sea chantey music in the background may add some fun to the illustration portion of this exercise.

A
(Swimming left)

B
(Swimming right)

Move three strips: make a fish.

Sea Chant Partner Activity

With a partner, discuss ideas for your chants. Write your chant by filling in the blanks below. Trade papers. Read your partner's chant and then illustrate the chant in the area below.

Way down yonder in the deep blue sea

I saw a _____ looking at me.

And when I looked up in the air

I saw a _____ playing there!

Author: _____

Illustrator: _____

Sea Chant activity page.

This chant activity may also be done as a class project on the overhead projector. The students can illustrate the class chant individually. These can be displayed around the room. Have various artistic mediums available for use in the illustrations to encourage the exploration of how they may be used to achieve different effects.

 A Magic Opportunity.
(Verbal-Linguistic; Interpersonal)

You can make a difference! Discuss how pollution of our waterways and beaches is affecting marine life. List these on the board. With the class in small groups, arrange for each group to go to the library and research water pollution on the Internet. Have them write one of the agencies listed here to find out more information about ways they can help stop pollution of our beaches, shores, and waterways. The children could also research how pollution affects marine life nearest their school. Have each group display their letter and any responses, along with a report to the class on their findings.

- Center for Marine Conservation, 1725 De Sales St. NW, Washington, DC 20036
- The Department of Environmental Management for your state. See government listings in your local phone book.
- The Oceanic Society, 218 D St. SE, Washington, DC 20003

TIPS FOR THE TELLER

The Fairies, the People, and the Sea

By Jenny Latimer

Retold and Adapted by Jeanne M. Donato

STORYTELLING METHOD

Puppetry

This imaginative story explains why the sea has waves and is salty. It also explains why people no longer see fairies or get close enough to play with them.

In preparing for this story the Teller may refer to the Puppetry Storytelling method detailed in Chapter 3. The students can make fairy and people puppets to help participate with the telling. The Teller will want to refer to the first Multiple Intelligence Activity following this story for ideas. With or without the puppets, the students can use their hands to create the motion of the sea waving. The students, holding their arms out in front of them on their laps, work together to synchronize a wave motion. Students on one side of the room slowly raise their hands from right to left over their heads and back to their laps. The students are seated and start to rise as their hands go up. They should be standing when their hands are over their heads and start to

Children participating in a story.

slowly sit down as their arms come down. When the first section of students' arms reaches over their heads, the next section starts the same movement. This gives the effect of one continuous wave rippling across the room. A similar wave is done by sports fans sitting in the bleachers at games. Go from one side of the room across the middle to the other end.

continued

TIPS FOR THE TELLER *continued*

Before beginning the story, the Teller may want to establish a signal such as a nod of the head or a hand gesture to indicate when everyone can join in making the wave with their arms and bodies. An asterisk indicates where in the story the audience will wave.

A discussion of the old stories and beliefs in fairies is a good starting point for this story.

Asking about the audience's experiences at being at the ocean will help set the tone for the discussion of the waves and the sea's salty taste. Tell the students: "This author has written a story that explains how all this came to be. See if you can remember what caused it and if it really could have happened."

The Fairies, the People, and the Sea

Once, a long time ago, people and fairies lived together in peace. It didn't matter that fairies had wings and were very small or that people had no wings and were very tall. In those days the sea was fresh water. It was sweet and delicious. The people and the fairies loved it and they loved each other.

They were all very happy, until one summer there was a terrible drought and the sea dried up, and all the places in that land where water came up from the ground stopped flowing. And so the people had no water. But the fairies had magic water that people could not drink or they would get sick. So the people moved away. And the fairies were sad.

The fairies went to an island in the middle of the sea, which was now a desert. They tried to think of some way to get the water back again so the people would come back. They could not think of anything, and they were so sad that they started to cry. Thousands, maybe millions, of fairies started to cry. They cried and cried and cried until soon they looked up through tear-filled eyes and saw the sea filled with their tears. Their tears had flowed down through the earth and awakened the water from below and that water filled the rivers with fresh, clear water.

The fairies were so happy they jumped in and swam around in the sea. But when they tasted the water they jumped back onto the island. They said to each other, "This water is not sweet. It is salty! But at least it is water." They were happy and content and they loved the sea, so they decided to give it a gift. They gave the sea the gift to be able to *wave. *(Teller does the wave with the audience.)* And the sea was happy. It *waved and waved and waved. And the fairies were glad.

The people did not know there was water in the sea, so they did not return. The fairies started to forget the people, and the people started to forget the fairies till only the sea remembered and *waved, beckoning to both.

Many years passed and the people longed for the memory of the sea. They wanted to go back to the land of their grandparents and see if anything remained of the sweet sea. They wondered if the sea had missed the people. They traveled over the mountains till they came to the top of the last mountain. There before them stretched the big, beautiful, **✳sea.** The sea was so happy to see the people that she **✳waved and waved** to them! And the people rushed down to the sea waving back.

The fairies saw the sea **✳waving and waving.** They looked up and saw the people by the edge of the sea waving their hands. And the fairies remembered the people that had left so long ago.

But these people looked different from their memories of the long ago people. The fairies, not sure what to do, hid and watched the people playing and the sea **✳waving.**

The fairies decided that one of them should try to talk to one of these new people. But no one was brave enough to go! All except one little fairy who was very friendly and a bit mischievous. She had strawberry red hair and wild sparkling green eyes. This little fairy wanted to see if she could make friends with these new people, just like the old fairies had been.

She looked for the new people in the forest and in the meadow, by the brook, and up on the cliffs; then she looked on the beach and she saw a boy about ten years old with wild, fire-red hair and big bright black eyes. He was standing barefoot in the sand, watching the sea **✳wave** and **✳waving** back. She could tell he was **✳enjoying it.** She went to join him with a smile. But when he saw her, he was very curious. He tried to catch the fairy; fortunately, she got away. She hid behind a tree; she wasn't giving up just yet. She peaked out and smiled; she saw the boy's eyes light up. And he watched carefully as she danced in the trees. He playfully started dancing too. She got a little closer and again he tried playfully to catch her. She darted behind a tree and danced into the woods and he followed, trying to catch her. He'd look behind a tree and she'd sneak up behind him and touch her wings to his face and he'd giggle and try again.

Meanwhile, the fairies had been watching from afar and they were afraid that they could get caught. They greatly feared these strange new people. So not one of them came out of hiding. And they decided it would be best never to speak to or to be seen by a person again. But that one little fairy and that one boy gleefully played peek-a-boo and tag through the years.

The fairies did not talk to the humans and the humans did not talk to the fairies. And so it is to this day. Some people even doubt the existence of fairies. But I know faries are real because when I was little I would sit on my grandpa's knee and would look up into his bright black eyes and look at his fire-red hair and he would tell me stories. And that is how I know this story and how I know that behind the next tree is a fairy hiding, watching. Maybe someday people will remember and the fairies will try once more and we will live again together, peacefully. But no matter what, the sea will always be there **✳waving** to all of us.

And that's the story of the fairies, the people, and the **✳sea.**

MULTIPLE INTELLIGENCE ACTIVITIES FOR . . .

The Fairies, the People, and the Sea

 Sea Fairies.
(Visual-Spatial ; Bodily-Kinesthetic)

The book *Faeries* tells us that August 7th was called "Lammas Tide" in King Arthur's time. It was believed that a human could see the fairy hills, which were hiding places for gold, rise up and reveal brilliant fairy lights. If one was very quiet, one could see the fairies march to another hill. Reenacting this event could make for the plot of a play. Making sea fairies involves tape, glue, and imagination. Provide two Band-Aids® to each child to wrap the end of one or more fingernails. Wrap one Band-Aid over the fingertip of each

child and a second around the finger and edges of the first Band-Aid. The Band-Aids will form a thimble shape over the tip of the finger. After the Band-Aids are fitted to the fingertip, wash the hand with soap and water. The Band-Aid thimble shape will come off easily and is now the perfect base mold for the sea fairy puppet. The students are encouraged to use waterproof markers to initial the insides of their puppet for later identification. The Band-Aid thimble may be decorated as it is, or the students may want to add layers of clay to create larger puppets. The boy puppet can be made from a cut-out of a paper doll. Cut out two holes where the legs would be, so when you poke

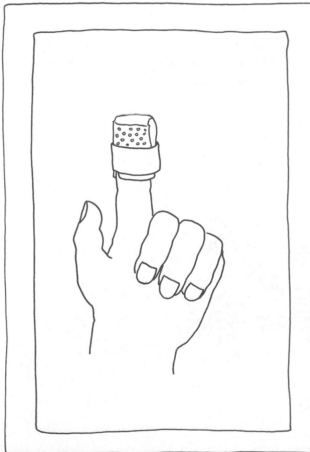

Band-Aid® finger puppets.

229

your fingers through the holes, they become the boy puppet's legs.

2 It Floats.
(Visual-Spatial; Naturalistic)

Would there be a difference between floating in a freshwater sea versus the salty sea of the fairies' tears? For this experiment you will need: two tall glass jars, one filled with fresh water and the other with ocean water. If you cannot get ocean water you can make it by dissolving two teaspoons of salt per two cups of water. Collect two of each object you want to observe, including pennies, plastic ink pen caps, plastic milk or juice carton lids, eggs, pieces of curly macaroni, etc. List your objects down the left side of a piece of paper. Divide the rest of the sheet into two columns and write Jar #1 Fresh Water and Jar #2 Ocean Water across the top. You are ready to experiment and observe. Start with pennies. Float one in each jar. Watch, observe, and write down or note your observations. Compare and share your observations. What affects the object's ability to float? Does shape make a difference in floating ability? Does size? Take equal-sized squares of aluminum foil. Float them in the jars as sheets and then crumble them into balls. Draw your own conclusions and share them. A wake-up thought: Which is heavier—a pound of pennies or a pound of feathers?

3 Oh, Dear! How Many Tears?
(Logical-Mathematical; Interpersonal)

The Sea Fairies cried and cried until they filled the sea. How many tears could that be? On a large bulletin board start a class project chart of numbers: "Their Names and Numbers." Start with one and work up to the highest number that would be a challenge for your class. For the younger classes, they may want to count their numbers 1–10 using Cheerios on a paper at their desk and count along with the teacher. The bulletin board project is best for introducing the numeral names. List the name for numbers from one million to one vigintillion (with 63 zeros). Find the largest scientific number known. The Sea Fairies cried tears. But tears are hard to count. For a class project, instead of tears, collect and count pennies, keeping a running numerical total of pennies collected. At the end of the project, the class can decide what to do with the pennies: add a book to the library, give to a charity, etc.

The Crab and the Lobster

Adapted by Susan Trostle Brand

STORYTELLING METHOD

Group Role-Play/Pantomime/Chant

In the fable of "The Crab and the Lobster," Crab is shy and cautious, while Lobster is bold and brave. Each has something to learn from the other. However, the outcome of the fable is that the Crab learns an important life lesson from the Lobster: taking small risks will broaden one's horizons and add excitement to life.

The Teller may introduce the fable with a brief description of minor risks he or she has taken in life, such as climbing a mountain, skiing, scuba dividing, riding a moped, and the like. Next, invite a few children to briefly describe a time they tried something new that initially scared them. Finally, inform them that the fable you will read or tell today is about a Crab who is frightened of life and about a Lobster friend who encourages him to try new adventures.

After the children are familiar with the simple story, select one child to become the Crab and another to become the Lobster. The Crab pantomimes by placing hands beside head and opening and closing them to represent pinching. The Lobster outstretches the arms, high above the head, and opens and closes hands to represent pinching. One child becomes the narrator. The remainder of the children, upon hearing the word "waves" read by the narrator, form a body wave. They stand in a circle around the Crab and Lobster and gradually rise as the adult signals them to do so. Upon hearing the word "winds," the same children make a loud whistling or howling sound, such as those of high winds.

In addition, the Teller may want to establish a signal such as a nod of the head or a hand gesture to indicate when the group of children can join in forming the waves or making the sounds. An asterisk indicates where in the story these actions occur.

The Crab and the Lobster

One stormy day, a shy and gentle Crab (*Crab makes low pinching gestures*) walked along the beach. He heard a splash and looked up. He was surprised to see Lobster (*high pinching gestures*) in the rough waters. She was preparing to set sail in her boat.

"Lobster," said Crab, "You are foolish to set sail on a stormy day such as this. I will keep you company if you must go out to seas. The ✱waves are high (*group wave*) and the ✱winds are ✱gusty (*howling sounds*)."

"Come along, Crab," said Lobster. Iím glad to have your company!"

The Crab and the Lobster boarded the sailboat. Soon they had traveled far from shore. Their boat was tossed and turned by the turbulent ✱waves The ✱wind yowled and howled (*howling noises*).

"Lobster!" cried Crab, "I am afraid. This is a terrible storm."

"Crab," said Lobster, "I love these high ✱waves. I love these wild ✱winds. I feel full of life and free from petty cares."

"Lobster!" cried Crab. "I think we are going to sink!"

"You are right, Crab," replied Lobster. "We are sinking. My boat is full of tiny holes. But remember, my friend, we are sea creatures. We have nothing to fear above or below the water and the ✱waves!"

Sure enough, within minutes, the little boat capsized. It became engulfed by another ✱wave and it quickly sank.

"Having fun?" called the excited Lobster.

"Help me!" cried the horrified Crab.

Poor Crab! He was upset and shaking. But not Lobster. Lobster knew exactly what to do. She took little Crab for a walk along the ocean floor.

Crab began to relax. The ✱waves were long gone. He no longer heard the howling ✱winds.

"What a wonderful adventure we have had, Crab," said Lobster. Crab nodded his head in agreement. The shy, gentle Crab wasn't used to so much excitement. But he had to admit that the memories of the huge ✱waves, the howling ✱winds, and his exciting day with Lobster would long remain among his favorites.

MULTIPLE INTELLIGENCE ACTIVITIES FOR . . .

The Crab and the Lobster

 Body Creatures.
(Bodily-Kinesthetic; Interpersonal; Musical-Rhythmic)

Children consult the story to create giant nautical body creatures. For example, the children form the crab by gathering a large circle with extended arms (claws). Two children, wearing dark-colored clothing, become the eyes. Other fun to form sea creatures include the lobster, an eel, a sea star, and a medusa. Practice "swimming" all together and retaining the shape of the sea creature. Later, when the body shapes are all formed, reenact the story of *The Crab and the Lobster*. While acting, children may sing new words to familiar tunes. The following song, written by first grade teacher Susan Daley, is sung to the tune of "The Wheels on the Bus."

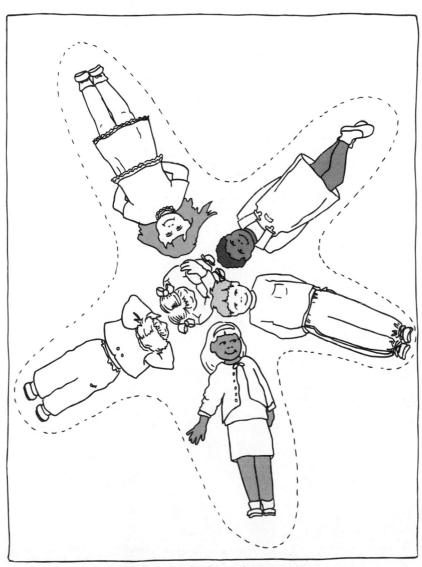

Children use their bodies to form a sea star.

233

The Crabs in the Sea

By Susan Daley, adapted by Susan Trostle Brand

(Sung to the Tune of "The Wheels on the Bus")
The crabs in the sea go snap, snap, snap,
Snap, snap, snap,
Snap, snap, snap;
The crabs in the sea go snap, snap, snap—
All through the day!

The dolphins in the sea go splash, splash, splash,
Splash, splash, splash,
Splash, splash, splash;
The dolphins in the sea go splash, splash, splash—
All through the day!

The lifeguard at the sea goes twitt, twitt, twitt,
Twitt, twitt, twitt,
Twitt, twitt twitt;
The lifeguard at the sea goes twitt, twitt, twitt—
All through the day!

 Edible Math.
(Logical-Mathematical; Verbal-Linguistic)

Provide each child with a nautical placemat and approximately 20 Goldfish crackers. Construct a large, fierce-looking tuna from poster board. Mount the tuna on a yardstick or dowel rod. As the tuna travels from one child to another, he eats the goldfish on the placemats. Invent verbal number problems to initiate the actions.

For example, the tuna travels to Fiona's table. The tuna says, "Fiona, the tuna just ate three of your goldfish. Tell me the number problem." Fiona answers, "Twenty minus three equals 17." From the "ocean" Fiona removes and eats three goldfish crackers. Then she counts the remaining fish to verify her answer. If Fiona's answer is correct, she may hold the tuna and create a new, edible number problem for someone at her table. The game can also be used to teach

Nautical addition and subtraction game.

addition, simply by adding more goldfish to the children's placemats.

 ### Terrific T-Shirts.
(Visual-Spatial; Naturalistic)

Purchase polyester and cotton (50/50) t-shirts (one per child) for the class (or ask parents to send a 50/50 t-shirt to school with the child). Have on hand fabric crayons, an ironing board and iron, and pictures of nautical creatures and scenes. Children may use the fabric crayons—pressed very firmly for the most transferable images—on paper to create colorful sea designs. They may either invent their own designs or use those which are provided. Inform them that the images, when pressed onto t-shirts, will be backwards; therefore, any printing on the papers must be done backwards to appear correct on the shirt.

When papers are completely colored (two per child; one for the front and one for the back) children print initials, in pencil, on the pages, also writing F for front and B for back. Invite a parent volunteer to transfer the colored pictures onto the fronts and backs of t-shirts, using a very hot iron (away from the children), and being certain to transfer the entire image onto the t-shirt. One teacher's class created the t-shirts the week before an Aquarium field trip in June. The entire class donned their beautiful and creative t-shirts for the trip!

TIPS FOR THE TELLER

The War between the Sandpipers and the Whales: A Tale from the Marshall Islands

By Margaret Read MacDonald

Adapted by Jeanne Donato

STORYTELLING METHOD

Chant

The total devastation of war is the theme of this folktale from the Marshall Islands, adapted here to the Chant Storytelling method discussed in Chapter 3. Pride and arrogance pit Whale and Sandpiper against each other. The story line engages the students while giving them ideas to discuss through the safe medium of a story. Anger increases as each character engages help for his or her cause. Whale and Sandpiper realize that the destruction will also affect their lives. The original question, of which side had the greater number, is left unanswered as they realize how trivial the dispute was.

As the students become more familiar with the story with each telling, they find creative ways to join in. To start, the Teller may want to have a display of an aquarium, a bucket of sand, seashells, and pictures of an island, whales, and sandpipers, along with other sea creatures. This story makes a great introduction to or culminating experience for a lesson on marine life and the seashore. Discussing the different creatures that can be found in and around the sea will also help the students feel more comfortable in suggesting other sea creatures and birds that are not mentioned in the original telling.

continued

TIPS FOR THE TELLER *continued*

Before beginning the story, the Teller may want to establish a signal such as a nod of the head or a hand gesture to indicate when everyone can join in the chanting. An asterisk indicates the text in which the class or audience participates. This text is printed on the chalkboard or a flip chart in advance so that they can easily see their parts.

The chants may be simplified with more repetition to help younger students catch on to the cadence and make it easier for them to follow along. Invite the students to join in the noises the characters make to call their friends, and have them mime the actions along with the Teller. It is wise to address one issue before the telling. Stress that the students will be acting out the actions and not really spitting. Remind them to be careful and considerate of their neighbors in their story actions. This will set the boundaries of acceptable behavior, help all the students feel more comfortable, and allow them to enjoy the story.

"The War between the Sandpipers and the Whales" is from *Peace Tales: World Folktales to Talk About* by Margaret Read MacDonald © 1992 by Margaret Read MacDonald. Reprinted by permission of Linnet Books, North Haven, Connecticut.

The War between the Sandpipers and the Whales: A Tale from the Marshall Islands

Every morning little Sandpiper went down to the beach for her breakfast. She would run into the water on her tall little legs and *(Teller mimes sipping water)* *Slup...slup...slup...* She would peck up a little minnow *(mime gobbling a minnow)*. Then she would run back up on the beach and wait. Into the water she would run again and *Slup...slup...* gobble up another tidbit.

Whale, who lived in the deep bay, saw Sandpiper running in and out of the water. Whale stuck his huge head out of the water and called to Sandpiper. "You! Little bird! Stay out of my water! The sea belongs to the *whales!*"

Sandpiper just ignored him. "The sea belongs to the *sandpipers* too. And there are lots more sandpipers than there are whales. So leave me alone!"

Whale was fuming and spewing. Sandpiper angered him. "More *sandpipers?* There are *many* more *whales* in the ocean than *sandpipers* on the *land!*"

"Not so!" said little Sandpiper. "There are more sandpipers!"

Whale was furious. "I will call my brothers. You will see!"

Whale came to the top of the water and spouted, *(Cup hands and call:)* ✳"Buuturu...buuturu..." Whale dove deep, deep into the bay. Whale turned to the east and sounded. ✳"**Whales of the east. Whales of the east. Come...come to this island!**"

Whale came up again. He spouted, ✳"Buuturu...buuturu..." He dove to the north. ✳"**Whales of the north. Whales of the north. Come... come to this island!**"

Whale came up one more time. He spouted, ✳"Buuturu...buuturu..." He dove to the south. ✳"**Whales of the south. Whales of the south. Come...come to this island!**"

In the east, in the west. in the north, in the south, his whale brothers heard. They began to swim toward that island. And when they had all come, that bay was so crowded with whales you could have walked across on their backs! They were packed so tightly into that bay.

Sandpiper was alarmed. "You *do* have a lot of brothers. But wait. I will call my sandpiper sisters!"

Little Sandpiper began to jump up and down and make her sandpiper call ✳"**Kirrir...kirriri...kirriri...kirriri... Sandpipers! Sandpipers! East! East! East! East! Come quick! Come quick! To this island! Sandpipers! Sandpipers! West! West! West! West! Come quick! Come quick! To this island! Sandpipers! Sandpipers! North! North! North! North! Come quick! Come quick! To this island! Sandpipers! Sandpipers! South! South! South! South! Come quick! Come quick! To this island!**"

And those sandpipers came flying in from the east, the west, the north, the south. And when they had landed, those birds covered the entire beach! They covered the trees! There were *so* many birds.

Were there more birds or more whales? More whales or more birds? It was impossible to say.

The whales talked among themselves, "We must call our whale cousins. *Then* there will be more sea creatures than *birds.*"

So the whales all came to the top of the water and spouted, ✳"Buuturu...buuturu..." They dove deep, deep. They called to the east, ✳"**Cousins to the east, Cousins to the east, come....come to this island!**" They came up and spouted, ✳"Buuturu...buuturu..." They dove, ✳"**Cousins to the west, Cousins to the west, come to this island!**" They came up. They spouted, ✳"Buuturu...buuturu..." "They dove, ✳"**Cousins to the north, Cousins to the north, come! Come to this island!**"

From the east, from the west, from the north, from the south, all the whale cousins began to swim toward that island. Dolphins heard. Dolphins came. Killer whales heard. Killer whales came. Porpoises heard. Porpoises came. Even the sharks came.

When all the whale cousins had arrived there were so many sea creatures that they surrounded the island on every side. As far as you could see in every direction there were sea creatures spouting and diving.

The sandpipers were frightened. "There are *so many* sea creatures. Quick! We must call all of our sandpiper cousins!"

The sandpipers began to jump up and down and make their call: ✻"Kirriri...kirriri...kirriri...kirriri... Sandpiper cousins! East! East! East! Come quick! Come quick to this island! Sandpiper cousins! West! West! West! Come quick! Come quick to this island! Sandpiper cousins! North! North! North! Come quick! Come quick to this island! Sandpiper cousins! South! South! South! Come quick! Come quick to this island!"

From the east, from the west, from the north, from the south, sandpiper cousins began to arrive. Gulls heard. Gulls came. Terns heard. Terns came. Cormorants heard. Cormorants came. Even the herons came.

When those seabirds had all arrived they covered the beaches and they stretched up into the mountains. There was not an inch of land on that island which was not covered by birds!

Were there more birds or more sea creatures? More whale cousins or more sandpiper cousins? No one could say.

Then the Whale had an idea. "If we whales could eat up the land, then those birds would drown! Then there would be more whales than sandpipers! Let's do it!"

The whales began to munch on the beach (*mime eating up the beach*). ✻"Scrunch...scrunch...scrunch" the beach was disappearing into their huge jaws.

Then the Sandpipers had an idea. "If we birds drank up all of the sea...the whales would die! *Then* there would be more sandpipers than whales! Let's do it!"

The birds flew down to the ocean. Each bird dipped its beak into the sea. They began to drink (*mime sipping water*). Those birds drank and drank (*draw out the words*). Their cheeks filled with water. They drank and drank. Their tummies filled with water. It was easier to drink than to munch. The birds finished *first!*

The birds looked down. The whales lay dying without water. The fish, too, all lay gasping. The tiny crabs, the starfish, all of the sea creatures, lay dying in the hot sun.

Suddenly, the birds thought of something. "Those tiny crabs, these sea creatures, that is our *food*. This is what we *eat*. If they die, *we* will die too. This is a *bad idea!* Quick! Spit out the water, spit back the ocean (*mime spitting out the water*). ✻Ptoooie...ptoooie...ptoooie...."The birds all spat back the sea.

The whales began to move again. The fish began to swim about. The little crabs and the starfish stretched out their legs and began to live.

"This was a *bad* idea!" said the whales. "The ocean is where we live. The beach is part of the ocean. We are destroying our own home. Quick, spit back the land (*mime spitting the sand back onto the beach*). ✻"Glurk...glurk...glurk...."The whales spat back the beach.

"This war was a bad idea," said Whale. "There is plenty of ocean for us all to share."

"Yes. A bad idea," agreed Sandpiper. "We almost destroyed our home!"

And so the whales and their whale cousins all swam away to the east, to the west, to the north, to the south. And the sandpipers and their cousins all flew away, to the east, to the west, to the north, to the south. And to this day no one knows the answer to the question:

Are there more whales or more sandpipers? Are there more sandpipers or more whales? And after all, it doesn't really matter. Such a little thing to start a war.

MULTIPLE INTELLIGENCE ACTIVITIES FOR . . .

The War between the Sandpipers and the Whales: A Tale from the Marshall Islands

 1 Lights, Cameras, Action!
(Bodily-Kinesthetic; Visual-Spatial)

After the class has become familiar with the story and the sequence of events, invite them to enjoy the story through creative drama exercises. Using the school stage area, spread the students out so they can get a feel for the space a stage offers. In a circle, have everyone practice moving like the whale and the characters presented in the story. Add the chant to the movements, with emphasis on characterization. Divide the class into sea creatures and birds. Subdivide the groups into different species such as different whales, dolphins, stingrays, bass, sharks, etc. Do the same with the birds. Have the groups move and chant in a manner that would identify their characters. Seat the students toward the back of the stage and have them listen for their cue to join in the story. The emphasis is the creative experience of becoming the sea and air creatures through movement and voice, not on the traditional costume and props of a formal play.

Rehearse the play scene by scene until all are familiar with their parts and the ideas have been incorporated. A tape of ocean sounds played in the background will add to the atmosphere as the Teller narrates the story. Using a microphone will enable everyone to hear their cues and enjoy vocalizing their characters. After a few practices the class will be ready to extend invitations to other classrooms. As the children's comfort and confidence levels increase, the class may elect to add costumes and present it as a formal play for the school or parents' night.

 2 Down in the Sea and Up in the Air.
(Visual-Spatial; Naturalistic)

The War between the Sandpipers and the Whales can involve more sea and air creatures than are mentioned in the story. Divide the class into two teams. One team will research and trace the shapes of sea creatures and the other team will do the air creatures. As teams, have them sort out the different shapes and retrace the best shapes onto heavy tag board. Label the shapes on their undersides.

Each team is now ready to play their own game of identifying their different creatures by shape alone. As they become familiar with the shapes have them exchange shapes with the other team. The ending can be a game of "name that shape" between the two original teams, or in groups of two.

For another colorful experience with shapes, invite the children to create stuffed fish mobiles to hang from the ceiling of the classroom.

 3 Mystery Shell.
(Verbal-Linguistic; Naturalistic)

Collect a set of shells of different sizes, shapes, and colors. Be certain to collect two of each kind of shell. Select one child, hiding his or her shell in a box, to be the Caller. All children initially stand. The Caller announces the properties of his or her shell, without displaying the shell to the classmates. When a property called does not fit the description of a child's shell, that child sits down. The Caller continues calling properties of his or her shell until all the children have sat down except for one. The child that remains standing should hold the shell, which exactly matches that of the Caller. The two students compare shells to ascertain the match. For the next round, redistribute the shells, giving each child a new shell. The child with the match from the previous game becomes the next Caller.

For example, the Caller says, "My shell is brown on the outside." Several children with different colored shells would sit down. The Caller continues, "My shell has a scalloped edge." Children with shells with smooth rims would sit down. The Caller would say, "My shell is pink on the inside." More children would sit down. The descriptions would continue until only one child with the matching shell remains standing.

AUGUST CHAPTER RESOURCES

Andersen, H. C. (1969). *The ugly duckling.* New York: Scholastic.

Babbit, N. (1967). *Dick Foote and the shark.* New York: Farrar, Straus & Giroux.

Bach, R. (1970). *Jonathan Livingston Seagull.* New York: Macmillan.

Baker, J. (1987). *Where the forest meets the sea.* New York: Greenwillow.

Baker, K. (1989). *The magic fan.* New York: Harcourt Brace.

Bang, B. (1978). *The old woman and the rice thief.* New York: Greenwillow.

Barber, A. (1990). *The mousehole cat.* New York: Macmillan.

Base, G. (1992). *The sign of the seahorse: A tale of the greed and high adventure in two acts.* New York: Penguin.

Benchley, N. (1973). *The deep dives of Stanley whale.* New York: Harper & Row.

Brett, J. (1996). *Comet's nine lives.* New York: Putnam.

Brodsky, B. (1977). *Jonah: An old testament story.* New York: Lippincott.

Burningham, J. (1970). *Mr. Grumpy's outing.* London: Cape.

Carle, E. (1987). *A house for hermit crab.* Natick, MA: Picture Book Studio.

Carrick, C. (1984). *Dark and full of secrets.* New York: Clarion.

Cherry, L. (1992). *A river ran wild.* New York: Scholastic.

Clements, A. (1988). *Big Al.* Saxonville, MA: Picture Book Studio.

Cole, S. (1985). *When the tide is low.* New York: Lothrop, Lee & Shepard.

Condra, E. (1994). *See the ocean.* Nashville, TN: Hambleton-Hill.

Cooney, B. (1990). *Hattie and the wild waves: A story from Brooklyn.* New York: Viking Penguin.

Cowan, C. (1997). *My life with the wave.* New York: Lothrop, Lee & Shepard.

Disney, W. (1995). *Pocahontas.* Santa Monica, CA: Disney.

Flack, M. (1977). *Story about Ping.* New York: Puffin.

Forest, H. (1986). The magic fish. On *Sing me a story.* Albany, NY: A Gentle Wind.

Forest, H. (1995). The magic mill. In H. Forest, *Wonder tales from around the world* (p. 195). Little Rock, AK: August House.

Forest, H. (1995). Sandpipers & Whales. In H. Forest, *Wonder tales from around the world* (pp. 39–47). Little Rock, AK: August House.

Forest, H. (1995). A Whale's Tale. In H. Forest, *Wonder tales from around the world* (pp. 1–9). Little Rock, AK: August House.

Froud, B., & Lee, A. (1978). *Faeries.* New York: Harry Abrams.

Gill, S. (1995). *Swimmer.* Homer, AL: Paws IV.

Glaser, M. (1983). *Does anyone know where a hermit crab goes?* Southbridge, MA: Knickerbocker.

Janszen, K. (1995). *Free Willy 2.* New York: Scholastic.

Johnson, C. (1955). *Harold and the purple crayon.* New York: Harper & Row.

Kellogg, S. (1976). *The Island of the skog.* New York: Dial.

Kellogg, S. (1977). *The mysterious tadpole.* New York: Dial.

Leonni, L. (1973). *Swimmy.* New York: Pinwheel.

Lionni, L. (1963). *Swimmy.* New York: Pantheon.

Littledale, F. (1985). *The magic fish.* New York: Scholastic.

MacDonald, G. (1946). *The little island.* Garden City, NY: Doubleday.

MacDonald, M. R. (1986). A whale of a tale. In M. R. MacDonald, *Twenty tellable tales: Audience participation folktales for the beginning storyteller* (pp. 1–9). New York: H. W. Wilson.

MacDonald, M. R. (1992). *The war between the sandpipers and the whales.* In M. R. MacDonald (comp.), *Peace tales: World folktales to talk about* (pp. 39–47). North Haven, CT: The Shoe String Press.

Magdanz, J. (1996). *Go home river.* Portland, OR: Alaska Northwest Books.

McCloskey, R. (1941). *Make way for ducklings.* New York: Viking.

McKissack, P. C. (1992). *A million fish...more or less.* New York: Knopf.

Michl, R. (1985). *A day on the river.* Hauppauge, NY: Barron's.

Noble, T. (1983). *Hansy's mermaid.* New York: Dial.

Oxenbury, H. (1982). *Beach day.* New York: Dial.

Pfister, M. (1992). *The rainbow fish.* New York: North-South Books.

Pratt, K. J. (1994). *A swim through the sea.* Nevada City, CA: Dawn.

Raffi. (1983). *Baby beluga.* New York: Crown.

Raffi. (1987). *Down by the bay.* New York: Crown.

Scieszka, J., & Smith, L. (1998). *Squids will be squids: Fresh morals, beastly fables.* Middlesex, England: Penguin Books.

Seuss, Dr. (1960). *One fish, two fish, red fish, blue fish.* New York: Beginner Books.

Spier, P. (1977). *Noah's ark.* New York: Doubleday.

Stevenson, R. L. (1992). *A child's garden of verses.* New York: Random House.

Stock, C. (1999). *Island summer.* New York: Lothrop, Lee & Shepard.

Trimble, M. (1999). *Malinda Martha and her skipping stones.* Los Altos Hills, CA: Images Press.

White, E. B. (1970). *The trumpet of the swan.* New York: Harper & Row.

Wilson, L. (1991). *Baby whale.* New York: Platt & Munk.

Wise, M. B. (1993). *The seashore noisy book.* New York: Harper & Brothers.

Yorinks, A. (1980). *Louis the fish.* New York: Farrar, Straus & Giroux.

Zamost, B. (1992). *Handstands in the sand.* San Leandro, CA: Sara's Prints.

September

✤

Making New Friends

A WAYFARING SONG

And who will walk a mile with me
Along life's weary way?
A friend whose heart has eyes to see
The stars shine out o'er the darkening lea,
And the quest rest at the end o' the day—
A friend who knows, and dares to say,
The brave, sweet words that cheer the way
Where he walks a mile with me.

-HENRY VAN DYKE
(EXCERPTED FROM THE COMPLETE
POEM "A WAYFARING SONG")

*S*eptember ushers in school days and apples, new friends and old. September heralds the ending of summer and signals the onset of autumn. The chill in the air tinges the leaves with shades of crimson and gold.

"September: Making New Friends" enlists Puppetry, Chant, Draw Talk, and Traditional Storytelling methods. Themes of universal caring and giving, autumn changes, and overcoming prejudice enlighten young minds this month.

Multiple intelligences tapped in activities such as Triaramas and Leaf Patterns are Naturalistic, Intrapersonal, Interpersonal, Verbal-Linguistic, Visual-Spatial, Bodily-Kinesthetic, Logical-Mathematical, and Musical-Rhythmic.

Good stories, like good friends, enrich our lives and brighten our days.

TIPS FOR THE TELLER

The Three Billy Goats Gruff

Retold and Adapted by Susan Trostle Brand and Michelle Berenson

STORYTELLING METHOD

Puppetry

This old, fascinating, classic tale, complete with puppets and a stage, is retold using a peaceful ending. A large, black-bearded Troll and three papier mâché Billy Goat puppets are needed. A puppet stage requires only two scenes: The Billy Goats' valley and river with blue sky above and, later, the other side of the bridge with the grassy meadow and blue sky. A curved bridge is affixed above the puppet stage and remains there throughout the story. The puppets are held above the bridge as they tramp across. The Troll pokes out his head twice, for both the tiny and the medium-sized Billy Goats. Near the end of

Children meet the puppets from
The Three Billy Goats Gruff.

the story, he hops upon the bridge, above the stage, to fight with the largest Billy Goat.

Two puppeteers manipulate the three puppets. A third assistant may be helpful for assisting in scenery changes. Voices of the three Billy Goats should be, alternately, shrill and tiny, medium and clear, and loud and commanding. For the Troll, a raspy, threatening voice works best. The addition of mood music at frightening places and, again, at the end of the story when peace is established is an entertaining option. Invite the audience to sing a favorite friendship song at the end, perhaps, such as "Make New Friends."

A versatile puppet theatre.

The Three Billy Goats Gruff

Narrator: Once upon a time there were three Billy Goats. They lived in a valley. The three goats were brothers, and their name was Gruff. There was a great Big Billy Goat *(goat appears over stage and bows)*, a Medium Billy Goat *(second goat joins first and bows)*, and a tiny, little Baby Billy Goat *(third goat joins first two above stage, and bows; all three goats exit)*. The goats found very little grass in the valley and soon they became very hungry. They wanted to go to the meadow on the other side of the river. There they could eat and eat and eat. They could grow nice and big and fat! But there was one problem. To get to the other meadow the Billy Goats had to cross over a bridge. Now, the bridge was not a problem, since it was a strong and sturdy bridge and it was not too long. But underneath that little strong and sturdy bridge lived a very mean and very ugly Troll *(enter Troll above stage; he growls and bows, then exits)*. The Baby Goat was afraid to cross over the bridge.

Baby Billy Goat: *(standing near end of bridge)* Ohhhhhh! I am not going to cross this bridge. I'd rather stay hungry. A mean and ugly Troll lives beneath it. I can hear him growling even as I speak!

Troll: GRRRRRRRRRRRRRRRRRRRRR!

Big Billy Goat: Don't be afraid, brother. You are much too small. Just tell the troll that you have a bigger and tastier brother who will soon cross the bridge. The troll won't hurt you then!

Baby Billy Goat: Okay, big brother. Here I go! *(tiptoes across bridge)* Trip-Trap, Trip-Trap, Trip-Trap *(assistant lightly taps wood behind stage)*.

Troll: WHO'S THAT TRIPPING OVER MY BRIDGE?

Baby Billy Goat: It is I, the Baby Billy Goat Gruff. I'm crossing the bridge to go to the meadow. There I will make myself fat.

Troll: Oh, no you're not! I am going to gobble you up, Baby Billy Goat!

Baby Billy Goat: Please don't gobble me up. I'm very tiny. Wait for my brother, Medium Billy Goat. He is much larger and tastier than I.

Troll: Well then, be off with you! *(Baby Goat completes crossing)*

Narrator: A little later the second Billy Goat Gruff decided he was getting too hungry to wait much longer. But he, too, was afraid to cross the bridge.

Medium Billy Goat: Ohhhh, I am so very hungry. I want to cross the bridge to join Baby Billy Goat. But I am quite afraid of the troll!

Big Billy Goat: Do not be afraid, brother. Just tramp over the bridge. If the Troll tries to stop you, tell him that you have a much bigger and much tastier brother who will soon be crossing the bridge. Then the troll will not bother you!

Medium Billy Goat: Very well. Here I go. Trip-Trap, Trip-Trap, Trip-Trap *(assistant taps wood more loudly behind stage as goat walks across bridge)*.

Troll: Who's that tripping over my bridge?

Medium Billy Goat: It is I, the medium-sized Billy Goat. I'm crossing the bridge because I am so very hungry. I am going to the meadow on the other side to eat and eat and make myself fat!

Troll: No, you're not! For I am hungry, too! And I am going to GOBBLE YOU UP!

Medium Billy Goat: Please don't gobble me up, Troll. I'm only a medium-sized goat! Wait for the next Billy Goat. He is much bigger!

Troll: Well, then, be off with you! *(Medium Goat completes crossing)*

Narrator: The third Billy Goat was hungry by now. And, unlike his two brothers, he was not afraid, for he was big and strong.

Big Billy Goat: TRIP-TRAP-TRIP-TRAP-TRIP-*TRAP (stomps across bridge as assistant bangs loudly on wood behind stage).*

Troll: WHO'S THAT TRIPPING OVER MY BRIDGE?

Big Billy Goat: IT IS I, THE BIG BILLY GOAT GRUFF. I'M VERY HUNGRY. I'M CROSSING THE BRIDGE TO GET TO THE MEADOW. THERE I WILL EAT AND EAT AND MAKE MYSELF FAT!

Troll: NO, YOU'RE NOT! FOR I AM GOING TO GOBBLE YOU UP! HERE I COME! WHOA!! WHOA!! I'VE SLIPPED! *(Troll hangs head-first off edge of bridge)* I'M FALLING! HELP ME! HELP ME!

(all three Billy Goats come to view falling Troll, who hangs upside down from bridge)

Big Billy Goat: Why should we help you, you old, ugly meanie?

Medium Billy Goat: Right, big brother! All that Troll's ever done is threaten and scare us! Our lives would be much easier and more peaceful without him! Let him fall into the river!

Baby Billy Goat: May I say something, brothers? *(brothers nod)*

I may be young, but I know something about life. I've learned that even when people are unkind to you, you should still be nice to them. We need to help the poor Troll before he dies!

Medium Billy Goat: Hmmm. I don't know about that.

Big Billy Goat: Baby brother is right! For a little guy, he sure is wise! I'm the biggest Goat. I'll help the Troll. You two stay here and wrap a blanket around him. He's had a bad scare. *(Big Goat pulls Troll onto the bridge; Medium and Baby Goats wrap a blanket around Troll)*

Troll: Oh, my! What a fright I've had! Serves me right, I guess, for being so mean to you goats. Thank you so much for saving my life!

Big and Medium Billy Goats: *(in unison)*

You were trouble to us at first sight;
All you wanted to do was fight;
We could have let you die in fright—
But Baby Goat taught us what was right!

Big Billy Goat: Would you like to come and play with us in the meadow, Troll?

Troll: *(clapping hands)* Well, well, I'd like that very much! No one has EVER asked me to be their friend before!

> I was once a mean old Troll,
> I thought that fighting was cool;
> Now that I have nice, new friends
> The green, green grass never ends!

Narrator: The three Billy Goats Gruff and the very ugly, but not-so-mean Troll went off to play together in the meadow. They lived happily ever after and became quite fat.

MULTIPLE INTELLIGENCE ACTIVITIES FOR . . .

The Three Billy Goats Gruff

 ### Charades.
(Visual-Spatial; Bodily-Kinesthetic)

Write the names of events, objects, and characters from *The Three Billy Goats Gruff* on several slips of paper. Fold papers. Place these papers inside a box or a model of a bridge. Children each select one slip of paper and pantomime the named thing for classmates, who try to guess the character, event, object, or emotion from the story. The first student to guess successfully becomes the next actor or actress. Ideas for charades include:

Characters and Events:
Small Billy Goat tiptoeing across the bridge
Medium Billy Goat walking across the bridge
Large Billy Goat stomping across the bridge
Troll shaking fists at Billy Goats
Troll hanging off edge of bridge
Troll and Billy Goats shaking hands; becoming friends

Objects and Places:
River
Bridge
Grass
Meadow

Emotions:
Confidence (large Billy Goat)
Timidity (smallest Billy Goat)
Anger (Troll)

Fear (small and medium Billy Goats)
Relief (all three Billy Goats when Troll becomes friendly)
Panic (Troll, hanging off edge of bridge)
Trust (first two Billy Goats who listen to their brother)
Gratitude (Troll, upon being saved by Billy Goats)

 ### Glad to Be Me.
(Intrapersonal; Interpersonal)

Review the special features and positive attributes of each of the four characters in the *The Three Billy Goats Gruff* story. Then discuss the fact that each child is also special in his or her own way. Each child draws him or herself (or use copies of school pictures) in the center of a large, white paper. Around the child, draw several lines, sufficient in number for each classmate to write one phrase or word on each of the lines. Each child writes a word or phrase about him or herself telling his or her best quality or personality characteristic. For example, Manuel begins his "Glad to Be Me" page by writing on one line, "good at sports." He passes his page on to his neighbor, who uses the next line and writes about Manuel, "helpful to others." Encourage each child to write something positive and unique and to write his or her name or initials beside the contribution.

A "Glad to Be Me" poster.

When every page is completed, you may mount and frame the autographed pictures and send them home. Prepare for many smiles and lots of good feelings about self and others!

 Triaramas.
(Visual-Spatial; Verbal-Linguistic)

Triaramas are paper displays that focus on a particular aspect of a story. They assist in developing comprehension and, simultaneously, promote students' direction-following, creative and artistic skills. You will need: 9″ × 9″ construction paper, paper scraps, glue, stapler, liquid markers, crayons, pencils.

A "Quadrarama."

Directions:
1. Fold the top right corner of the square of paper downward to the lower left corner. Fold the top left corner of the remaining triangle downward to the lower right corner.
2. Open paper. Turn the paper so that you are looking at a diamond shape instead of a square.
3. Cut along the fold line in the center of the bottom half of the diamond, stopping where the fold lines meet in the center.

4. On the top half of the diamond (two triangular sections) draw a scene from the story.
5. Fold the two bottom sections together, overlapping them completely. Glue.
6. Add stand-up parts to enhance the triarama, such as trees, fences, animals, buildings, and characters with dialogue bubbles.

Note: Four triaramas can be joined to form a Quadrarama, as shown in the illustration.

TIPS FOR THE TELLER

Pigs...Bears

By OUAT (Once Upon a Time) Storyteller Mike Myers
Adapted by Jeanne M. Donato

STORYTELLING METHOD

Chant

Pigs...Bears is a delightful, original story in which the pigs and bears become friends and delight in each other's company. Some characters in the story assume that the pigs and bears would not want to sit in the movies, dine, or dance together. The pigs and bears continue to enjoy their friendship throughout the story, because they see each other as delightfully different.

Following the model in Chapter 3 for Chant Storytelling, the Teller reviews the stories of *The Three Pigs* and *The Three Bears*. Then the Teller asks, "What would happen if the pigs and the bears met each other in another story? How are pigs and bears different? How are they alike? Do you think different animals could become friends? What qualities do the animals in this story have that make for being a good friend? Conclude by saying, "You are going to discover the answer!"

After the discussion, the Teller explains that during the story there will be opportunities for the children to become the voices that chant "Pigs...bears...pigs...bears...pigs...bears." Before beginning the story, the Teller may want to establish a signal such as a nod of the head or a hand gesture to indicate when everyone may join in the chant. An asterisk indicates the text in which the class or audiencce participates. This text is printed on the chalkboard or a flip chart in advance so that they can easily see their part.

Pigs...Bears

I am walking, walking, walking in the woods. Pine needles squish and crinkle as I'm walking, walking, walking. The smell of pine fills my senses. The sunlight dances through the tall pines, making the ground glitter and dance.

I come up to two little houses, a brick house with a straw roof, shutters made of sticks and a squat, round oak door. The second house is forest green with a large gold lock on the front door. Wild red roses climb to the top of this very tall house.

Behind the two houses there are blueberry bushes, a vegetable garden, fruit trees, and a stream so small that it cannot babble. A big picnic table with a fire truck red umbrella sits between the two backyards like a bridge of friendship. It passes over the stream.

And I'll bet you didn't know that the three pigs live right next door to the three bears. ❋**Pigs...bears...pigs...bears...pigs...bears.** They are the best of friends. All summer long they have picnics together under that red umbrella, playing cards every Wednesday night. They always share work and fun and food.

The pigs are named Patty, Paul, and Priscilla. They are porkers.

Patty chose sticks.

Huffinpuff!

Paul thought straw was the quickest way to build a house.

Huffinpuff!

Priscilla was the pig that built the brick house.

Huffinpuff and Huffinpuff and huffinpuff and huff and puff and a nice wolf stew.

Priscilla is the pinkest pig in the history of pink pigs. She wears a tutu and a Kermit the Frog t-shirt.

The bears' names are Bunchy, Barrella, and Basey Bear. They are grizzlies.

Bunchy is gigantic, enormous, and hairy. Nobody ate *his* oatmeal!

Barrella has soft brown eyes, as soft as the bed she sleeps in. Barrella is always on a diet that consists of eating all the time. She is as large as a barrel. That's how she got her name.

Basey Bear is the baby bear with the broken chair. He wants to be a "basebear" player for Chicago. Basey is a goofy looking bear with leaves and stuff stuck in his fur. He isn't just goofy looking; he is really goofy, but he doesn't work for Disney. Some days he puts his shoes on the wrong feet, and he never figures it out.

Priscilla is Basey's best friend. Priscilla loves to sing a song from one of the biggest pigs of England's past. It goes, "I'm Henry the oink I am, Henry the oink I am I am, I got married to the widow next door, she's been married seven times before." Basey Bear liked her singing.

Basey Bear is Priscilla's best friend. Basey Bear also loves to sing. Almost everybody puts their fingers in their ears when Basey sings, "I'm Henry the one two three, I am. Something something something."

Priscllla plays catch with Basey Bear when he asks. Priscilla doesn't put her fingers in her ears when Basey Bear sings, though. They are best friends.

All Priscilla had to do was put her snout up in the air and sniff four times. She could point to the nearest honey tree for Basey Bear. Then Basey would climb the tree and come down with a zillion mad bees stuck in his fur and completely honey-sticky from head to toe. Priscilla Pig likes honey, too. They are best friends.

One Wednesday night, Priscilla and Basey were sitting at the picnic table playing "pig-nochle" and declaring trump. Priscilla said that they should go into town to see a movie and have some fun. Everyone agreed: ❋**Pigs...bears...pigs...bears...pigs...bears.** On Friday night, they had an early snack and walked into town. It was the first time they had seen the lights of the city and they oohed and ahhed at everything. After walking, walking, walking for a long time they could see the bright lights of the Bijou Theatre. It was all red and purple neon lights with hundreds of light bulbs forming an arc around the marquee, and the name of the movie was *Planet of the Humans*. Bunchy Bear walked up to the ticket booth and, right away the ape in the booth asked "Three tickets?"

Bunchy said, "No, I want six." ✱**Pigs...bears...pigs...bears...pigs...bears.**

The ape got a funny look on her face and said, "OK."

They looked at the posters of coming attractions framed on the red velvet walls and went through big double doors into the theater.

An usher walked over to them and said, "Bears sit on *this* side and pigs sit on *that* side."

Bunchy said, "We are friends and we want to sit together." ✱**Pigs...bears...pigs...bears...pigs...bears.**

The usher took them to the first row, where you have to look straight up to see the movie.

Basey Bear and Priscilla asked for money to go to the concession stand. Patty Pig and Barrella Bear reached into their purses and gave them money to buy popcorn for everyone and something for themselves. Priscilla Pig got frozen garbage on a stick, and Basey Bear got baby bees dipped in honey, and a monstrous bucket of popcorn.

Just before the movie started, they could hear the audience behind them whispering, ✱**Pigs...bears...pigs...bears...pigs...bears.** But, when they turned around, nobody said anything.

When the movie was over Paul Pig said, "I'm hungry as a bear. Let's find someplace to eat." So they did. They walked up the street until they came to a fancy restaurant called Chez Louis. They walked in. The maitre d' said, "Table for three?"

"No." Said Bunchy-Bear. "There are six of us." ✱**Pigs...bears...pigs...bears...pigs...bears.**

"But the pigs usually sit in *this* dining room, and the bears sit in *that* dining room."

Bunchy Bear replied, "Well, we are friends and we want to sit together." ✱**Pigs...bears...pigs...bears...pigs...bears.**

The maitre d' took them into the dining room. All the tables were covered with fine linen, fancy china, silver flatware, and crystal glasses. Everything was absolutely elegant. The waiter came to the table and poured water into the glasses and gave them menus. The menus were very big and everything was written in French. Since none of them read French, Bunchy Bear scratched his head, pointed to a table nearby and said, "We'll have what they are having."

As they sat there they could hear voices whispering, ✱**Pigs...bears...pigs...bears...pigs...bears.** But, when they turned around, nobody said anything.

They didn't listen to those voices, and they had a meal to remember. Salmon with dill sauce, little potatoes, peas, hot rolls, and afterward the waiter brought them a flaming dessert and the bill. Bunchy Bear paid for everything with his Animal Express card.

They walked down the street until they came to a purple and orange flashing neon sign that said, "Dance...Dance...Dance...Dance...Dance..."

And Barrella Bear said, "Let's go in. I would love to go dancing." So they did.

Bunchy turned to Barrella Bear and asked, "May I have this dance?"

Barrella replied, "I'd be happy." Clumsily they pawed at the dance floor. Paul Pig looked at Patty Pig and asked, "May I?"

"Yes," replied Patty. Off they twirled with their tails in a curl.

Basey Bear looked at Priscilla Pig and said, "Wanna dance?"

"Certainly," replied Priscilla.

They did the bear-cha-cha, the pig twist, and as they spun and had fun the voices came back, **✱Pigs...bears...pigs...bears...pigs...bears.** They stopped dancing. They looked around. Nobody said anything. So they had fun and danced no matter what those voices said.

They left the dance hall arm in arm. They had a wonderful night in town. Do you know why they were such good friends? Nobody ever taught them that they weren't supposed to be friends. **✱Pigs...bears...pigs...bears...pigs...bears.**

MULTIPLE INTELLIGENCE ACTIVITIES FOR . . .

Pigs...Bears

 ### It's Very Nice to Meet You.
(Musical-Rhythmic; Interpersonal)

Have the children sit down in a large circle. This allows everyone to feel part of the group. The following questions are suggestions to help lead a discussion to help the children contemplate and share what it feels like to go to a new school or grade and meet new classmates, or a new teacher.

Share a time when you felt like the "new" person. How do you greet a friend when you meet them walking down the street? Elicit "wave your hand" as one of the answers. This makes a great lead-in to the "It's Very Nice to Meet You!" song. This is a very easy and effective song, sung accompanied by a guitar or an autoharp, with the children clapping the rhythm and waving.

Discuss with the class the idea that the more we get together with new people, the more opportunities we have to discover and enjoy new friends like the pigs and bears did. The class may want to collect coffee cans to make drums; combs covered with wax paper attached with rubberbands will make a hum-a-zoo; and rice placed inside the coffee cans will make rhythm rattles when shaken.

It's Very Nice to Meet You!

*(Tune: "Buffalo Gals Won't You Come Out Tonight"
—Traditional) Words by Jeanne Donato*

As I was walking down the street, down the street, down the street

A very good friend I chanced to meet and
(Pause, for the child to say his/her own name)
was his name-oh!

Take your hand and wave hello, wave hello, wave hello.

Take your hand and wave hello. It's very nice to meet you!

This rhythm band will lend itself to many activities such as singing and marching to these friendship songs. The children may decide to share and sing their friendship song in honor of a new classmate, to greet other classrooms, at a school assembly, or for a parent-teacher night. Acting out the story *Pigs...Bears* will add to the friendship festivities.

② New Friends.
(Musical-Rhythmic; Bodily-Kinesthetic)

Make a bulletin board titled "New Friends." After the first telling of *Pigs...Bears,* lead the class into the discussion questions: "What do the animals in this story have that would make them good friends?" "What qualities would you look for in a new friend?" List the children's suggestions on heart-shaped cards and display on the board. Encourage them to read and discuss each quality. Some good friendship words include: Caring, Kind, Thoughtful, Listening, Fun, Considerate, Warm, Giving, Sharing, Loving, etc.

Another way to celebrate the fun of discovering new friends and to use the friendship words is to have the children sing and dance to "The Friendship Song." Guitar chords are included.

The Friendship Song
(Tune: "New River Train—Traditional")

1. Making friends is more fun with one

   A

   Making friends is more fun with one

   D   **G**

   For when you make one, there's lots of [insert friendship word here] and fun

   D   **A**   **D**

   Making friends is more fun with one.

   D

2. Making friends is more fun with two

   A

   Making friends is more fun with two

   D   **G**

   For when you have two, there's lots of [insert friendship word here] here to do

   D   **A**

   Making friends is more fun with two.

3. For when you have three, there's lots of [insert friendship word here] to see

4. For when you have four, there's lots of [insert friendship word here] and more

5. For when you have five, there's lots of [insert friendship word here] all your lives

6. For when you have six, there's lots of [insert friendship word here] in a fix

7. For when you have seven, there's lots of [insert friendship word here] like heaven

8. For when you have eight, there's lots of [insert friendship word here] of late

9. For when you have nine, there's lots of [insert friendship word here] so fine

10. For when you have ten, there's lots of [insert friendship word here] my friends

Friendship Dance:
1. Review "The Friendship Song."
2. Dance as follows:

   Formation: Ten children form a circle facing outward. Each child is given one of the friendship quality hearts from the bulletin board.

   Verse 1: One child is picked to be the lead child. He or she skips around the outside of the circle, during the first verse. The child sings the quality of a friend written on his or her heart when the refrain, "there's lots of [friendship word]" is sung. All the children sing the verses, clap in rhythm to the music and/or play their instruments.

   Verse 2: The lead child continues to skip around the circle. When the refrain, "for when you have two (three, etc.)" is sung, the lead child stops and picks one of the children nearest him or her. They join hands. At the refrain, "there's lots of..." the new friend sings the friendship word written on his or her heart. They continue skipping around the circle facing the children remaining in the circle.

   Verses 3–10: Follow the same pattern till all the children are included. The children are now holding hands skipping in a large circle facing inward.

   Rotation: The rest of the class sings the song and plays their rhythm instruments. A new group of dancers are chosen until everyone has had a chance to dance and play an instrument.

Delightfully Different.
(Interpersonal; Musical-Rhythmic)

Discuss the concept of how different objects can have similar qualities; size, color, etc. Display a picture of a rainbow and discuss the different colors that are needed to make one. Note that each color is different and yet adds to the beauty of the rainbow. On a flip chart, use rainbow colors to list the different ways that people in our human family are different and yet similar to each other. These qualities are referred to in the "Different" song activity.

Introduce choral singing in the following song, by Julie Garnett. This activity lends itself to many creative presentations. The Leader sings the first line, the students repeat it, and everyone joins in singing the last lines, as they act out each of the actions mentioned in the refrains. Divide the children into two groups, facing each other. Each group of children chants (and later, sings) their part of this favorite song as they all join in the movements. The letters (A) and (B) refer the accompanist to the corresponding part in the music.

Different

Words and music by Julie Garnett

"Different" (© 1999 Tigerlily Music. From Julie Garnett's cassette *Starry Eyed*. Melody line arranged by Jean Liepold).

255

(A)

Leader: Clap your hands for being different
Students: Clap your hands for being different
All: Clap your hands for being different
All: Different everyone

(A)

Leader: Stamp your feet for being different
Students: Stamp your feet for being different
All: Stamp your feet for being different
All: Different everyone

(B)

Group 1: The color of our skin
The clothes we like to wear
We all have different eyes
We all have different hair
A voice that's high or low
We all have different names
How boring it would be if we were all the same

(A)

Leader: Wave your arms for being different
Students: Wave your arms for being different
All: Wave your arms for being different
All: Different everyone

(A)

Leader: *(spoken)* How high can you hop?
Leader: Hop, hop, hop, for being different
Students: Hop, hop, hop, for being different
All: Hop, hop, hop, for being different
All: Different everyone

(B)

Group 2: We come in different shapes
All ages, heights, and styles
We all like different food
We all wear different smiles

Some ways we're the same
We laugh, we love, we cry
But we're different like the colors
of a rainbow in the sky

(A)

Leader: Clap real soft for being different
Students: Clap real soft for being different
All: Clap real soft for being different
All: Different everyone

(A)

Leader: Clap real loud for being different
Students: Clap real loud for being different
All: Clap real loud for being different
All: Different everyone

(A)

Leader: *(spoken)* Get on up and dance
Leader: Dance, dance, dance, for being different
Students: Dance, dance, dance, for being different
All: Dance, dance, dance, for being different
All: Different everyone

(A)

Coda

Leader: *(spoken)* Everybody
Leader: Dance, dance, dance, for being different
Students: Dance, dance, dance, for being different
All: Dance, dance, dance, for being different
All: Different everyone

Leader: That's what makes it fun
All: We're different everyone!

TIPS FOR THE TELLER

The Most Beautiful Thing in the World

Retold and Adapted by Susan Trostle Brand

STORYTELLING METHOD

Draw Talk

The Most Beautiful Thing in the World, retold and adapted from the folktale of the same name, is a moving story of the Chinese king of Yong-An and his three sons. As the king grew old, he informed his sons that he would choose one of them to wear his crown. He gave each son one hundred gold coins. The first two sons buy a beautiful picture and a precious pearl. The third son, however, encounters many poor and homeless people near his home. He spends all of his gold on helping them and, therefore, has no gift to bring his father. In the meantime, word has traveled to the king about the kind heart of the youngest son, who is ultimately rewarded with his father's crown. The greatest gift was that of friendship.

This story can be told using a number of storytelling approaches. Because of the small number of characters and simple plot, it lends itself well to Puppetry. A small group of children, likewise, may Group Role-Play the story. A third alternative, the one selected for this chapter, is the Draw Talk method. The Teller uses five sheets of 24" by 36" newsprint on which he or she draws six major scenes from the story. These may be sketched onto the paper before the telling. Using red, purple, gold, and green liquid markers, the Teller weaves the story, through words and synchronized drawings, which culminates with the crowning of the third son. The Teller may color some images in advance to shorten the story's length.

Introduce the story using the story introduction model, described in Chapter 3. You may also inform the group that this story is about a kingdom in China called Yong-An, which in English means "forever peace."

The Most Beautiful Thing in the World

Page one: One day, the king of Yong-An was sitting on his throne *(draw king on chair)*. The king wore a beautiful robe of red, purple, and gold *(draw robe as you say each color)*. On his head he wore a golden crown with a large purple jewel in the center *(draw crown and add jewel)*. He said, "My sons, I grow old. Soon I must choose one of you to wear my crown. To win that crown, you must bring me the most beautiful thing in the world."

Page two: The first son came to the king *(draw son)*. He kneeled before his father. The son wore a purple robe *(draw robe, using purple marker)*. On his head, he wore a pointed purple hat. He had black hair, a small mustache, and a pointed beard. His hands were folded on his chest *(draw each item as it is named)*.

The second son came to the king and kneeled before him. The second son wore a green robe. On his head, he wore a pointed green hat. He had black hair, a thin face, a thin mustache, and a tiny beard. His hands were folded on his chest *(draw each feature and item as you name it)*.

The third son kneeled before his father. He wore a bright red robe. On his head, he wore a pointed red hat. He had black hair with long sideburns. He wore a little smile on his sweet face. He had no mustache and no beard. He folded his hands across his chest *(draw each item and feature as you say it)*.

The king gave the first son one hundred coins. He placed the coins in a purple box *(draw gold coins in purple box)*. The king gave the second son one hundred coins. He placed the coins in a green box *(draw gold coins in green box)*. Next, the king gave the third son one hundred coins. He placed the coins in a red box *(draw gold coins in red box)*. The king told his three sons, "You have nine days. Go. Seek. Find." The three princes hurried away.

Page three: On a white horse, the oldest prince rode from one market town to another, seeking but not finding. He fingered tasseled tapestries and stroked silken robes but saw nothing worthy of his father's throne. The ninth morning, he came to the house of a painter. The painter *(draw artist)* wore a red robe *(draw red robe)*. On his head, he wore a pointed red hat *(draw hat)*. In his hand he held a paint brush *(draw paint brush)*.

A square picture lay on a table before the artist *(in purple, draw square paper atop table)*. The first son, in his purple hat and purple robe, gazed with admiration at the picture *(draw smiling son)*. He said, "Surely this must be the most beautiful thing in the world!"

He traded his gold for the painting and rode toward the palace.

Page four: On a black horse, the middle prince rode into the mountains, seeking but not finding. The last night, he saw white smoke and a light coming from a cave. Quiet as a shadow, he led his horse toward the light. In the cave, he found an enormous purple dragon *(draw purple dragon)*. Under the dragon's chin glowed a perfect pearl with gold lights around it *(draw gold pearl and add sun rays around it)*. "Surely this pearl is the most beautiful thing in the world!" the prince said. "But how shall I gain it?"

The prince knew the dragon would not sell his treasure. So that night, he caught and roasted nine swallows. At sunrise, on the ninth day, he laid the swallows on a large leaf *(draw gold swallows and green leaf)*. The swallows were a gift for the dragon.

Hungrily, the dragon ate the swallows. Then he dropped the pearl at the prince's feet. Bowing to the dragon, *(draw son kneeling over leaf)* the prince tucked the gleaming pearl into his sash. Then how he rode toward the palace!

Page five: Meanwhile, the youngest prince walked among his father's people, seeking beauty but finding only sadness and great need *(draw street with several run-down shacks with yellow straw roofs)*. He saw people with ragged clothing *(draw sitting people in yellow and green clothing)*. Some cried from hunger. Some had no homes and had to sleep in the streets *(add sleeping people)*. Wanting to help, the prince gave one gold coin after another *(draw youngest prince)*. Hungry people ate. Those who wore ragged clothes bought new robes. Ones who lacked shelter built homes.

There was joy in the city. As the youngest prince gave away his last coin, his brothers came riding by. "Ah, foolish one, come with us," they said.

Page six: At the palace, the king sat waiting. He wore his gold robe and golden crown *(on throne, draw king wearing gold robe and gold crown)*. The oldest son showed the painting *(draw long purple scroll painting)*. "Magnificent!" said the king. The middle prince showed the pearl *(draw glowing golden pearl)*. "Perfect!" said the king.

The youngest prince hung his head *(draw prince, kneeling before his father)*. "Father, I am sorry," he said. "I have no beautiful thing to show you."

"Ah, you are wrong, my son," the king said. "Word of your kindness has come daily." He smiled at his youngest son *(draw smile on king)*.

Page seven: The king looked at his youngest son. The son still wore his red robe, but he had removed his pointed red hat. The king gazed at his black hair and his gentle smile *(draw youngest son as you talk)*.

"You have shown me the most beautiful thing of all—friendship, and a caring heart. Because of this friendship to those in need, you deserve the crown," the king said.

Thus, the king placed the golden crown atop the head of his youngest son *(draw gold crown atop head of son)*. The new king ruled long and with justice in Yong-An.

MULTIPLE INTELLIGENCE ACTIVITIES FOR . . .

The Most Beautiful Thing in the World

 1 It's a Small World.
(Musical-Rhythmic; Interpersonal)

Introduce the children to sign language. You may choose to begin with the letters of the sign language alphabet. Later, as children gain familiarity, help them to learn the song, "It's a Small World," in sign language (see Sign Language Alphabet).

 2 Hug O' War.
(Verbal-Linguistic; Interpersonal)

Outdoors, provide a long rope. Divide the children into two teams. Play a game of tug-of-war. Back inside, discuss the way the winning team feels. Then the losing team tells how it feels. Next, children find examples, in newspapers and magazines, of wars and violence, in which people suffer as a result of struggles to control. Invite children to brainstorm peaceful solutions to conflicts and suffering, at home, at school, and in the world. You may decide to adopt a group in your community such as a shelter or a nursing home, and show them support via cards, good deeds, and visits.

Tell children that you have a poem about an activity in which everyone wins. Introduce Shel Silverstein's poem "Hug O'War." Follow the poem reading with hugs for all!

Hug O' War

I will not play at tug o' war
I'd rather play at hug o' war,
Where everyone hugs
Instead of tugs,
Where everyone giggles
And rolls on the rug,
And everyone kisses,
And everyone grins,
And everyone cuddles,
And everyone wins.

"Hug O' War," in *Where the Sidewalk Ends,* is used with permission of HarperCollins Publishers, Copyright © 1974 by Evil Eye Music, Inc.

 3 Hello Around the World.
(Musical-Rhythmic; Verbal-Linguistic)

Teach the children this song related to universal friendship and multiculturalism. Afterward, help children to discover additional words, climates, clothing, and customs from other countries. The children might conduct research and prepare a large chart, comparing several aspects of different countries.

Sign Language Alphabet

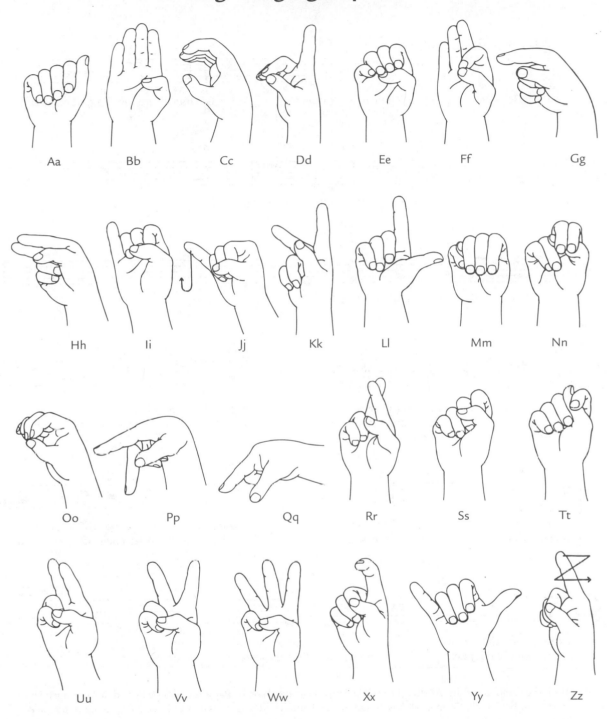

Sign Language alphabet.

Hello to All the Children of the World

"Hello to All the Children of the World" (From *Wee Sing Around the World* by Pamela Conn Beall and Susan Hagen Nipp, Copyright © 1994 by Pamela Conn Beall and Susan Hagen Nipp. Used by permission of Price Sloan & Stern, Inc., a division of Penguin Putnam Inc.)

TIPS FOR THE TELLER

How the Leaves Got Their Colors
Retold and Adapted by Jeanne M. Donato

STORYTELLING METHOD
Traditional/Chant

This story is a retelling of an old Native American Cherokee tale. The trees are given their choice of colors to wear to greet The Great Sun when he returns from the North Country. They are warned not to take the colors too early or they will fall asleep and lose their leaves. Their concerns for getting the colors that they want overshadow their duty to stay awake to greet the Sun. The trees that become friends remain awake by helping each other and are given the gift of remaining evergreen.

This telling is done with movement and facial gestures. In telling the story you can invite the children to join in the North Wind's refrain of "Watch, wait, and stay awake." Before beginning the story, the Teller may want to establish a signal such as a nod of the head or a hand gesture (in imitation of the wind) to indi-cate when everyone can join in the chanting. An asterisk indicates the text in which the class or audience participates. This text is printed on the chalkboard or a flip chart in advance so that they can easily see their part. During the first telling you may want to also verbally invite the class or audience to join in.

Set the tone of the story with a discussion on friendship and the qualities of a good friend. Ask the children to listen and note the qualities of friendship that the trees manifest to help them at the end of the story.

Refer to Chapter 3 for information on the Traditional and Chant methods of storytelling. Display a collection of actual or artificial autumn leaves as an introduction to this story. Discuss their properties and link children's prior knowledge to this topic.

How the Leaves Got Their Colors

Once, a very long time ago, all the trees in the forest were green. The Great Sun decided to give the trees the gift of many colors to celebrate his return from the north. He chose the brilliant colors of the sunrise and sunset and gave them to the North Wind saying, "Take these colors to all the trees so they may share them. But warn them that it takes much energy to wear such beautiful colors. If they dress them too early, they will fall asleep and lose their leaves. Tell them that I will send signs so they will have enough time to prepare for my return."

The North Wind swept over the trees whispering the news. He buried the colors under the ground where the trees could find them.

"But how will we know when to get ready?" the trees murmured.

"Be patient. ✱Watch, wait, and stay awake. You will know the signs when you see them," answered the Wind as he blew back to the North.

The trees rustled with excitement. "Did you see those beautiful colors? Why, I don't know which one to choose!"

In the cool evening air, the Catalpa fanned itself with its large, heart-shaped leaves and sighed, "I love bright yellow. Yes, yellow mixed with my green will be just perfect for my leaves! I must make sure that I get all the yellow my leaves will need. The animals are gathering the berries from the bushes. It is getting cool enough. I feel a frost in the air. I'm sure of it." And so the Catalpa tree hurriedly drew the bright yellow of the sun up into its leaves. Dancing and swaying in the wind, it called to the others, "Look at me! No one has leaves that look as splendid as mine! The Great Sun will notice me first when he returns."

The other trees shook their branches and whispered, "Why, the frost has not even kissed the grass at night! Foolish Catalpa has dressed much too early!" The warm days passed and the trees watched as Catalpa's heart-shaped leaves drooped and fell from the branches. Soon Catalpa fell asleep with barren branches.

"Foolish Catalpa dressed too early!" the other trees reminded themselves. But within their trunks they wondered, "What if more trees decide to dress early? We may not get our choice of color." And so, uneasily, the trees watched each other and waited for signs of the Great Sun's return.

The Sumac, which grows low to the ground, was first to notice frost's kiss on the mossy ground. "Oh!" he cried, "winter is near! That means the Sun will return soon!" And he drew the burning red color into his leaves, lighting up the forest with a blaze of color. Sumac took so much red that he is still called the fire-bush. He burned until both he and his leaves dropped off in sleep.

When the birds started to leave their nests and gather to fly south, the Elm and Beech trees rushed to soak up the russet yellows. The Birches and Poplars drew in the pure gold, while the Nut trees vied for the brightest yellows. Standing amid the forest with their delicate leaves shimmering, they rustled, "Oh what glorious colors! Don't we look splendid?" But, as the days passed, they grew tired and fell into a listless slumber. Their leaves dropped as the North Wind passed by rustling their branches.

The North Wind shook his head and whispered to the other trees, "Whoooo! ✱Watch, wait, and stay awake! Winter is not yet here. It is not time for the Sun to return!"

The other trees in the forest became alarmed murmuring, "But what if there is not enough color left? What will become of us?"

The nights grew longer and the days shorter. The Sassafras fretted, "This must be the last sign of the Great Sun's coming. Surely, if we wait any longer we will not be ready to greet him!"

The Maples shook their branches, fretting, "If the Sassafras is going to take some of the colors there may not be enough left for us. We don't want to be left out! We must grab some for ourselves! Now!" And they drew up the blazing oranges, lemon yellows, and flame reds sending the forest into a riot of color as they shook their leaves in the cold breeze. Confident, they watched as the North Wind stripped the colors from the trees that had not waited till now and laughed at the others who had not joined them. Weeks passed as, one by one, their leaves floated to the ground in a brilliant shower covering the ground. One by one, they nodded asleep.

The Oaks, disdainful of the other trees' impatience, waited. They listened for the sounds of acorns dropping on the ground and the chattering of squirrels scampering over the fallen leaves to gather them. Hearing this, the proud Oaks agreed, "This must be the final sign! We cannot wait for the other foolish trees!"

"But winter's snows have not even covered the ground," whispered the Pines, Hemlocks, Spruce, and Cedars.

"What does it matter?" replied the haughty Oaks. "We are strong and quite capable of holding on to our leaves. The others have taken most of the colors. If we do not act now you may try to take the colors for yourselves. We cannot take that chance!" With that, the mighty Oaks drew in the remaining reds from scarlet to wine, adding warm bronze and browns to their leaves.

The Pines, Hemlocks, Spruce, and Cedars realized that there were no colors left for them. Sighing, they closed their branches to protect each other against the wind and rain and to shelter the few birds left in the forest. They whispered to each other, "The Great Sun asked us to stay awake to greet him. We must not disappoint him. If we help each other we will be able to do it. Remember that we need to **✼watch, wait, and stay awake.** We can do this together!" And so the remaining trees huddled through the long dark nights bending under the blankets of snow that winter spread over them. Whenever one of the trees started to drift off to sleep the others would rustle their boughs and whisper, **✼"Watch, wait, and stay awake.** We can do this together. Surely, the Sun will be returning soon. Do not give up now!"

As the days grew longer, the North Wind danced over the forest and blew one last icy blast to announce the Great Sun's return. He saw that the foolish trees had lost their leaves and fallen into a deep slumber. Their leaves lay brown and brittle under the snow. The proud old Oaks, half-asleep, clung stubbornly to a few tattered, dry leaves. Only the Pines, Hemlocks, Spruce, and Cedars shook their treetops and shivered with anticipation. "The Great Sun is here at last!" they whispered.

The sun's rays shone over the trees. He slowly melted the blanket of snow that covered all the Pines, Hemlocks, Spruce, and Cedars. He asked, "Why didn't you dress yourselves in the other colors that I sent?"

The Pines, Hemlocks, Spruce, and Cedars tipped their bows and answered, "We watched for your signs and helped each other to remain awake to greet you. But, when the time came, there were no more colors remaining. We are sorry if we have disappointed you."

The Great Sun lengthened his rays and replied, "Disappointed? Why, I am most pleased that you friends have worked together to greet me! The other trees did not trust each other or themselves to share their colors. You were willing to give up those colors to help each other and remain awake. Because the other trees fell asleep, they will lose their colorful leaves every winter. But you faithful trees will keep your leaves and beautiful color forever. From now on, as friends, you will be known as 'evergreens.' And when others behold your color, during the long winter, they will be reminded of the strength and loyalty of your friendship."

And so it has been to this very day.

MULTIPLE INTELLIGENCE ACTIVITIES FOR . . .

How the Leaves Got Their Colors

① Mix and Match Leaves and Trees.
(Naturalistic; Visual-Spatial)

Draw the trunks and branches and label eight different trees on posters around the room (for example: oak, maple, catalpa, beech, elm, hemlock, pine, sumac). Display a picture of each tree's leaf or needle. Invite the children to go on a walk through a park or arboretum as a class or with their families. Ask them to collect leaves or needles from some of the poster trees and bring them to class. With supervision, cut a piece of wax paper large enough to cover each leaf. Lay it on old newspaper. Cover it with an old cloth dishtowel and

A festive holiday card created from a fern tip.

iron the leaf with a hot iron. This will help preserve the leaf. Help the children identify and label their leaves and hang them on the matching tree. A variation is to mix up the leaves and have the children match them to the correct trees after they have learned to identify their shapes. Towels, waxed paper, an iron, old newsprint, tape, and poster paper will be needed for these projects.

An artistic variation of this activity is to take the group on an early fall fern walk. Cut off the top, triangular 3 inches of each fern. A beautiful evergreen tree emerges. Then, on folded white note cards, each child uses white glue to attach the "tree" to the front of the card. Next, the children paint diluted white glue on to the front of the "trees" to preserve their color and add holiday sheen. Add messages inside, and send to friends and relatives. A great gift idea! Materials needed to prepare for this activity include white glue diluted with water, paint brushes to apply the glue, white note cards, and ferns.

 ## Dancing Leaves.
(Bodily-Kinesthetic; Musical-Rhythmic)

Try this exercise! As the class stands in a circle and practices movements, ask them to imagine what it would be like to be one of the trees waiting for the Great Sun's return. How would the catalpa, maple, oak, pine, sumac, etc., sway in the wind, waiting and longing for the beautiful colors? How would they feel the colors as they draw them up

through their roots into their branches? How would the trees move their branches to express how they feel about their new colors? And now, as they become sleepy, how will the branches move as they lose their leaves in the rain or wind? After the class has experienced the movements as a group, play a recording of "Bizet's Intermezzo" from Carmen, Act III. It sets the actions for the entire scene from showing off the leaves, to falling asleep as the leaves drop off. For a variation, have the children visualize becoming leaves as they dance in the wind on their way to the ground while the music plays. Before class, tape the recording several times. This tape will allow time to engage in the activity without having to reset or replay the music.

 ## Leaf Patterns.
(Naturalistic; Logical-Mathematical)

Take the leaves collected by the class and have the children create a wall or window montage of falling leaves. They may also cover the leaves with a piece of paper. Take a crayon and rub it over the paper, creating a leaf rubbing design. Encourage the children to arrange rubbings of the different leaves on one paper, creating patterns and designs with the colors and shapes of the different leaves. For instance, one child may create an oak-elm-birch pattern; another may create a hemlock-spruce-pine-cedar pattern. Various colors may be added to enhance the emerging patterns.

SEPTEMBER CHAPTER RESOURCES

Aliki. (1982). *We are best friends*. New York: Mulberry.

Andreas, E. (1954). *Pinocchio* (Adapted). New York: Wonder.

Asbjornsen, P. C., & Moe, J. E. (1991). *The Three Billy Goats Gruff*. New York: Harcourt Brace.

Baylor, B. (1977). *Guess who my favorite person is*. New York: Scribner.

Beall, P. C., & Nipp, S. H. (1994). Hello to All the Children of the World. In *Wee Sing Around the World*. New York: Price Stern & Sloan.

Brett, J. (1992). *Goldilocks and the three bears*. New York: Dodd, Mead & Company

Brown, M. (1957). *The Three Billy Goats Gruff*. New York: Voyager.

Brown, M. (1967). *The neighbors*. New York: Scribner.

Brown, M. (1994). *Arthur's first sleepover*. Boston: Little, Brown.

Capucilli, A. S. (1997). *Biscuit finds a friend*. New York: HarperCollins.

Carlson, N. (1994). *How to lose all your friends*. New York: Puffin.

Clifton, L. (1980). *My friend Jacob*. New York: Dutton.

Cohen, M. (1967). *Will I have a friend?* New York: Macmillan.

Cohn, J. (1987). *I had a friend named Peter*. New York: Morrow.

Crimi, C., & Munsinger, L. (1999). *Don't need friends*. New York: Random House.

Desbarats, P. (1968). *Gabrielle and Selena*. New York: Harcourt Brace.

Faro, T. G. (1990). *Everyone asked about you*. New York: Philomel.

Fleming, V. (1993). *Be good to Eddie Lee*. New York: Philomel.

Flory, J. (1974). *We'll have a friend for lunch*. Boston: Houghton Mifflin.

Freeman, D. (1968). *Corduroy*. New York: Puffin.

Garland, S. (1994). *I never knew your name*. New York: Houghton Mifflin.

Garnett, J. (1999). Different. On *Starry eyed: Songs for learning & fun for kids and their families*. Cranston, RI: Tigerlily Music.

Girard, L. W. (1991). *Alex, the kid with AIDS*. Morton Grove, IL: Albert Whitman.

Hoban, R. (1969). *Best friends for Frances*. New York: Harper & Row.

Hutchins, A. R. (1994). *Picking apples and pumpkins*. New York: Scholastic.

Kubler-Ross, E. (1982). *Remember the secret*. Berkley, CA: Celestial Arts.

Leaf, M. (1997). *The story of Ferdinand*. New York: Penguin Putnam.

Lewis, J. (2000). *Jan Lewis' fairytales: The ugly duckling, little red riding hood, Cinderella, the three little pigs*. New York: Silver Dolphin.

London, J. (1993). *Into this night we are rising*. New York: Puffin.

McPhail, D. (1990). *Lost!* Boston: Little, Brown.

Polacco, P. (1994). *Pink and say*. New York: Scholastic.

Schenk deRegniers, B. (1974). *May I bring a friend?* New York: Atheneum.

Silverstein, S. (1974). *Where the sidewalk ends*. New York: Harper & Row.

Stimson, J., & Rutherford, M. (1988). *Oscar needs a friend*. Hauppauge, NY: Barron's.

Thomas, P. (2000). *Stop picking on me*. Hauppauge, NY: Barron's.

Waber, B. (1975). *Ira sleeps over*. New York: Houghton Mifflin.

Waddell, M. (1990). *We love them*. Cambridge, MA: Candlewick.

Walker, B. K. (1993). *The most beautiful thing in the world*. New York: Scholastic.

Will & Nicolas. (1989). *Finders keepers*. New York: Harcourt Brace.

October

Shivers and Quivers

MY SHADOW

I have a little shadow that goes in and out with me,
And what can be the use of him is more than I can see.
He is very, very like me from the heels up to the head;
And I see him jump before me, when I jump into my bed.

The funniest thing about him is the way he likes to grow—
Not at all like proper children, which is always very slow;
For he sometimes shoots up taller like an India-rubber ball,
And he sometimes gets so little that there's none of him at all.

He hasn't got a notion of how children ought to play,
And can only make a fool of me in every sort of way.
He stays so close beside me, he's a coward you can see;
I'd think shame to stick to nursie as that shadow sticks to me!

One morning, very early, before the sun was up
I rose and found the shining dew on every buttercup;
But my lazy little shadow, like an arrant sleepy-head,
Had stayed at home behind me and was fast asleep in bed.

-ROBERT LOUIS STEVENSON

*W*hooosh! Eeeeeeeeeeeek! Whrrrrrrrrrrrrr! Creeeeeeeeeeeek! HSSSSSSSSSSS! October is vampires and bats, goblins and ghosts, and things that go "shrieeeeeeeeeek!" in the night.

In "October: Shivers and Quivers," children delight in witnessing four stories told in Chant, Felt Board, Adapted Pantomime, Character Imagery, Musical, and Group Role-Play. They meet Old Rattle Bones, the witch with red lips, a trickster spider, and a devious museum curator.

Visual-Spatial, Verbal-Linguistic, Bodily-Kinesthetic, Musical-Rhythmic, Logical-Mathematical, Naturalistic, Interpersonal, and Intrapersonal intelligences are targeted in activities involving a Treasure Hunt, a Witch's Brew, String Pumpkins, and a Web of Friendship.

Experience the spine-tingling thrill of October storytelling!

TIPS FOR THE TELLER

Old Rattle Bones

By Susan Trostle Brand

STORYTELLING METHOD

Musical/Group Role-Play

A story told with musical instruments and voice sounds, *Old Rattle Bones* keeps the children involved and eagerly attentive. The children may self-select, or the adult may appoint parts for each new telling of the Halloween tale. In order for the children to first become familiar with the story, however, the adult reads the story to the group at least once.

Before beginning the story, the Teller may want to establish a signal such as a nod of the head or a hand gesture to indicate when the class or audience responds to the cue words by playing musical instruments, making sounds, and/or delivering that character's signature line. A list of the parts and what each does is printed on the chalkboard or a flip chart in advance so that the class or audience can easily see their parts. An asterisk indicates the cue

words throughout the text. When the children indicate readiness to participate, use the following parts and instruments and—let the storytelling begin!

Old Rattle Bones/skeleton/rattle: Shakers
loud Music: Play rock & roll
thunder: Drums
Halloween: Whooooooo!
rain: Pie tins
all make sounds: All instruments and friends plus home, rain, Halloween, and thunder play
Glenda Ghost: BOOOO!
Winona Witch: Hee, Hee, Hee
Benny Bat: Flap, Flap (flap arms)
Victor Vampire: Yummy blood!
house/home (group voices): Creak, Creak
people: ha, ha, ha!

Old Rattle Bones

Once, there was a very old, nearly deserted *house. In this very old, nearly deserted *house lived only a very, very old *skeleton. The name of this very, very old *skeleton was *Old Rattle Bones. He was *so* old that, when he walked, his bones rattled.

One *Halloween night *Old Rattle Bones became lonely. He longed for the good old days when his friends *Glenda Ghost, *Benny Bat, *Winona Witch, and *Victor Vampire had lived with him in his old, deserted *home. They had left him, and moved far away, over 200 years ago. They wanted to scare people all over the world. But Old Rattle Bones was shy. He was afraid to leave his safe, very old, deserted home. So he lived all alone.

*Old Rattle Bones hoped that on *Halloween night, all of his old friends would be nearby in his neighborhood and all around the town, haunting and scaring everyone in sight. *Old Rattle Bones thought and thought. Then *Old Rattle Bones made a brave decision. For the first time in five hundred years, he decided to step outside and see the sights of Halloween. Perhaps he would even find his old friends!

*Old Rattle Bones stepped outside his very old, deserted *house. He knew at once that something had changed. The sky still looked the same. It was dusk, and the sun was a huge orange ball, setting in the west. And, in the east rose the moon, a full white ball in the sky with a face that seemed to frown down on *Old Rattle Bones. Yet, nothing else was the same. Huge colored objects rolled down roads on round wheels. They honked their horns at *Old Rattle Bones. What could they be? Beside the roads were smokestacks and factories and mills and tall, tall buildings. *Old Rattle Bones coughed and sputtered at the fumes and smoke around him.

*Old Rattle Bones wandered down the busy street. He *rattled his bones beside a night club which played some very strange, *loud music. Then, to make matters worse, it began to *rain. At first, it sprinkled and showered; then the *rain became louder and louder and harder and harder. It *thundered. It *thundered again. *Old Rattle Bones became very frightened. He decided he had had enough. *Old Rattle Bones was going back *home.

Just then, strange looking *people carrying umbrellas walked toward him. Ladies with long hair and men with short hair stared and laughed at *Old Rattle Bones. "What a great Halloween costume!" they said. They pulled and tugged at *Old Rattle Bones. The people hurt his backbone and his leg bones and his arm bones. One child looked very hard at *Old Rattle Bones. "Mommy," he said, "this *skeleton is not a costume. This *skeleton is *real!* And it is *alive!*"

*Old Rattle Bones was nervous. He *rattled like he had never *rattled before. The *rattling scared the people. *Old Rattle Bones rattled so loudly that he even scared himself. The child's mother and father and all the other *people in the crowd stopped their tugging and pulling. They knew that the child was right. This was a *real* skeleton.

"Ahhhhhhhhhhhhh!" said the funny-looking *people. Horrified, they ran away in the *rain and the loud *thunder. Old, wet *Rattle Bones ran swiftly back *home, rattling all along the way, far, far from the funny-looking *people.

When his safe old *home was in sight, *Old Rattle Bones stopped to catch his breath. He looked ahead, and a wonderful sight beheld his eyes. It was his old friends, *Glenda

Ghost, ✽Benny Bat, ✽Winona Witch, and ✽Victor Vampire. But his old friends were covering their eyes. They looked very frightened, indeed.

✽"Old Rattle Bones!" they said, "We haven't seen you in hundreds of years! Was the horrible ✽rattling sound coming from *you?*"

"I'm afraid it was, friends," admitted ✽Old Rattle Bones. And I humbly apologize for scaring you. It's just that I've not ventured outside for five hundred years and everything looked so different now. My ✽rattle is always louder when I'm frightened. I guess it's been a scarrrrry night for everyone!"

✽Old Rattle Bones invited his friends ✽Glenda Ghost, ✽Benny Bat, ✽Winona Witch, and ✽Victor Vampire back into his old deserted ✽home. They chewed on toenails and sipped on blood of vultures. For dessert, they enjoyed Gizzard of Beast Pie. ✽Old Rattle Bones told his friends all about his scary ✽Halloween adventures. His friends laughed and laughed. They told ✽Old Rattle Bones about computers and cars and factories and television and movies and travel in outer space. They decided to return to visit ✽Old Rattle Bones every year, at ✽Halloween. And, just for fun, they played some music to remind them of the good old days. Here is how it sounded on that rainy ✽Halloween night (all make sounds).

MULTIPLE INTELLIGENCE ACTIVITIES FOR . . .

Old Rattle Bones

 ### Shivery, Quivery Tales.
(Verbal-Linguistic; Bodily-Kinesthetic)

On the chalkboard or a pocket chart, display the following words. Invite children to write a shivery, quivery tale using as many of the following nouns and verbs as they like; encourage them to add other words of their own choice. When the stories are finished, the children illustrate, share, and enact their story creations.

Nouns

ghost	bat
spider	skeleton
black cat	monster
witch	vampire

Verbs

howl	hiss
fly	howl
scream	thump
screech	thud

 ### Create a Monster.
(Visual-Spatial; Bodily-Kinesthetic)

This activity is both great fun and educational. One child or an adult lies on the floor atop a large sheet of white mural paper. Another child traces the figure on the floor using a pencil. Place the completed body tracing atop a large table top or other flat surface.

Ask the children to name this monster. Then, using liquid markers, youngsters complete the monster figure by adding body parts to it. Hanging a labeled human skeleton poster near the monster figure may inspire children to add bones and muscles with their correct names to the figure. Others may draw and color the liver, pancreas, spleen, heart, lungs, hair, eyes, fingernails, and so on. Children's artwork may be realistic or imaginative. When the monster is completed, display for all to admire during the Halloween season!

273

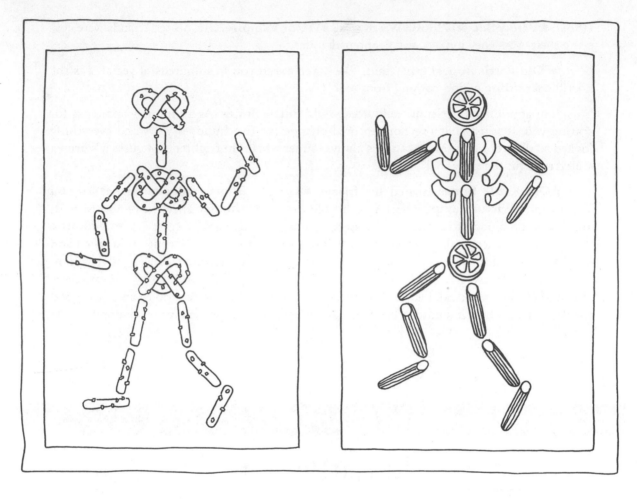

Forming pasta and pretzel figures following "Old Rattle Bones."

As a variation, create a smaller monster or skeleton figure using pretzels or pasta.

 Scrap Paper Wonders.
(Naturalistic; Visual-Spatial)

Children discuss the fact that, to many folks, "junk" is beautiful. Lead them in a group discussion of recycling and litter control. Next, go outdoors on a clean-up and recycle walk. Children take large paper bags and, into the bags, place scrap paper, newspapers, candy wrappings, and other assorted trash items. For cleanliness, you and the children may wish to wear plastic gloves when handling trash. Upon returning, the group creates colorful scrap paper Jack-o-lanterns, ghosts, witches, bats, vampires, and the like. The creations may be either flat (mounted on cardboard or poster board) or three-dimensional, to resemble junk sculptures.

Using recycled trash to create a bat.

Mobile with recycled paper.

TIPS FOR THE TELLER

Red Lips
Retold and Adapted by Jeanne M. Donato

STORYTELLING METHOD

Chant/Adapted Pantomime

Telling "Red Lips" using the Chant and Adapted Pantomime methods.

Children are able to safely look at and overcome their fears through listening to stories. This old jump story can be found throughout the United States. The listener is able to vicariously experience Rosemary's nonchalant attitude in the face of building tension. After three nightly visits by a strange old woman, Rosemary watches as the old woman insists on showing her what she does with her long fingernails and red lips. The jump, or surprise, part of the story comes when the old woman shouts, "I'll show you! Burrrrrrrr! Happy Halloween, Rosemary!"

Reviewing the Chant method in Chapter 3 will help the Teller prepare the class to join in the story. Before beginning the story, the Teller may want to establish a signal such as a nod of the head or a hand gesture to indicate when everyone can join in the chanting, perhaps using separate signals for the two chants. An asterisk indicates the text in which the class or audience participates. This text is printed on the chalkboard or a flip chart in advance so that they can easily see their parts.

The Pantomime method will be adapted to the chanting portion of this story. It is an excellent aid in drawing the students into the story with pantomime participation. The Teller may lead a discussion on Halloween and the customs of dressing up to trick or treat. A display of a witch's hat and broom, and a plastic cauldron or pumpkin will set the mood. Review the chant with the class.

The Teller may want to use signs found in an American Sign Language book. Make the class aware that direct word-for-word translations of ASL signs from spoken English make no sense. Make it clear to the class that if ASL signs are used, this is not the correct way to sign and that these signs or signals are only being used as memory prompts for the chant and participation parts of the story. The Teller may also want to pantomime some of the action in the story as part of the telling. The repeated sequence where Rosemary shuts and locks her window against the old woman lends itself especially well to pantomiming.

Review the chant showing the class signs that you decided on for the words in the chant. Demonstrate the various pantomimes that will accompany the chant and have the class practice. For example: for "the old, old woman," the Teller may crouch over and hold hands out like claws. For "black, black hair" the Teller may use the ASL sign for black tracing the right eyebrow from left to right with the forefinger and then making up a gesture to suggest

continued

TIPS FOR THE TELLER *continued*

long hair. For the "white, white, face" the Teller may want to slowly move the index finger counterclockwise around the face. For "long, long fingernails" the Teller may choose to mime long curved fingernails. "Red, red, lips" is suggested by pointing to the lips; the Teller may want to wear bright red lipstick, if appro-priate, for this telling or have a pair of red wax lips that are sold in stores at Halloween. Rosemary may be shown as the letter "R," by crossing the middle finger over the index finger on the right hand, and drawing it twice down along the right chin as the ASL sign for girl.

Red Lips

I have a cousin named Rosemary who is very brave. She's not afraid of anything! Rosemary lives in Atlanta, Georgia, where it is still warm around Halloween time. It is so warm there that people sleep with their windows open with the screens in. This is the story that Rosemary told me.

Three days before Halloween, Rosemary still couldn't make up her mind about what costume to wear to go trick-or-treating with her friends. Now, Rosemary's bedroom is on the first floor of their house. The streetlight outside of her window filters through the trees, casting soft shadows around her room so she doesn't need a night-light. She can hear the town clock chime the hour from her bedroom, so she always knows what time it is.

On this particular night, Rosemary was still awake when the clock struck twelve! She heard a scratching and scraping sound on the screen outside her window. Rosemary got out of bed and walked across the floor to see what was making all the noise. When she looked out her window she saw:

✽**an old, old, woman, with black, black, hair, a white, white, face, red, red, lips, and long, long, fingernails.**

As her fingernails clawed at the screen, the old woman hissed, ✽**"Rosemary! Do you know what I do with these long, long fingernails, and these red, red lips?"**

Rosemary shook her head and said, "No." Then she shut the window, locked it, closed the curtains, went to bed, and fell asleep! What would you have done? *(Elicit a few audience responses.)* I know that I wouldn't have been able to stay in that room! But not my cousin Rosemary, nothing bothers her! She's not afraid of anything!

The next morning at breakfast, Rosemary told her Mother that she had finally made up her mind. She wanted to dress up like an old witch for Halloween! She asked her Mother if she would help her find a long black wig and cape.

That night Rosemary fell asleep with the window open because it was so warm. When the town clock struck midnight, something shuffled through the leaves outside. It began to scratch and claw at her window and woke her up! Rosemary jumped out of bed, went over to the window and saw:

✻an old, old, woman, with black, black hair, a white, white face, red, red lips, and long, long fingernails.

As the old woman's fingernail clawed through the screen she pushed her face up against it and snarled: ✻"Rosemary! Do you know what I do with these long, long fingernails, and these red, red lips?"

Rosemary shook her head and said, "No." Then she shut the window, locked it, closed the curtains, went to bed and fell asleep! I don't know about you, but I certainly wouldn't have been able to stay in that room. I would have run out of there screaming for dear life! But not my cousin Rosemary, she's not afraid of anything!

At breakfast, Rosemary asked her Mother if she could find some long, long fingernails and some red, red lipstick for her costume.

That night all the children went out trick-or-treating and Rosemary collected a whole bag full of candy! When she got home, she poured her candy onto the kitchen table for her Mother to check to make sure it was safe. Rosemary's Mother warned her not to eat too much candy, but Rosemary took five big candy bars into her bedroom. What are your favorite candy bars? *(Elicit responses from the listeners.)* Well, Rosemary got ready for bed. She read some scary stories while she ate all five candy bars and then tried to go to sleep.

Rosemary tossed and turned. Her stomach ached from eating so much candy all at once. When the town clock struck midnight, poor Rosemary was still awake. She heard something shuffling through the dry leaves outside her window. Then she heard scratching on the window screen. The scratching and clawing got louder and louder until the screen rattled to the floor! Rosemary got up and she saw:

✻an old, old woman, with black, black hair, a white, white face, red, red lips, and long, long fingernails.

The old woman had pushed her head, shoulder, one arm, and one leg through the open window and crawled through! She looked at Rosemary and her voice creaked as she cackled "Rosemary! Tonight, I'm going to show you what I do with these long, long fingernails, and these red, red lips!

Then, lifting her long, long fingernails to her red, red lips she buzzed her lips over her finger and cackled, "Burrrrrrrrrr! Happy Halloween, Rosemary!"

MULTIPLE INTELLIGENCE ACTIVITIES FOR . . .

Red Lips

 Scary Monster.
(Musical-Rhythmic; Bodily-Kinesthetic)

Introduce the class to their "Imagination Bags." Form a circle by holding your left arm out from the left side of the body and touching the left hand to the left hip. Reach into the circle with your right hand and fish around as if pulling a large bundle out. Explain to the class that these are their "Imagination Bags." Explain that anything can be found in them but that today we are all going to pull out our scariest monster outfits

and put them on. Tell them to pull out their monster suits as the Teller mimes unrolling it and putting on a one-piece "monster" jump suit. Mime adjusting the hood, fluffing up the ears and tail. Carefully pull the zipper up the front, like a jacket, and ask the class to flex their claws as you flex your claws. Ask them to shake the hair on their heads, roll their eyes, and roar. Encourage them to stomp around the room as big, scary monsters. Describe the monster in the following song and have the class move and act out the song as they sing it.

Monster

I am a scary monster I am such a horrible sight. I am a scary monster I can roar with all my might. My face is very ugly see how I show my teeth my fingernails are long and sharp *(spoken)* guess what I like to eat? I am a scary monster I am such a horrible sight. I am a scary monster I can roar with all my might my hair is green and messy 'cause I don't like to wash it. All the better for SCARING YOU When I

279

shake my head and toss it. I am a sca-ry mon-ster I am such a hor-ri-ble sight. I am a sca-ry mon-ster I can roar with all my might. My feet are ve-ry ve-ry big real-ly good at stomp-ing You'd bet-ter give me lots of room when ev-er I go romp-ing. I am a sca-ry mon-ster I am such a hor-ri-ble sight. I am a sca-ry mon-ster I can roar with all my might.

("Monster" from the recording *Can You Sound Just Like Me?* © 1983 Smilin' Atcha Music. Written by Red and Kathy Grammer. Distributed through Red Note Records, 1-800-824-2980.)

The music and words to "Monster" by Red and Kathy Grammer can also be found on the tape *Can You Sound Just Like Me?* The Teller may either play the tape several times or sing it with the class as everyone joins in this creative monster dance.

② Snap Apple Night.
(Visual-Spatial; Bodily-Kinesthetic)

In Colonial times, apple games were so popular on Halloween that it was also known as Snap Apple Night. Children played games by bobbing, snapping, or peeling apples. On Snap Apple Night they would hang apples from a string along a rope stretched across the room. They would then swing and spin the apples while others tried to snap at the apple and eat it with their hands held behind their backs. The winner was supposed to be the first one to marry. To enjoy the challenge but make it easier on the teeth, place a rope across the classroom and tie strings to the rope so that they hang down. Tie donuts to the end of the strings. Measure the length of the string and adjust it to match the height of the contestant's mouth. Have the class keep score of how many tries it takes for the student to eat the whole donut without dropping any of it on the floor. The student's hands must stay behind his or her back while trying to snap and eat up all of the donut. The donut is swung back and forth to get the student started. The one who accomplishes the goal in the fewest tries is the winner. Another old-fashioned apple game children enjoyed playing around Halloween time went as follows. Each person would take a turn at paring an apple peel in one long piece. The peel was swung slowly around the head and thrown over the left shoulder. If it fell unbroken, it was supposed to form the initial of the girl or boy's future mate.

3 **Tangram Creatures.**
(Logical-Mathematical; Visual-Spatial)

A tangram is a Chinese puzzle enjoyed by many famous people. President John Quincy Adams and the writer of *Alice in Wonderland*, Lewis Carroll, both enjoyed playing with tangrams. A tangram is made by cutting one large square into a square, a rhomboid, and five triangles. You can also use a die cutting machine to make tangram pieces. Black construction paper would be best for this project or have the students color the pieces before they cut out the tangram shapes. Ask the students to use the tangram pieces to form a witch and a cat. Include a solid pattern of the witch and cat without showing the lines. Challenge the students to solve both puzzles. Have them glue their solutions on to yellow or orange paper to display them when finished. As a further challenge, invite students to make up their own tangram shapes. The patterns are found in the illustration that follows.

Halloween tangram pictures.

TIPS FOR THE TELLER

No Kids in the Gallery!

By Michelle Berenson
Adapted by Susan Trostle Brand

STORYTELLING METHOD

Character Imagery

No Kids in the Gallery! is a story about mystery and art. This suspenseful story is adapted for Character Imagery Storytelling. The story lends itself well to this dramatic method because of its high degree of action and because of its reliance upon one main protagonist, the daughter of an art museum security guard.

The Teller, while narrating the story's introduction, dresses as an eight-year-old girl wearing blue jeans, a t-shirt, sneakers, and ponytails. A discussion about curiosity may ensue at this time, as the Teller invites the audience to tell about times when they were especially interested in learning more about something (e.g., December holidays or birthdays). Then the Teller leads into the theme of the story, as he or she completes dressing for the audience. Complete the introduction by telling the group that this story is about a very curious little girl who loves art.

No Kids in the Gallery!

Hi, I'm Charlotte *(point to self)*. I'm eight years old and I love art *(smile and hug self)*. My dad is really tall *(gesture with hand high in air)*. I live with him in a pretty brick house *(frame house with hands)*. He is a security guard at a very large *(spread arms wide apart)* art museum *(from large box shape with hands)*. On Saturdays, Dad *(gesture Dad)* takes me *(point to self)* to work with him. It's not a long ride *(gesture long winding road while shaking head)*. Sometimes I ride in Dad's car *(frame large car)*. Other times, on nice days, when the sun is shining *(form circle in sky with hands; make sun rays with fingers)*, I ride my bike to the museum *(pretend to ride bike around room)* and park it along the side of the building *(pretend to park bike)*.

A while ago, the only problem was, Dad never *(shake head "no")* let me see the artwork *(frame pictures while shaking head)*. I had to sit in the security office all day long, watching boring TV shows *(sit on chair or floor and place fists beneath chin, frowning)*. Everyone at the museum was so mean to me! *(stand up and shake fists)*. When I wasn't in the security office, all they ever said was, "Charlotte, be quiet!" *(make shhhhh motion with pointer finger at lips)* or

"Charlotte, don't touch that!" *(shake pointer finger, on hand on hip)* or Charlotte, stop running!" *(Put hand up, police officer style.)*

Then I had to go back to the boring *(stretch arms and yawn)* old security office and watch that boring *(yawn again)* old TV again. When I looked at my watch *(look at watch)* and it was six o'clock *(hold up six fingers)*. I was glad! *(Clap hands.)* Now I could go home! *(Frame house.)*

One day was *not* boring at the museum *(frame large box shape)*. It was the day the great Leonardo DaVinci painting the Mona Lisa *(point to mouth as you smile demurely)* was arriving for a special exhibition! I had learned about the famous Mona Lisa in art class *(gesture painting)* at school *(frame rectangular school house)*, so I was very excited *(clap hands and jump up and down)*. Maybe Dad would let me see *(frame hands around eyes)* the painting!

It was a pretty Saturday in October *(gesture sun shining)*. I decided *(point to temple)* to ride my bike *(pretend to ride)* to the museum *(gesture large box)* on the day the Mona Lisa *(smile demurely and create frame with hands)* arrived. "Dad," *(hold one hand high)* I asked, "couldn't I go and see the Mona Lisa? *(frame and smile)* This is a very special day!" *(Two thumbs up.)*

"Well, okay," agreed Dad *(gesture high)*. "But I'll need to go with you. Children *(gesture low)* are not *(move hand horizontally)* allowed in the galleries without an adult" (gesture high).

The Mona Lisa *(point to smile on your face and frame picture)* was amazing! I couldn't believe how real she looked. And the colors! *(clasp hands)* They were beautiful *(spread hands gracefully)*.

Dad *(gesture high)* needed to get back to his job. He ordered me to go to the security office (gesture small box) and wait for him to finish up at six o'clock *(show six fingers)*. But I guess I did something wrong *(partially cover eyes)*. I did *not* go back to the office. I stayed in front of Mona Lisa for a long, long *(gesture long string with hands)* time.

All of a sudden, I jumped! *(jump into air)*. A shrill voice behind me said, *(change body position)* "What are you doing here? *(point finger sternly)* Children are not *(shake finger)* allowed in the exhibits without adults."

It was Miss Smitten, the evil *(make monster face and position with body and hands)* museum curator. She wore her usual black blazer *(point to chest)* and long black velvet skirt *(gesture down legs)*, and her long, black hair *(flowing motion around head)* was tied into a severe bun *(show circle with two hands)* on top of her head (pat top of head). Miss Smitten *(evil face)* tugged me by the ear (point to ear) and dragged me into the security office *(gesture small box)*.

Dad was angry *(shake fist)* that I'd not listened to him and had stayed in front of the Mona Lisa painting *(frame picture)*. I had to sit in that small, boring *(yawn and stretch)* office for the rest of that day.

The next Saturday was sunny *(gesture sun)* again, so I rode my bike *(pretend to ride around the room)* to the museum. To my surprise (open mouth wide and spread hands), Dad *(gesture high)* let me *(point to self)* go with him on his rounds that morning.

We pushed *(pushing motion)* open the door *(frame door)* to the exhibit hall *(frame rectangular hall)*. That's when we made our awful discovery *(cover eyes)*. The painting was missing! *(Point upward and open mouth as if to gasp.)*

Dad *(gesture high)* and I raced back *(run to another area of room)* to the security office. He called 911 on the phone *(press three buttons and hold phone)*. About five minutes later *(hold up five fingers)* detectives and police came rushing through the museum to the exhibit hall *(rush around room)*. Dad sent me back to the security office *(gesture small room)* to wait. I ambled slowly back (*wander slowly to a designated area of room*). I looked down (*look down*) and saw a tiny (*pinch thumb and index fingers together before eyes*) patch of fabric stuck on the exhibit hall door (*frame door*). It was velvet, just the same as Miss Smitten always wore!

"Dad, Dad! (*cup hands around mouth and shout*). I found a clue!" I shouted. "Miss Smitten stole the painting. This fabric is from her black velvet skirt!" (*flowing gesture down legs*).

"Now, Charlotte," said Dad, (*shake head*) "You can't accuse her of stealing just because you don't like Miss Smitten" (*gesture monster face*). Besides, Miss Smitten has been traveling (*extend arms to show plane*) in South America (*gesture downward*) for one week! (*hold up pointer finger*). Please wait at the security office!" he told me (*hands outstretched*).

That's when I heard (*cup ear*) the voice. It was Miss Smitten (*monster face*). She was whispering to someone (*cup mouth*).

(*Change body position to represent Miss Smitten.*) "Everyone thinks I'm on vacation in South America, Juan! No one will ever guess that I (*point to self*) stole the Mona Lisa painting (*frame picture*). They'll never (*shake head*) think to look in the old mill building (*frame building*) downtown. But we've got to move it today (*shake finger*) and hop on the plane (*fly around one area of room*) down to Argentina (*point down*) at once, before they find out!" she whispered.

I swiftly tiptoed down to the exhibit hall (*tiptoe to designated room area*). I told Dad (*gesture high*) about Miss Smitten and Juan and where they could find the Mona Lisa painting (*frame picture*). I told them to hurry (*shake hands beside head*) because she was leaving soon for Argentina (*gesture plane*)!

Dad (*gesture high*) couldn't believe what he was hearing (*cup ear*)! He quickly told the police what I'd (*point to self*) told him. The police sped away in their cruiser (*pantomime speeding police car*) to the old mill building downtown (*frame large building*). And guess what (*hands open to audience*)? Dad (*gesture high*) and I (*point to self*) got to ride along in the police car (*smiling, "drive" around the room*).

When we arrived we were just in time to catch the thieves, Miss Smitten (*monster face*) and her friend, Juan (*mean face and hands on hips*). And, in their hands was a large, flat, square box (*gesture box*). The police tore open the box (*tearing motions*). Inside was the Mona Lisa painting! (*frame picture*) The police (*point finger*) said, "Hands up (*hands in air*); you are both under arrest!"

Miss Smitten (*change position*) looked shocked (*look dismayed*). She wailed, "I confess; I stole the Mona Lisa! (*Frame picture.*) How did you find out?" (*Shrug shoulders and shake head.*) The police (*point finger*) took Miss Smitten (*monster face*) and Juan (*hands on hips*) to jail (*prison bars*). I (*point to self*) was pretty famous (*arms outstretched*) after that day! Now I have a badge of my own. It says (*polish "badge" at chest*), "Assistant Security Guard." And, best of all (*clap hands*), I get to see all the art I want, all day long! (*sweeping motion of arms*).

MULTIPLE INTELLIGENCE ACTIVITIES FOR . . .

No Kids in the Gallery!

1 Witch's Brew.
(Logical-Mathematical; Verbal-Linguistic)

Invite children to invent recipes for their favorite Witch's Brew. They may include bat wings, vampire blood, broom straw, spider legs, cobwebs, wiggly worms, and the like. Share the recipes and, perhaps, bind them together, complete with illustrations, into a big class book. Later, as you share *No Kids in the Gallery!*, sip some delicious brewed tea using the following recipe (have youngsters help you measure and blend ingredients earlier):

Spiced Brew Hot Tea

1 cup (decaffeinated) brewed or instant tea
2 cups Tang
1 cup sugar
1 cup lemonade mix
1 tsp. cloves
1 tsp. cinnamon

Mix the above ingredients and use about 2 teaspoons per cup of boiling water. Serve very warm or hot.

2 String Pumpkins.
(Naturalistic; Visual-Spatial)

No Kids in the Gallery! provides an inspiring background for class discussion and activities involving autumn and Halloween traditions. First, hold an outdoor scavenger hunt, inviting children to find (previously-hidden) evidence of October, such as colored leaves, miniature pumpkins, acorns, Indian corn, tissue ghosts, and plastic spiders. Provide paper bags for their treasures. Upon returning, children display their findings.

Continue the October theme with a festive art project. Provide large, round balloons for the children to inflate. Tie balloons closed. The children wrap their balloons with orange string. Tie string securely around the balloons several times, and, when completed, tie the end of the string to a nearby strand to form a knot. Paint cornstarch, which is mixed with water, onto the string/balloon; cover completely. Allow the balloons and starch to dry for several days. When dry, prick and break the balloons. The dried orange string will remain firm in a circular shape to resemble a pumpkin. Attach empty toilet tissue rolls, painted green, at the tops of the balloons to resemble the stem. Paint on black eyes, nose, and mouth to form a jack-o'-lantern. Then, when the paint is dry, using a knife and with help from an adult, the children cut a circular opening near the tops of their string pumpkins. Using the stem as a handle, lift this lid and stuff pumpkins one-half full with orange tissue paper. Fill pumpkins with the treats and other surprises found on the scavenger hunt. The jack-o'-lanterns make creative gifts or displays!

3 Treasure Hunt.
(Visual-Spatial; Verbal-Linguistic)

Read Robert Louis Stevenson's *Treasure Island* to the class. Then, as a follow-up, prepare a word, symbol, and/or picture map of the classroom and surrounding outdoor area. Children form teams of two and take their maps and small shovels on a Treasure Hunt where an adult has previously hidden an October treat for the class. Be certain that adults closely supervise children as they proceed on their Treasure Hunt. For younger children, perhaps use a sandbox with buried treasure for the children to discover.

For example, the Treasure Map and related notes might read:

1. Begin at the teacher's desk.
2. Find a note beneath the teacher's chair. Follow the instructions on this note.

Fun with cornstarch, string, and balloons.

3. Behind the old maple tree, walk seventeen steps. Find a note.

4. Find a large white stone. Look underneath.

5. Proceed to the group of birch trees. Find the tallest one. Look for the note.

6. Find a circle of leaves. In the center of the circle is a pail.

7. Turn over the pail. The note under the pail will lead you to the buried treasure.

8. At the X, use your shovel to dig six inches below the earth. Here you will find a treasure for the class.

9. Bring the treasure back to the class, share it, and describe your Treasure Hunt adventure!

TIPS FOR THE TELLER

Skinny as a Spider's Waist

Retold by Kevin D. Cordi

Retold and Adapted by Susan Trostle Brand

STORYTELLING METHOD

Felt Board/Chant

Anansi stories are favorites among children and adults alike. Anansi stories are traditional myths about a mischievous father spider named Anansi, and his spider family. Set in Africa, these stories convey charm, adventure, and mystery, a combination which results in delightful and vivid Felt Board Storytelling.

In order to tell this story the Teller prepares the following felt board pieces, using bright and dark colors that contrast against the background (blue sky and green trees of the jungle): Anansi, Leopard, Monkey, food pots, drum, Lion, yarn ("rope"), Tiger, Turtle, Parrot, Rabbit, Elephant, trees, and sky.

For each new animal a new voice is introduced. For example, the Monkey might chatter, the Lion might use a powerful, low voice, the Rabbit a soft, timid voice, and the Elephant a low and loud voice. The use of a spider puppet for a story introduction is recommended. A discussion about arachnids versus insects might transpire.

Throughout the story, Anansi talks to his great drum. First, he asks the drum to tell him when the food is ready. As the story ends, he bewails his fate when, alas, his waist becomes very thin due to his greed. These conversations between Anansi and his drum give the Teller an opportunity to use the Chant Storytelling method to supplement the felt board. Before beginning the story, the Teller may want to establish a signal such as a nod of the head or a hand gesture to indicate when everyone can join in with Anansi's drum chant. A separate signal may be used for each of the two chants. An asterisk indicates the text in which the class or audience participates. This text is printed on the chalkboard or a flip chart in advance so that they can easily see their part.

Skinny as a Spider's Waist

Deep, deep in the African jungle, the sky (place sky) was blue. Underneath the bright blue sky grew many green trees and bushes (place trees and bushes). And in this deep jungle lived a spider (place Anansi). His name was Anansi.

He did not look like an ordinary spider that you might see today. Anansi had a large head and a large waist. Some animals said he grew big because he hated to do work. He was even called Lazy Anansi by the other animals.

One day Anansi was lying around watching all the other animals busy at work. From the East, a great sound was heard. The animals rushed past Anansi. He watched as a yellow spotted Leopard (place Leopard) carried bananas on its back. Soon Leopard was far from sight (remove leopard). Monkey (place Monkey) carried sweet potatoes in a bag. By the handle, she carried a large pot (place pot on Monkey's tail) on the end of her long, windy tail. Anansi was curious. He asked Monkey, "Where is everyone going with all that food?"

Monkey replied, "Don't you know we are having a feast? It is the great feast of the West. Everyone is helping so that we can have the best feast ever! Anyone can come. And anyone who comes will have plenty to eat! Now I have to run, Anansi (remove Monkey).

Anansi loved feasts. The problem was, he did NOT like to help. He just like to eat. Anansi thought, "I do not want to help. How will I know when the food is ready to eat?"

Anansi pulled out his drum. He began to play. It helped him think. He played and sang:

❋ Great drum, great drum
Tell me what I need to know
Tell me when the food is ready
And then I will go.

As Anansi played, Lion (place Lion) marched across the jungle. He had a full orange mane around his face and he walked very proudly. Lion was carrying a pot of beans (place pot in Lion's paws). Anansi loved beans. He stopped Lion.

"Lion, could you do me a small favor?" asked Anansi.

"Sure, Anansi," said Lion. "but be quick. I don't want to be late for the feast. I must help everyone prepare the food."

Anansi continued, "Could you take this rope (attach yarn to Anansi) I have attached to me and tie it around you? Then pull on the rope when the food is ready for the feast."

Lion was confused. He asked, "Why don't you just come now, Anansi?"

Anansi lied, "I am busy."

The Lion agreed to help Anansi. He took one end of the rope (attach yarn to Lion) Anansi offered to him. Soon, carrying the rope and the food pot, Lion was out of sight (remove Lion).

For a while all was quiet. Anansi waited. The animals had left, but only for a moment. From the West more animals rushed past Anansi. First, orange Tiger stormed by. Next followed beautiful red, yellow, and green Parrot. Turtle crawled by carrying berries in a small pot on his back. Rabbit hopped along. Before long, Tiger, Parrot, Turtle, and Rabbit were out of sight *(place and remove each as you state name)*. They were in a hurry to help prepare the food for the feast.

Each animal carried food and pots. Just when wrinkly, gray Elephant *(place Elephant)* marched along. "Elephant, where is everyone going in such a hurry?" asked Anansi.

"We are going to the great feast of the East," replied Elephant in her low, booming voice.

Now Anansi had a problem. Two feasts! One feast of the West and one feast in the East! He could not be in two places at one time, now could he? Well, maybe he could. "Elephant," asked Anansi. "Could you do me one small favor?"

"What is it?" answered Elephant.

"Could you take this rope *(attach yarn to Anansi)* and tie it around you? I am attached to the other end. Then could you pull on your end when the food is ready?"

"Why don't you come along now, Anansi?" asked the puzzled Elephant.

"I have work to do," lied Anansi.

Elephant agreed to help Anansi. She took one end of the long white rope *(attach yarn to Elephant)*. Then Elephant marched away *(remove Elephant)* to help prepare food at the feast of the East.

Anansi took out his drum. He played and sang:

❃ **Great drum, great drum**
   Tell me what I need to know
   Tell me when the food is ready
   And then I will go.

Anansi waited and waited. He did not work. He just thought of all the food he was going to eat. Just then the rope from the West began to pull him to the West *(tug on yarn)*.

Anansi jumped up. "The food is ready! I must go."

At the same time the rope from the East began to pull him to the East *(tug on other yarn)*. "Oh, no!" Anansi yelled.

The ropes pulled and pulled *(continue tugging on yarn)*. With each pull Anansi's waist became smaller and smaller *(cinch Anansi's waist with yarn)*. No longer did Anansi have a big waist. There was nothing he could do to stop it. Anansi was so greedy to want to eat in both places that the rope made his waist become small. He did not eat that day. However, he sat down and he played his drum and sang:

❃ **Great drum, great drum**
   How foolish I have been
   Because of my greed
   My waist is very thin.

Ands so it has been that way to this very day. A spider has a large head and a small waist. It is a reminder of the day that Anansi forgot that greed will never fill an empty belly.

MULTIPLE INTELLIGENCE ACTIVITIES FOR . . .

Skinny as a Spider's Waist

 Edible Arachnids.
(Visual-Spatial; Logical-Mathematical)

Children measure, cut, and arrange ingredients to form creepy spiders for a tasty Halloween snack. For added fun and to enhance their story comprehension, invite them to decorate the spiders as they appear in the book *Anansi the Spider* by McDermott, or similar to the felt board spiders. You will need black licorice sticks, rules, scissors, or dull knives, mini-cupcakes, candy corn and assorted candies, and paper plates. Youngsters help to ice the mini-cupcakes with dark brown frosting. To the icing, they add candy of various shapes, sizes, and colors to resemble the bodies of the spiders in the story. If desired, encourage children to create other new and unusual spiders.

Children measure 5-inch legs using the rulers, provided. They cut them to size with dull knives or scissors, and insert eight of them—four per side—to the bodies of their spiders. Viola! Easy, edible arachnids!

A Spider on the Floor!
(Musical-Rhythmic; Visual-Spatial)

Using cardboard egg cartons, cut one two-egg section for each child. Provide string or yarn, liquid

Cupcake creativity at Halloween.

A Spider on the Floor

There's a spi-der on the floor, on the floor. There's a

spi-der on the floor, on the floor. Who could ask for an-y more Than a

spi-der on the floor? There's a spi-der on the floor, on the floor._____

"Spider on the Floor" (© 1977 Egos Anonymous, All Rights Reserved. Used with permission).

markers, pipe cleaners, and hole punchers. Have the children color and decorate their egg carton sections to form spiders. To make legs, they may punch eight holes into the edges of the egg carton sections, and wind the ends of eight colorful pipe cleaners into the holes. (Curl spiders legs, if desired). They may poke a small hole into the top, at the center of the spider's head, and insert a 15-inch length of yarn or string, secured with a large knot. Invite children to sing the song "A Spider on the Floor" (print and display in advance on large chart paper) as they dangle their spiders and use expressions to follow the song's words.

3 Web of Friendship.
(Interpersonal; Intrapersonal; Verbal-Linguistic)

Locate the dialogue in the story *Skinny as a Spider's Waist.* Invite each child to read the dialogue of one character in the story. Inform children that they are going to use dialogue in the project to follow.

Children take turns lying down on the floor and, using long mural paper, tracing the bodies of each other. Next, they cut out their own life-sized shapes and paint clothing and faces on them. Allow to dry. When all paper bodies are dry,

ask children to use "dialogue bubbles" for a given purpose and attach the bubbles near the mouths of their bodies. Arrange bodies atop a silver or white "web" of yarn background, perhaps, to create a Web of Friendship.

One class invited parents in for a Halloween Open House. Each speech bubble instructed the child's parents to find something of which the child was proud within the classroom. Another seasonal use for dialogue bubbles is for the children to report on "Things That Scare Me," "Favorite Halloween Candies," and "What I Like Best/Least About Halloween."

Body tracing with dialogue bubbles.

291

OCTOBER CHAPTER RESOURCES

Aiken, S. (1987). *The moon's revenge.* New York: Knopf.

Alexander, L. (1992). *The fortune-tellers.* New York: Dutton.

Appelt, K. (1996). *Bat jamboree.* New York: Morrow.

Aruego, J. (1970). *Juan and the Ausangs: A tale of Philippine ghosts and spirits.* New York: Scribner.

Asch, F. (1985). *Bear shadow.* New York: Scholastic.

Babbitt, N. (1970). *The something.* New York: Farrar, Straus & Giroux.

Barth, E. (1972). *Witches, pumpkins, and grinning ghosts: The story of the Halloween symbols.* New York: Clarion.

Belting, N. (1969). *Winter's eve.* New York: Holt, Rinehart & Winston.

Benjamin, A. (1979). *1,000 Monsters.* New York: Scholastic.

Berenstain, S., & Berenstain, J. (1995). *The Berenstain bears count their blessings.* New York: Random House.

Berenstain, S., & Berenstain, J. (1982). *In the dark.* New York: Random House.

Birch, C. (1984). *Nightmares rising.* Southbury, CT: Frostfire.

Bodkin, O. (1995). *The Banshee train.* New York: Clarion.

Branson, D. (1998). *The monster encyclopedia.* Bridgeport, CT: Greene Bark.

Brown, M. W. (1998). *The little scarecrow boy.* New York: HarperCollins.

Brown, R. (1981). *A dark, dark tale.* New York: Dial.

Bunting, E. (1986). *Scary, scary Halloween.* New York: Clarion.

Bunting, E. (1973). *Night of the gargoyles.* New York: Clarion.

Bunting, E. (1987). *Ghost's hour, spook's hour.* New York: Clarion.

Byfield, B. (1973). *The haunted ghost.* Garden City, NY: Doubleday.

Carle, E. (1984). *The very busy spider.* New York: Putnam.

Dillon, J. (1992). *Jeb scarecrow's pumpkin patch.* Boston: Houghton Mifflin.

Gag, W. (1928). *Millions of cats.* New York: Coward, McCann, & Geoghegan.

Galdone, J. (1977). *The Tailypo, a ghost story.* New York: Clarion.

Garnett, J. (1992). I'm batty about you. On *That's o.k.* Cranston, RI: Tigerlily Music.

Grammer, R. (1983). Monster. On *Can you sound just like me?* Brewerton, NY: Red Note Records.

Grindley, S. (1985). *Knock, knock, who's there?* New York: Dragonfly.

Hazbry, N., & Condy, R. (1983). *How to get rid of bad dreams.* New York: Scholastic.

Heide, F. P. (1969). *Some things are scary.* Illustrated by Robert Osborn. New York: Scholastic.

Heide, F. P., & Van Clief, S. W. (1968). *That's what friends are for.* Illustrated by Brinton Turkle. New York: Four Winds.

Himonelman, J. (1994). *I'm not scared.* New York: Scholastic.

Howe, J. (1990). *There's a monster under my bed.* New York: Aladdin.

Johnston, T. (1995). *Alice nizzy nazzy: The witch of Santa Fe.* New York: Putnam.

Jones, D. W. (1989). *Stopping for a spell.* New York: Puffin.

Joy, F. (1992). The spell of the green ghost. In F. Joy, *Whole language celebrations.* Carthage, IL: Good Apple.

Justice, J. (1992). *The ghost and I: Scary stories for participatory telling.* Cambridge, MA: Yellow Moon.

Keleven, E. (1998). *A monster in the house.* New York: Dutton.

Libby, L. (1996). *I remember when I was afraid.* Sisters, OR: Quester.

Liro, N. J. (1994). *Who's afraid...? Facing children's fears with folktales.* Englewood, CO: Teacher Ideas Press.

MacDonald, M. R. (1988). *When the lights go out: Twenty scary tales to tell.* New York: H. W. Wilson.

Martin, B., & Archambault, J. (1986). *Barn dance.* New York: Holt.

Mayer, M. (1976). *There's a nightmare in my closet.* New York: Dial.

McDermott, G. (1972). *Anansi the spider.* New York: Holt, Rinehart & Winston.

McKissach, P. C. (1992). *The dark-thirty: Southern tales of the supernatural.* New York: Scholastic.

Merriam, E. (1987). *Halloween ABC.* New York: Simon & Schuster.

Michaels, S. (1992). *102 haunted house jokes.* New York: Watermill.

Oaks, J., & Oaks, J. T. (1989). Here come the skeletons. On *Flora Joy presents five original chillbump stories.* Garland, TX: CAM Audio.

O'Keefe, S. H. (1989). *One hungry monster.* New York: Scholastic.

Preston, T. (1999). *The lonely scarecrow.* New York: Dutton.

Russell, B. (1996). *Spider on the floor.* In Raffi, Songs to read. New York: Crown.

Russell, B. (1977). Spider on the floor. On *Spider on the floor.* Sillery, Quebec: Egos Anonymous.

Schutz-Gruber, B. (1993). *Voices on the wind.* Ann Arbor, MI: Author.

Schwartz, A. (1984). *In a dark, dark, room and other scary stories.* New York: HarperCollins.

Sendak, M. (1963). *Where the wild things are.* New York: Scholastic.

Seuss, Dr. (1961). What was I scared of? In *The Sneetches and other stories.* New York: Random House.

Smith, M. (1991). *There's a witch under the stairs.* New York: Lothrop, Lee and Shepard.

Stevens, K. (1985). *The beast in the bathtub.* Milwaulkee, WI: Gareth Stevens.

Stevenson, J. (1983). *What's under my bed?* New York: Greenwillow.

Stevenson, R. L. (1932). *Treasure island.* Garden City, NY: Doubleday.

Tashjian, V. A. (1969). *Juba this and juba that*. Boston: Little, Brown.

Trimble, M. (1998). *Witchy's turned around house*. Los Altos, CA: Images Press.

Van Allsburg, C. (1992). *The widow's broom*. New York: Scholastic.

Viorst, J. (1973). *My mama says there aren't any zombies, ghosts, vampires, creatures, demons, monsters, friends, goblins, or things*. New York: Atheneum.

Waber, B. (1972). *Ira sleeps over*. Boston: Houghton Mifflin.

Withers, C. (1966). *The tale of a black cat*. New York: Holt, Rinehart and Winston.

Yolen, J. (1989). *Best witches: Poems for Halloween*. New York: Putnam.

Young, R., & Young, J. D. (1990). *Favorite scary stories of American children*. Little Rock, AK: August House.

Zeifert, H., & Smith, M. (1989). *In a scary old house*. New York: Puffin.

November

Food for Thought

THANKSGIVING DAY

Over the river and through the wood
To Grandmother's house we go.
The horse knows the way to carry the sleigh
Through the white and drifted snow.
Over the river and through the wood,
Oh, how the wind does blow.
It stings the toes and bites the nose
As over the ground we go.

Over the river and through the wood
To have a full day of play.
Oh hear the turkeys gobbling,
For it's Thanksgiving Day.
Over the river and through the wood,
Trot fast my dapple gray;
Spring o'er the ground just like a hound,
For this is Thanksgiving Day.

Over the river and through the wood
And straight through the barnyard gate.
It seems that we go so dreadfully slow;
It is so hard to wait.
Over the river and through the wood,
Now Grandma's cap I spy.
Hurrah for the fun; the pudding's done.
Hurrah for the pumpkin pie!

–LYDIA MARIA CHILD
(ADAPTED FROM THE COMPLETE
POEM "THE NEW-ENGLAND BOY'S
SONG ABOUT THANKSGIVING DAY")

Giving thanks, remembering our past, and sharing all mark the generous gifts of November. The frost dusts the orange pumpkins as the squirrels scurry through the crunchy leaves. Pumpkin pie, roasted turkey, and family and friends fill our harvest days with joy.

"November: Food for Thought" urges us to snuggle in for the winter with a good book. Discovering the true meaning of Thanksgiving, becoming aware of different types of Thanksgiving celebrations, and learning to cooperate willingly with others form bonds of appreciation and friendship this month. The Storytelling methods used include Group Role-Play, Adapted Pantomime, Draw Talk, and Traditional.

The Logical-Mathematical, Interpersonal, Intrapersonal, Musical-Rhythmic, Naturalistic, Bodily-Kinesthetic, Verbal-Linguistic, and Visual-Spatial multiple intelligences engage the children while simultaneously fostering their empathy and creativity.

Just as November's harvest provides food for the body, so do stories and storytelling provide food for the mind and soul this month.

TIPS FOR THE TELLER

The Little Red Hen

Adapted by Susan Trostle Brand

STORYTELLING METHOD

Group Role-Play

A tale about an industrious and clever chef, *The Little Red Hen* has delighted young audiences for generations. *The Little Red Hen* has the last laugh, and the last bite of bread, when her friends refuse to help her with the cooking.

The story organization and plot lends itself well to several storytelling methods, including Felt Board, Puppetry, Traditional, and Character Imagery. For variety, the Teller and the children may wish to vary the method(s) used to tell this story.

When told as a Group Role-Play story, the following characters are used: Narrator, Little Red Hen, Chick (Little Ned), Mr. Pig, Mr. Duck, and Mrs. Turkey (more farm animals may be added, if desired). For a play production, add animal costumes, props, and scenery; encourage the designated animals to sing and pantomime.

The Little Red Hen

Narrator: Our story is called "The Little Red Hen." It is an old tale about a hen *(hen enters, curtsies)*, a chick named Little Ned, a pig *(enters; bows or curtsies)*, a duck *(enters; bows or curtsies)*, and a turkey *(enters; bows or curtsies)*.

(All animals except Hen and Chick exit.)

Little Red Hen: *(looks into cupboard)* My, oh, my! I see that I am nearly out of bread. I must make some more at once. But baking bread is a very slow, long process. I wish I had some help. Hmmmmmm. Which farm animal friends might we ask to help us bake the bread, Ned?

Chick (Little Ned): Ask Mr. Pig, Mama. All he does all day long is roll in the mud. He has plenty of time to help us.

Narrator: So the Little Red Hen and her son, Little Ned, walked to Mr. Pig's pen *(enter Mr. Pig)*.

Little Red Hen: Good morning, Mr. Pig. Will you help us bake some bread? It's nine o'clock and time to be fed.

Mr. Pig: I'm a big, fat pig. I roll in the mud all day. My mama says I really should jog; but, then, how will I ever become a hog? No, I'm sorry, Little Red Hen and Little Ned. I'm much to busy to help bake your bread *(rolls on floor in "mud.")*.

Little Red Hen: Very well, then, Mr. Pig. Good day.

Little Ned: You'll be sorry!

Narrator: The Little Red Hen and her son, Little Ned, went back *home (walk home)*. Mama hen thought about who else might help to bake the bread.

Little Red Hen: Hmmmmm. Do we have any other friends who might help us bake the bread, Ned?

Little Ned: Ask Mrs. Duck, Mama. All day long she wades and paddles in the water. She has plenty of time to help us.

Narrator: So the Little Red Hen and her son, Little Ned, went to visit Mrs. Duck *(enter Mrs. Duck)*.

Little Red Hen: Good morning, Mrs. Duck. Will you help us bake some bread? It's nine o'clock and time to be fed.

Mrs. Duck: I'm a water-lovin' duck. All day long I fish and play. I'd like to catch a whale someday! No, I'm sorry, Little Red Hen and Little Ned. I'm much too busy to help bake your bread.

Little Ned: You'll be sorry!

Narrator: So the Little Red Hen and her son, Little Ned, walked back home. They were becoming very disappointed in their friends.

Little Red Hen: Do we have any other friends who might help us bake the bread, Ned?

Little Ned: Ask Mrs. Turkey, Mama. All she does all day long is walk around the barnyard, gobbling and strutting, strutting and gobbling. She has plenty of time to help us bake the bread.

Narrator: So the Little Red Hen and her son, Ned, walked to the barnyard home of Mrs. Turkey *(enter Mrs. Turkey)*.

Little Red Hen: Good morning, Mrs. Turkey. Will you help us bake some bread? It's nine o'clock and time to be fed.

Turkey: I'm a proud, important turkey. My feathers are red and brown. Though times are good and times are bad, I'm never one to wear a frown. No, I'm sorry, Little Red Hen and Little Ned, I'm much too busy to help bake your bread.

Little Ned: You'll be sorry!

Narrator: Sadly and slowly, the Little Red Hen and her son, Little Ned, walked back home. They were very disappointed in their friends.

Little Red Hen: Well, Ned, We've asked Mr. Pig, Mrs. Duck, and Mrs. Turkey. It's getting late, and time is running short. Will *you* help me bake the bread, Ned?"

Little Ned: I'm a sweet little chick. I'm hard-working and clever. I'll be glad to help you, Mama; we'll make the best bread ever!

Narrator: So, Little Ned, and Little Red Hen began to make the bread. They planted the seeds *(plant seeds)*. They gathered the wheat *(gather wheat)*. They ground the wheat into flour *(grind wheat)*. They made the flour into a thick, white dough *(kneed dough)*. They placed the dough into a baking *dish (place Play Doh or clay into baking dish)*. They waited and sang songs *(sing songs)* and played games *(play games)*.

Little Red Hen: Ned, I smell fresh bread. I think it is nearly finished! *(checks bread in "oven")*. Yes! It is ready to eat!

Little Ned: It smells delicious, Mama. I'll help you cut the bread and place it on a serving platter *("cut" bread and place onto platter)*.

(Enter Mr. Pig, Mrs. Duck, and Mrs. Turkey.)

Mr. Pig: Say, what's that delightful aroma? Come to think of it, I'm pretty hungry. A pig can grow tired of rolling in the mud and eating slop all day, you know!

Mrs. Duck: Say, I smell something verrrry tasty! Come to think of it, I'm pretty hungry, too. A duck can grow tired of swimming and splashing and fishing all day, you know!

Mrs. Turkey: Say, it's nice, warm bread, fresh out of the oven.

Mr. Pig, Mrs. Duck, Mrs. Turkey: *(in unison)* Can we help you eat the bread, Little Red Hen and Little Ned?

Little Red Hen: I am very sorry. You didn't help us plant the seeds. You didn't help us gather the wheat. You didn't help us grind the wheat into flour. You didn't help us kneed the flour into dough. You didn't help us bake the bread. You didn't even help us slice the bread. You cannot help us *eat* the bread.

Mr. Pig, Mrs. Duck, Mrs. Turkey: *(in unison)* Ahhhh, shucks! Guess we learned a lesson: we were too busy to help the hen; the duck was in her pond, the pig was in his pen. If we wanted to eat the bread, we should have listened to Little Ned! Good day, Little Red Hen. Good day, Little Ned.

Narrator: The Little Red Hen and Little Ned had a most delicious feast that day of fresh, homemade bread. And they ate it *all by themselves!*

MULTIPLE INTELLIGENCE ACTIVITIES FOR . . .

The Little Red Hen

 Creative Collections.
(Logical-Mathematical; Interpersonal)

Invite youngsters to bring to class their favorite small collections (one collection per child). Children sort each collection according to a specified property, such as size, shape, color, texture, or age. Next, children help each other count the items in the collections by ones, twos, fives, and tens. Then, tally the total number of items in each group and in the entire class. Display collections for all to admire and discuss. Allow each child to tell why he or she collects this item and why it is special to him or her. Suggestions for collections: stones, amusement park or raffle tickets, stamps, postcards, shells, buttons, baseball cards, small dolls or animal figures, polished glass, butterflies, leaves, pencils, boats, thimbles.

2 **"When I Grow Up" Photo Books.**
(Intrapersonal; Verbal-Linguistic)

Reread and discuss the story of *The Little Red Hen* and how she worked hard to create something delicious. Ask children to share their work and career aspirations with the class. Then, on sepa-

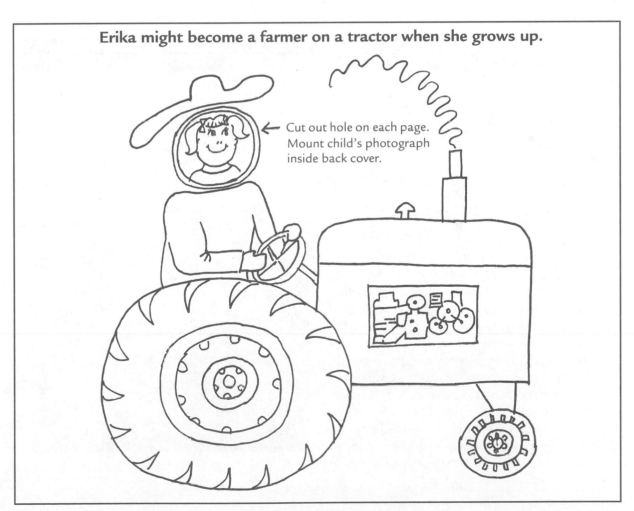

Erika might become a farmer on a tractor when she grows up.

← Cut out hole on each page. Mount child's photograph inside back cover.

Child is star of each book page.

rate sheets of paper, glue magazine pictures of various occupations. The children replace the faces of the people in the pictures with small school photos of themselves. It is exciting for children to see pictures of themselves engaged in their chosen careers. Compile pictures and written caption descriptions into a class book.

3 Sensory Seasons.
(Naturalistic; Verbal-Linguistic)

Divide the group of children into four groups: Spring, Summer, Autumn, and Winter. Each group writes a seasonal poem using all the senses—smelling, touching, tasting, seeing, and hearing. Take a sensory nature walk to explore the surroundings and to garner ideas. For example, one second-grade autumn group created the following sensory poem, set to autumn music.

This is Autumn

Smelling warm, spicy pumpkin pies and orange bonfires,

Touching squishy insides of a pumpkin to make a scary jack-o'-lantern,

Tasting brown caramel apples and chewy chocolate candy bars,

Seeing my red brick school and smiling faces of friends, old and new,

Hearing "Touchdown" at our team's football game and the *crunch, crunch, crunch* of leaves beneath my feet—

This is Autumn!

TIPS FOR THE TELLER

This story available on **Storytelling Video!**

Stone Soup
Adapted by Susan Trostle Brand

STORYTELLING METHOD

Adapted Pantomime

Stone Soup is an old favorite tale about trickery, magic, and—of course—soup. Told in the Pantomime Storytelling method, the Teller may dress in neutral-colored clothing and take on the roles of the food, the old woman, and the funny little man, while at the same time using words, body movements, and gestures to weave the story. Suggested pantomime gestures, movements, and/or facial expressions for many nouns and verbs appear in parentheses following the first appearance of the particular words. The cue words themselves are set in boldface type.

"Stone Soup" told through Adapted Pantomime method.

continued

TIPS FOR THE TELLER *continued*

A motivating introduction to the story is to bring a large electric cooking pot into the classroom and set it before the children on a table. Surround the pot with fresh vegetables, such as potatoes, carrots, onions, and cabbage. Inform the children that, after the story, the class will all make some delicious soup using the ingredients they see.

Finally, pass around a large, clean white stone. Invite the children to brainstorm ways in which stones might be used. The children may offer ideas such as paperweights, surfaces for creative painting, skipping them to form concentric circles in a pond, holding down corners of a tent, and hammering nails into a wall. Tell them that one more use for a stone is that of making "Stone Soup" and that the story that you will tell today is entitled "Stone Soup."

Stone Soup

Once upon a **time** *(point to wrist watch)* there was a **funny little man** *(hunch over and make a funny face)*. He had no **home** *(frame roof)*. But he **traveled** *(pretend to walk)* **far** *(point into distance)* and **wide** *(stretch arms at sides)*. He told **stories** *(extend hands from mouth)* and sang silly little **songs** *(sing, "La, la!")*. He was so **funny** *(smile broadly)* that everywhere he went, he made people **laugh and laugh** *(bend over, laughing and holding stomach)*.

One *(hold up pointer finger)* day he decided to **walk** *(walk in place)* through the deep, deep **woods** *(draw parallel lines in air with both hands)*. Tall **trees** *(gesture two parallel lines with hands)* grew all around him. The man **shivered** *(shiver)*. He was **cold** *(rattle teeth)* and **hungry** *(hold stomach and make sad face)*. Big **snowflakes** *(spread fingers)* **fell** *(fall to floor)* all around him. A few snowflakes even landed on his **nose** *(point to nose)*.

"What am I to do?" *(spread hands outward at shoulders)* he asked. Just as he asked this, he saw a **curl** *(curl pointer finger into air)* of smoke **rising** *(point up)* into the **sky** *(spread arm above head)* ahead. He **walked** *(walk forward)* a little farther. Then he saw a cozy little **cottage** *(frame roof)*. He was so **happy** *(jump once, smiling, and clap hands)*!

He **knocked** *(make fist and knock into air)* on the **door** *(frame rectangle)* of the **cottage.** He **waited** *(make fist below chin; look at watch)*. The door began to open. A **grouchy old woman** *(hunch over; look cross)* appeared before him.

"What do you want?" she **snapped** *(snap fingers)*.

"I have been walking in the tall trees of the woods all day, ma'am. I am very **cold** and very **hungry**. May I **come in** *(gesture forward)*?

"You may **come in** and **warm yourself by the fire**," *(rub hands together)* she said. "But I am very **poor** *(looking down, tilt head to side; cross arms over chest)*. I have no **food** *(extend palms of hands)* in this house for you to **eat**" *(pretend to put food in mouth and chew)*.

The **little man** was **happy** to be invited inside the **cottage**. But he could tell that the **old woman** was not **poor**. She had very big **cupboards** *(frame large squares with hands)*. He felt sure that they had **food** inside them. Somehow he must find a way to get her to **share** *(hold hands with self)* that **food** with him.

First *(hold up pointer finger)* he told her some funny **jokes** *(put one hand on hip and outstretch the other while smiling)*. **Second** *(hold up two fingers)*, he sang her some funny **songs** *(cross hands over chest and sing, "Laaa!")*. Then he told her a very funny **story** *(extend hand from mouth)*. The **old woman laughed** and **laughed** *(laugh aloud)*. She **laughed** until she **cried** *(rub hands at eyes and sniffle)*.

"Now, why don't we have some good, hot **soup**?" *(make slurping sound while pretending to hold soup spoon to mouth)* asked the clever man.

"I told you, I have **no food**," *(shake head; make finished gesture, pulling arms apart with palms facing floor)* replied the old woman.

"**No problem** *(shrug shoulders)*, ma'am," said the **man**. "I brought my own **soup**-making ingredients. See?" The man **held up** *(lift hands)* three small white **stones** *(make circles with thumb and four fingers)*.

"But those are only **stones**!" said the surprised **woman**. "You cannot make the **soup** from **stones**!"

"Oh, **yes** *(nod head)* I can" answered the **man**. "If you will be so kind as to bring me a **big pot** *(make large circle with arms in front of body)* I will show you how. You might add some **water** *(make wave motions with hands)* to the **pot**, if you can spare some. These **stones** are magic. **You** will **see**" *(circle eyes)*.

The **old woman** found her largest **pot**. She **filled** *(pretend to pour)* it with **water**. She **carried** *(pretend to carry heavy pot)* it to the **man**. The man **dropped one, two, three stones** *(count as you pretend to drop stones)* into the **pot**. Then, using a big **spoon** *(pretend to hold spoon into the air)* he **stirred** *(make stirring motions)* those three **stones** and the **water**.

"May I ask **one** small favor?" said the **man**. "I have made **soup** with these same **stones** many times before. The **stones** are losing a bit of their **flavor** *(smack lips)*. If you have just a **teeney** *(pinch thumb and pointer fingers together)* bit of **cabbage** *(form round head with hands)* it will be much more **flavorful**. However, if you have no **cabbage**, it is perfectly fine. The **soup** will taste **good** *(rub stomach)* on its own.

The woman was **happy** to oblige. She was **thrilled** *(clap hands and nod head, smiling broadly)* with the idea of making **soup** from practically **nothing** *(spread hands at sides)*. She brought the **man** a whole **head of cabbage**.

The man **added** *(pretend to throw in cabbage leaves)* the **cabbage** to the **pot**. He **stirred and stirred**.

"Why, this **soup** is fit for the **richest people** *(tilt head up, looking elegant)* in the world," exclaimed the **man**. In fact, only last week, I served it to the **king** *(form crown atop head)* and **queen**!" *(wave gaily)*. The only difference was that I added just a **wee bit of meat** *(form circle with curved hands, joining fingertips)* and a few **potatoes** *(form small circle with one hand)* and **carrots** *(make chopping motions)* to their soup. But, no matter. Our **soup** will be **fine** *(make A-OK sign with thumb and pointer finger, other fingers outstretched)* just as it is."

"**No** *(shake head vigorously)*, indeed!" said the **woman**. "That which is fit for the **king** and **queen** is **not** *(shake head)* too good for **me**" *(point to self)*. And, with that, she brought the **man** a large piece of **roast beef** *(make meat gesture)* and many fine **potatoes**.

The **man stirred and stirred**. "Oh, this **soup** is almost **perfect** *(form A-OK sign)* now!" he said.

"Almost **perfect**!" asked the **woman**. "How can you make it **perfect**?"

"Why, if you have just a **tiny bit of butter** *(pretend to spread bread)* it will be **absolutely perfect** *(make two A-OK signs)* ma'am," said the **man**.

"**Of course**!" replied the **woman**. She **brought** the man a **whole stick** *(make long stick form with hand and arm)* of top quality **butter**. The smiling **man dropped** *(pretend to drop ingredients)* **the butter** into the **pot** of **stones**, boiling **water, meat,** and **vegetables** *(make chopping motions)*. He **stirred and stirred**. Finally, the **soup** was **finished** *(spread hands apart, palms facing floor)*. The **man dished** *(pretend to use ladle)* it out into **two large bowls** *(show two bowl shapes with joined, curved hands)* being careful to leave the **stones** behind in the **pot**. The **old woman** and the **man ate and ate** *(pretend to eat and enjoy soup)*.

When they were nearly **finished eating** *(pat stomach)* the old woman **shook** *(pretend to shake outstretched hand)* the man's hand. "Thank you for showing me how to make this delicious **soup**, sir," she said.

"**No trouble** *(flap hand downward)* at all, my dear," answered the **man**. "As you can **see**, it is very easy. All you need is a couple of **stones** and a little of **this** *(click fingers on left)* and a little of **that**!" *(click fingers on right)*.

The **man** could not help **smiling** *(smile broadly)* as he ate yet another **bowl** of the wonderful stone **soup**.

MULTIPLE INTELLIGENCE ACTIVITIES FOR . . .

Stone Soup

 Delicious Stone Soup.
(Bodily-Kinesthetic; Logical-Mathematical)

Place a large, scrubbed, and boiled stone in the electric cooking pot used to introduce the story. Add two or more gallons of water to the pot and boil. Distribute vegetables that the children have brought in, several plastic knives, paper plates, paper towels, and measuring cups. Children chop and measure ingredients and add to the boiling water in the cooking pot to make their own delicious Stone Soup. Use several cans of vegetable soup or beef bullion cubes as the soup base. When the soup is finished, distribute soup in plastic soup bowls, add soup crackers, and enjoy!

 Try to Make Me Laugh.
(Interpersonal; Intrapersonal)

In the story, the funny little man tricked the old woman by making her laugh. Invite the youngsters, likewise, to try to make their friends laugh. Form a large circle of chairs in the center of the room. One child is "it." He or she tries for ten seconds to make a classmate or friend of his or her choice laugh by making funny faces and using silly words. No touching is allowed. If "it" is unsuccessful, he or she travels to another classmate and tries for ten seconds to make this classmate laugh. When "it" is successful, the child who laughs becomes the new "it." This is a fun party game, sure to produce many laughs!

③ Food Phonemes.
(Musical-Rhythmic; Verbal-Linguistic)

Using the following song/poem, children supply their own food names beginning with the sequential letters of the alphabet. Continue the song around the circle until each child has a turn to sing a verse with his or her name and food. Later, construct an illustrated class songbook using each of the child's contributions.

As a follow-up to the Food Phonemes activity, ask children to write original recipes. Writing recipes is enjoyable and creative for children. Ask each child to write one recipe for his or her favorite food. Be prepared for some unusual combinations and ingredients! Then ask the children to illustrate

> ## "A, My Name is Anna"
> *(sung to the tune of "The Farmer in the Dell")*
>
> A, my name is Anna,
>
> My friend's name is Al,
>
> We come from Arkansas,
>
> And we eat avocados!
>
> B, my name is Bernie,
>
> My friend's name is Beth,
>
> We come from Baltimore,
>
> And we eat bananas!
>
> C, my name is Connie, (etc.)

their recipes using crayons, liquid markers, or creative craft materials. Compile all of the class recipes into an enticing class book. Some teachers photocopy the recipe booklets and send them home for the children to read with their parents.

As an alternative idea, ask children's parents to send in one favorite recipe from home. Compile all class recipes together into booklets and send home the "published" recipe books as special occasion gifts for the families.

TIPS FOR THE TELLER

Old Man Rabbit's Thanksgiving Dinner

By Carolyn Sherwin Bailey

Adapted by Susan Trostle Brand

STORYTELLING METHOD

Draw Talk

This delightful story helps the student discover one of the important lessons in life: that we derive greater satisfaction in being helpful than in being helped. Old Man Rabbit's only concern is to get enough food for himself. When he becomes aware that other animals are in need he decides to make a dinner to share with them. He enjoys being involved with the preparation and serving of the dinner for his friends. When they thank him for his generosity he is deeply touched to know that his dinner was indeed a Thanksgiving dinner. Listeners will be captured by the author's skillful appeal to the senses and her emphasis upon the spirit of kindness, which makes for a true Thanksgiving.

Reading about the Draw Talk Storytelling method in Chapter 3 will help the Teller to prepare the flip chart for preparation and gather all the needed materials. A fall display of a cornucopia with colorful dried leaves, gourds, pumpkins, and fruit will help set the scene. A discussion of Thanksgiving as a holiday and what the children are looking forward to will direct the focus to the preparation and the dinner. Introduce the concept of "sharing" the dinner with others. Invite the students to listen with their eyes and ears to discover how Old Man Rabbit changes.

Old Man Rabbit's Thanksgiving Dinner

Page One: Old Man Rabbit *(draw rabbit)* sat at the door of his little house *(draw door and house)*, eating a nice, ripe, juicy turnip *(draw a turnip)*. It was a cold, frosty day, but Old Man Rabbit was all wrapped up, round and round, with yards and yards of his best red wool muffler *(draw muffler)*, so he didn't care if the wind whistled through his whiskers and blew his ears up straight *(draw tall ears)*. Old Man Rabbit had been exercising, too, and that was another reason that he was so nice and warm.

Page One, "Old Man Rabbit's Thanksgiving Dinner."

Page Two: Early in the morning he had started off, lippity, clippity, down the little brown path *(draw path)* that lay in front of his house and led to Farmer Dwyer's corn patch. The path was all covered with shiny red leaves *(draw leaves)*. Old Man Rabbit scuffled through them and he carried a great big bag over his stomach *(draw bag)*. In the corn patch he found two or three fat, red ears of corn *(draw corn)* that Farmer Dwyer had missed, so he dropped them into his bag. A little farther along he found some purple turnips and some orange carrots *(draw turnips and carrots)* and quite a few russet apples *(draw apples)* that Farmer Dwyer had arranged in little piles in the orchard. Old Man Rabbit went in the barn, squeezing under the big front door by making himself very flat. He filled all the chinks in his bag with potatoes *(place potatoes in bag)* and he took a couple of eggs *(draw eggs in paws)* in his paws, for he thought he might want to stir up a little pudding for himself before the day was over.

The Old Man Rabbit started off home again down the little brown path, his mouth watering every time his bag bumped against his stomach, and not meeting anyone on the way because it was so very, very early in the morning.

Page Three: When he came to the little house he emptied his bag and arranged all his harvest in piles in his front room; the corn in one pile, and the carrots in the second pile, the turnips in the third pile, the apples in the fourth pile, and the potatoes in the fifth pile *(draw piles of food as each is named)*. He beat up his eggs and stirred some flour with them and filled it full of currants to make a pudding.

Page Four: And when he had put his pudding in a bag and set it boiling on the stove, he went outside to sit a while and eat a carrot *(draw Rabbit sitting outside)*, thinking all the time what a mighty fine old rabbit he was, and so clever, too.

Page Two, "Old Man Rabbit's Thanksgiving Dinner."

Page Three, "Old Man Rabbit's Thanksgiving Dinner."

Well, while Old Man Rabbit was sitting there in front of his little house, wrapped up in his red muffler and munching the carrot, he heard a little noise in the leaves. It was Billy Chipmunk *(draw Chipmunk)* traveling home to the stone wall where he lived. He was hurrying and blowing on his paws to keep them warm.

"Good morning, Billy Chipmunk," said Old Man Rabbit. "Why are you running so fast?"

"Because I am cold, and I am hungry," answered Billy Chipmunk. "It's going to be a hard winter, a very hard winter—no apples left. I've been looking all the morning for an apple and I couldn't find one."

And with that, Billy Chipmunk went chattering by, his fur standing straight out in the wind.

Page Four, "Old Man Rabbit's Thanksgiving Dinner."

No sooner had he passed than Old Man Rabbit saw Molly Mouse *(draw Mouse)* creeping along through the little brown path, her long gray tail rustling the red leaves as she went.

"Good morning, Molly Mouse," said Old Man Rabbit.

"Good morning," answered Molly Mouse in a weak little voice.

"You look a little unhappy," said Old Man Rabbit, taking another bite of his carrot.

"I have been looking and looking for an ear of corn," said Molly Mouse in a sad little chirping voice. "But the corn has all been harvested. It's going to be a very hard winter, a very hard winter."

And Molly Mouse trotted by, out of sight.

Pretty soon Old Man Rabbit heard somebody else coming along by his house. This time it was Tommy Chickadee *(draw Chickadee)* hopping by and making a great to-do, chattering and scolding as he came.

"Good morning, Tommy Chickadee," said Old Man Rabbit.

But Tommy Chickadee was too much put out about something to remember his manners. He just chirped and scolded, because he was cold and he couldn't find a single crumb or a berry or anything at all to eat. Then he flew away, his feathers puffed out with the cold until he looked like a round ball, and all the way he chattered and scolded more and more.

Page Five: Old Man Rabbit finished his carrot, eating every single bit of it, even to the leaves. Then he went in his house to poke the fire in his stove and to see how the pudding was cooking. It was doing very well, bumping against the pot as it bubbled and boiled, and smelling very fine indeed.

Page Five, "Old Man Rabbit's Thanksgiving Dinner."

Old Man Rabbit looked around his house at the corn and the carrots and the turnips and the apples and the potatoes, and then he had an idea. It was a very funny idea, different from any other idea Old Man Rabbit had ever had before in his life. It made him scratch his head with his left hind foot, and think and wonder; but it pleased him, too—it was such a very funny idea.

First he took off his muffler, and then he put on his gingham apron *(draw apron on Rabbit)*. He took his best red tablecloth from the drawer and put it on his table, and then he set the table with his gold-banded china dinner set. By the time he had done all this, the pudding was boiled, so he lifted it, all sweet and steaming *(draw steam)* from the kettle and set it in the middle of the table *(draw table and kettle)*. Around the pudding Old Man Rabbit piled heaps and heaps of corn and carrots and turnips and apples and potatoes *(draw each food on table, separately as each is named)* and then he pulled the cord on his dinner bell *(draw bell)* that was all rusty, because Old Man Rabbit had very seldom rung it before, and he stood in his front door and he rang it very hard, calling in a loud voice:

"Dinner's ready! Come to dinner, Billy Chipmunk, and Molly Mouse, and Tommy Chickadee!"

Page Six: They all came, and they brought their friends with them. Tommy Chickadee brought Rusty Robin *(draw Chickadee and Robin)* who had a broken wing and had not been able to fly south for the winter. Billy Chipmunk brought Chatter-Chee *(draw Chipmunk and squirrel)* a lame squirrel, whom he had invited to share his hole for a few months, and Molly Mouse brought a young gentleman Field Mouse *(draw male and female mice)* who was very distinguished looking because of his long whiskers. When they all tumbled into Old Man Rabbit's house and saw the table with the pudding in the center they forgot their manners and began eating as fast as they could, every one of them.

It kept Old Man Rabbit very busy waiting on them. He gave all the currants from the pudding to Tommy Chickadee and Rusty Robin *(point to birds)*. He selected juicy carrots for Molly Mouse and her friend *(point to mice)*, and the largest apple for Billy Chipmunk *(point to Chipmunk)*. Old Man Rabbit was so busy that he didn't have any time to eat a bite of dinner himself, but he didn't mind that, not one single bit. It made him feel so warm and full inside just to see the others eating.

When the dinner was over, and not one single crumb was left on the table, Tommy Chickadee *(point to Chickadee)* hopped up on the back of his chair and chirped:

"Three cheers for Old Man Rabbit's Thanksgiving dinner!"

"Hurrah! Hurrah!" they all twittered and chirped and chattered. And Old Man Rabbit was so surprised that he didn't get over it for a week. You see, he had really given a Thanksgiving dinner without knowing that it really and truly was Thanksgiving Day *(print the words "Happy Thanksgiving" at the bottom of page six)*.

Page Six, "Old Man Rabbit's Thanksgiving Dinner."

MULTIPLE INTELLIGENCE ACTIVITIES FOR . . .

Old Man Rabbit's Thanksgiving Dinner

1 Weather Wisdom.
(Naturalistic; Logical-Mathematical)

Old Man Rabbit observed changes in nature and knew that it was time to store food for the winter. The Pilgrims and early Colonists did not have modern weather service to help predict the weather. They had to depend on developing their Naturalistic Intelligence to help them prepare for changes in the weather. They observed animal behavior and nature to predict the weather. Join the fun! Gather old weather lore that people used to believe would help them predict weather changes. Look for these signs in nature or in animals that are around for a month. Keep observations in a class notebook. Check the eastern sky each morning and plan weather walks where everyone may look and record weather indicators and clues. Record the weather signs observed and the type of weather that occurred. Keep a chart to compare your observations with the reality of the weather. How accurate were the old sayings and beliefs?

Here are some weather signs and sayings, for your chart, to help you start your observations:

1. Red sky in the morning—Sailors take warning. Red sky at night—Sailors delight.
2. A sunny day is on the way When you see cobwebs on the hay.
3. A storm is coming soon if you see a hazy halo 'round the moon.
4. Mackerel sky, soon wet or dry.
5. If the leaves show their underside, Rain is coming. Run and hide.
6. Seagulls flying from the sea. A storm is brewing, best hurry.
7. Rain before seven, quits by eleven.
8. If a woolly bear caterpillar's stripes are wide, A mild winter we'll abide.
9. First frost will come three months after the first katydid's hum.
10. When the clouds are black and the grass bends low, A storm is coming, better go!
11. Birds fly high, skies are dry.

2 Old Man Rabbit's Secret.
(Interpersonal; Intrapersonal)

Discuss with the class what gave Old Man Rabbit such joy and happiness. Invite them to join in Old Man Rabbit's Thanksgiving fun. Care and share! Initiate a canned food drive from your class for a local food bank. Bring a surprise to another class. Check with the other classroom teacher (if applicable) to make sure a popcorn surprise will fit into his or her schedule. Choose a day for the popcorn surprise. Collect juice drinks or fresh apple cider, cups, napkins, bowls, and popcorn. Arrange with an adult to microwave the popcorn or bring a hot air popper into class to use. Pour the popcorn into the bowls. Pour the drinks into the cups and place on trays. Others in the class may want to decorate the trays with fall leaves and place mats woven with colorful construction paper strips. Then arrange to visit the other classroom and share your popcorn feast with them.

3 Crazy Colors.
(Bodily-Kinesthetic; Musical-Rhythmic)

The author's use of color is so vivid in this story. This color game is fun-filled exercise that will help develop visual, auditory, and listening skills. You will need four colors of construction paper. Red, yellow, light blue, and purple are recommended in consideration of those students who may be color blind to red and green. Have the class pick a leader, and decide what movements will be assigned to each color. (Example: red: stop; yellow: glide; light blue: hop; purple: spin.) Arrange the class in a circle where they can all see the leader holding the colored construction paper. When the leader holds up one color the children move around in the circle with the appropriate movement.

Review the colors and corresponding movements. Have the class watch and move according to the color help up by the leader. Variations of this game can include assigning different rhythm instruments, gestures, or vocal sounds for each of the colors. Music can be played softly in the background for further enjoyment.

TIPS FOR THE TELLER

The Strawberry Thanksgiving
Retold by Jeanne M. Donato

STORYTELLING METHOD
Traditional

This story is a retelling of a traditional Narragansett legend passed down from the oral tradition. It introduces the listener to one of the several Thanksgiving feasts, celebrated throughout the year by Native Americans long before the arrival of the Pilgrims. Thanksgiving is a time to celebrate the richness and wisdom that comes to us from our many different traditions. *The Strawberry Thanksgiving* has its own special message of love and forgiveness.

The Traditional method of storytelling in Chapter 3 is chosen for this story. The Teller may choose to dress as a Pilgrim or early settler to introduce the story. A display of fall fruits and a picture of old Plimoth (Plymouth) Plantation in Plymouth, Massachusetts, along with a display of northeastern Native American artifacts and pictures will help set the time frame. It will also serve as a reference for a question and answer discussion such as "Who celebrated the First Thanksgiving?" or "Where did the idea for a Thanksgiving Celebration originate?" Invite the students to listen to discover the answers.

The Strawberry Thanksgiving

Feasts of Thanksgiving and harvest festivals have been celebrated in many cultures throughout the world. So when the Pilgrims asked Squanto to invite the chief of the Wampanoags, Massasoit, and his followers to share in their Harvest Festival, it was a custom that his people celebrated throughout the year.

When Chief Massasoit and ninety of his braves attended the Pilgrims' Harvest Festival they brought with them five deer as a gift. Sharing gifts of friendship, food, games, and dancing were all part of the many traditional Thanksgiving feasts that the Native American people celebrated. Chief Massasoit explained to the Pilgrims that his people also gave thanks to the Great Spirit during bountiful seasons, but most importantly, they gave thanks when times were hard.

The powerful Narragansett tribe, which later befriended Roger Williams, the founder of the Rhode Island colony, also celebrated many Thanksgivings throughout the year. One of these Thanksgivings is celebrated to this day during the month of June. It is called the Strawberry Thanksgiving. During this Thanksgiving festival the people gather to share food, songs, dances, and stories. This is one of these stories.

Many moons ago when the earth was new, a Brother and Sister lived with their Grandmother. Their lives were rich in happiness, for they enjoyed and respected each other. Their wetu (house) was filled with aque'ne (peace).

Then one day the spirit of laziness entered their lives and they thought only of their own comfort. No longer were they willing to help or share. Grandmother gave them each a gathering basket and sent them into the forest to search out food. When they came to a place where the ma'yi (path) split they could not agree on which one to take.

Words flew between their hearts, leaving tiny scars of anger, till the Sister turned her back on her Brother and rushed down the ma'yi (path) towards the rising sun. The Brother turned his back and followed the ma'yi (path) facing the setting sun.

The Brother traveled till he found a stream. There he waited and watched, trying to catch a fish. The warm spring air hung in silence about him. The nippa'wus (sun) seemed to stand still in the kee'suck (sky). He missed his Sister's companionship. When he caught a fine fat trout, only the empty echo of the hills greeted his shout of joy. He thought of his Sister alone in the woods and regretted his rashness in letting her go off alone. What would Grandmother and the others think of him? "Oh Great Spirit," his heart prayed, "please help me to find my Sister safe."

As if the Great Spirit were answering his plea, Kaku'kont (a crow) cawed from his perch high atop a tall pine tree. He swooped down and flew off in the direction of the rising sun. The Brother quickly followed. But no matter how fast he ran he could not catch up with his Sister. For everyone knows how fast a person can walk when he or she carries anger in his or her heart.

Now the Sister had walked fast and far towards the rising sun. She did not notice the birds calling for her attention or their gifts of colored feathers hanging here and there from the trees. She did not slow when the trees burst into blossom or when the wind showered her with their soft petals. Not even the pungent smell of the pines as she brushed by their soft needles stopped her.

As she walked she began to remember the goodness of her Brother. She missed him and wished they had not argued. Tears of sadness wet the grass as she walked. When she looked ahead for the ma'yi (path) she realized mat mayanu'nno (there was no way.) Realizing she was lost, fear and regret flooded over her. How she missed her Brother and her Grandmother.

While the girl cried, the Great Sprit blew on the tears that had fallen where she walked. The tears grew into green running vines that carpeted the ground with soft white blossoms shaped liked tiny stars. These stars burst into tiny, red, heart-shaped berries.

When the Sister stepped on one of these strange berries, its aroma made her smile, for it reminded her of happiness. She reached down and picked one of the berries. The tiny heart with its seeds on the outside reminded her of the scars that angry words leave. She closed her eyes and tasted the berry. Its taste reminded her of the sweetness of love. Oh how she wished that she could share this gift with her Brother. She stopped to gather the fruit.

When the Brother found his Sister, her basket was filled to overflowing with the strange new fruit. She looked up without speaking and shared one of the berries with him. When he tasted it, he too tasted the gift of love and forgiveness.

Happiness flooded their hearts as they gave thanks to the Great Spirit for the gift of wutta'himneash (strawberries). They returned to their Grandmother and shared this gift with their people.

Every June the Narragansett people celebrate the wutta'himneash (strawberries) Thanksgiving. They give thanks to the Great Spirit every time they eat wutta'himneash (strawberries). For they believe that whenever people share and eat wutta'himneash (strawberries) they must forgive, forget, and remain netompau'og (friends).

The Strawberry Thanksgiving

 1 **The Strawberry Friendship Dance.**
(Musical-Rhythmic; Bodily-Kinesthetic)

With rhythm instruments, play and sing the chant for the students. This dance works best with even numbers. Have some students play and sing while the others dance, taking turns. Next, invite them to form a circle. Make it tight enough that they can reach out and tap the student in front of them. They may start out going counterclockwise and then will stop, turn, and go clockwise. Start on the first beat with the foot on the outside of the ring. Bend the knees slightly, and shuffle from the outside and inside foot in unison. The weight of the foot should shift onto the ball of the foot then bring the heel down with a sharp rhythmic beat. When it comes to the line "Give me a pat on the shoulder," on the word "friend," everyone should tap the person in front of him or her on the shoulder and turn to face the opposite direction falling into the rhythm of the dance. Everyone shouts "Ho!" and starts chanting the chorus: "Hey ya,..."

Strawberries

We have ga - thered the straw - ber - ries____ come and feast to your

heart's con - tent, Give me a pat on the shoul - der, friend, and

all your troub - les will end. Hey ya hey ya hey ya hey ya.

"Strawberries" (traditional Narragansett song. Melody line arranged by Jean Liepold).

Dance Directions:

(Dance in a circle going in a counterclockwise direction while singing:)

We have gathered the strawberries.
Come and feast to your heart's content.
Give me a pat on the shoulder, friend,
(Pat the person in front of you on the shoulder.)
And all your troubles will end. Ho!
(Turn and dance in the opposite direction.)

Chorus:

Hey ya, Hey, ya, Hey ya, Hey ya.
(Repeat the song moving while dancing in this new direction.)

 ## The First Thanksgiving?
(Verbal-Linguistic; Interpersonal)

When we research a question it can open our eyes. This question will lead the class on a group project as they discover that other colonists celebrated harvest festivals in the New World before the Pilgrims' well-known Thanksgiving. The idea of a Thanksgiving feast is nothing new for Native American tribes, which hold several Thanksgiving feasts all through the year. Research books in the library to discover other colonial settlements that may have celebrated harvest festivals earlier. Locate any Native American families attending your school or living nearby who would be willing to speak to the class. Your State Council on the Arts will have a listing of Native Americans living in your state who will come to share their culture with your class and speak to your class about their Thanksgiving feasts. Work on a display and chart that lists pictures and information on the different Thanksgiving festivals that the class discovers. Find and share some of the legends and wisdom of these feasts. Prepare a list of questions for your speaker ahead of time. Follow up with a class thank-you note. Include thoughts on what the students have learned.

3 Catch a Dream.
(Visual-Spatial; Interpersonal)

The Sioux people hang dream catchers above their beds or in their homes to sift their dreams and visions. They believe that the good in their dreams will be captured in the web and be carried with them. To make a model of a dream catcher you will need the following material: strips of thin willow branches or similar soft, pliable wood approximately 15 inches in length; a pan of water deep enough to cover and soak the willow strips overnight; tape; wire; white yarn about a yard in length; beads that can be threaded onto the yarn; scissors; feathers; and ribbon.

Instructions: Soak the strips of willow branches in water overnight to soften. Cut the branches into 15-inch lengths. Lay three strips together and fasten together at one end. Braid the three sections into one strand. Connect the two ends, forming a circle, and secure with tape, glue, or wire. Next, tie a strand of yarn to the outside of the willow hoop and thread it across the circle and wrap around the opposite side. Weave a spider's web pattern with the yarn, adding beads along the weaving for decoration. Tie off the web. Add a yarn thread at the top of the dream catcher to hang it

Dream Catchers.

up. Feathers and ribbons may be used to hang off the bottom of the dream catcher for decoration.

Display your dream catcher on the board. The Sioux Native Americans believe that the dream catchers are a web that help people to reach their goals and make good use of their ideas, dreams, and visions. Ask the students to reflect on their ideas, dreams, and visions for a better world. Share these and write these ideas down. Display them along with the dream catchers.

NOVEMBER CHAPTER RESOURCES

Amery, H. (1990). *Usborne farmyard tales: Scarecrow's secret.* London: Usborne House.

Anosky, J. (1993). *Every autumn comes the bear.* New York: Atheneum.

Barth, E., & Arndt, U. (1975). *Turkeys, Pilgrims and Indian corn: The story of Thanksgiving symbols.* New York: Houghton Mifflin.

Berenstain, S., & Berenstain, J. (1995). *The Berenstain bears count their blessings.* New York: Random House.

Brink, C. R., & Wolff, A. (1964). *Goody O'Grumpity.* New York: North-South Books.

Bunting, E. (1988). *How many days to America? A Thanksgiving story.* New York: Clarion.

Carle, E. (1979). *The very hungry caterpillar.* New York: Putnam.

Cowley, J. (1996). *Gracias, the Thanksgiving turkey.* New York: Scholastic.

Croll, C., & Ross, K. (1995). *The story of the pilgrims.* New York: Random House.

Galloway, M. R. U. (1990). "The legend of the strawberry." In *Aunt Mary, tell me a story: A collection of Chero-* kee legends and tales as told by Mary Ulmer Chiltoskey. Cherokee, NC: Cherokee Communications.

Grindley, S. (1985). *Knock, knock, who's there?* New York: Dragonfly.

Harness, C. (1992). *Three young Pilgrims.* New York: Aladdin.

Jackson, A. (1997). *I know an old lady who swallowed a fly.* New York: Dutton.

Jennings, P. (1993). *Strawberry Thanksgiving.* Cleveland, OH: Modern Curriculum.

Koller, J. F. (1999). *Nickommoh! A Thanksgiving celebration.* New York: Aladdin.

Lionni, L. (1967). *Fredrick.* New York: Dragonfly.

Peters, R. M. (1992). *Clambake: A Wampanoag tradition.* Minneapolis, MN: Learner.

Robbins, M. L. (1996). *Native American tales and activities.* Huntington Beach, CA: Teacher Created Materials.

Ruccki, A. (1992). *Turkey's gift to the people.* New York: Aladdin.

Sendak, M. (1963). *Where the wild things are.* New York: Scholastic.

Sewall, M. (1995). *Thunder from the clear sky*. New York: Aladdin.

Simmns, W. S. (1989). *The Narragansett*. New York: Aladdin.

Tashjian, V. A. (1969). *Juba this and juba that*. Boston: Little, Brown.

Travers, D. F. (1991). *The Thanksgiving primer: A complete guide to re-creating the first harvest festival for your family, friends or church*. Plymouth, MA: Plymouth Plantation.

Van Leeuwen, J. (1995). *Across the wide dark sea: The Mayflower journey*. New York: Aladdin.

Warren, J. (1995). *Stone Soup*. Everett, WA: Author.

Waters, K. (1989). *Sarah Morton's day: A day in the life of a Pilgrim girl*. New York: Aladdin.

Waters, K. (1993) *Samuel Eaton's day: A day in the life of a Pilgrim boy*. New York: Scholastic.

Waters, K., & Kendall, R. (1996*). Tapenum's Day: A Wampanoag Indian boy in Pilgrim times*. New York: Scholastic.

Weinstein-Farson, L. (1988). *The Wampanoag*. New York: Aladdin.

Wigginton, E. (1972). "Weather signs." In *The Foxfire book*. Garden City, NY: Anchor Books.

Wilbur, C. K. (1978). *The New England Indians*. Chester, CT: Globe Pequot.

December

Holidays Around the World

CHRISTMAS BELLS

I heard the bells on Christmas Day
Their old, familiar carols play,
    And wild and sweet
    The words repeat
Of peace on earth, good will to men!

And thought how, as the day had come,
The belfries of all Christendom
    Had rolled along
    The unbroken song
Of peace on earth, good will to men!

Till, ringing, singing, on its way,
The world revolved from night to day,
    A voice, a chime,
    A chant sublime
Of peace on earth, good will to men!

-HENRY WADSWORTH LONGFELLOW

*D*ecember, the last month of the year and the final chapter of this book, conjures childhood memories of family gatherings, holiday festivities, gift exchanges, and delicious seasonal foods. December brings Chanukah and Christmas, Kwanzaa, St. Lucia Day, and many, many other international holidays. Celebrate!

In "December: Holidays Around the World," children discover a variety of multicultural holidays. The Teller enlivens the holidays by engaging the children in Chant Storytelling and by depicting stories using the Traditional and Puppetry Storytelling methods.

As youngsters concoct Lucious Latkes and create Angels of Kindness they experience December holidays in tangible and ever-so-memorable ways using the Visual-Spatial, Musical-Rhythmic, Logical-Mathematical, Bodily-Kinesthetic, Interpersonal, Verbal-Linguistic, Naturalistic, and Intrapersonal multiple intelligences.

The gift of storytelling makes every day a holiday.

Saint Lucia Day: A Swedish Tradition

By Jeanne M. Donato

STORYTELLING METHOD

Traditional

Saint Lucia Day is derived from a compilation of Swedish traditions and legends. In this story set in America, a grandmother shares with her twin grandchildren her memories of celebrating Saint Lucia's Day in Sweden. She explains the customs and traditional food and drink served during this holiday and shares her excitement about the preparations and customs she practiced in Sweden as a young girl. Grandmother also tells the children her favorite legends of Saint Lucia. She explains the history of the celebration and how it has evolved to the present day, and her grandchildren are invited to participate in the tradition as it is handed down to them.

The Traditional method described in Chapter 3 will help the Teller prepare for the presentation of this story. Make a recording of "Santa Lucia" and play it softly in the background or sing it before the introduction of the story. Display a map of the world and point out where Sweden is located. Inquire if anyone in the classroom is of Swedish descent or knows of anyone who may have come from Sweden. A discussion of traditions and customs from different countries will offer an opportunity for explaining Saint Lucia Day as a Swedish tradition. Display a Saint Lucia's wreath with electric candles lit, and serve ginger snap cookies as a snack. Print words to the song so all can join in singing it at the beginning and end of the telling. These preparations will help the students to appreciate the customs. Invite them to compare this celebration, held on December 13, with other winter traditions and customs celebrated during this time. When we learn about the stories and traditions of other countries, we learn to respect and appreciate them.

Saint Lucia Day: A Swedish Tradition

The aroma of freshly baked saffron buns, cinnamon, and ginger teased the twins into Grandma Freda's cozy kitchen.

"Oh, Grandma!" cried Jodie and John. "Why are you making desserts and coffee so late in the day? May we help you?"

"Yes, yes, yes," laughed their Grandma. "You can help me make the pepparkakor for tomorrow while the Luciakatter cools," Grandma answered, pointing to the warm saffron buns.

"What does pepparkakor and Luciakatter mean, in English, Grandma?" asked the Twins. "Why are you making them tonight?"

Grandma smiled and answered, "Those pinwheel-shaped saffron buns are called Luciakatter. It means Lucia cats or light-cats, in Swedish. Pepparkakor are what you call gingersnap cookies. The coffee is good thick traditional Lucia kaffee. I am getting everything ready for a real Swedish Saint Lucia Day to surprise your mother and father. It will be just like my family did when we lived in Sweden."

"But Grandma," the Twins exclaimed. "We've never celebrated that holiday here in America. What is it?"

Grandma Freda answered, "Tomorrow is a very special holiday in Sweden. There, on December 13, everyone in Stockholm joins in celebrating Saint Lucia Day. After cleaning the houses from top to bottom, the mothers bake the Luciakatter and pepparkakor and brew the Lucia kaffee the day before. Here, sit down at the table and I will tell you all about it. The two of you are old enough to celebrate Saint Lucia Day. Would you like to help me with the surprise?"

"Oh, yes!" the Twins answered excitedly as they moved their kitchen chairs closer to their Grandmother. "What do the children in Sweden do on Saint Lucia Day, Grandma? What was it like when you were a little girl? What do we get to do?"

"Wait! Wait! Not so many questions all at once," Grandma laughed. "Now let me see. Where should I begin? Hundreds of years ago, when the Swedish people used the older Julian calendar, December 13, Saint Lucia Day, fell on the longest, darkest night of the year, called the winter solstice. They used this calendar up to the 1300s, so this gives you an idea of how old these traditions are. An old saying goes that 'even the cow from hunger bites the manger three times.' In those old days, the people feared that the sun would never return. They believed that this night was filled with frightening creatures and evil spirits, which roamed the world causing mischief. Saint Lucia Day is an old Christian custom that has combined with ancient folklore traditions to create a warm and joyous day. It started as a simple home-centered celebration, marking the end of the long darkness and the return of the sun's light.

"You've noticed that, during the winter, it starts to get dark early and the days get shorter. Well in Sweden, where I was born, the days are shorter still and folks must put the lights on as early as three o'clock in the afternoon! That is why we call them 'dark nights.' But in the summer time daylight lasts half through the night.

"There are many legends about how this tradition started. My favorite one is about Saint Lucia and the shipload of food.

"Hundreds of years ago, during the long, icy winter, famine swept the land. The people in Sweden were so hungry that all they had left to eat was bitter bread made from ground-up tree bark. So much snow had fallen that the mountains were impassable. The harbor was frozen and no ship could sail in or out to bring food to the starving people. December 13, the winter solstice, was the ancient celebration of the sun god Freya's birthday and the return of his light. Yet, the darkness was growing longer than anyone could remember and the people feared that their ancient sun god would never return to warm the earth.

"Some traveling Christian priests from Ireland were also stranded and starving in Sweden. They preached against the old pagan ways and beliefs. The people feared that the famine was sent to punish them for listening to these foreigners.

"The preachers told the people stories of God and his saints. They announced that God's power was stronger than that of the old gods. They said that they would pray for a miracle to rid the land of famine on the day following the winter solstice. This was also the feast day of Saint Lucia, whose name means 'light.' The preachers told the people the story of her life and death. The Swedish people admired the courage and compassion shown by this beautiful young Sicilian maid. They could imagine her glowing figure, crowned by a halo of light as she walked through dark caves to feed the poor and needy. The priests encouraged the people to pray for a miracle from God in the name of Saint Lucia. They taught them the old Neapolitan boat song, 'Santa Lucia.' The people took heart, prayed, sang, and waited.

"Early the next morning, so the legend goes, a great shining light was seen from a ship that glided across the icy harbor. A beautiful young woman, all dressed in white, stood at the helm. Her face was so radiant that there was a glow of light around her head and the darkness departed. The stars themselves seemed to come down from the heavens and dance in the sky. Legend says it was Saint Lucia bringing love, hope, and light back to the world. Her ship, filled with food, saved the poor, starving people of Sweden. To this day, 'Santa Lucia,' is the traditional song that marks this celebration."

"Wow!" exclaimed the Twins. "That was a great story, Grandma. But how do the children in Sweden celebrate Saint Lucia Day?"

"Well," Grandma explained, "Saint Lucia celebration is traditionally a family celebration, though now it is celebrated in homes, schools, churches, and cities throughout Sweden. Each family chooses one of their young daughters to be their Saint Lucia. If a family does not have a young girl, a relative or neighbor may be Lucia. She is dressed in a white flowing gown with a lace collar and a red ribbon tied at the waist. On her head she wears a wreath of lingonberry leaves with lighted candles carefully attached to it.

"She is accompanied by 'star boys' dressed in long white robes. They wear tall, cone-shaped hats covered with stars and carry long poles with a star and ribbons on top to represent the stars that danced in the sky. The white-gowned children sing Lucia carols as they go from room to room waking everyone up. They carry Lucia kaffee, Luciakatter, and pepparkakor and serve it to everyone in the household.

"When I was young, Saint Lucia Day was very exciting. The older students would go out about six o'clock in the morning and 'Lucia' their teachers. The fun was to catch their teacher in bed, sing them songs, and serve them cookies and coffee.

"All the children brought their Lucia and star-boy gowns to class. We would put on our gowns, light candles, and sing Lucia carols. The teachers would read stories, and the older students would 'Lucia' each classroom. The wonderful smells of the Lucia kaffee, Luciakatter, and pepparkakor filled our classrooms. After the celebration, school would be dismissed early. It marked the beginning of our festive Christmas holidays. Our vacation ended on Tjugondad Knut, or Saint Knut's Day, January 13, a week after the Epiphany."

"Wow!" the Twins exclaimed. "You got a long vacation."

"Now, look and see what I have made for the two of you. Your own Lucia and star-boy gowns!" smiled Grandma Freda. "Try them on and we will see how they fit. Perfect!" Grandma opened a large box and carefully laid out a wreath made of boxwood. "It's hard to find lingonberry leaves here in America, so boxwood greenery will have to do. The frame for the wreath is from when I was a little girl. I put these small electric candles on it. They run on batteries. These modern inventions are much safer than real candles. Now off to bed with both of you. We have to get up at 5:30 tomorrow morning to get ready to surprise your parents."

The next morning, the wonderful smell of Grandma Freda's kaffee and the glow of candles on the table filled the kitchen. The Twins entered the kitchen excitedly with their flowing white gowns. Grandma put the cone star hat on John's head and handed him a pole with a star on the tip and ribbons streaming down. Next, she carefully placed the Lucia crown on Jodie's head and switched on the candles. A beautiful glow filled the darkened kitchen. Grandma handed the tray filled with Lucia kaffee, Luciakatter, and pepparkakor to Jodie.

John, holding his star wand, led the procession down the hallway. Next came Jodie, all aglow in her Saint Lucia crown. Grandma followed carrying a candle. Quietly, they sang the "Saint Lucia" song as they opened the door to their parents' bedroom. And the ancient tradition of Saint Lucia's Day continued.

MULTIPLE INTELLIGENCE ACTIVITIES FOR . . .

Saint Lucia Day: A Swedish Tradition

 1 ### Let Your Light Shine.
(Visual-Spatial; Musical-Rhythmic)

Play the music softly in the background as you prepare the props needed for Lucia and star boys. To make the star wands, use a star pattern to mark and cut stars from brightly colored poster board. Collect rulers, straws, or long dowel rods and glue a star on the top of each one. Glitter, tinsel, and long strands of silver Mylar ribbon will add a festive and personal touch to the wands. Making the Lucia crowns can vary in degree of difficulty, depending on the ability of the students. The crowns may be made of live boxwood greens attached to a circular wire frame. A pattern for a Christmas wreath may be reproduced on colored construction paper cut out and glued to fit each child's head. Cutting artificial green garland in strips to be wired together to make a wreath is most effective. Paper candles can be taped to the wreaths. More advanced groups may want to wire five battery-operated candles into the wreath. The class will become familiar with the melody of the song by singing it during these projects.

Child models Saint Lucia Day crown.

Santa Lucia

Now 'neath the sil-ver moon, O - cean is glow - ing, O'er the calm

bil - low Soft winds are blow - ing. Here balm - y breez-es blow Pure joys in -

- vite us And as we gent-ly row All things de - light us. Hark how the

sail-or's cry Joy - ous - ly ech-oes nigh. San - ta Lu - ci - a

San - ta Lu - ci - a Home of fair Po - e - sy Realm of pure

Har-mo-ny San - ta Lu - ci - a San - ta Lu - ci - a

"Santa Lucia" (traditional Italian boat song. Melody line arranged by Jean Liepold).

2 **Prepare Some Pepparkakors.**
(Logical-Mathematical; Bodily-Kinesthetic)

This is a creative exercise in measurement, observation, order, and directions! Make a paper star for a pattern. Copy the outline onto heavier tag board

and cut out. Be sure to have access to an oven. Gather cookie sheets, cooking spray, spatulas, wax paper, plastic knives, bowls, mixing spoons, measuring cups and spoons, and cooling racks. Follow the directions for this traditional recipe for gingersnaps. Roll out the dough on individual pieces of wax paper so each child may trace the outline of a star from the tag board pattern with a plastic knife.

 Pepparkakors

1 3/4 cups butter
2 tbsp. baking soda
2 tbsp. ginger
1 cup evaporated milk
6 cups flour (approximate)
Tiny colored beads made of sugar to decorate the stars.

2 tbsp. cloves
3 1/2 cups white sugar
1 cup Karo syrup (dark)
2 tbsp. cinnamon

Melt butter and cool in a large mixing bowl. Add syrup, evaporated milk, and sugar. Mix spices and soda with the flour in another bowl, and mix into the liquid mixture. Cover with a cloth and let dough set overnight in the refrigerator.

Heat oven to 350 degrees. Take dough out and let it warm up a little. Sprinkle the wax paper with flour and roll out the dough very thin. With adult supervision, let students trace their star shapes and cut them out with plastic knives. Have them decorate their stars with the small colored sugar beads with a design of their choice. Bake on greased cookie sheets 5 to 7 minutes. Watch cookies carefully, as they may burn.

 ③ Let's Celebrate.
(Interpersonal; Musical-Rhythmic)

This activity is an excellent culmination for this story. Gathering all of the materials from the above activities, have the class decide how they would like to participate in this celebration. Their Lucia Day celebration may be just in the classroom, they may invite other classes to join in, or they may share it as an activity for the entire school. Make and send invitations. Reprint the words to the music "Santa Lucia" for the class. Have them decide how they would like to sing the song. Practice singing it as a group or divide it into parts with each group taking a different verse.

The class can decide what tasks are needed for the celebration, such as a group of star boys, with props, to lead the procession and decide the route it will take; a group of Lucias, with wreaths; trays of cookies to share; printed words to the song for guests to join in, etc. Set the date and time for the Lucia procession to take place. You may want to video or take photos to add to the class yearbook for the end of the year. A simpler form of the procession is done, with one Lucia and a few star boys, while the rest of the celebrants walk single file holding hands and singing the song as they weave in and out the rooms. In Sweden, the children end by circling a Christmas tree. Adapt freely to suit the needs of the class.

TIPS FOR THE TELLER

The Kwanzaa Story
By Susan Trostle Brand

STORYTELLING METHOD

Chant

For seven days in late December and early January, many households celebrate the joy of African harvest and culture. These households also celebrate the joy of being a family. Kwanzaa means "First Fruits of the Harvest." Now, most folks call Kwanzaa a festival of lights and, on each of seven days, a candle is lit: three red on the left, a black in the center, and three green on the right. The seven-candle candleholder is called a Kinara.

In *The Kwanzaa Story* the African language of Swahili is used to present the seven cherished principles of the Kwanzaa celebration. Kwanzaa is presented here, as in life, as an annual festival of shared harvest, shared memories, and shared beliefs.

Told in the Chant Storytelling method described in Chapter 3, this story uses an adult to tell the story and a child to help with the candle props. The child responsible for the candle props may wish to place paper flames on paper candles for each corresponding day in the story on a velcroed kinara.

Candles are "lit" beginning with the middle (black) candle and then alternating between red and green candles.

Before beginning this story, the Teller may want to establish a signal such as a nod of the head or a hand gesture—perhaps a thumbs up or pointing to a wristwatch—to indicate when everyone can join in the refrain, "Now it's Kwanzaa!" An asterisk indicates this text. This refrain is printed on the chalkboard or a flip chart in advance so that the class or audience can easily see their part. Also prepare the audience for the story with a display of various Kwanzaa artifacts, such as an African shirt, a flag, a map of Africa, a calendar, and African beads.

The Kwanzaa Story

Kwanzaa is a Swahili word that means "First Fruits of the Harvest." Some folks call Kwanzaa a "festival of lights." Kwanzaa falls in late December and lasts for seven days in which family and friends celebrate the joy and richness of African-American culture! The first day of Kwanzaa, on December 26th, is called Umoja *(child "lights" middle black candle)*. Daddy calls, ✳"Now it's Kwanzaa!" Daddy helps me dress up in an African shirt. Daddy dresses like an African king. Mama dresses like an African queen.

The second day of Kwanzaa, on December 27th, is called Kujichagulia *(child "lights" red candle directly left of middle)*. Nana calls, ✳"Now it's Kwanzaa," and visits us with good things to eat. She brings stewed chicken and dumplings, candied sweets, red, black and green Kuumba salad, and "Karamu" cookies.

The third day of Kwanzaa, on December 28th, is called Ujima *(child "lights" green candle, just right of middle, black candle)*. Mama says, ✳"Now it's Kwanzaa!" Daddy flies our red, black, and green flag. Mama hangs our map of the motherland, Africa.

The fourth day of Kwanzaa falls on December 29th. It is called Ujamaa *(child "lights" middle red candle)*. I call, ✳"Now it's Kwanzaa!" And I light the colorful Kwanzaa candle.

Then Mama says, ✳"Now it's Kwanzaa!" We tell family stories each night at this special holiday time. Uncle Moses calls me to sit on his lap. He tells me stories and reads me books about Africa.

The fifth day of Kwanzaa is December 30th *(child "lights" fifth candle, which is the next-to-end green candle)*. It is called Nia. Mama says, ✳"Now it's Kwanzaa!" Nana and I spend time together stringing African beads. They are blue, red, black, purple, and green. We make colorful bracelets and necklaces.

On December 31st we celebrate the sixth day of Kwanzaa, Kuumba *(child "lights" end red candle)*. My uncles and aunts call, ✳"Now it's Kwanzaa!" They come to visit us from all over the country. Many cousins also come wearing smiles and holding gifts. We have a great feast tonight called "karamu."

The first day of the new year is the last day of Kwanzaa. It is on January 1st *(child lights final green candle on right)*. Its name is Imani. My cousins say, ✳"Now it's Kwanzaa!" We share gifts, called zawadi, and hugs. We sing and play games. Grandfather says the "Tamshi La Tutaonana," the farewell speech given at the end of the Kwanzaa celebration. The speech helps us all remember the values of Kwanzaa, which are *(point to each candle, in the order in which it was lit)*:

1. **Umoja** (Unity): Helping each other and maintaining unity

2. **Kujichagulia** (Self-Determination): Deciding things for ourselves

3. **Ujima** (Collective Work and Responsibility): Working together responsibly and cooperating to solve our problems

4. **Ujamaaa** (Cooperative Economics): Building and supporting businesses

5. **Nia** (Purpose): Developing our community and maintaining a reason for living

6. **Kuumba** (Creativity): Leaving our community more beautiful

7. **Imani** (Faith): Believing in ourselves, our ancestors, and our future

We think of all the fun we have had and hope that soon it will be next year when, again, we will all say, ✽**"Now it's Kwanzaa!"**

MULTIPLE INTELLIGENCE ACTIVITIES FOR . . .

The Kwanzaa Story

 ### Habari Gani.
(Verbal-Linguistic; Musical-Rhythmic; Interpersonal)

In Swahili, Habari gani means "What's new?" or "What's the news?" On each day of Kwanzaa an adult or child asks, "Habari gani?" Another child then replies with a principle for that day. He or she then defines the principle and points to the candle which represents that principle. For example, on the sixth day of Kwanzaa an adult asks, "'Habari gani?" The child replies, "Kuumba!" Then the child defines Kuumba as creativity or beautification of the community. The child then indicates the red candle on the far left of the kinara (candleholder). He or she asks, "Habari gani?" to another child, and the game continues.

To accompany the game, teach the children the words to this traditional song, which may be sung as each principle is identified:

This Little Light of Mine

This little light of mine,

I'm going to let it shine.

This little light of mine,

I'm going to let it shine,

Let it shine, Let it shine.

Shine on First Day, Umoja,

I'm going to let it shine.

Shine on First Day, Umoja,

I'm going to let it shine,

Let it shine, let it shine, let it shine!

Shine on second day, Kujichagulia,

I'm going to let it shine.

Shine on second day, Kujichagulia,

I'm going to let it shine

Let it shine, let it shine, let it shine!

Continue singing, substituting the given Swahili word for each of the seven days in the verse of the song.

 ### Flags of Many Lands.
(Visual-Spatial; Naturalistic)

Display a large paper or cloth flag of Africa. Ask youngsters to guess the significance of each color—red, black, and green. Then explain that red symbolizes the blood of the African people and their struggles. The black color is for the face and skin of the African people. The green color symbolizes the hopes of the African people for a bright future.

Next, invite children to work in pairs or teams to identify one country on a large map, which is displayed in the classroom. The children locate and create the flag of their chosen country, research the significance of its colors and share facts with classmates about their chosen country on a Retrieval Chart. Display the international flags proudly and, perhaps, hold an International Holiday Foods Celebration (invite parents and other family members!) to culminate your study of flags, cultures, customs, and climates.

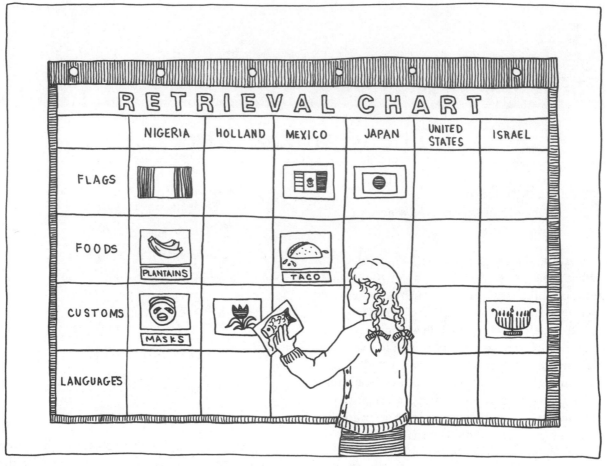

Collaborative groups research and share fun facts about other lands.

3 Strings of Love.
(Visual-Spatial; Logical-Mathematical)

Provide string or unwaxed dental floss and many green, black, red, gold, and purple (and other assorted color) beads. The children create beauti-ful "Strings of Love" necklaces as gifts for loved ones. Encourage children to string beads in patterns, such as green, blue, black or red, gold, purple, etc. Assist children in identifying and using patterns that suit their developmental levels.

TIPS FOR THE TELLER

A Baker's Dozen

Retold by Jeanne M. Donato

STORYTELLING METHOD

Traditional

This story is an adaptation of a Colonial Dutch-American folktale. A Baker calls on St. Nicholas for inspiration and profits from the idea to sell cookies in the shape of the old saint. When he decides to close his shop early, an Old Woman demands that he stay open to sell her a dozen cookies. They have a dispute over how many cookies make up a dozen. She leaves the shop vowing that bad luck will teach him how to be generous. After a year of bad luck, the Baker meets the Old Woman again. He has learned his lesson on generosity and sells her, a "Baker's dozen," twelve cookies plus one more for good luck.

This telling is done with vocal changes, facial gestures, and body movement to depict the different characters. Refer to Chapter 3, which discusses the Traditional method of storytelling. An awareness of where objects such as the door, display window, and counter are placed in the story will help both the Teller and children to visualize the setting.

The following information will help the students with the vocabulary used in this story. "Dutch" is a nickname for the people who live in Holland, or the Netherlands. In Colonial times, the Dutch traded and settled in America. They called their colony New Netherland after their old home in Holland. The town of Beverwyck, where this story takes place, is present day Albany, the capital of New York state. Some Dutch words that we still use today are: boss, snoop, and cookie. This is a story about counting and how many cookies are in a baker's dozen.

Children listen intently to a story.

A Baker's Dozen

In Old Beverwyck the Dutch settlers celebrated their gift-giving day on December 6, St. Nicholas' Day. Baker Baas was busy preparing for the holiday. He thought and thought. If he could create a new recipe or pastry, more people would come to his shop.

"By St. Nicholas, I need help!" he cried as his rolled out his cookie dough. "Nothing seems to be working! Even my dough is crooked!" And as Baker Baas started to pull the dough up and start over again, he stopped. "What is this? The shape of that cookie reminds me of someone. If I add some raisins for eyes, icing for a beard, and a coat, by Saint Nicholas, I'll have a cookie that looks like the old Saint himself! What a great idea!"

Baker Baas quickly took some tin and fashioned it into the cookie's shape. "Now I will be able to make a lot of them at once. Oh, the money I will make!"

Word about Baas's fanciful Saint Nicholas cookies spread up and down the Hudson River valley. Throughout the month of December, Baker Baas was kept busy making his famous cookies. He worked New Years Eve day till his moneybox was full and his shelves near empty. Satisfied, he decided to close his shop early and go home to take his ease. It was not worth staying open to sell some leftover cookies.

He swept the floor and prepared to close. As he prepared to draw the blinds and lock the door, the bells on the door jingled as it blew open. There, in the midst of the cold swirling snowflakes, stood an old, bent woman dressed all in black.

Out of breath, she exclaimed, "I am so glad to make it here on time. I need one dozen of your famous St. Nicholas cookies!"

"I am sorry, madam, but I am closed and all sold out. Come back some other day. Now kindly leave. I am in a hurry to get home before it gets too dark," replied Baker Baas as he moved to close the door.

The Old Woman begged, "Look, there on the shelf! You have a dozen left. I'll take those. I have traveled such a long way to purchase your cookies. Please help me."

"Oh all right," grumbled Baker Baas, "But be quick about it. I do not have all day to waste! Let me see your money." The Baker took the old woman's money, counted out twelve cookies and placed them in the Old Woman's small cloth sack. "There," he said. "Now be off with you!"

The Old Woman opened her sack and slowly counted the cookies. "I do not have a baker's dozen here! I only have twelve cookies. You owe me one more!"

"You paid for a dozen cookies and I gave you a dozen. Now leave!" cried the Baker. "I do not have time to waste on you or this foolishness!"

"I asked for and expected a baker's dozen in keeping with the spirit of the holidays," replied the Old Woman, glaring back at the Baker. "A baker's dozen is twelve plus one more for good luck and good fortune."

"Spirit of the holidays? A baker's dozen? What nonsense! Do you think I have nothing to do but give my cookies away to the likes of you? I am an honest man. One dozen means twelve cookies and not one more. I gave you one dozen cookies. You will not get one extra cookie from me!" cried the exasperated Baker.

"You have one extra cookie left over. What would it hurt to share some generosity for the sake of Saint Nicholas himself, who blesses us all? Or do you need to learn a lesson?" replied the Old Woman.

"What lesson? Are you trying to threaten me? I have what I have through my own hard work and no help from the likes of you. Now be off before I lose my temper," yelled Baker Baas.

The Old Woman shook her finger at the Baker and said, "We will see what it takes for you to learn how to count with generosity." And she left the shop.

Baker Baas ran to the door and looked up and down the snow-covered street. He saw no footsteps or sign of the Old Woman. Baker Bass locked the door. He looked at the cookie left on the shelf and muttered, "I would rather throw that cookie out than give it to that old witch. Spirit of the holidays indeed. She could learn a lesson on hard work from me!"

Baker Baas found his wife out of sorts when he told her about the Old Woman. And she fretted, "Maybe she was right, dear. The idea of a baker's dozen would be a nice way to offer generosity for all that we have."

"What would you know about business!" Baas huffed as he retired to his bed.

That year a series of strange misfortunes plagued Baker Baas. No matter what he did, Baas's cakes would not rise, bread fell flat, pies burned, and his icing ran thin. But when his brick oven collapsed, he began to worry about this year of unusual bad luck.

New Year's Eve found Baker Baas working late in his shop, hoping to make a few more sales and fretting over the few coins in his moneybox. He muttered, "By Saint Nicholas, I wish I knew how to turn my luck around."

The bells jingled softly as the door opened. There, in the cold, stood the same Old Woman demanding a dozen Saint Nicholas cookies. "My, I see that things have changed around here, Baker Baas. Well, never mind. I have come to buy a dozen of your Saint Nicholas cookies, if you please."

The Baker hurriedly counted out twelve cookies and placed them in the Old Woman's sack. Then he paused and added one more, saying, "Most people think thirteen is an unlucky number. That is why I have always been reluctant to add an extra one to my dozens. But a Baker's Dozen makes for good will just in case one of the cookies breaks. I know you will understand, madam. Happy New Year."

The Old Woman accepted the bag with a stern smile and said, "I see you have learned your lesson well. Mark my words. A baker's dozen will come to be known as a symbol for the spirit of generosity. I have always believed thirteen to be a lucky number. And I predict that thirteen colonies will band together someday to make a brave new nation. The new nation will remind people of how lucky the number thirteen can be. Happy New Year to you, Baker Baas!" The bells on the door jingled as it closed, and the Old Woman was seen no more.

MULTIPLE INTELLIGENCE ACTIVITIES FOR . . .

A Baker's Dozen

 Then and Now.
(Logical-Mathematical; Naturalistic)

This activity invites students to explore how tradespeople, over the centuries, developed their methods for counting, grouping, and measuring objects that they used. What did the shapes, weights, and lengths used by these people have to do with how these methods evolved? Divide the class into groups to research one trade group each. Examples are road construction workers, seamstresses, carpenters, plumbers, confectioners, bakers, etc. When they have discovered some of these measuring items used by various professions, ask them to decide how to share what they've learned with the class. Some possibilities include a skit, display, report, rhyme, or physical challenge to do the actual measuring. On the bulletin board display a list of measurement terms learned. Explore the library for the latest books on measurement and counting.

 Create a Skit.
(Interpersonal; Bodily-Kinesthetic)

Creative drama offers students a chance to stretch their imaginations with improvisation. Warm-up exercises may include movements found in the story; for example, moving like someone in a hurry, trudging through snow, mud, or over slippery ice or acting out sweeping, cooking, baking, rolling dough, or counting and bagging bakery items. Have the students divide the story into scenes: baker meets old woman; baker and wife at home; baker and wife in the shop while unfortu-nate things happen to them during the year; baker meets old woman again. Choose partners and have the class act out the three scenes, also swapping roles. Ask the students to imagine "what if...." What if the baker was generous the first time? What if the old woman was a generous and understanding spirit that granted wishes? What if the wife was in the shop instead of the baker? The list is endless. Invite the students to share their interpretation with another group. Invite them to share their interpretations of the different scenes with their whole class or other classes.

 Word Wonders.
(Verbal-Linguistic; Visual-Spatial)

Did you ever wonder where some of the words in our language come from? Display a wall map of the world on the bulletin board. Print the names or draw the shape of countries on cards and distribute them to students or teams. The goal is to have the class construct a challenge game (written or verbal) that all can play. Students connect words with their country of origin. Then, on the cards indicating the country name or shape, students write or draw a picture of the world. The cards are collected and posted on the wall map. When all the information has been collected and reviewed, the cards are removed and used as a memory challenge game. One player holds up the picture or word on the card and the other player must guess what country that word comes from. The goal is for both members to encourage each other to master all of the cards and answers.

TIPS FOR THE TELLER

A Stranger's Gift
Retold by Peninnah Schram and Steven M. Rosman
Adapted by Susan Trostle Brand

STORYTELLING METHOD

Puppetry

This enchanting Chanukah story is an old retold tale from Persia. Because of its simplicity and few characters, it is easily retold using sock or stick puppets and two scenery backgrounds. The first scene is that of Azaria's street, where children collect little Chanukah gifts from the neighbors; the second scene is that of the inside of Azaria's home.

The protagonists are Azaria, a young and sincere boy, and the stranger, an old and bedraggled man. Other characters include Azaria's mother and father and Azaria's four neighbors from whom he collects treats which he, in turn, gives to the needy stranger. Two puppeteers are needed to manipulate the puppets for these characters. A third child is needed to help change the scenery. A final child (or child's voice) is needed to narrate the non-dialogue parts of the story. Suggested props include small bags of nuts, and seeds; one large bag of seeds, candles, nuts, and gold candy coins; and, for the adult puppet, Azaria, a small book.

The story is introduced by Azaria, who asks the children if they have ever helped someone in need. After listening to a few answers, Azaria explains that he has helped a stranger in need and that the results have been surprising. Azaria asks the children to watch the show to learn more about this stranger and his adventures.

"A Stranger's Gift" is from *Eight Tales for Eight Nights: Stories for Chanukah*. Reprinted by permission of the publisher, Jason Aronson, Inc., Northvale, NJ © 1990.

A Stranger's Gift

(display neighborhood scene with removable sun)

Azaria: *(excited)* The sun is going down in the sky now. Once the sun is gone, another night of Chanukah will arrive. On Chanukah, we village children go from house to house, collecting little gifts from all our Jewish neighbors. Usually the neighbors give us bundles of roasted nuts and seeds. We are so happy and excited about our special treats! Now the sun is gone. It is time!

Narrator: Azaria stepped outside, onto the street. He heard his friends laughing. They were comparing gifts in their bags. Azaria's friends had left before he did. They had already begun knocking on doors farther up the street.

(enter two friends)

Female Friend: "Oh, Look! I have five bags of nuts in my bag."

Male Friend: "And look at mine! I have three bags of seeds and two bags of nuts" *(exit friends).*

Narrator: Azaria was eager to begin knocking on doors to collect his treats, too. But after three steps he saw something that made him suddenly stop. There in the road sat a single, lonely figure. It was an old, old man *(enter man puppet)*. He was draped in a tattered robe. Under his bushy white beard the stranger's skin was red and chapped. His eyes were sad and full of tears.

Azaria: *(thinking aloud to self)* I think I know that man. I remember him from the synagogue on Shabbat. Even though he was dressed in rags, the rabbi treated him like an honored guest and gave him the special seat near the holy Ark. That man really needs a friend now. He is sad and cold and shivering.

(Azaria walks to man and gives him his hand.) Hello, sir. I am Azaria. I would like to be friends with you. Please wait here. I will be right back *(remove stranger).*

Narrator: With great speed, Azaria ran to the next house on the street. There, he collected nuts and seeds that were wrapped and waiting for him for his Chanukah treat. He ran to the next house and the next. At each house, he collected more and more nuts and seeds, all gaily wrapped for Azaria for his Chanukah treat.

Azaria: Thank you!" *(display first house)* Thank you! *(display second house)* Thank you! *(display third house).*

Narrator: When Azaria was finished visiting each of the neighbor's houses, he ran back to the old, sad stranger *(return stranger).*

Azaria: *(to stranger)* I have come back my friend, just as I promised. And look what I have brought for you *(gives stranger large bag of treats)*. I have only one more house to visit. Please wait here; I will be right back *(remove stranger).*

Narrator: *(display fourth house)* Azaria rushed to the final house to collect his treats. He wanted to give one last gift to the sad stranger. He thanked the kind people in the last house and hurried back to the stranger.

Azaria: My friend! My friends! Look! I have brought you another treat from the final house. Here are more nuts and seeds for you. My friend! *(Pause.)* "My friend?" *(Pause.)* "My friend?" *(Pause.)*

Narrator: Azaria was puzzled. His friend was gone. Azaria wandered along the windy streets, calling and looking for his lost friend. Finally, he grew very tired and walked back home, carrying only his final treat.

(change scenery to inside Azaria's house)

Azaria: Mother, Father, I am home *(enter Mother and Father).*

Father: Azaria! Come here. We have something to tell you. While you were gone, someone came by and left this huge bag for you *(place large bag beside Father and Azaria).*

Azaria: *(surprised and excited)* Who left this bag?

Mother: We do not know. A great gust of wind blew through the house. It rattled the windows and glasses. It caused the candles to flicker. Then there came a knock at the door. We collected our wits and made our way to the door. There was no one to be seen. There was no one there at all. But we found this bag with your name, Azaria, written on it. Here, Azaria. Open the bag. See what is inside!

Azaria: *(tears open bag with enthusiasm as candles, nuts and seeds, separately wrapped, spill out)* I have never seen anything like it! Nuts and seeds and candles! There are enough here for one year! But there is something else! Oh, look! Mother! Father! It is gold! Three gold coins. One for each of us! *(Arazia shows coins; exit Mother, Father, and Azaria)*.

Narrator: Azaria knew that he had not been dreaming. But who could have brought such a gift? For many years he wondered about that gift. He wondered, too, about the stranger he had helped out on the street that cold Chanukah night. Azaria grew older and older. Before long, he was a man himself *(enter adult Azaria)*.

Azaria: *(holding small book)* Reading helps me understand. I now know and understand what happened on the Chanukah night, long ago, when I was just a boy. Here, in my book, it explains, "One who has helped a stranger may have helped an angel. That was no ordinary stranger. That old, sad man was an angel—my angel."

MULTIPLE INTELLIGENCE ACTIVITIES FOR . . .

A Stranger's Gift

 1 Spinning Dreidels.
(Visual-Spatial; Logical-Mathematical)

Although ancient dreidels were made from clay, children can easily make dreidels from poster board and pencils. First, divide a 4-inch by 4-inch square of poster board into triangles by using a pencil to draw a neat *X* in the middle of the square. In each of the four triangles, children write a Hebrew letter: Nun, Gimel, Hay, and Shin. Insert a pencil into a small hole in the center of the poster board so that about an inch of the pencil, just above the point, remains above the hole. Attach a flag, tag, or clip to the pencil as a pointer. This will point to a Hebrew symbol when the dreidel stops spinning. Youngsters spin the dreidel on the pencil point, keeping score as they play.

After a predetermined time, the player with the most gelt (pennies, chocolate coins, buttons, etc.) wins the game (see illustration).

 2 Lucious Latkes.
(Naturalistic; Logical-Mathematical)

Potato pancakes are fried in oil to remind us of the miracle of the oil that burned for eight days in the temple in Jerusalem many years ago. List the following recipe on a large sheet of chart paper. Before beginning to cook, discuss the origins of each food: potatoes, onions, eggs, flour, salt, and oil. Next, together, the children and an adult soak, measure, stir, pour, and fry ingredients to make tasty Hebrew latkes.

 Latkes

(makes approximately 18 potato cakes)
6 large potatoes, 2 small onions, 2 eggs, 4 tbsps. flour, 1 tsp. salt, vegetable oil.

339

The Dreidel Game

A dreidel is a four-sided top showing four Hebrew letters—nun, gimel, hay, or shin. The letters stand for New Gadol Hayah Sham, which means "A Great Miracle Happened There." Each letter also stands for a Yiddish word that indicates what each player does during his turn in the game.

1. To begin, give each player five chips. These can be gelt, peanuts, or pennies. In the middle of the playing area, place several chips.
2. Each player takes a turn spinning the dreidel.
3. When the dreidel stops, the player does what the letter on top of the dreidel indicates.

   Nun—*nisht* (nothing). Take nothing.
   Gimel—*gantz* (everything). Take everything.
   Hay—*halb* (half). Take half.
   Shin—*shtel* (put in). Put one in the pile of chips in the middle.

4. If the pile is empty, or has only one chip, each player puts a chip into the pile before the next spin.
5. The game ends when one player wins everything and the others have nothing.

Learning the significance of Hebrew symbols.

1. Soak the potatoes in a bowl of water for about half an hour. Then drain and peel the potatoes.
2. Grate the potatoes and onions. Put them into a large bowl, pouring off any remaining liquid.
3. Add the eggs, flour, and salt. Let the mixture sit for a few minutes until it thickens.
4. In a large frying pan heat several tablespoons of oil. Add seven or eight separate tablespoons of latke mixture and flatten each with a spatula.
5. Brown latkes in oil. Then turn them over to brown the other side.

6. When both sides are golden brown, remove from the frying pan. Drain them on paper towels. Use remaining mixture to make additional latkes.
7. Serve latkes with applesauce or sour cream.

3 Angels of Kindness.
(Visual-Spatial; Intrapersonal)

Into cone-shaped paper drinking cups, insert and attach wooden ice cream spoons. Create angels inspired by the one found in the story *A Stranger's Gift*. Provide buttons, yarn, fabrics, glitter, ribbons, and streamers. If desired, add wings made of nylon netting. Encourage children to design unusual angels, such as the one in the story, who are different in appearance from those typically depicted.

Invite each child to name his or her angel as it is completed. Display all angels on a table. When a child performs an act of kindness or goodwill toward another child, without being requested or reminded to do so, an adult hangs his or her angel from the ceiling. Good deeds and/or angel names might be printed upon each of the angels before they are hung. Constructing a class book describing each act of kindness performed by the various angels might culminate this touching activity.

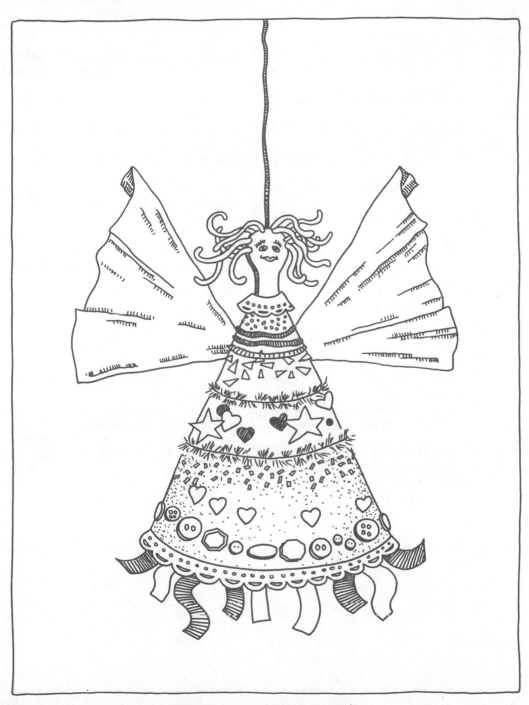

Ice cream spoon/drinking cup angels.

DECEMBER CHAPTER RESOURCES

Albyn, C. L. (1993). *The multicultural cookbook for students.* Phoenix, AZ: Oryx.

Barber, A. (1990). *The mousehole cat.* New York: Aladdin.

Beal, P. C., & Nipp, S. H. (1984). *Wee sing for Christmas.* San Francisco, CA: Chronicle.

Beal, P. C., & Nipp, S. H. (1994). *Wee sing around the world.* Los Angeles: Price Stern & Sloan.

Borchers, E. (1965). *There comes a time.* Garden City, NY: Doubleday.

Brett, J. (1989). *The mitten.* New York: Putnam.

Cheng, H. T. (1976). *The Chinese New Year.* New York: Holt.

Chocolate, D. M. (1992). *My first Kwanzaa book.* New York: Scholastic.

Clements, A. (1990). *Santa's secret helper.* New York: Scholastic.

Croll, C. (1996). *The little snowgirl: An old Russian tale.* New York: Paper Star.

De Paola, T. (1978). *The clown of God.* New York: Harcourt Brace.

De Paola, T. (1995*). Country angel Christmas.* New York: Scholastic.

Domanska, J. (1975). *Din dan don: It's Christmas.* New York: Greenwillow.

Durell, A., & Sachs, M. (1990). *The big book of peace.* New York: Dutton.

Forest, H. (1998). *The baker's dozen: A colonial American tale.* Orlando, FL: Harcourt Brace.

Goode, D. (1990). *Diane Goode's American Christmas.* New York: Dutton.

Greenberg, M. H., Wugh, C., & Wugh, C. G. (1991). *A Newberry Christmas.* New York: Delacorte.

Handforth, T. (1938). *Mei Li.* New York: Doubleday.

Hays, E. (1992). *The Christmas eve storyteller.* Leavenworth, KS: Forest of Peace Books.

Hill, E. (1983). *Spot's first Christmas.* New York: Putnam.

Hoban, L. (1982). *Arthur's Christmas cookies.* New York: HarperCollins.

Hoffman, E. T. A. (1991). *The nutcracker.* New York: Crown.

Hoffman Corwin, J. (1995). *Harvest festivals around the world.* Parsippany, NJ: Silver Burdett Press.

Jackson, K. (1989). *Two-minute Christmas stories.* New York: Golden Books.

Leighton, M. R. (1994). *An Ellis Island Christmas.* New York: Puffin.

Lewis, S. (1987). *One-minute Christmas stories.* New York: Doubleday.

Malcolmson, A. (1941). *Yankee Doodle's cousins.* New York: Houghton Mifflin.

McGovern, A. (1960). *Treasury of Christmas stories.* New York: Scholastic.

McKissack, P. C., & McKissack, F. L. (1994). *Christmas in the big house, Christmas in the quarters.* New York: Scholastic.

Morris, A. (1998). *Shoes, shoes, shoes.* New York: Mulberry Books.

Nayer, J. (1998). *The eight nights of Hanukkah.* New York: Troll.

Newcombe, J. (1991). *A new Christmas treasury.* New York: Viking.

Noble, T. H. (1984). *Apple tree Christmas.* New York: Dial.

Odge, M. (1957). *Hans Brinker and the silver skates.* New York: Simon & Schuster.

Olley, J. (1978). *Reader's Digest: American folklore and legend.* Pleasantville, NY: Reader's Digest.

Robbins, R. (1960). *Babbouska and the three kings.* New York: Parnassus.

Sabuda, R. (1996). *The twelve days of Christmas: A pop-up celebration.* New York: Simon & Schuster.

Schram, P., & Rosman, S. M. (1990). "A stranger's gift." In *Eight tales for eight nights: Stories for Chanukah.* Northvale, NJ: Jason Aronson.

Simon, C. (1990). *The boy of the bells.* New York: Doubleday.

Steele, P. (1966). *The world of festivals.* Skokie, IL: Rand McNally.

Wernecke, H. (1992). *Christmas customs around the world.* Philadelphia: Westminster.

Wojciechowski, S. (1995). *The Christmas miracle of Jonathan Toomey.* Cambridge, MA: Candlewick.

Glossary

accommodate— The process of changing existing knowledge in order to incorporate new knowledge.

adapted pantomime storytelling— A storytelling method in which gestures, facial expression, and body movement accompany words while the Teller weaves a story.

aesthetic enjoyment— The appreciation of a combination of fantasy and reality which has been presented in a creative and engaging manner, using some art form that stimulates the senses.

alphabet letter recognition— The ability to name or otherwise identify written alphabet letter forms.

assimilate— To recognize and store new information in the brain using existing mental constructs.

attention span— The ability to stay focused on the task at hand for concentrated periods.

auditory discrimination— The ability to discern differences among and between sounds and messages.

auditory memory— The ability to recall sounds or messages previously heard.

authentic assessment— Evaluation which is collected in a natural, on-site, and ongoing manner in order to develop an accurate learning profile of a student and which may include, for example, writing samples, art samples, tapes of oral reading, checklists, rubrics, self-evaluation, and videotapes of learners' engagement in work.

authentic literature— Books using characters, pictures, vocabulary, and stories that closely resemble the reader's frame of reference and/or the real world.

authentic settings— Environments that closely approximate the learner's real world.

balloon storytelling— The teller manipulates a balloon to accentuate one aspect or character of the story, either for sound effects or to present a tangible image to the audience.

Bodily-Kinesthetic Intelligence— The ability to handle physical objects, move and interpret body movements, manipulate objects, and establish a connection between the mind and body.

catharsis— Emotional release and relaxation regarding life events, fears, and or challenges through one's identification with some aspect of the reading.

Chant Storytelling— Before the telling, the Teller establishes a gesture, which indicates that the audience joins in on a repetitive phrase, song, or sentence(s). The audience participates in the Teller's narrative by chanting the words at these designated times.

Character Imagery Storytelling— Stories told in first person, past tense, in which the Teller dresses as the protagonist during the introduction and acts as the protagonist through voice and body imaging throughout the telling.

chunking— The brain's ability to perceive a pattern and remember a coherent group of items as a single chunk of information or item.

cognitive learning— Consciously finding simple, rational relationships between spoken language and letters to make logical connections and reason.

cognitive structures— That elements that collectively comprise schemata.

comprehension— The ability to understand the meaning of words or passages one hears or reads.

Concept Map— A graphic representation used to determine students' prior knowledge about a topic, including attributes, relationships, history, and personal experiences.

concrete operations stage— The time in a child's life, ranging approximately from ages four through seven, in which a child learns best through real, rather than written or spoken, experiences.

constructivism— A theory involving the child's active involvement in his or her learning.

343

dramatic story reenactments—Using children's retelling of stories and/or parts of stories in order to develop their skills of recall of story line, cause and effect, and sensitivity to characters' predicaments and feelings.

Draw Talk Storytelling—Stories which are told by drawing the main ideas and objects in the story in sync with the narrative.

emergent literacy—An evolving process involving the child's gradual acquisition of literacy competencies, including speaking, listening, writing, and problem-solving, which eventually results in the child's formal reading.

empowerment—One's sense of control over life circumstances and life decisions.

Existential-Spiritual Intelligence—This is the newest multiple intelligence being considered by Howard Gardner. It is the ability that allows one to know the invisible, outside world and ask philosophical, fundamental questions about our existence and purpose in life.

explicit results—Effects of children's engagement in reading and literacy experiences which are both readily observable and significant.

expressive language—Language that is spoken, usually to convey emotions or thoughts.

Felt Board Storytelling—Stories are told using felt pieces and a large, contrasting felt board. Felt pieces are placed and removed in synchrony with the words which tell the story.

genre—A classification of literature selection which may include, for example, folktales, historical fiction, picture books, picture storybooks, fantasy, realistic fiction, poetry, and the like.

gestalt hemisphere—The part of the brain that deals with rhythm, music, intuition, images, color, patterns, emotion, empathy, feelings, and language comprehension. It can see the whole picture and can deal with many tasks at once. It gathers information from images, can process many types of information simultaneously, uses spatial perception, and looks for patterns. It is commonly referred to as the right-brain, or right hemisphere. Some learners have these parts transposed and the Gestalt abilities are found in the left hemisphere of the brain.

grammatical knowledge—A kind of language information that allows the child to construct sentences and predict the way a sentence might go.

graphical representations—Visual information organizers for expository text and fiction. They help the students to use and process knowledge using higher-order thinking skills, analysis, synthesis, and evaluation. Some examples of graphic representations are Venn Diagrams, and Concept Maps.

group/dyad storytelling—Children in small or large groups or in a team of two retell a story using one or more of the storytelling methods explained in Chapter 3 of this text, such as Felt Board, Draw Talk, Puppetry, Character Imagery, Pantomime, and so on. When children are new to storytelling, group/dyad telling is usually most successfully conducted after children witness an adult or adults telling the same story.

Group Role-Play Storytelling—In groups of two or more people, individuals each assign themselves or are assigned to one or more characters from a story. They dramatize the story, slightly adapting the words and/or sequence and acting it out before an audience. The use of a script, scenery, costumes, and props during Group Role-Play Storytelling is optional.

higher-level thinking skills—The learner's ability to comprehend information that extends beyond the literal (factual) level.

horizontal learning experience—The integration of reading into many other life experiences and content areas.

implicit results—Effects of children's engagement in reading and literacy experiences which are not readily observable but are nonetheless significant.

Interpersonal Intelligence—The ability to learn through working and interacting with others.

Intrapersonal Intelligence—The ability to know oneself and one's own abilities. Self-assessment and metacognition are part of this learning process.

journal writing—Recording personal thoughts, reflections, spontaneous ideas, and reactions in a diary or log in words or drawings on an ongoing basis. These thoughts can then be read to note the change and growth of opinions, attitudes, or ideas over time.

language experience approach (LEA)—A whole-to-part process involving the child's dictating a story based upon a real-life event and the adult's recording the story as the child tells it. Later, the adult and child read the sentences together, and then the child reads them independently.

learning logs—A journal documenting skills acquired by the student during reading, a content area lesson, or a real life learning experience, used to promote higher level thinking, such as analysis, synthesis, problem solving, application, decision making, and evaluation. These logs may contain verbal and visual representations of these thinking processes.

left hemisphere—*See* Logic Hemisphere.

limbic system—The second brain in the Triune Brain Model also called the paleomammalian or feeling brain. All information passing into long-term memory is processed through this system.

linguistic awareness—The process by which students develop knowledge about the nature of their language.

literal questions—Those that deal with the facts as they are written and/or spoken.

logic hemisphere—The part of the brain that deals with the parts of speech, reading, writing, and language, and that recognizes words, letters, numbers, technique, literal interpretation of words, and is time-oriented. It sees parts and details and prefers sequential, rational thinking.

Logical-Mathematical Intelligence—The ability to use deductive and inductive reasoning, to understand complex relationships, and solve abstract problems.

metacognition—The action of thinking about thinking what information is to be learned, and how it is acquired and processed.

mind-mapping—a graphic representation in which the subject is in a central image. The main themes of the subject branch out from the central image. Key images or words are printed on associated lines. Lesser topics are attached to the higher level branches. Used in brainstorming new ideas, for clearer thinking.

multiple intelligences—Howard Gardner's Theory of Multiple Intelligences posits that the brain is designed to process several distinct forms of learning styles referred to as: Bodily-Kinesthetic, Intrapersonal, Interpersonal, Logical-Mathematical, Musical-Rhythmic, Naturalistic, Verbal-Linguistic, and Visual-Spatial (the Existential-Spiritual Intelligence is not completely defined at this time.) Each of the intelligences is autonomous, in that distinct brain areas are dedicated to processing its function, and yet closely interrelated. A more dominant intelligence can be used to improve a weaker intelligence. A blending of the intelligences must occur to achieve significant learning.

Musical Storytelling—Children are assigned a section of a song and/or a musical instrument in advance of the telling. During the telling, upon a signal from the teller, children play their instruments and/or sing at the appropriate times.

Musical-Rhythmic Intelligence—The ability to use musical elements in learning.

Naturalistic Intelligence—The ability to see differences and similarities in forms, recognize and classify natural and cultural artifacts, such as clothes, and understand relationships in the environment.

neural pathways—A set of connected neurons in the brain that form a path that speeds the passage of electrical signal back and forth, integrating and generating information.

Pantomime Storytelling—A storytelling method in which gestures, facial expression, and body movements substitute for words while the Teller weaves a story.

personal portfolio—Unlike other assessment portfolios, this one is like a scrapbook of things that interest the student. It may contain the student's personal journal entries summarizing their thoughts. It may include notes or quotes or ideas that inspire them. Students may include writings about experiences and people that touched them throughout the year in their personal and academic life. It helps students to reflect upon who they are and what they have done.

phonemes—Speech sounds represented by letters or groups of letters.

phonemic awareness—The ability to hear the sounds that make up words.

phonics—A method of teaching reading, pronunciation, or spelling based upon the science of speech sounds and their production, transmission, and reception, and their analysis, classification, and transmission.

phonology—The sounds, rhythms, inflections, and meter of words.

pourquoi stories—Named from the French word for "why," this type of story answers the question of how or why something is such as "why the sea is salty."

praxis—The different uses of words.

process writing—A step-by-step collaborative writing procedure that begins with a rough draft and ends with the child's published story.

projection—By means of a literature description or image, the listener or reader identifies with one of the main characters of the story and, as the story unfolds, imagines him or herself in a new role or way of living.

Puppetry Storytelling—Puppets and a stage combine to create a story using props, a background, and often music and sound effects.

reading readiness—A term formerly used in reference to a child's ability to read, usually at a set age, as determined by his or her acquisition of predetermined skills.

receptive language—Language that is received and understood via listening.

representational thought—The spoken or written word, which symbolizes and substitutes for direct experiences, persons, and objects.

retrieval chart—A large wall display containing information found and printed by student research groups. This long-term display is usually cumulative and, as more information is found, the students display these additional findings.

right hemisphere—*See* Gestalt Hemisphere.

rubrics—Sequentially-numbered scoring devices which contain written criteria and descriptions for achieving each number.

schemata—Ever-changing mental constructs that result from experiences and learning.

semantic—Pertaining to the meaning of words in a sentence or passage.

story frame—Similar to an outline, a story frame provides guided captions for the student, who sequentially completes the missing information in writing, thereby creating a whole story summary.

story map—A combination of linear words, pictures, or a combination of both that express the student's perception of the story's basic structure, covering the beginning, middle, and end, including any recurring patterns.

story structure—The organization of material in a literature selection, including, for example, cause and effect, sequence, main idea and details, classification, and comparison.

story web—A visual display that develops students' in-depth understanding of a story's plot, characters, scenes, main ideas, and details. The subject of the story is written or pictorially represented in a circle in the center of a large, blank sheet of paper. Related descriptions, phrases, and ideas that students brainstorm on the story's topic are written or drawn on lines branching off from the center circle.

style—The tone or mood of the author's writing.

syntactic—Relating to the rules of grammar and the ordering of words accordingly within a sentence.

syntax—The way in which linguistic elements, such as words, are arranged to form phrases and sentences.

theme—The broad topic of a literature selection.

Traditional Storytelling—Stories which are told by the Teller without the use of props.

Triune brain model—An early model of the brain's development proposed by Dr. Paul MacLean. He posited that the brain evolves developmentally into three distinct areas, based on evolved functioning and developmental patterns. These areas of the brain are referred to as the reptilian brain, the paleomammalian or limbic brain, and the neo-mammalian or neocortex brain.

Venn diagram—Two large, intersecting circles that are used to compare two concepts, objects, places, persons, groups, or events. The left circle contains facts about one item. The right circle contains contrasting properties about another item. At the intersection of the two circles are listed the similarities of the two items under comparison. The names of the items under comparison are listed atop each of the two circles.

Verbal-Linguistic Intelligence—The sensitivity to the sounds, structure, meanings, and functions of words and language.

visual discrimination—The ability to discern differences among and between images one sees.

visual memory—The ability to remember and recall images previously seen.

Visual-Spatial Intelligence—The ability to perceive, recreate, imagine, or modify a visual concept graphically.

References

Chapter 1

Adams, M. J. (1990). *Beginning to read: Thinking and learning about print.* Cambridge, MA: Boly, Beraneu & Newman.

Adams, M. J., Fooray, B. R., Lungberg, I., & Beeler, T. (1997). *Phonetic awareness: A classroom curriculum.* Baltimore, MD: Paul Brookes.

Baker, A., & Green, E. (1987). *Storytelling: Art and technique* (2nd ed.). New York: R. R. Bowker.

Bredekamp, S. (Ed.). (1997). NAEYC issues revised position statement on developmentally appropriate practice in early childhood programs. In *Young Children, 52,* 34–40.

Cambourne, B. (1988). *The whole story: Natural learning and the acquisition of literacy in the classroom.* New York: Ashton Scholastic.

D'Aulaire, I., & D'Aulaire, E. P. (1992). *Books of Greek myths.* New York: Bantam Doubleday Dell.

Durkill, D. (1993). *Teaching them to read* (6th ed.). Needham Heights, MA: Allyn & Bacon.

Fisher, B. (1998). *Joyful learning.* Portsmouth, NH: Heinemann.

Gardner, H. (1993). *Multiple intelligences: The theory in practice* (p. 71). New York: Basic.

Gardner, H. (1983). *Frames of mind.* New York: Basic.

Glazer, J. (1991). *Literature for young children.* Columbus, OH: Merrill.

Gunning, T. G. (1998). *Best books for beginning readers.* Needham Heights, MA: Allyn & Bacon.

Johnson, J., Christie, J., & Yawkey, T. (1987). *Play and early childhood development.* Glenview, IL: Scott Foresman.

Morrow, L. M. (1997). *Literacy development in the early years.* Needham Heights, MA: Allyn & Bacon.

Piaget, J. (1962). *Play, dreams, and imitation in childhood.* New York: Norton.

Piaget, J. (1952). *The origins of intelligence in children.* New York: Norton.

Routman, R. (1988). *Transitions: From literature to literacy.* Portsmouth, NH: Heinemann.

Smilansky, S. (1968). *The effects of sociodramatic play on disadvantaged preschool children.* New York: Wiley.

Smith, F. (1983). *Essays into literacy.* Portsmouth, NH: Heinemann.

Strickland, D., & Morrow, L. (Eds.). (1989). *Emerging literacy: Young children learn to read and write.* Newark, DE: International Reading Association.

Trostle, S., & Hicks, S. (1998, Fall). The effects of story reading versus storytelling on vocabulary and comprehension in British primary school children. *Reading Improvement, 35*(3), 27–36.

Valencia, S., Hiebert, E., & Afflerbach, P. (1994). *Authentic reading assessment: Practices and possibilities.* Newark, DE: International Reading Association.

Yashima, T. (1955). *Crow boy.* New York: Viking.

Chapter 2

Adams, M. J. (1990). *Beginning to read: Thinking and learning about print.* Cambridge, MA: Boly, Beraneu & Newman.

Bettelheim, B. (1976). *The uses of enchantment.* New York: Knopf.

Caine, R. N., & Caine, G. (1991). *Making connections: Teaching and the human brain.* Alexandria, VA: Association for Supervision and Curriculum Development.

Checkley, K. (1997, September). The first seven and the eighth: A conversation with Howard Gardner. *Educational Leadership, 55*(1), 98–113.

Clay, M. M. (1991). *Becoming literate: The construction of inner control.* Portsmouth, NH: Heinemann.

Fogarty, R. (1997). *Brain-compatible classrooms.* Arlington Heights, IL: SkyLight Training and Publishing.

Gardner, H. (1983). *Frames of mind: The theory of multiple intelligences.* New York: Basic.

Gardner, H. (1993). *Multiple intelligences: The theory in practice.* New York: Basic.

Glasser, W. (1986). *Control theory in the classroom.* New York: Perennial Library.

Hannaford, C. (1995). *Smart moves: Why learning is not all in your head.* Arlington, VA: Great Ocean.

Jensen, Eric. (1998). *Introduction to brain-compatible learning.* San Diego, CA: The Brain Store.

Kline, P. (1988). *The everyday genius: Restoring children's natural joy of learning—and yours too.* Arlington, VA: Great Ocean.

Lazear, D. (1991). *Seven ways of knowing.* Arlington Heights, IL: Training & Publishing SkyLight.

Livo, N. J. (1996). *Troubadour's storybag: Musical folktales of the world.* Golden, CO: Fulcrum.

Morrow, L. M. (1989). *Literacy development in the early years: Helping children read and write.* Englewood Cliffs, NJ: Prentice-Hall.

Nelson, O. (1989). Storytelling: Language experience for meaning making. *Reading Teacher, 42*(6), 386–90.

Roth, K. (1998). *The naturalist intelligence: An introduction to Gardner's eight intelligences.* Arlington Heights, IL: SkyLight Training and Publishing.

Russell, P. (1976). *The brain book.* New York: Dutton.

Snowman, S. R. (1996). *Rising to the challenge: A styles approach to understanding adults with ADD and other learning difficulties.* Plymouth, MA: Jones River.

Sylwester, R. (1995). *A celebrations of neurons: An educator's guide to the human brain.* Alexandria, VA: Association for Supervision and Curriculum Development.

Chapter 3

Martinez, M. (1993). Motivating dramatic story reenactments. *The Reading Teacher, 46,* 682–88.

Chapter 6

MacDonald, M. R. (1982). *The storyteller's sourcebook: A subject, title, and motif index to folklore collections for children.* Detroit, MI: Neal-Schuman.

Index

"A, My Name is Anna" (song), 304
Abe Lincoln and the Bullies (retold by Donato), 79–84
   activities, 82–84
   story, 79–81
   storytelling method, 79
Abe's Buzzin' Song, 83–84
Accommodation, 3
Adapted pantomime, 9, 28–30, 40
   attire for, 28, 29
   creative/thematic approaches, 42
   group/dyad, 30
   preparation for, 28, 30
Aesthetic enjoyment, 11
Alphabet letter recognition, 3
Amazing Amphibians activity, 92–93
American Sign Language, 261
Amphibians, 92–93
Angels of Kindness activity, 340–41
Apple Graphing activity, 198
Appleseed, Johnny, 194–99
Approximation, 7
Around the World Friendship Cookies activity, 76, 78
Assimilation, 3
Attention span, 3
"At the Sea-Side" (Stevenson), 218
Auditory discrimination, 3
Auditory memory, 3
"Auguries of Innocence" (Blake), 118
Authentic assessment, 11–12
Authentic literature, 8
Authentic settings, 6–8
   approximation, 7
   demonstration and modeling, 7
   engagement, 7–8
   expectations, 7
   feedback or response, 7
   immersion, 6–7
   responsibility, 7
   use and practice, 7
Author, Author! activity, 190
"The Average Child" (Anonymous), 22

A Baker's Dozen (retold by Donato), 333–36
   activities, 336
   story, 334–35
   storytelling method, 333
Balloon storytelling, 38, 41, 44
Band-Aid finger puppets, 229
The Barnyard activity, 185
"The Barnyard" (Burnham), 185
Be a Star activity, 88–89
Bettelheim, Bruno, 19

"The Blue Tail Fly" (song), 83–84
Bodily-Kinesthetic Intelligence, 17, 18–19
"Body Beat" (Brand and Donato), 186
Body Creatures activity, 233–34
Bog activity, 178
Bojabi (retold by Brand), 120–25
   activities, 123–25
   story, 120–23
   storytelling method, 120
The Brownies and the Tailor (retold and adapted by Donato), 162–67
   activities, 167
   story, 163–66
   storytelling method, 162
Bubbles (non-edible) recipe, 116
Bunny Baskets activity, 180–81
Bunny Hop Tag, 180

Cambourne's model of language learning, 6, 8
Catch a Dream activity, 318
Catharsis, 4, 8, 10
A Celebration of Neurons: An Educator's Guide to the Human Brain (Sylwester), 16
Center for Marine Conservation, 226
Ceremonial Masks activity, 76
Chant storytelling, 10, 34–36, 41
   creative/thematic approaches, 43
   group/dyad, 35–36
   introduction to, 35
   preparation for, 35
Character Imagery, 10, 30–31, 40
   creative/thematic approaches, 42
   group/dyad, 31
   introduction to, 31
   preparation for, 30
Charades activity, 247
The Children's Rainforest, 123
Chinese Calendar activity, 57–58
The Chinese New Year: How the Animals Were Chosen (retold and adapted by Donato), 55–59
   activities, 57–59
   story, 55–57
   storytelling method, 55
"Christmas Bells" (Longfellow), 320
Chunking, 15
The City Mouse and the Country Mouse (Aesop), 148–52
   activities, 151–52
   story, 149–50
   storytelling method, 148
Coffee Filter Butterflies, 124–25
Cognitive learning, 16
The Colonial Twist activity, 214, 216
Colors activity, 313–14

Comprehension, 3, 4
  development of, 8
  meaning and, 15–16
  storytelling and, 10–11
Concept Maps, 4, 20
Concrete operations stage, 11
Constructivist approach, 3
A Co-Op Play, 160–61
"The Crab and the Lobster" (adapted by Brand), 231–35
  activities, 233–35
  story, 232
  storytelling method, 231
"The Crabs in the Sea" (song), 234
Crayon-Press Class Quilts, 151
Creative Collections activity, 299
Cuchulainn. *See Finn and Cuchulainn* (retold and adapted by Brand)
Cute Keepers activity, 203

The Dance of the Brownies activity, 167
A Dandy Bog Salad, 177
Daniel O'Rourke and the Pooka's Tower (retold and adapted by Donato), 98–102
  activities, 101–2
  story, 98–101
  storytelling method, 98
DEAR. *See* Drop Everything and Read (DEAR)
Delightfully Different activity, 255–56
Did You Hear the News? activity, 190–91
"Different" (song), 255–56
Down in theSea and Up in the Air activity, 239
Dramatic story reenactments (DSRs), 31
Draw Talk, 10, 31–33, 40
  creative/thematic approaches, 43
  group/dyad, 32–33
  introduction to, 32
Dream catchers, 318
Dreidel activity, 339, 340
Drop Everything and Read (DEAR), 6, 7
DSRs. *See* dramatic story reenactments (DSRs)

Edible Arachnids activity, 290
Edible Math activity, 234–35
Emergent literacy, 3
Emotion, 15–16
Empowerment, 7
Engagement, 7–8
Existential-Spiritual Intelligence, 21
Expectations, 7
Explicit results, 3
Expressive language skills, 4–5, 11

The Fairies, the People, and the Sea (Latimer), 226–30
  activities, 229–30
  story, 227–28
  storytelling method, 226–27
Fairy tales, 28

Family Coat of Arms activity, 155–56
Family Trees activity, 151–52
Feedback, 7
Felt Board storytelling, 10, 36–38, 41
  creative/thematic approaches, 44
  group/dyad, 37
  introduction to, 36–37
  preparation for, 36
Find the Wee Folk activity, 101–2
Finn and Cuchulainn (retold and adapted by Brand), 103–7
  activities, 106–7
  story, 104–5
  storytelling method, 103
The First Thanksgiving? activity, 317
Fish activity, 224
Flag activities, 216, 331–32
Flags of Many Lands activity, 331–32
Flannel board. *See* Felt Board storytelling
Fluent reading, 8
Folk tales, 28
Food Phonemes activity, 304
The Fourth of July (retold and adapted by Donato), 211–16
  activities, 214–16
  story, 212–14
  storytelling method, 211
Frames of Mind: The Theory of Multiple Intelligences (Gardner), 16
Friendship activities, 291, 316–17
Friendship bracelets, 93–94
Friendship cookies, 76, 78
"The Friendship Song," 254
The Frog Prince (Grimm), 89–94
  activities, 91–94
  story, 90–91
  storytelling method, 89
The Frogs Go Hopping activity, 91–92
Frontier village shoebox diorama, 82

Gardner's theory of multiple intelligences, 12, 16–20
  bodily-kinesthetic intelligence, 17, 18–19
  existential-spiritual intelligence, 21
  interpersonal intelligence, 19–20
  intrapersonal intelligence, 19
  logical-mathematical intelligence, 17, 18
  musical-rhythmic intelligence, 17–18
  naturalistic intelligence, 20–21
  verbal-linguistic intelligence, 17, 20
  visual-spatial intelligence, 19
Genre
  awareness of, 8–9
  defined, 9
George Washington's "Lifeguard": The Legend of Simeon Simons (Donato), 84–89
  activities, 88–89
  story, 85–87
  storytelling method, 84–85

Gestalt hemisphere, 19, 21
Giant Classroom Pen Pals activity, 106–7
Gingerbread Person Cookies recipe, 78
Glad to Be Me activity, 247–49
Grammatical knowledge, 15
Graphic representations, 19
Group Role-Play, 10, 27, 41

Habari Gani activity, 331
Habitat activity, 177–78
Hat activities, 54
Hay Foot, Straw Foot activity, 209
Hello Around the World activity, 260, 262
"Hello to All the Children of the World" (song), 262
Here, There, and Everywhere activity, 151
Higher-level thinking skills, 4
Horizontal learning experience, 5
How the Leaves Got Their Colors (retold and adapted by Donato), 263–67
    activities, 266–67
    story, 263–65
    storytelling method, 263
How Would You Say It? activity, 64
Hug O'War activity, 260
"Hug O'War" (Silverstein), 260

Ida Lewis: Keeper of the Light (Donato), 199–204
    song, 200
    story, 200–202
    storytelling method, 199–200
I Have a Dream (Brand), 65–70
    activities, 69–70
    story, 66–68
    storytelling method, 65–66
I Like You the Best (Hanley), 74–78
    activities, 76–78
    story, 74–75
    storytelling method, 74
I Love You Coupons, 78
Imagination, 15–16
Immersion, 6–7
Implicit results, 3
I'm Thinking of a Town activity, 115
Interpersonal Intelligence, 19–20
Intrapersonal Intelligence, 19
Irish Festival, 107
Irish Tunes and Traditions activity, 106
It Could Be Worse! (retold and adapted by Brand), 182–86
    activities, 185–86
    story, 183–85
    storytelling method, 182–83
It Floats activity, 230
It's a Small World activity, 260, 261
It's Very Nice to Meet You activity, 253

Jack and the Beanstalk (retold and adapted by Brand), 132–38
    activities, 136–38

story, 132–36
    storytelling method, 132
Johnny Appleseed (adapted by Brand), 194–99
    activities, 196–99
    story, 195–96
    storytelling method, 194
Johnny Appleseed meets Miss Rumphius activity, 199
Johnston, Tony, 28
Journal writing, 19
"July Is..." (Brand), 192

Keep it Ship Shape activity, 204
Kibungo: Beast of the Rainforest (da Silva), 126–31
    activities, 130–31
    song, 129
    story, 127–29
    storytelling method, 126
Kibungo's Animal Hunt activity, 130
King, Martin Luther, 65–71
Kung Hei Fat Choy activity, 58
The Kwanzaa Story (Brand), 329–32
    activities, 331–32
    story, 330–31
    storytelling method, 329

Language development, 8
    expressive, 11
    receptive, 11
Language Experience Approach (LEA), 6
Language learning, Cambourne's model of, 6, 8
Latkes recipe, 339–40
LEA. *See* Language Experience Approach (LEA)
Learning, 15–16
    cognitive, 16
    logs, 19
    storytelling and, 21–22
Leaves activities, 266–67
Let's Be Problem-Solvers! activity, 69
Let's Celebrate activity, 328
Lets Pretend activity, 101
Let Your Light Shine activity, 325–27
Lewis, Ida, 199–204
Life Goes On activity, 156–57
Lights, Cameras, Action! activity, 239
Limbic system, 16
Lincoln, Abraham, 79–84
Linguistic awareness, 15
The Lion and the Mouse (Aesop), 139–44
    activities, 142–44
    story, 140–42
    storytelling method, 139
Lion Hunt activity, 143–44
Literacy, authentic assessment of, 11–12
Literal questions, 4
"Little Birdie and Mother" (Tennyson), 146

Little Bunny Foo Foo (retold and adapted by Brand), 178–82
  activities, 180–82
  story, 179–80
  storytelling method, 178
The Little Bunny Who Wished for Red Wings (retold and adapted by Donato), 157–62
  activities, 160–62
  story, 158–60
  storytelling method, 157
Little Rabbit Foo Foo (Rosen), 178
The Little Red Hen (adapted by Brand), 296–300
  activities, 299–300
  story, 296–98
  storytelling method, 296
Logical-Mathematical Intelligence, 17, 18
Logic hemisphere, 21
The Lovely New Year Flower Dance activity, 58–59
Lucious Latkes activity, 339–40

Magical Mixables activity, 115–16
Magic Fish in the Sea (Forest), 220–26
  activities, 224–26
  song, 221
  story, 221–24
  storytelling method, 220
A Magic Opportunity activity, 225–26
The Magic Shamrock Game, 101
Magic Wands activity, 181–82
Marshall Islands, 235–40
Masks activity, 76
Math Sleuths activity, 191
Meaning, comprehension and, 15–16
Memory, 15–16
Metacognition, 19
Mind-mapping, 19
The Mind's Eye activity, 110
Modeling, 7
Monster activities, 273–74, 279–80
"Monster" (song), 279–80
The Most Beautiful Thing in the World (retold and adapted by Brand), 257–62
  activities, 260–62
  story, 258–59
  storytelling method, 257
Mouse activity, 142
Multicultural storytelling, 28, 39
Multiple intelligences. *See* Gardner's theory of multiple intelligences
Musical-Rhythmic Intelligence, 17–18
Musical storytelling, 38–39, 41, 45
My Dream for the World activity, 69
"My Shadow" (Stevenson), 269
Mystery Shell activity, 239–40
My Story Map, 116–17

Native American symbol writing, 76–77
Naturalistic Intelligence, 20–21

Nature and Family Trees activity, 151–52
Neural pathways, 15
New Friends activity, 254
No Kids in the Gallery! (Berenson), 282–86
  activities, 285–86
  story, 282–84
  storytelling method, 282

Oceanic Society, 226
Oh, Dear! How Many Tears? activity, 230
Oh No! activity, 110–11
Old Man Rabbit's Thanksgiving Dinner (Bailey), 305–14
  activities, 313–14
  story, 305–12
  storytelling method, 305
Old Rattle Bones (Brand), 271–75
  activities, 273–75
  story, 272–73
  storytelling method, 271
O'Rourke, Daniel, 98–102

Pantomime. *See* adapted pantomime
Papier mâché puppets, 34
Pasta and Cheese recipe, 115
A Patriotic Jug Band activity, 208
Peacemaker windsocks, 69, 70
Peace Tales: World Folktales to Talk About (MacDonald), 236
Pepparkakors
  activity, 327–28
  recipe, 328
Personal portfolios, 19
Phonemes, 5
Phonemic awareness, 5
Phonology, 20
Pigs...Bears (Myers), 250–56
  activities, 253–56
  story, 250–53
  storytelling method, 250
Play it Again activity, 130–31
The Pot That Would Not Stop Boiling (retold and adapted by Brand), 111–17
  activities, 115–17
  story, 112–15
  storytelling method, 111–12
Pourquoi stories, 18
Praxis, 20
Preschool children
  benefits of reading aloud to, 3–5
  maximizing potential of, 5–6
  reading and, 3–6
Problem-solving activity, 69
Process writing, 20
Projection-type stories, 9–10
Pumpkin activity, 285
Puppetry, 33–34, 40
  creative/thematic approaches, 43
  group/dyad, 34

introduction to, 33
papier mâché puppets, 34
preparation for, 33
The Purple Hat (Brand and Brand), 51–54
  activities, 54
  story, 51–53
  storytelling method, 51

Quill Pen activity, 209–10
Quilt activity, 151
The Quilt Story (Johnston), 28

Rainsticks, 130–31
Rattlin' Bog (retold and adapted by Donato),
    172–78
  activities, 177–78
  song, 175–76
  story, 174
  storytelling method, 172–4
Reading
  aloud, benefits of, 3–5
  development of, 8
  fluent, 8
  maximizing children's potential through, 5–6
  preschool children and, 3–6
  promoting lifelong, 8–9
  school-aged children and, 6–8
  storytelling versus, 9–10
Reading readiness, 3
Recycle and Renew activity, 124
Red Lips (retold and adapted by Donato), 276–81
  activities, 279–81
  story, 277–78
  storytelling method, 276–77
Representational thought, 4
The Rhyming Song, 167
Riddle activity, 64
A Riddle for Winter (Lipman), 59–64
  activities, 64
  story, 60–63
  storytelling method, 59–60
"Romance" (Stevenson), 72
Row, Ida, Row activity, 203–4
Rubrics, 12

Saint Lucia Day: A Swedish Tradition (Donato), 322–28
  activities, 325–28
  story, 323–25
  storytelling method, 322
"Santa Lucia" (song), 327
Save the Rainforests activity, 130
Schemata, 3
School-aged children
  approximation and, 7
  demonstration and modeling with, 7
  engagement and, 7–8
  expectations, 7
  feedback/response, 7
  immersion and, 6–7
  reading and, 6–8
  responsibility and, 7
  skill use and practice, 7
Scrap Paper Wonders activity, 274–75
Sea Chants activity, 224–25
Sea Fairies activity, 229–30
Seasons activity, 300
Self-esteem, 8
Semantics, 8, 16, 20
Shake a Leg! activity, 154–55
Shape activity, 142–43
Shivery, Quivery Tales activity, 273
Shower curtain art, 136, 137
Showers of Flowers activity, 136, 137
Sign Language alphabet, 261
Silverstein, Shel, 136, 138, 187–91, 260
Simeon's Tasty February Treat activity, 88
Simons, Simeon, 84–89
Skinny as a Spider's Waist (retold by Cordi; retold
    and adapted by Brand), 287–91
  activities, 290–91
  story, 288–89
  storytelling method, 287
Skit activity, 336
Snap Apple Night activity, 280
"Snowflakes" (Longfellow), 49
Spiced Brew Hot Tea recipe, 285
Spider activities, 290–91
A Spider on the Floor! activity, 290–91
Spinning Dreidels activity, 339, 340
Spring has Sprung! activity, 138
SSR. *See* Sustained Silent Reading (SSR)
Stone Soup (adapted by Brand), 300–304
  activities, 303–4
  story, 301–3
  storytelling method, 300–301
Story Frames, 186
Story maps, 19, 116–17
Story structure
  awareness of, 8–9
  defined, 9
The Storyteller's Source Book (MacDonald), 111
Storytelling
  adapted pantomime, 9, 28–30, 40, 42
  approaches to, 27–39
  background information, 26
  balloon, 38, 41, 44
  benefits of, 10–11
  chant, 34–36, 41, 43
  character imagery, 30–31, 40, 42
  creative/thematic approaches, 42–45
  draw talk, 10, 31–33, 40, 43
  as entertainment, 9
  felt board, 36–38, 41, 44
  group role-play, 27, 41
  learning and, 21–22
  musical, 38–39, 41, 45
  nature-related explanations, 9
  preparation for, 26–27

Storytelling (*cont.*)
    projection, 9–10
    puppetry, 33–34, 40, 43
    story reading versus, 9–11
    techniques summary, 40–41
    traditional, 9, 27–28, 40, 42
Story webs, 19
"A Stranger's Gift" (retold by Schram and
    Rosman; adapted by Brand), 337–41
    activities, 339–41
    story, 337–39
    storytelling method, 337
"Strawberries" (song), 317
The Strawberry Friendship Dance activity, 316–17
The Strawberry Thanksgiving (retold by Donato),
    314–18
    activities, 316–18
    story, 315–16
    storytelling method, 314
Strings of Love activity, 332
Style
    awareness of, 8–9
    defined, 9
"Summer Sun" (Stevenson), 170
Sustained Silent Reading (SSR), 6
Sylwester, Robert, 16
Symbol Savvy activity, 214, 215
Syntax, 8, 16, 20

Talking Book Covers activity, 123
Tangram Creatures activity, 281
"Thanksgiving Day" (Child), 294
Theme
    awareness of, 8–9
    defined, 9
Then and Now activity, 336
"This is Autumn" (poem), 300
"This Little Light of Mine" (song), 331
Three Billy Goats Gruff, The (retold and adapted by
    Brand and Berenson), 244–49
    activities, 247–49
    story, 245–47
    storytelling method, 244
Three *Rs:* Rhyme, Rhythm, and Repetition, 5
The Three Wishes (retold by Donato), 108–11
    activities, 110–11
    story, 108–10
    storytelling method, 108
Traditional storytelling, 9, 27–28, 40
    creative/thematic approaches, 42
    folk/fairy tales, 28
    group/dyad, 28
    multicultural, 28, 39
Treasure Hunt activity, 285–86
Triaramas, 249
Try to Make Me Laugh activity, 303–4

T-Shirts activity, 235
Twist Me and Turn Me activity, 167

The Unicorn (Silverstein), 187–91
    activities, 190–91
    song, 188–90
    story, 188
    storytelling method, 187
The United States activity, 196–97
"The United States" (song), 197
The Uses of Enchantment (Bettelheim), 19

Venn diagrams, 20
Verbal-Linguistic Intelligence, 17, 20
Village activity, 82
Visual discrimination, 3
Visual memory, 3
Visual-Spatial Intelligence, 19

"The War between the Sandpipers and the
    Whales: A Tale from the Marshall Islands"
    (MacDonald), 235–40
    activities, 239–40
    story, 236–38
    storytelling method, 235–36
Washington, George, 84–89
"A Wayfaring Song" (van Dyke), 242
Weather Wisdom activity, 313
Web of Friendship activity, 291
The Weight of a Snowflake (retold by Donato),
    64–65
What Did Simeon Simons See? activity, 88
Whatif? activity, 136, 138
"Whatif" (Silverstein), 136, 138
"What is Green?" (O'Neill and Weisgard), 107
What Make a Difference? activity, 64
Whatsit activity, 160
"When I Grow Up" Photo Books, 299–300
Why Not Call It Cow Juice? (Krasner), 153–57
    activities, 154–57
    story, 153–54
    storytelling method, 153
"The Wind" (Stevenson), 96
The Wishing Game, 161–62
Witch's Brew activity, 285
Word Wonders activity, 336
"The World Turned Upside Down" (song),
    208

A Yankee Doodle Legend (retold and adapted by
    Donato), 205–11
    activities, 208–11
    story, 206–7
    storytelling method, 205
You Don't Say activity, 111
You Were There activity, 82